Sketches of History, Life, and Manners, in the United States

Young Ladies' Academy, at the Convent of the Visitation, in Georgetown, Dist. of Col.

SKETCHES

OF

HISTORY, LIFE, AND MANNERS,

IN THE

UNITED STATES.

—◦◦◦—

BY A TRAVELLER.

—◦◦◦—

NEW-HAVEN :

PRINTED FOR THE AUTHOR.

....

1826.

JOHNSON REPRINT CORPORATION
111 Fifth Avenue, New York, N.Y. 10003

JOHNSON REPRINT COMPANY LTD.
Berkeley Square House, London, W1X6BA

SERIES IN AMERICAN STUDIES

Editor-in-Chief: Joseph J. Kwiat

PROGRAM IN AMERICAN STUDIES

UNIVERSITY OF MINNESOTA

U.

First reprinting 1970, Johnson Reprint Corporation

Printed in the United States of America

TO THE PUBLIC.

THE author of these "Sketches," begs leave to apologize for the unavoidable delay of its appearance, owing to the lamented death of Mr. Wiley, of New-York: also, that the matter of the book does not exactly come up to the prospectus, as regards the western states, for this reason,—when the proposals for this, as well as two other works, were published, the author was unapprised of the extensive matter embraced in the work, and found it impossible to comprise any thing like a satisfactory description of the atlantic and western country, in a book of this size, and that one part of the design must be given up to make room for the other. The author therefore thought it best to exchange that part least interesting, which is the western country, excepting a few remarks only in the first of the book, which it is hoped will be found interesting, particularly the history and geography of places, which have never been noticed by any other writer. The author further begs leave to state, that the whole of the work has undergone an abridgement, to bring it within the proposal. In addition to the foregoing reason for expunging the western instead of the atlantic country, from the present work, the author is influenced by the prospect of remunerating the public by two other works, which will shortly appear, relating wholly almost to the western states.

The work herewith presented to the public, contains a description of the public institutions, manners and appearance of the inhabitants, and the history of the principal places visited by the author, with sketches of the principal characters, physical remarks on the country, &c.

SKETCHES, &c.

—❦—

JOURNEY FROM HUNTSVILLE TO VIRGINIA.

HAVING been advised to try the mineral waters in Virginia for my health, I set out on horseback from St. Stephens, in Alabama, July the 1st, 1823, intending to take the stage at Huntsville. With a view to divert my mind from melancholy reflections, to which it was disposed from ill health, I resolved to note every thing during my journey, worthy of remark, and commit it to writing, and to draw amusement and instruction from every source. In doing this, I shall not imitate most journalists, in such remarks as " cloudy, or fair morning," and where we stop, dates, &c. This is all the preface I deem necessary.

Upon my arrival at Huntsville, I was told that the stage left there at day-light next morning. Huntsville is well known to be one of the largest towns in the state : it is on the north side of Tennessee river, about ten miles distant. It is handsomely situated on an eminence, has a commodious square in the centre, as have all the towns in the state. On this square is an elegant brick court-house, a market-house, and two fire engine-houses. The town is principally built of brick. Around the square, several wealthy merchants have drawn themselves, and do much business. There are four churches, one for Presbyterians, one for Methodists, and two for blacks, two female academies, and one for young men. The land in the neigh-

2

bourhood of Huntsville, yields considerably in fertility, to the land on the south side of Tennessee river,
though it maintains the same beautiful, undulative
surface, with large fields of cotton.

After resting a few hours, I sallied out to refresh
myself with a walk, and meeting with Col. Pope, accepted an invitation to spend the night with him. Col.
Pope is amongst the wealthiest men in the state of
Alabama, and lives in princely style. If any man is
to be envied on account of wealth, it is he. His house
is separated from Huntsville, by a deep ravine, and
from an eminence overlooks the town from the west;
on the east lies his beautiful plantation, on a level
with the house. Although the ascent to it is considerable, yet when you are there, it is a perfect plane. He
has, however, injured the beauty of his situation, by
surrounding it with the lombardy poplar. If I admired the exterior, I was amazed at the taste and elegance displayed in every part of the interior; massy
plate, cut glass, china ware, vases, sofas, and mahogany furniture of the newest fashion, decorated the inside.

To those unacquainted with the wealth of this new
country, the superb style of the inhabitants, generally, will appear incredible. Mrs. Pope is one of
your plain, undisguised, house-keeping looking females; no ways elated by their vast possessions, which,
I am told, are the joint acquisition of her and her husband's industry. Report says, she is benevolent and
charitable, and her looks confirm it. Next morning
found me in one of my splenetic fits: I resolved to
shake it off in the stage, and set off in it, accordingly,
for the sweet springs.

Three passengers besides myself. This consoled
me a little, as it afforded an opportunity of indulging
observations, on the variety of character, which now
presented itself, in the persons of the strangers. One
was a young gentleman from Abington, Virginia.
Another was from East Tennessee, and the third was
of Huntsville, and an Irishman. Travellers in stages

are (at least in this part of the country,) not long in making up their acquaintance. The young man of Abington, whose name is B——, was one of your noble, fine looking men, and though stout, possessed of much personal beauty, and grace of manner. He was good natured, moderately improved, yet still enough so for his age, being very young: he was shortly after this, married to the young and beautiful Mrs. Trigg, of Wythe. Our Irishman was a comical, gay, lively man, of about thirty, a little crazed when sober, a good deal so when tipsy. The Tennesseean was a middle aged man, of the inferior order, he was ugly, ignorant, and in short, he was a complete boor, if it be good English. Clown, as he is too surely, he must have the back seat, the only one with a back belonging to the stage, which was nothing but an old rattletrap. However, this made no difference : I was prejudiced against him at first sight. Meantime I was relieved by the driver, who informed me, we would soon meet the Nashville line, which was more comfortable.

For the distance of a mile, after leaving Huntsville, the road is causewayed with huge logs, and so soon as the stage was on it, we were sadly jolted. Our Irishman acted the merry Andrew to perfection, uttering as many " Oh laws" as Sancho, after his discomfiture by the mule-drivers. " Oh Lord, sir ! do speak to your horses, and tell them to go more softly ; Oh law, O ! they are the most uncivil horses ever I saw." The horses were actually the best of their kind, and seemed to understand every word of their master perfectly. After we were clear of the causeway, the road, though level, was narrow and crooked, often interrupted with stumps of trees : going at the rate we went, it required the utmost skill to avoid them. When the driver would see danger before him, he would address his horses with " look sharp," or " take care," that moment the animals would be seen looking up the road, and would avoid the danger, with all the caution of reasonable beings.

The first day brought us to Winchester, in Tennes-

see. Winchester is the seat of justice for Franklin
county; it is a handsome village, many of the buildings are well built, of brick. It contains a Court-
House, a church, a post office, an academy and other
schools. The land is beautiful and fertile. From
Huntsville to this place, forty miles, the soil and its
productions are the same, viz. rich and level. Here
we change our driver, as is the practice; I dislike the
practice.

Next morning before day, all on the road again, in
health and good spirits. Our Irishman having invig-
orated his spirits, with a portion of the spirits of corn,
was doubly amusing; his tongue outwent the wheels
of the stage, and his countenance defied description.
It was ludicrous enough, to see him earnestly ruma-
ging his pocket-book, while some dowdy fat woman
endeavoured to keep up with the stage, to " get the
letter from her father, mother, or acquaintance,"
whilst he voeiferated the driver, for not stopping
his horses, till he gave the lady the letter. Anon
he has some awkward boy or girl, by the way-side,
staring at " has Jim come from mill yet?" When he
could make us laugh no other way, he would insist upon drinking out of the horse-bucket, and that after the
horses had done, for which he was sometimes censured by the driver, with " sir, why did'nt you drink before I watered my horses." What a happy knack some
people have! I have often wondered whether it affords such characters the same amusement it does
others, as their aim appears solely to amuse the company. This man of happy disposition, once independent (as I have since understood,) well reared and educated, is now not worth a cent, and yet how merry
he is! Is not a disposition like his a fortune.

MacMinville.—The second day brought us to Mac-
Minville, the seat of justice for Warren county. The
land is low and flat. After leaving Winchester, you
see no more cotton fields. The soil, though equally
rich, gradually changes from a redish to a black color,

presenting a flat, even surface, from thence to
Cumberland mountain, which occasions bad water,
and sickness, but produces Indian corn in abundance. Here the Huntsville stage-line ends, and the
Nashville stage takes in the travellers. But if it be
too full, as is sometimes the case, the Huntsville stage
passengers have to remain at MacMinville till the next
stage. The Nashville stage brought but three passengers, and our Irishman going no farther, we got a
seat, as it happened. I was gratified that our Tennessee
boor had to give up the back seat, which was the exclusive privilege of those first in the stage. I had
much rather have dropped the Tennesseean, as we
were now nearly laden with the baggage of the strangers, he being very heavy, and had not three ideas in
his head.

Our new fellow travellers were, a young Doctor who
lived in Knoxville, a Mr. Mager (or Major,) who lived in Philadelphia, to which city he was returning, after a three years residence in New-Orleans, as agent
for his father. He was modest, genteel, and communicative, with a countenance glowing with benevolence and good humour. I don't know when I was
more disappointed; I had always understood, that the
young men of Philadelphia were inanimate, ignorant,
reserved, and unsociable; a greater contrast, perhaps,
never existed than the present. The charms of this
amiable stranger, left a lasting impression on my
memory. Our third and last stranger, was, I believe
a merchant, clerk, or something like that, direct from
Nashville, but where his place of residence, I never
learned; for although two days in company, he did
not in that time, speak more than half a dozen words.
He was one of your close calculating, suspicious, distant, contracted men, his countenance a complete
contrast to the openness and candour of our Philadelphian. The young Dr. of Knoxville, in few
words, was a pert little fop, and an ignoramus besides. Such are the travellers that now joined us.

2*

We set out from MacMinville* long before day, and long before we reached Sparta, a little village, where we were to change horses, and breakfast, it rained excessively. At length we reached Sparta, at the foot of Cumberland mountain. Sparta is the seat of justice for White county, it has some very neatly built houses, of brick, contains a church, a court-house, a post office, and unfortunately for us, two taverns. My friend of Abington, proposed to take breakfast at one of these, a different one from that at which the stages were wont to stop; the fare, he said, was much better, and withal, cheaper: this however, would have had but little weight with us, but the proprietor was a worthy man, and a new beginner. We therefore closed with his proposal. But this circumstance put it out of our heads to enter our names, at the stage office, which was kept at the other tavern, and here the new driver, a huge, rough, red headed fellow, comes posting upon us in a violent passion, swearing he would leave us, and in fact he was very near it; he did wait, however, until some of our party ran to enter our names on the way-bill. While they were absent, he and *our* tavern-keeper had nearly come to blows, because he did not apprise us of our duty. But as the tavern-keeper waxed warm, the other grew cool, and upon the interference of the travellers, the storm blew over. I suspected, what I afterwards found true, that the mighty offence, was that we gave the preference to the new tavern. This was the meanest driver I met with on the route.

Near Sparta they have found salt water, from which they already make a considerable quantity of salt. Within a few miles, also, there is a spacious cave, called the arch cave, a great natural curiosity, having an arch-way under ground, the distance of a mile in length, through which persons may walk upright, from one end to the other. An opening being

* A village, called after M'Min, Governor of Tennessee. It is growing fast.

at each end, sufficiently wide to admit one person. Some salt-petre has been made at this cave, and a great quantity, I am told, might be made were it properly attended to. At Sparta, and at the new tavern too, we met several members of the Legislature, on their way from East Tennessee, going on to Murfreesborough, to hold their session. We were sorry to impart bad news to them, but it was little less than our duty to do so. Their house in which they intended to convene, viz. the state-house, was just burnt to the foundation, only two nights before; the gentlemen who joined us at MacMinville, saw its remains smoking on the morning of the succeeding day. Respecting this dreadful business, different opinions prevail; some suspected the people of Nashville, and some the people of Jefferson, in order, as was supposed, that the seat of Government would be moved, at least the approaching session. But in this, if this was the view, they were disappointed, as I have since learned, they convened in a church.

Cumberland Mountain.—This was an unlucky day throughout, we were so heavily laden, the mountain to ascend, and the rain had rendered the road deep and difficult. Such being the case, we had to walk on foot a great part of the way up the mountain, all but our Tennessee clown, who feigned himself sick; but I shall ever think he was any thing else than sick, and worse than all this, we have to travel all night. The Cumberland mountain, where we cross it, is sixty miles wide. About day-light we arrived at the foot of "Spencer's Hill," by far the steepest part of the mountain. When you are on the summit of this part of Cumberland, you have a grand view of this stupendous pile. The eye ranges over the whole, without control, to an immense distance, the mountain throwing itself into a thousand different shapes and curvatures, assuming different hues, as they are near or remote. I was much pleased at the enthusiastic effusions of our Philadelphian, to whom the sight was new, he

having never witnessed a scene like this. I was glad
that it afforded him pleasure, but for myself, I have
little partiality for mountains; I have suffered too
much amongst mountains; they are splendid objects to
look at, and sound well in theories, but nothing wears
worse than mountains, when you take up your abode
amongst them. True, you can have a delicious pheas-
ant, a venison, or a trout now and then, but these
delicacies are greatly overbalanced by the cold blasts
of the winter, killing your lambs and calves by dozens,
chilling vegetation, overwhelming every thing with
snow, and a thousand other inconveniences, killing up
your horses clambering over them, to bring you from
a distance. articles of necessity, rewarding your hard
labour with a scanty bundle or two of buckwheat
perhaps, or rye, and a few Irish potatoes. I confess
I cannot admire mountains as I hear many do.

Spencer's Hill.—This hill took its name (as the story goes) from a man by the name of Spencer, who
with his family was travelling westwardly, and encamped for the night on this hill, that having built his
fire over a snake den, the snakes, annoyed by the heat,
came out in the night and bit him in such numbers,
that he died immediately. In the pangs of death he
awoke, called his wife and bid her get up quickly,
and save herself by flight, which she did. It appears
incredible that the snakes should wreak their vengeance on the man, whilst the woman escaped unhurt.
A number of legendary tales are related of this memorable mountain, such as people being frozen to death
in the snow, killed by the Indians, &c. Though there
are several houses and farms on it, the land is thin,
and the accommodation is wretched, hardly fit for
waggoners.

When you gain the eastern limit of Cumberland,
you have an extensive view of East Tennessee, Clinch
River, Kingston, and Campbell's Fort; all are present at once, to view. It was truly grand and picturesque. The Fort rises conspicuous above the rest, it

being situated on a high hill, descending rapidly at all points. What a scene this for the fancy and pen of a poet! while I have neither leisure nor talents to exhibit it in simple prose.

The Cumberland mountain leaves you on the bank of Clinch River, a beautiful smooth-flowing stream, about 250 yards wide, navigable its whole length, which is a little less than 200 miles. While crossing Clinch (which you do in a boat) you witness another display of the rich and beautiful scenery which abounds in this country. Kingston lies before you—the majestic Tennessee shows itself below, having just joined Clinch river, while Campbell's Fort appears at the same time looking down upon the junction of these noble streams, from its lofty eminence to the right, decorated with fruit trees and shrubberies, like the guardian genius of the place.

Kingston, the seat of justice for Rowan county, E. Tennessee, is built on that point of land formed by the junction of Holston and Clinch rivers. It is a handsome little town, of about forty houses; a post-office and a fine spring are all the objects of notice within it. Having travelled forty-four hours without sleep, we arrived at an inn a few miles west of Knoxville, at 10 o'clock at night, where, more dead than alive, I threw myself on a bed, without undressing, to await the hour of starting. We arrived at Knoxville to breakfast, and my friend of Abington and myself resolved to stop till the next stage, to refresh ourselves with sleep, for the want of which we were almost exhausted. I must not forget to mention that we passed Campbell's station a few miles below Knoxville, and the pleasure I had in seeing and talking with Col. Campbell, who gives name to it and to the Fort mentioned before. I had a message to him from his daughter, Mrs. Col. Wright, of Alabama. The good old man came out to meet me with a smiling countenance. He appeared to be between sixty and seventy, hale and active, tall and straight as an Indian.— Happy should I have been to have spent some time

with him, but the stage drove on, and we parted. I
ought to have mentioned too, that we set down our
Tennessean in the road, the preceding night, being
near his home.

Knoxville.—Here our fellow travellers, of Nashville, parted from us, the one who belonged to Knoxville having arrived at the end of his journey—Mr.
Major and his friend pursuing their's to the north.—
I never shall forget the former, particularly an expression of his, on a dispute which took place between
the passengers : " Let us have peace." He spoke
with such persuasive sweetness that harmony was
soon restored. I never was more struck by so few
words, and from so young a man.

Knoxville is the largest town we have seen since
we left Huntsville. It is situated on the Holston river, below its junction with French broad. It contains
four churches, for as many denominations, a court-
house, offices, a prison, two printing offices, a bank,
a college, an academy, and several schools. It has
twelve stores and 300 houses, several of which are of
brick, besides barracks for 500 men. They have a
watch, but the town is not lighted. The college is
handsomely endowed by Congress, and is in a flourishing condition. The manners of the citizens are
very pleasing, and much more refined than those of
Huntsville, though with not half their eclat. The ladies are easy and artless, very much so,—and what is
highly honorable to the citizens, and what I never
met with before, the different sects of christians unite
in worship! These must be christians indeed! The
land near the town is very poor pine land, though I
am told that large bodies of good land lie on the river.

We put up at Boyd's—a man who in every respect
deserves the patronage of the public. He keeps a
table spread with plenty and variety, and what was
our bill ? 50 cents per day, including extra charges.

While we remained in Knoxville (which was three
days) I had an opportunity of indulging an inclination

I had long entertained of contemplating human nature in a new guise. At the house where we put up,
was a lady eighty years of age. This was the first
opportunity in my life I had had of judging for myself
respecting a subject of which I had often heard and read,
viz.—that persons of her age were measurably dead
to those vivid affections and feelings of the heart,
which are common to the species of junior years; that
the powers of the mind become relaxed and enfee-
bled by long exercise. She was a stout hale woman,
could see to sew with a needle, and read without glas-
ses, though she told me (reluctantly I thought) that
she had used spectacles for thirty-five years. One
afternoon as she and I were sitting together in a pleasant portico, I drew her into conversation with a view
to ascertain what were her ideas on moral and divine
truths, her opinion with respect to a future state, and
what were her views of christian duties, faith, charity,
&c. She was much averse to this conversation, though
she was fond of talking on other subjects. After some
time she answered to the several questions, but with
much incoherence, and only replied by monosyllables.
Before I was done with her she appeared to have a
mental view of the duties of a christian, but it was
long before I could draw it from her, in doing which,
I had to advance several texts of scripture again and
again. But of the practice of a christian, she was either entirely ignorant or averse! I had a fair opportunity of deciding on this point; though I had, as I
thought, aroused her attention to this particular the
evening before. I stepped into the kitchen one
morning, to send one of the servants for something I
wanted, and this old lady happened to be present.
She drew near to me, and looking earnestly in my
face, exclaimed, " he can't go, he's got his work to
do." This negative of her's proved to me nothing
more than her selfish, uncharitable disposition, as
there were half a dozen servants then idle in the
kitchen. Upon our return to the parlour, I seized
the opportunity this circumstance afforded, to prove

to her her want of christian charity. I found it easy
to convince her, but the impression was momentary.
The result proved what I had often heard, " that old
people are callous to the duties of a christian."

During our stay at Knoxville, a beautiful female
from the Northern States, accompanied by her husband and two beautiful children, passed through the
town. Her husband has an interest in the salt works,
already mentioned, near Sparta, he is a man of some
wealth, and although a Yankee, had purchased several slaves as he came through Maryland, with a view
of making his fortune at the salt works. Poor simple-
ton! he will lose his children, and very probably his
wife, the first year, and the next he will break; the
place being generally fatal to foreigners. This day's
stage (I mean the fourth) brings one passenger, and
with him we pursue our journey.

Our new fellow traveller was by far the best company we had had yet; he was all frolic, fun, life and
spirits, that never flagged. He was different from our
Irishman in this, he never drank a drop of spirits.
He was not long in our company, before he imparted
to us three of his maxims, one was " that he never
drank," the second, " that he never played cards,"
and the third, " that he never gave or took paper
money." All this was well. He, I soon discovered,
would keep me from the hypo, so long as we remained together. He had been accustomed to travelling,
and that too in a stage : he had never learned to ride
on horseback. He was a Yankee, he said, but I do
not believe him hardly yet; neither his conversation
nor manners had any appearance of the Yankee. If
he really was a Yankee, he was the most gentlemanly
of the country I had ever seen. I hinted this to him.
" I hope," said he, " you would'nt judge us all by the
d—n little Yankee pedlars, that go through the country." He was about twenty-three years of age, well
made, his complexion dark, his features handsome, and
countenance all expression. He had what is called a
" laughing" black eye. He was a merchant from

Demopolis, going on to New-York, to purchase goods. Demopolis is a town in Alabama, in that part of it that was ceded conditionally to the French. I was glad to hear this; I had heard much of those emigrants, and now I had an opportunity (so far as I chose to rely) of hearing the truth: well, here we have the story of the Frenchmen.

" When they first began to clear their vineyard," he said, " they sent five men three miles for a rope, and having previously provided axes, about twenty-five or thirty of them in a body proceed to business. In the first place one ascends the tree which is to be fallen, and ties the rope hard and fast to the top; he then descends, and ten or a dozen of them take the end of the rope, whilst the others commence cutting, and perform a portion of the task in rotation. They cut all round, up and down, crossways, and lengthways, the tree; meantime the rope division kept pulling. At length down came the tree, killed two and crippled several. From that day to the present, no entreaty, or persuasion, can prevail on them to resume the business of clearing, or any attempt at falling timber. They have gone so far as to cultivate some little patches," he said, " for vegetables, but cutting with an axe, with them, is out of the question. When they are obliged to have a tree felled for firewood or other purposes, they hire the Americans to do it for them. They were, he continued, the most indolent, contemptible, and intractable people, to be found in any country: That Lefever, after doing all that a man of his patience and ability could do, left them in despair, with a broken heart! They were not only ignorant but given to all manner of vice; apply themselves to no manner of business for a livelihood, except strolling about with a few strings of beads or buttons, and such trifles, to sell, covered with rags and dirt." I inquired where they came from, and how Lefever could think of making any thing out of such abandoned people: He replied that some were immediately from France.

3

and some were picked up in our seaports. He said they had no more judgment in matters of farming, or planting, than children; and that government was adopting measures to get rid of them, and let those have the land who may turn it to better account. It is said to be the best land in the State. We laughed enough at his droll description of the French; hardly sensible of the jolting and swiftness of the stage. He had purchased a tremendous watermelon at Knoxville, and after we had done laughing he sat the melon in the driver's water-bucket. It was so large that he could only get a part of it endways into the bucket; setting it therefore between his knees, he began to slice it into pieces, which he distributed liberally between us and the driver, and commenced eating himself, and singing alternately. Somewhere on the road, he had inquired for melons; the man of whom he had inquired, desired his daughter (a woman grown) to go to such a place, and she would find one. The girl was not long in finding the melon, and in the eagerness of her joy she exclaimed, before she was near the house, " Oh law, daddy, its a roarer." The humour of the thing struck him at the moment, and he and my friend of Abington began to sing, " A bucket full of watermelon, we're neither drunk nor mad nor felon," and the chorus, " my daddy is a roarer O," as loud as a trumpet, the horses going almost at full speed. I was really deafened with them, but could not refrain from laughter to see the doors and windows fly open, and crowded with amazed spectators, while the dogs barked, and the stage flew on, without giving them time to gratify curiosity. When I remonstrated with them, the Alabamian said, " O, never mind, it will be a new epoch; the people on the road will say hereafter, " the year (or as the case may be) after the roarers went along."

Upon gaining Virginia, the country is principally settled with Germans and their descendants; therefore, as soon as you are in Washington county, Va. you have Dutch (as they are called) drivers, Dutch inns, and Dutch every thing. These mischievous plagues still kept up the roaring, and our Dutch driver, to whom this roaring was a new thing, would look round, with evident signs of amazement. Sometimes he would mutter to himself, sometimes go slow, and then put his horses to their best speed, as if he would outride the noise, or by that means bring about a cessation. But all in vain—the faster he drove the louder they sang, till their voices were exhausted. After making inquiry where we were to sleep that night, and the driver, pleased to find they were rational beings, had satisfied them on that point, they agreed between themselves to rest until they came within hearing of the house. Accordingly they raised the roaring, and continued until the horses stopt at the gate. Meanwhile some dozen Dutch men and women, the brothers and sisters of the driver, with the father and mother, attracted by the noise, were paraded in the yard, with looks of terror and amazement; and the moment the horses stopt, the old man accosts him—" Vy Shake (Jake) vot sot ov beebles is you cot, is it ta tifle, oder mat beebles ?" Jake muttered something, as I replied, " yes, we had one poor fellow, whom we were taking on to the lunatic hospital." The old man had just time to say " which is he," when seeing none but well-dressed, genteel looking people jump out of the stage, his terror gave way to joy. The next day I was rid of the roarers, as Mr. B. of Abington, arrived at his place of residence, and his friend, of Alabama, wishing to rest, accepted an invitation from him, to spend a day or two at Abington, I pursuing my journey alone.

East Tennessee, resembles the western part of Virginia, being nothing but alternate mountains and rivers. We cross no mountain, however, but the Cumberland, our road following the Holston river, which appears and disappears at intervals. The land on those rivers, however, is fertile, and yields hemp, corn, tobacco, wheat, rye, oats, flax, sweet and Irish potatoes, fruit, such as apples, pears and peaches, all sorts of garden vegetables, particularly melons, that exceed those of any country I have seen, both in size and flavor.   East Tennessee exports flour, indian corn, Irish potatoes, whiskey, bacon, cider, apples, cider-royal, Tennessee-royal, hemp, tobacco, iron, beef, butter, cheese, beeswax, lard, feathers, indian-meal, onions, and great quantities of plank, scantling, and other timber.   These articles they exchange mostly for cotton, either in Alabama or New-Orleans, and this they again exchange for merchandise.   The merchants have to waggon their goods from Philadelphia, as they cannot ascend the river, without great difficulty.   We met a number of those waggons every day, ten and twelve teams together.   They were so heavily laden, and the weather so warm, that they never travelled more than ten and twelve miles per day.   The poor horses, I was sorry for them; the skin, in many instances, being rubbed off with the gears.   The road is wretchedly bad, too, particularly after you get in Virginia: and here the stage passes six times every week, carrying the U. S. Mail; that is, three go to Nashville, and three return in one week, and yet, no one repairs the road.   I should think it nothing but right, and just, that government should improve this miserable road, or make a better.

Notwithstanding the great advantages derived from increasing demand for its produce, East Tennessee is at a stand.   In many places, improvement has ceased, the houses going to decay, and many of them tumbling down.   Their little towns have a melancholy appearance, and evidently show that they are no longer the residence of industry or enterprise.   Even in Knoxville, although some new buildings are erected, yet many others are mouldering into dust.

I passed the head of Holston, yesterday, after tracing it from the shoals, where it is three miles in width, to a small creek, and finally to its source, which is two small springs, one on each side of the road, in Washington County, Virginia.   Tennessee river waters five States,* Virginia, North-Carolina, Tennessee, Alabama, and Kentucky. A gentleman related to me a singular anecdote of this river, which I never heard or read of, until I went to Alabama. One, upon whose veracity we may rely, says that there is a place called the painted rock, which is not far above (if I mistake not,) where it passes through Cumberland mountain. This rock presents toward the river, a perpendicular surface of great height from the water's edge, with written characters in red paint, equally distant, both from the top and the bottom, and far beyond the reach of any person, either from above or below, nor can they from the distance, ascertain in what language the characters are written. This phenomenon has given rise to various conjectures : some imagine that a part of the rock has been broken off by some shock of nature, upon which some adventurous individual might have once stood and left this memento of his temerity. Others think it has been done by means of a long pole. The Indians who live near the place can give no account of it.

Newbern.—Here I turn to the left, my way to the Springs lying through Giles county, Va. And here too I had the pleasure of once more meeting my friend of Demopolis, and I hope it will not be the last. I shall never forget this agreeable and pleasant stranger.

Washington, Wythe, and Montgomery.—These counties of Virginia, meet the traveller in succession upon leaving the state of Tennessee. Industry marks the face of the country, and in many parts opulence and taste ; great part of them, however, as before observed, are settled by Germans. In these three counties three things are peculiar to them, viz : more natural children and more fleas I'll venture to say, than can be found in any ten. The third peculiarity

* I might say six, as it touches Mississippi.

3*

is their " sweet melodious voices ;" their accent is distinguished by a sonorous, smooth-flowing sound,
which is actually enchanting—it is music. They do
not themselves appear conscious of this endowment
of nature, which is free from affectation. I remarked this peculiarity in them when I formerly passed
through this part of Virginia some years since ; also
in those who visit our country for the purpose of
traffic. I have travelled through several of the states,
and never witnessed any thing equal to this natural
excellence. They likewise surpass in personal beauty ; they are handsome fine looking men, very much
in appearance like the Kentuckians, though they excel even these in expression of countenance. In addition to all this, they are a well informed, hospitable
and polite people. But from these advantages we
must except the poor ignorant Dutch, who, though
industrious, and in many instances wealthy, are
grossly ignorant, and immoral, particularly their females ; it is among them that those natural children
abound ; to the advantages of the former, perhaps the
misfortunes of the latter may be ascribed.   But
whence come all the fleas ? Heaven knows, for they
torment me even while I am writing. But to return,
I shall mention but one instance of this immorality,
which may serve for the rest.

As I drove through these counties to this place
(Newbern,) my eye was attracted by a beautiful farm ;
we had passed several handsome farms that day, but
this exceeded them all in beauty and size. I inquired of a countryman, (who had taken a seat in the
stage to ride a few miles) who owned that beautiful
farm, he replied " a Dutchman by the name of Blessing," (I think.)   " He must be wealthy," said I, how
many slaves must he have to cultivate all this land ?"
What was my astonishment at hearing that the farm
was cultivated by his daughters principally, and that
he had no slaves. " And why don't some of you
young men," said I, " beguile him of some of those fine
girls ; they must be worth having, they are a fortune

themselves." " Yes," he said, "they were a fortune
in one respect, they had children enough." " And how
many have they ?" five, was the answer, " yes, an ta
vill soon pee some more," said the driver. He had six
daughters, and all but one which was not grown, had
had children ; some two or three, and the young one it
was, " that promised another shortly ! !" This countryman said—nay, I saw one of them myself, with a
black child—"that there were several instances of their ↙
having children by black men." This is the effect
of that ignorance that universally prevails among the
Germans; this too, in a country where the enlightened Prestons live—where the classical, the eloquent,
and highly polished Dr. Floyd, Gen. A. Smyth, and
many other enlightened and intelligent people live—
where the great and wise Maj. Sheffy once lived.
Strange that those eminent characters, prompted by
fellow feeling, or some feeling that would have for its
object the improvement of their neighbors, whose morals are entirely subverted for the want of education,
should not make some exertion to remove the evil.   In
extenuation, however, it must be observed, that the
Dutch (so called) generally, throughout America,
evince an insuperable aversion to learning. I expressed myself to the young man in the stage, in terms
of abhorrence at this gross immorality. "Vy I 'm sure
its no harm," said the poor ignorant driver. But I
will give them up, and see what I can make of Giles
county, through which it seems I am to pass to the
Springs. After spending several days at Newbern, I
bid my kind and worthy friend, Mr. Tiffany, adieu.

Giles County.—Giles is a poor, hilly, broken, thinly settled county. I was agreeably surprised at the
passage of New River, through Peter's Mountain : the
scenery it presents is truly romantic—the only thing
worthy remark on the road to the Salt Sulphur, where
I arrived very much fatigued. And here I have the
fleas again, notwithstanding the neatness of the landlady, who is an excellent house keeper. They cer-

tainly must delight in a cold climate, the whole of this
country, and particularly this, (Monroe,) being elevat-
almost to the clouds. Here are people from almost
every state in the Union, going to, and coming from
the different mineral springs, which abound in these
everlasting mountains. Some come for health, and
some for pleasure. In Paulding's "Letters from the
South," you have a very correct portrait of these watering places; a better description could not be given.
In this county (Monroe) are no less than four different
mineral springs. Here are the Salt Sulphur and the
Sweet Sulphur within a mile of each other—the Red
Sulphur, which is said to be the most efficacious of
them all, within eighteen miles, and the Sweet Spring
within twenty. Besides these, there are the White
Sulphur and the Blue Sulphur in the adjoining county
of Greenbriar, and in the county of Bath, about forty
miles north-east of this place, are the Hot Springs, and
Warm Spring about four miles distant one from the
other. How admirably has Providence provided resources for every part of the globe. This bleak, inhospitable, and dreary country, remote from commerce
and navigation, destitute of arts, taste, or refinement,
derives great advantages from these springs. Thousands of dollars are left here annually by those wealthy
visiters; and in the mean time, as they are mostly people of taste and refinement, they bring a fund of amusement and instruction home to the doors of its inhabitants. The northern people are reserved and distant; the Virginians frank, open and sociable, and
their ladies are very agreeable; the South Carolinians
still more so. Of all people I have met with, they
are the most pleasing in their manners; they are however annoyed with the cold and the fleas. It is not
uncommon to see a South Carolinian wrapped up in
a cloak, in the middle of August.

Although I was myself perplexed, between the fleas
and the cold together, I could not forbear smiling at
the other sufferers, particularly a French gentleman.
Sitting in my chamber one day, and these insects the

topic, he would close his eyes to personate sleep, and then pass his hands with flippant motion over different parts of his body, " dare, and dare, and dare ;" according to him, they missed no part of his body, " per dew da be von diable ting, no possible to sleep for dem, da are not von fla to insect, how you call dat ? da are da fla (flea,) to make hase away, I defy you to catch dem." One of the servants happened to be present, while he was execrating them in his way, and observed, " you get them at the stables sir, if you would refrain from visiting the stables, you would be free from them ;" " you go in b—l," said he to the servant, " da are congenal to all place."

Meeting with my old friend D., I rode out with him through the country a few miles, and having letters to write, we called at a little town near the spring, where I was told that a post office was kept. Unluckily for me, it was the quarterly term of their court, which was held at this town. One tavern only in the place, and every room engaged by the lawyers, and what nots of the country ; all but one, which no one would have, as it was immediately over the bar room, and which necessity compelled me to accept. Goldsmith says, a tavern is the true picture of human infirmity. In history we find only one side of the age exhibited to our view, but in the accounts of a tavern, we see every age equally absurd, and equally vicious. Several men were assembled in the room beneath me. They were talking, singing, laughing, drinking, and swearing, all at the same instant of time. Being compelled to write, I, like the countryman who sat down on the bank of the river, in the pleasing expectation, that the rapidity of the current would soon exhaust the stream, by which means he might pursue his journey, sat with the pen in my hand, and the paper before me, waiting for some fortunate intermission in the noise below, or that they would finally close and disperse to their respective homes,—all in vain !

As I could hear the most of what was said, and sung, it came into my head, (since I could do no bet-

ter,) to take down the conversation as it struck my
ear, in short hand, and see what a budget of nonsense
it would display on paper. The reader has, no
doubt, seen the conversation of a club, written by
Goldsmith; this was not half so entertaining, but it
was equally absurd. Two men were disputing on
the orthography of Mississippi; two others appeared
to be shoemakers, one of whom seemed to question
the skill of his brother chip. Another was accusing
one who sat near him, of stealing a march with his
neighbor's daughter, as I took it; and another was
calling for more whiskey, and a song. "I say it's
Mas-mas-sa-masa-sep-sep-py-py, Massaseppy. I'll
tell you what 't is Jake, you never lasted a shoe in
your life, so, and I never said that before. What the
d—l could you be doing there at that time. Come
Jim, give us that song. Landlord bring us a half pint
of whiskey. Well, I'll hold you a half pint that it's
Mic-ci-ci-micci-pi-pi. I can last a shoe. Of the
morning and the man in the range. Silence, Jim's
goin till give us a song. One night I dreamed I lay
most easy down by a murmuring. Micippi, and I'll
stand to it till the day of doomsday, that it's mas.
I'll be d——d, give me the same leather, and the same
thread, and if I can't. D—n it man, what's the use
of denying the. D———n seize ye, can't ye listen
to the song. Truth. "One night I dreamed I lay
most easy, down by a murmuring river side." Well,
I'll bate (bet) you a gallon the best whiskey in the
Union; done, that it's mic. Make a shoe that'll
out-last. If I had'nt eyes, you might persuade me.
"Whose spreading banks were spread with daisies,
and the stream it gently glide." I'll hold you all the
whiskey in the Union that it begins with. Out wear,
any shoe that ever you made. Out of my senses.
Give us another half pint. Hic-kup an hic-kup.
M—— you'r a l—r."

The Landlord now interfered, and sent the two
spellers, who appeared to be very drunk, out of the
house. By this time Court adjourned, a crowd entered

the house, and the whole scene became one continual
buz, in which not one word could be distinguished:
It must be observed, as a clue to the conversation taken down, that the speakers are noticed in regular
rotation as they are announced at the beginning.
First, the two were spelling—second, the shoemakers
—third, the man who accused the other of stealing his
neighbor's daughter, in the absence of her father—
fourth and last, the man of fine music, and his friend;
the word " truth," however, is an exception, it belongs to the man who accused his neighbor, &c.

Writing being out of the question, I consoled myself by taking a seat at the window and viewing the
scenery of the surrounding country, which is highly
picturesque. Farms, or gentlemen's seats, perhaps,
(I know not which,) appear at intervals on the side of
the mountains, which are not so steep as to preclude
cultivation; neither does their proximity offend the
eye. While I was musing on the scene before me, my
attention was attracted by a party in the street. A
poor invalid of the springs, who appeared to be in the
last stages of a consumption, was riding up street, directly under my window. Some distance behind, rode
four ladies abreast, the self same way; they were none
of your finical, fine spun, scrupulous ladies; this was
evident at first sight; they were fine lusty looking females, that might average a hundred and sixty weight.
They all rode on trotting horses; they whipped on
pretty brisk, and soon gained upon the young man ;
as they drew near, his horse being a little fiery, began
to display his mettle, by attempting to escape from his
imaginary danger. His rider, however, had strength
enough to check him by reining him up; the horse
finding himself over-ruled in his first design, resolved,
at least, to examine the nature of the case, and wheel-
ing now to the right, and now to the left, I expected to
see the young man thrown from his back; and in the
eagerness of my alarm for him, I was actually putting
my head out of the window to call to the ladies " to
have mercy and not ride over the good man," when

Mr. D—— (who had likewise been looking on,) with-
held me, saying I might as well attempt to control the
wind. The young man finding himself in danger,
(though afraid to look behind him,) screwed himself
up in a heap, and holding fast to the pummel of the
saddle, resigned himself to his fate.; meanwhile his
fair foes advanced in unbroken rank, with resolution
and firmness, apparently without pity or remorse for
his situation, when fortune relieved him by an unexpected movement of his horse to one side. I asked
Mr. D—— " where that female troop intended to go
that night," as I perceived they were bound for the
country somewhere. He replied, " home, to be sure."
" They cannot live far then," said I, " as they have
delayed their departure so late, the sun must be
down." What was my astonishment when he informed me that two of them lived nineteen miles at least,
and the others nine or ten. " These are ladies for
you," no attendance of any sort. "But," said I, " I
should be afraid of the wild beasts ; I should be afraid
that a wolf, a bear, a raccoon, or some such terrible
animal would light on my head, out of a tree, as I rode
under it : I should think they ought to be armed, at
least, in a country infested as this is with wild beasts.
" And if mothers ride at this rate," said I, " at what
rate must the daughters ride ? they do not thus
brave danger, unattended by the other sex." He
surprised me still more when he replied " that it was
quite common to see young women of that country,
jump on a horse hardly broke to the bridle, and gallop ten or fifteen miles by themselves, and sometimes
attended only by another of their own age and sex !
So much for the ladies of Monroe.

This is a poor little village, remarkable for nothing
but a very elegant brick court-house, and the residence of the renowned A. B. and his famous rival
C——, Esq. both of whom have amassed great
wealth in the line of their business, which is that of
merchants and speculators. The former, however,
it appears, as longer engaged, is by far the wealthi-

est. He was carrying every thing before him with
a high hand, when he met with a formidable rival in
the person of Mr. C. who commences the business
in the same town: B. flies to the country, and plants
other stores; C. does the same; all advantages are
sought on both sides, and every measure is resorted
to, to 'fleece the people and increase their own coffers.
The latter, however, yields greatly to the former in
point of wealth and mercantile talents, while he has
the advantage of B. in speculative arts. Both set
out poor, and from small beginnings have succeeded
without a parallel, taking into view the nature of the
country in which they have so eminently distinguished their talents. B. is an emigrant from Ireland,
from whence he arrived twenty-four or twenty-five years
since. They used to call him the greasy pedlar, it is
said; they may now call him the greasy merchant.—
He commenced his career in these back countries when
ginseng was in great demand, and these mountains
abound in it. He took it from the people's doors,
whereas they, before that, had to take it to Staunton.
He did the business of several counties, bringing in
goods from Philadelphia in waggons, and taking every thing in exchange from the people. The whole
of this country teeming with cattle, ginseng, and peltry, this enterprising man wrested these articles of
commerce from the lower country merchants. He
possessed every qualification of a great merchant; he
was well educated, of pleasing manners, possessed all
the warm hearted generosity of his country, and was
long distinguished as an open and fair dealer. With
no competitor to oppose him, no wonder then, such as I
have described him, that he outstripped the wind; nor
is it known at this time how much he is worth;—it is
supposed to amount to millions. He has, however,
lost the confidence of the people, who begin to awake
from that state of vassalage in which they have been
held by him and his rival. Report says that he has
lost, too, the charater of an upright and fair dealer.
I have more than once observed this of the Irish, that
when they have remained long in America, particularly

if they become rich, they lose those characteristics for
which alone they are estimable ; I mean that frankness
and generosity which so eminently distinguish their nation ; perhaps those are plants that will not thrive in our
climate.   C—— is an American, a Kentuckian (I think.)
He is descended from a respectable family ; and having
lost his father, was reared, educated, and protected by
an uncle ; but his talents, at an early age, soon rendered
him independent of friends ; and shocking, (if it be true)
the first object of his speculation was the destruction of
this uncle ; I mean as respects his fortune.   I have just
seen him ; he is a great contrast to his rival, in appearance ; he is one of your finest looking men, of elegant
address, and very handsome.   Whereas B—— goes
with his head down, more like a criminal going to execution than any thing else.   But, however they may
differ in other respects, it seems they agree in one, which
is to grind the poor.   Those who are so unfortunate as
to fall in their debt, receive no mercy at their hands,
while they have insensibly beguiled the people of almost every thing they possessed—the natural result of
competition.   This perhaps is right—agreeably to Pope
it is so.   The taste those people have for foreign finery,
and foreign luxuries, roused them to industry ; their labor, it is true, has gone into other hands, but it is losing
nothing, it is in safe keeping.   Meantime their children
are springing up, already practising the arts of cunning
and speculation, inured to shift for themselves, while
those of the sovereigns of the soil are reared in indo-
lence, ease and luxury ; it is quite probable that in
time these will fall an easy prey to those whose fathers
were fleeced by theirs.   This has already been the case
in all countries, but more particularly in the United
States ; this refluent quality is co-existent with wealth,
and right it should be so.   By this means every one has
his share in time.   Not a doubt in my mind but that this
young fry here, (I can see it in them,) actuated by a spirit of revenge, ambition, and that insuperable envy, resulting from disparity of wealth, will in time possess
themselves of the hard earnings of their fathers, and
so on.

I have picked up several anecdotes and historical sketches of this part of Virginia, and shall throw them together in order at my leisure hours. As this is to become the channel of communication between the eastern and western states, it on that account deserves some notice; but as I am going to take a trip to the Ohio river perhaps, at least to the Kenhawa, I shall begin with that country.

Accordingly, after spending a few days at the springs, which did not answer my expectation, I set out with with my friend D. to the west. I shall pass over Greenbriar, and the celebrated Grayson county, through which we passed, until I return, if ever. Our course lies a little north of west; the ground rises gradually higher, and the waters, instead of running westerly, come meeting us, repelled by the mountains, to seek a more favourable passage to Greenbriar river, which lies behind us. As we advance, the land is more sterile, and the climate much colder. Much of the country consists of savannahs, covered with luxurious grass, which feeds large numbers of cattle. On these savannahs no trees grow; they are, however, covered with a small shrub, which shelters the grass, no doubt, both from the drying heat of the sun in summer, and the freezing cold in winter. Farms appear in many places, which produce wheat, rye, oats, flax, and the best Irish potatoes.

At length this savannah land totally disappears and you are on a mountain named Suel. This mountain takes its name from a man by the name of Suel, who first discovered Greenbriar river, and was killed by the Indians on this mountain. It is much like Cumberland mountain, in Tennessee, and is in fact the same, being a continuation of it, but not so high. Like Cumberland, it is settled, and produces fine wheat, oats, rye, and potatoes. The people who have settled here for the purpose of living by travellers, afford good accommodation, are well informed, and keep very neat beds and chambers, at which I was much astonished. This mountain is covered principally with chestnut timber of prodigious size. Where you find chestnut you find inhabi-

tants, but in some places you find neither: such parts
display nothing to the eye but a dreary waste, with here
and there a stunted pine tree, stript of its foilage by
some dreadful convulsion, where the little bird of winter sits and chimes his solitary notes, and sometimes
perches on the holly, which is abundant. You often descend into deep vallies, shaded to fearful darkness with
lofty spruce and laurel. One of them is very justly
called "the shades of death"—I thought it might aptly
be applied to more than one. Through these deep re-
cesses, streams of the purest water roll in headlong torrent.

The whole of this mountain, however, looks like
winter although it is now the last of August; we were
quite chilly, at least, I was. Mr. D. informed that the
cold is so intense on this ever-reigning winter mountain,
as to freeze people who have the hardihood to attempt
crossing it in the winter season. He related two instances within his own knowledge. "A Mr. Mayers, a
lawyer, travelling from Kenhawa to Lewisburg, in Greenbriar, became so benumbed with cold, that he was unable to speak, or guide his horse, which turned of his
own accord to a house, were he was taken from the
horse and restored by proper applications." The other instance was, of a man who was returning to Kenhawa (where he lived) to Richmond, in the winter, and in
crossing this mountain he had both his ears bitten off by
the frost: when he arrived at home he had the circumstance recorded in court, lest some doubts might at a
future day be suggested. This did not, however, screen
him from the sarcasm of a lady, who told him that "the
Almighty did that which the laws ought to have done
long before." This happened some years ago.

At length, from the summit of a frightful chasm, formed by the passage of New river through this mountain,
you behold that foaming river rolling far beneath your
feet, while with shivering fear and dizzy head, you
wind your way down to it. This is the second instance
I have witnessed of this daring river forcing its way
through mountains. Some huge rocks, I see, however,
have set it at defiance, over which it rushes with mad-

dening fury, sending forth a noise which echoes from cleft to cleft. I should like to see a boat stem that torrent!! After much riding and walking in zigzag, angles and semi-angles, we reached the river, which we crossed in a boat, with great ease and safety, it having assumed a smooth and slow current. By the same zigzag which brought us to the river we ascend the mountain on the opposite side, nor are you completely off of it until you reach Kenhawa river, which is nothing more than the river just mentioned, but does not assume that name till after receiving Gauley, a small river which discharges itself into New river, about six miles above the falls, twenty-eight miles from where we crossed New river, and about seventy-eight from Lewisburgh, the county seat of Greenbriar county. Within four miles of the falls, where our road strikes Kenhawa river, we cross a part of the mountain named Cotton Hill, which may aptly be compared to Spencer's Hill, on Cumberland mountain. After passing Cotton Hill, the scenery becomes beautiful and picturesque beyond description. For the distance of two miles you pursue a small stream, which increases as it goes, and brings you to Kenhawa: but the scenery in this distance compensates you for the fatigue underwent in reaching it. This stream runs between two moderate hills, which are clothed with flowers of a thousand different hues; meanwhile it swells as you advance, forming innumerable grotesque appearances. Sometimes it runs with nimble speed over a smooth solid rock of about twenty paces, which looks as it were planed by man, on which not the smallest pebble appears. In a moment you see it interlucent, some of the wildest rocks in nature: anon it flows gently over a dam that seems to defy the ingenuity of man, both in symmetry and design. Presently it precipitates itself from a vast height, in one entire sheet: again it buries itself, and you think you have seen it for the last time, when you behold it curling ahead, in Hogarth's line of beauty. Thus, after amusing the traveller with ten thousand gambols, it leaves him at the falls of the great Kenhawa river, the grandeur of which absorbs, for the moment, every earthly thought.

4*

This famous river, after surmounting a variety of ob-
stacles, this amazing rock over which it tumbles, being
the last, flows in smooth and silent pride. The fall is
over one entire rock, about fifteen feet perpendicular.
Below the falls, it is deep, and from two hundred and
fifty to three hundred yards wide. This majestic river
flows between two mountains of moderate elevation, which
are perfectly barren, and almost perpendicular. The
bottom land, at first narrow, (I mean at the falls,) widens
towards the mouth of the river, to the distance of two
miles, and as rich as any in the world, producing from
seventy to one hundred bushels of maize to the acre.
I am told, that, to the depth of eight and from that to
twelve feet deep, little difference exists in the nature
and color of the soil. The growth is butter principally.
Few springs are found on Kenhawa river; and those
that are found are said not to be wholesome; the people therefore, drink river water generally. This is very pleasant, if taken out of the river in the evening, and
left in the open air during the night, it becomes very
cold; and if sat in a shade or in a cellar, it is very pleasant drink the whole of the succeeding day. I did not,
however stomach it so well below the salt-works, particularly as I saw several carcases of dead horses floating on the surface of the stream. While I was viewing
these one day, I asked some black women who were
washing clothes on the bank, how they could relish the
water in which these putrefied bodies were floating.—
" Oh," said they, " da purifies de vater, and makes it
sweet."

Kenhawa County.—With a degree of high-wrought
enthusiasm, I hastened on, regardless of every object
beside, to the salt-works, and the celebrated burning
spring, which are on the bank of Kenhawa river, about
twenty-eight miles below the falls. This burning spring
is no spring at all—how it came to assume the name is
strange; and instead of one there is seven, which are nothing more than this. " The surface of the earth is worn
away by some means, (probably by setting it on fire so
often as is done,) into a hollow, not a foot in depth;

this cavity receives the rain water, which is kept from sinking by the air that blows violently through a number of small apertures in these cavities." The holes through which the air issues are round, and about the size of one's little finger ; they looked precisely as though they were bored with a spike gimlet. I saw but two of those springs as they are called ;* one had water in it, the other was dry. We heard the bubbling of the water ere we saw the spring, which being agitated by the wind from beneath, keeps it in continual motion, resembling water when boiling very fast. The noise is like that produced by blowing through a tube with one end in water. This water was evidently no other than rain water, which probably fell the preceding day ; it was very turbid indeed, occasioned, no doubt, from its violent agitation, and to this, perhaps, may be ascribed, the wearing away of the earth. From this spring no stream arises, nor any vestige to show that ever one flowed from either of those which I saw. From the one that contained no water I could discern, very plain, the air issuing through those apertures already mentioned, which were as numerous as the holes in a riddle, and from both issued the most nauseous smell in nature, something like the wipings of a foul gun, but much more insupportable. These places were discovered by boatmen, who were seeking for wood to kindle a fire after night, with a torch in their hands, and happening to carry the torch near one of them, communicated a flame to it ; it happened to have water in it at the time, and hence I suspect took the name of the Burning Spring. There is no difference in the burning of the air, (for it is the air that burns,) with respect to their being with or without water ; the flame is equally strong in both cases, and when set on fire will burn for months if not extinguished by rain. The flame is usually about two feet in height. Boatmen frequently boil their meat over these springs by setting them on fire, and hanging the pot over them. I would not be surprised if an explosion should take place in the neighborhood of these springs some day, particularly if the air should by any

The others were not far off, but my curiosity was satisfied.

means become heated or confined. No opinion has
been expressed respecting this phenomenon, or any
pains taken to ascertain the nature or cause of its existence.

Salt-works.—The salt-works in this county are another natural curiosity ; they abound on both sides of the
river, for the distance of twelve miles. This is another
evidence of the providential care of the Deity. Here
is a spot, that were it not for this article of commerce,
and the facility with which it can be sent to market,
would be destitute of almost every comfort and convenience of life. Immense quantities of salt are made
here annually ; upon an average about one million of
bushels, which employ one thousand hands. This salt
is sent down Kenhawa river in boats to every part of
the western country, and exchanged for articles of consumption. It appears, however, notwithstanding this
great bounty of nature, that very few of the proprietors
have realized any solid advantage from it ; owing, perhaps, to want of capital in the commencement, want of
skill, or want of commercial integrity, or perhaps to all
three.

The salt water is obtained from the bottom of the river by means of a gum,* which is from eighteen to twenty feet in length, and from four to five feet wide ; these
gums are from the sycamore tree. They are prepared
by making a crow at one end, and a head to fit it tight.
This being done, about twenty hands repair to the place
where it is to be sunk, which is at the edge of low water, on the river; not any where, for the salt water is
only found within certain limits. But to return, all hands
proceed with provisions, and plenty to drink, to the
place. The gum is first placed in the water on one end,
(the one with the crow,) a man is then let down into it by
a windlass, and digs round the edge with an instrument
suited to the purpose ; when he fills a bucket with the
sand, gravel, or earth, which he meets in succession ;
the bucket is immediately drawn up, emptied, and let

*An American term for a hollow tree, after it is taken from the forest.

down again, and so on till the gum descends to a rock, which is uniformly at the same distance. As the man digs, the gum sinks; but no man can remain in it longer than twenty or thirty minutes, owing to the excessive cold that exists at the bottom; and another one is let down, and so on in rotation, till their task is performed. In the mean time a pump is placed in the gum to pump out the water as the men work, which otherwise would not only hinder, but drown them. This pump is kept continually at work; about eight or ten days and nights are consumed in this operation; the head is then put in, which effectually excludes the fresh water; and a man from a lofty scaffold commences boring through the rock, which takes some time, as the best hands will not bore more than two feet per day, and the depth is from one to two hundred and fifty, and in some instances three hundred feet, through a solid rock! The moment he is through, the salt water spouts up to a great height, and of stronger or weaker quality as it is near or remote from a certain point on the river, which is the place where salt water was first discovered. Their manner of boring is nothing more than an iron of great strength, and of considerable length, made very sharp at one end, while the other end is fixed into a shaft of wood, and a heavy lever fixed to this; the performer stands still on the scaffold and continues to ply the augur (as it is called) in a perpendicular direction. This part of the business is not so laborious as the other; nor does the performer require that relief which is indispensable in sinking the gum; but he must have some dozens of augurs continually going to and from the smith's shop. I saw several of these at work, and likewise those at the gum; it is impossible for any one to guess what a wretched appearance those poor creatures make when they are drawn out of this gum. They are unable to stand, and shiver as if they would shake to pieces; it can hardly be told whether they are black or white, their blood being so completely chilled. The trouble of making salt, after salt water is obtained, is trifling. When the man finishes boring, a tin tube is placed in the rock, and by means of a machine, which is worked by a horse, the

water is thrown into cisterns, from which it is committed
to the boilers.   This water is so strong that they make
it into salt twice in twenty four hours!   All their wood
being consumed, they are now boiling with coal, which
abounds in their mountains.

These salt-works have very recently been established.   Some few years since, in the latter part of a very
dry summer, the river being lower than it was ever
known since it was settled by white people, the top of
an old gum was discovered at the edge of low water, and
salt water issuing out of it.   In many places, where the
fresh water had left it, it was incrusted into salt by the
heat of the sun.   It is supposed that the Indians, when
they were in possession of the country, sunk the gum,
and perhaps made some attempts at making salt.   Col.
David Ruffner, a very enterprising man, was the first
that established salt-works in Kenhawa, at the place
just mentioned; after him several others; but the old
well, as it is called, that is, where the gum was discovered, is by far the strongest water, and it is weaker in
proportion as it is distant from it, either up or down the
river.   Col. Ruffner invented a machine which forces
the water up hill, to the distance of three miles, for
which I understand he obtained a patent.   The salt
made here is not so fair as that made at King's works,
in Washington county, but it is much stronger, and better for preserving meat.   I saw this proved in Alabama; the meat (that is, bacon,) that was cured with the
salt from King's works, spoiled, while that which was
salted with the Kenhawa salt, did not.   Great quantities
of it is consumed in Alabama; they take it in boats
down the Ohio and up the Tennessee river.   A great
quantity is likewise taken up the Cumberland to Nashville.   But what astonishes me, is, that they have to
bore double the depth now to what they did at first;
even at the old well, the water sunk, and they were
compelled to pursue it by boring; this is the case with
all of them.

These salt-works are dismal looking places; the
sameness of the long low sheds; smoking boilers; men,
the roughest that can be seen, half naked; hundreds of

boat-men ; horses and oxen, ill-used and beat by their
drivers ; the mournful screaking of the machinery, day
and night; the bare, rugged, inhospitable looking mountain, from which all the timber has been cut, give to it
a gloomy appearance.* Add to this the character of
the inhabitants, which, from what I have seen myself,
and heard from others, lack nothing to render them any
thing but a respectable people. Here have settled people from the north, the east, and the west of the United
States, and some from the nether end of the world.—
However refined, however upright, however enlightened, crafty and wicked they might have been previous to
their emigration, they have become assimulated, and mutually stand by each other, no matter what the case is,
and we be to the unwary stranger who happens to fall
into their hands. I never saw or heard of any people but these, who gloried in a total disregard of
shame, honour and justice, and an open avowal of
their superlative skill in petty fraud ; and yet they are
hospitable to a fault, and many of them are genteel. I
see men here whose manners and abilities would do
honour to any community, and whilst I admired, I was
equally surprised that people of their appearance should
be content to live in a place which has become a by-
word. But their females in a great measure extenuate
this hasty sketch. As nature compensates us in many
respects for those advantages she denies us in others,
and in all her works has mingled good with evil, you
have a striking instance of this in the female part of the
society of this place. In no part of the United States,
at least where I have visited, are to be found females
who surpass them in those virtues that adorn the sex.
They possess the domestic virtues in an exemplary degree; they are modest, discreet, industrious and benevolent, and with all, they are fair and beautiful ; albeit, I
would be sorry to see one of those amiable females become a widow in this iron country, in which, however,
for the honour of human nature be it remembered, there
are a few noble exceptions amongst the other sex, which

* The river, which is extremely beautiful, is the only relief to the
scenery.

may justly be compared to diamonds shining in the
dark.

As this famous county is to be a link in the chain
which is to connect that part of Virginia east of the
mountains with the whole of the western country, I have
been at some pains to pick up every thing respecting it.
As curiosity leads one to trace things to their origin,
such as the history of countries, and remarkable events,
I have traced this part of Virginia as far back as the
year seventeen hundred and seventy-four, to the memorable battle of the Point, fought between the whites and
the Indians, at the mouth of this river.   I have seen several men who were in that bloody and hard fought battle, and have just returned from viewing the ground on
which it was fought.   I have seen that part occupied
by the "Augusta militia," commanded by Gen. Lewis,
and that by the Indians.   I have seen the bones of the
latter sticking in the bank of the Ohio river; part of
the bank having fallen in where the battle was fought
discloses their bones sticking out in a horizontal position : the engagement lasted from sunrise till dark ; the
victory was claimed by the whites.   From this bank,
which is a hundred feet, or thereabouts, in height, I
had a view of the beautiful river Ohio : at this place it
is said to be five hundred yards wide.

This river, which is justly celebrated for its beauty
and utility, flows in a smooth current as silent as night ;
not the least noise can be heard from it ; not the smallest
ripple is seen. This, and its limpid appearance, the rich
foliage which decorates its banks and looks as though it
were growing in the water, by reason of its luxuriance,
completely conceals the earth, and constitutes its
beauty.   If the reader can imagine a vast mirror of endless dimension, he will have an idea of this beautiful river.   It is so transparent that you may see pebbles at the
bottom ; not a rock or stone of any size, has a place in
the Ohio.   Kenhawa is a very handsome river, being
generally as smooth as the Ohio, but by no means so
limpid ; it has a greenish appearance ; you cannot see
the bottom, except at the shoals. And more than all this,
I have seen the celebrated heroine, Ann Bailey, who

richly deserves more of her country, than a name in its
history.

This female is a Welch woman, and is now very old.
At the time Gen. Lewis's army lay at the Point, a station on Kenhawa river, Ann would shoulder her rifle,
hang her shot-pouch over her shoulder, and lead a horse
laden with ammunition to the army, two hundred miles
distant, when not a man could be found to undertake the
perilous task—the way thither being a perfect wilderness, and infested with Indians. I asked her if she was
not afraid—she replied, " No. she was not; she trusted
in the Almighty—she knew she could only be killed,
and she had to die some time." I asked her if she never met with the Indians in her various journies, (for she
went several times.) " Yes, she once met with two, and
one of them said to the other let us kill her, (as she
supposed, from the answer of the other,) no, said his
companion, God dam, too good a soger, and let her
pass :" but how, said I, did you find the way,—" Steered by the trace of Lewis's army, and I had a pocket
compass too." " Well, but how did you get over the
water courses ?"— Some she forded, and some she
swam, on others she made a raft: she " halways carried
a hax and a hauger, and she could chop as well has hany
man ;" such was her dialect. This is a fact that hundreds can attest. A gentleman informed, that while the
army was stationed near the mouth of Elk, he' walked
down that river to where it intersects with Kenhawa,
for the purpose of fishing ; he had not remained long
there before he heard a plunge in the water, and upon
looking up, he discovered Ann on horseback swimming
toward him ; when the horse gained the landing, she
observed, " cod, I'd like to a swum." She was quite a
low woman in height, but very strongly made, and had
the most pleasing countenance I ever saw, and for her,
very affable. " And what would the General say to you,
when you used to get safe to camp with your ammunition." " Why he'd say, you're a brave soldier, Ann,
and tell some of the men to give me a dram." She was
fond of a dram. When I saw the poor creature, she
was almost naked ; she begged a dram, which I gave to

5

her, and also some other trifle. I never shall forget
Ann Bailey. The people here repeat many sayings of
hers, such as "the howl upon the helm on the bank of
the helk"—that is, an owl on an elm upon the bank of
Elk river.

History.—Kenhawa county consists of two strings
of inhabitants, upon Kenhawa and Elk rivers. It
was reclaimed from the Indians and the buffaloes, by
degrees, with the loss of many lives by the former,
until Gen. Wayne subdued them. The buffaloes were
so numerous on this river, that they made large roads
through the bottoms. Elks, deer and bears were likewise numerous. None of the buffaloes are to be seen
now, but bear and deer are still numerous, and elks are
often seen on the head of Elk river, which empties into
Kenhawa river at a little town called Charleston, the
seat of justice for this county.* It is navigable its
whole length, two hundred miles. In this town are four
stores, two taverns, a court-house, a jail, and an academy; the three last are of brick; and a post-office, a
printing press, and some very handsome buildings. The
first permanent settlement was made in 1786, though
they had to defend themselves with forts, or at least one,
which was built near where a Mr. Jones now lives, called Jones's ferry. Mr. Morrice, a Mr. Cea, this Jones,
and Col. Donnally, the hero of Donnally's fort, were
the first; others soon followed, but M. was the head
man; he had a boat-yard, built boats, and sold them to
people who emigrated to the west. He had money at
interest, and was the successful rival of Col. D. They
never agreed; M. carried every point, he was looked
up to by the people, and what he said was the law, let
that be what it might. Courts of justice were established, magistrates appointed, and all as this lord of the
land dictated. Some person, however, who had a bond
on M., had the audacity to sue him. The court sat in
an old house, or cabin rather, as the story goes. Some

* I saw one which was caught when it was young on Elk river. It
was quite gentle, and went at large, though nearly grown; it belonged
to Col. Ruffner.

suits were disposed of, before M.'s suit was called. At
length the suit was called, and one of the magistrates
came down, or rather got up, went out behind the house,
and awaked a brother chip, who was lying on the
ground drunk, saying "get up! M.'s suit is coming on."
Another magistrate was lying drunk on the floor; he
was roused by the sheriff; at length they have a court,
and proceed to business. The case was argued on both
sides by their respective attornies, and the jury was
sent out to a blacksmith's shop. You have seen these
shops; they generally have a log cut out of some length,
on the opposite side from the door; at least they have
in the western country, but what the use of it is, I never learned, unless it be to hang their work on; or, perhaps, let in the air in warm weather; but to the purpose.
After the Jury were fastened in, M. gets a three gallon keg full of whisky, and thrusts it in through this window, saying to the Jury, "now do your best." They
were not long, we may suppose, in agreeing; when
they came into the court, their verdict was, "we, the jury, find for the defendant!!" The lawyer for the plaintiff was thunderstruck; nothing was clearer, a plain
bond! He grated his teeth, and cursed them all to himself; returned the plaintiff (which was equally extraordinary,) his fee, jumped on his horse, and was never seen
there afterwards. Thus was Kenhawa settled, and thus
was justice administered, and with little variation continues the same. Many suits have been eight, ten, and
some fifteen years on the docket. The new modelling
of the judiciary, has, however, of late, measureably relieved the people.

Climate.—The climate on Kenhawa river is very hot
in summer; the thermometer rising from ninety to a
hundred; not a breeze relieves you from suffocating
heat; when it does, it uniformly brows up the river from
the north west; these breezes, however, seldom prevail
except in the fall and winter months. This great difference between the climate and that of Greenbriar and
Monroe, of which it is several miles north, must be attributed to that of its being much lower, and hemmed in

on each side by perpendicular mountains. This climate ceases at the Ohio river. To the nature of the climate, and the richness of the soil, may be ascribed that surprising exuberance of vegetable productions, which is not exceeded by any country. Tobacco overgrows itself; wheat and rye grow to such bulk, that its weight brings it to the ground before it comes to perfection; Irish potatoes are cultivated, but are not good; all garden vegetables succeed beyond description; and in no part of the United States are to be found better peaches; apples are not much attended to; indeed, little attention is paid to agriculture, in this county; the salt business engrosses the principal part of the force. Kenhawa is said to be unhealthy; at some seasons of the year (but this does not happen every year,) it is subject to intermittent fevers.

Here are three great high ways, contiguous to each other, viz : one on the north side of the river, leading from Ohio, Indiana and Missouri, to the eastern states. Another on the south bank, leading from Kentucky and Illinois, likewise to the eastern states; and the river itself. The river is covered with boats, some going up, and some going down. The roads are likewise much travelled, particularly in the fall of the year; that on the south side of the river, is alive from morning till night, with people, horses, cattle, but principally hogs; myriads of hogs are driven by this way annually, to the east. They commence driving in September, and from that till Christmas, you can look out no time in the day without seeing a line of hogs. This road is one of the most unpleasant in the world to travel at that time; the river on one side, the mountain on the other, and both so near, that it confines the traveller to one narrow space; which, from the yielding quality of the soil, added to the absence of the sun, the rays of which are totally interrupted by the mountain, is a perfect quagmire. This circumstance has given rise to many ludicrous stories, of people being buried alive; and others travelling on the backs of cattle, hogs, &c. that have sunk into it. From what I have seen myself of this road, even at this season of the year, I am inclined to credit its ill fame.

On our way from Ohio, we travelled on that side of the river. When we drew near to Charleston, it being very dark, we could just perceive something before us, which appeared not to move; but whether it was man or beast, or what, we could not discover. At length, as we approached nearer, we found it to be a man, whose horse had stuck fast in the mud. It was laughable to hear him cursing the horse. " Blast you," said he, " can't you go neither back nor forward." It appeared that he was a citizen of the town, and, like ourselves, had been delayed till dark, by the badness of the road, when his horse plunged into a mud-hole up to the girth, and was unable either to advance or retreat. We could not think of leaving him in such a piteous condition ; but how to relieve him was a question of some difficulty. At length, he was compelled to dismount in the mud, which took him up to his knees ; and with some difficulty, he extricated his horse. They tell an anecdote (indeed, they tell hundreds,) of a Scotch gentleman, who was travelling this road, and who, it seems, was not aware of those fallacious mud-holes, cried out to his horse, as he was sinking into one of them, " ho'd ! ho'd ! gin I had aff my close, we'll swum, I'm thinkin ; dom ye for a blind bast, gin ye could'nt see the quick sand." It was said that the horse was really blind.

After spending two weeks at Kenhawa, I returned easterly, taking a circuit through Nicholas and Pocahontas. At length I find myself in Lewisburg.

Lewisburg.—Lewisburg is four miles west of the Alleghany Mountain ; contains a handsome stone court-house and jail, two clerks offices, two churches, one for presbyterians and one for methodists, one academy for young men, and one for young ladies, two taverns, four retail stores, a post-office, a printing office, and forty dwelling-houses, chiefly of wood. In this small town four different courts hold their sessions, to wit : a Superior Court of Chancery twice a year, the Superior Court twice a year, the United States Court twice a year, and the inferior courts for the county. These courts, and the number of travellers who pass through

5*

this place, from the west to the east, and from east to
west, and the vast numbers of hogs, horses, and cattle,
that are drove through it from all parts of the western
country, gives it an air of liveliness, for about ten months
in the year.

The state of Virginia is now engaged in making a
road from the head of navigation, that is, the nearest
point of intersection with James river. It is, when
completed, to come in at the falls of Kenhawa. This
road passes through Lewisburg. The intention of this
undertaking, I am told, is to draw the trade of the western states. It appears to be the design of Virginia, to
come in for a share of that commercial interest, hitherto
engrossed by the states north of her. She contemplates
transporting merchandise by water to Covington, a
small town on Jackson's river, at the point of intersection with this road, and from thence by waggons, to the
falls of Kenhawa, where a line of steam boats is to convey it to different parts of the western country. The
merchandize is to be exchanged for the produce of the
west. I have not been able to trace the scheme further
than this. But in my humble opinion, it will be long
ere Virginia will be able to furnish the western states,
upon this or any other plan, as low as they will be furnished by the northern. She has clear evidence of this,
in the universal practice of the merchants of West Virginia, and Tennessee, who lay in their goods at Philadelphia, which is nearly double the distance to Richmond; and besides, Virginia commands navigation for
nearly two hundred miles in that direction by James' river. Why she has not realized this advantage I am not
able to say. It appears, that from the little I have been
able to learn of Virginia, though she by no means wants
genius or public spirit, yet, she wants that genius necessary to promote commerce. They say here that it
is designed to connect the waters of James river and
Kenhawa, by cutting a canal through the Alleghany
mountain, from Dunlap's Creek, on the east, to Howard's
Creek, on the west of it. As the Alleghany presents
but a slight elevation at this place, and these streams
are but a few miles asunder, this might easily be done

But then another obstacle presents itself; these streams
are nearly dry seven months in the year; and, upon an
average, frozen two months in every year, and from
their great fall, although they swell to a prodigious degree very often, yet they swell and subside in a few
hours. I have seen enough of this, having lived among
mountains nearly all my life. A boat would get but a
few miles, before she would find herself stationary till
the next swell; and whether a boat could stem those
impetuous torrents at all, is a great question with me;
running down the sides of the mountains as they do, nothing less than a double portion of steam would be able
to propel them; experience, however, is the only test of
all things.

The Alleghany mountain, as already observed, is so
low that if it were not for the streams flowing in opposite directions it would not be perceivable. But although low, it spreads out to an immense width; it is nothing less than this mountain that extends to Kenhawa
river, 90 miles, although called by other names. Those
ridges are much higher than the Alleghany; Greenbriar
river rises near the main ridge, on the west of which it
runs at a hurrying rate for 200 miles, being hemmed in by
the vast bed of mountains just mentioned. It discharges
itself into New river, several miles above the junction of
that river, with Gauly. On the bosom of this vast mass
of mountains are the six counties of Virginia, known by
the names of Greenbriar, Monroe, Nicolas, Pocahontas,
Giles, and Tazewell, elevated to the clouds, resembling
each other in every thing: Greenbrier, however, as she
is the mother of the whole, commands most wealth, having the advantage in good land. But with respect to
the appearance of the inhabitants, their pursuits and
manners, they are alike, and to these we may add Alleghany, also clipped from the wings of Greenbriar.
These counties have been erroneously confounded with
the western country, whereas there is as much difference
between the people of the western states and those, as
there are between any two people in the union. The
inhabitants of the western states are an enterprising,
systematical, industrious people, to which they are stim-

ulated by the fertility of their soil, and numerous navigable rivers. These last are likewise distinguished for energy of mind, politeness of manners, and application to business; whereas the former exhibit a striking contrast to all these traits. These counties, remote from commerce and civilized life, confined to their everlasting hills of freezing cold, all pursuing the same employments, which consist in farming, raising cattle, making whiskey, (and drinking it,) hunting, and digging *sang*,* as they say, present a distinct republic of their own, every way different from any people.

Appearance.—The young people, of both sexes, are very fair and beautiful, and many of them well formed: the men are stout, active, and amongst the best marksmen in America. They are, both male and female, extravagantly fond of dress; this, and their beauty, only serves to expose their unpolished manners, and want of education. They have no expression of countenance, nor do they appear to possess much mind. One great proof of this, is, that all places of honor, profit, or trust, are monopolized by strangers: even here, in Lewisburg, where Rev. M——, (who is also a foreigner,) has been daily employed as the principal of an academy, the only one in the republic, for fifteen years, several foreigners have stepped in and have made great fortunes: and, by the way, too, here are the Messrs. B. and C. the two great mercantile heroes already mentioned. They are taking in the people of Greenbriar with admirable skill. Having rendered Monroe insolvent, they have come to try the range, (to use one of their expressions,) of Greenbriar, and bid fair to strip her as bare as they have her daughter. But this is the fault of the people; that taste they have for dress, foreign manufactures, coffee, tea, &c. will prove their ruin. I passed through this county about thirty years since, when the people hardly knew what tea or coffee was; in fact, many of them did not; and now there is no family but what uses coffee and tea, and in no country under heaven have they more delicious milk, or more abundant.

* Ginseng.

At that time nothing but domestic cloth was worn, and
now every one in one hundred men, (out of the country,
too,) which I counted to-day, at preaching, were clothed
in foreign manufactures ; but one only, a member of congress, had on domestic.*

Since I have been here, I have been astonished to
see loads of crockery ware, tea-cups, and such things,
purchased by people who lived twenty, thirty, and in
one instance fifty miles off, put them in the saddle-bags
or tie them up in a kerchief : and a woman will think
nothing of setting them in her lovely lap, holding them
with one hand and the rein of an unruly horse in the
other, and set out for home in a round trot, at sunset,
which, perchance, may be fifteen or twenty miles distant. The pernicious effect of this growth of foreign
luxuries already begins to show itself ; twenty, perhaps
forty, for one, die now to what was known when they
lived on their own wholesome viands, and dressed in
their own coarse but warm and substantial domestic
cloths, which are still made, indeed, but brought to the
stores and exchanged for frippery, which is not sufficient to defend them against the cold of this region.
Consumptions are now common, whereas, thirty
years ago, sickness of any sort was almost wholly unknown. The climate is also fatal to black peole. But
the most astonishing circumstance which distinguishes
this country, and one that has often been remarked, is
that it never has produced one tolerable smart man.
From Montgomery to Harrison, there never has been
reared one man of abilities of any sort, while Kenhawa,
inferior as it may be, has produced one of the brightest
stars of American genius, I mean Henry Ruffner, L.L. D.
a man of profound erudition, who would do honor to
any country ; he is the son of Col. Ruffner, mentioued
in these sketches. I am told he is professor of Greek,
in Washinton college, Va. This cannot be the effect
of climate ; if it be, how do we account for the opposite
result in Switzerland, and other cold countries, which has
produced some of the greatest geniuses in the world ;
nor can it be the effect of education, as genius exists
without it. Indeed, West Virginia has dealt out genius

* Hon. William Smith.

with a sparing hand : with the exception of John Breck-
enridge, I am told she has never produced one man
that might be called great.

But, to return to my Grison republic ; their dialect
sets orthography at defiance, and is with difficulty understood ; for instance, the words *by*, *my*, *rye*, they pronounce as you would *ay*. Some words they have imported, some they have made out and out, some they
have swapped for others, and nearly the whole of the
English language is so mangled and mutilated by them,
that it is hardly known to be such. When they would
say *pretence*, they say *lettinon*, which is a word of very
extensive use amongst them. It signifies a jest, and is
used to express disapprobation and disguise ; " you are
just lettinon to rub them spoons—Polly is not mad,
she is only lettinon." Blaze they pronounce *bleez*, one
they call *waun*, sugar *shugger* ; " and is this all it ye got ?"
handkerchief *hancorchy*, (emphasis on the second sylla-
ble ;) and " the two ens of it comed loose ;" for get out
of the way, they say get out of the road : Road is universally used for way ; " put them cheers, (chairs) out of
the road." But their favorite word of all, is *hate*, by
which they mean the word thing ; for instance, *nothing*,
" not a hate—not waon hate will ye's do :" What did
you buy at the stores, ladies ? " Not a hate—well you
hav 'nt a hate here to eat." They have the *hickups*,
and corp, (corps,) and are a *cute* people. Like Shaks-
pear, they make a word when at a loss : *scawm'd* is one
of them, which means spotted. They have rock houses
and rock chimneys, &c. &c.

It would cure any one of the spleen to take a day or
two in the country near the border of this republic.—
" Billy, tell Johnny he must bring Sammy home ;" if
you were to tell them there were no such words, they
would put you down as a fool. Their houses are adorned throughout with netting and fringe of coarse cotton,
and the *han'tawel* : This last puzzled me much ; I
thought it meant one exclusively for the hands, but it is
distinguished from a spacious one that sticks by the four
corners to the wall, near the door or window, (if there
be one in the house.) Thus disposed, a looking-glass,

of neat device, about four by six inches, is confined in
the centre; and by this last, hangs suspended, by one
end, a long narrow lucid housewife, with some dozen
pockets, consisting of as many different colors.   These
are grappled by a comb-case, but you would never
know it by the name; it is not made of horn at all, but
of paste-board, on the outside of which is pasted a bit
of painted paper; this comb-case is about the size of a
lady's reticule, and differs from it in shape only in this,
that the part next the wall terminates in a triangle, by
which it is suspended amongst its fellow ornaments.
The ingenuity, taste, and pride, of the females, seems to
be centered in this group of fineries—meantime you are
addressed by the mistress of the family, " I reckon you
are a most starved," while she is busied in preparing
you something to eat: while this is doing, you are suffering the torments of the ordeal, from the impertinent
curiosity of the whole family, in asking " What may be
your name? where you are going? from whence you
came? and whether you are married? and have you
any children? and whether your father and mother be
alive?"   At length a small table is drawn into the centre of the same arpatment you are in, while the noise
produced by it, jars every nerve in your body.   This
table is covered, (in many instances, with a cloth black
with grease and dirt,) ten or a dozen plates, (I'll say
nothing of them,) are placed on it, and finally one or
two small dishes, on which is piled fried meat, to the
height of a modern pyramid, with a hay-stack of sliced
bread upon a plate.   At one end of the table is another
pile of besmeared, becracked, cups and saucers, which
seem to maintain their place on the edge of the table
by magic.   You are now asked to sit down, with the
man, his wife, and four or six dirty boys and girls,
around a table about large enough for two persons; and
what's to be done, now? If you offer to touch the pyramid of bread to help any one of the party, great part
of it tumbles over the table.   But this is unnecessary, for
each one reaches over the table with the utmost facility
and helps himself; now and then, his sleeve, as black
as your hat, coming in contact with the meat and bread,

while their faces and noses are enough to set you against
eating, forever; and as for the meat, you might as well
try to insert your knife into a brick-bat. The coffee,
however, and butter are fine, and nothing would affront
them more than to offer them pay; meanwhile if you
happen to lay any of your clothing where they can get
hold of it, if to soil it sends it to perdition it must go
there; they take it in their dirty hands again and again,
turn it over and over, and when one has besoiled it another one must satisfy his curiosity. If you tell them
the most interesting anecdote, they pay no more attention to you than if you were muttering Greek; take up
the most amusing book and read to them, it is the same
thing, and two-thirds of them would be *afraid* it was not
a good book.

History—Greenbriar river, which gives name to the
county of that name, was discovered in the year 1749, by
two enterprising hunters, by the name of Suel and Carver. These two men crossed the river and selected a
cave, on a creek, which has, since that time, been called Carver's, after the latter, as the former gave name
to the mountain, on which, he was, long after this,
however, killed by the Indians. These two men, it
appears, lived in a cave for several years, but
at length they disagreed on the score of religion,
and occupied different camps. They took care, however, not to stray far from each other, their camps
being in sight. Suel used to relate that he and his friend
would sit all night without sleep, with their guns cocked ready to fire at each other: "And what could that
be for?" said one to him, "Why because we could 'nt
agree." "Only two of you, and could you not agree?
what did you quarrel about?" "Why about rela-gin."*
One of them, it seems, was a presbyterian, and the
other, of the church of England. Greenbriar county,
from which, all those I have mentioned, were taken, was
settled by emigrants from Augusta county, Va. The
first settlers were by the names of "Yokum, Cea, Lawrence, and Clendening." Cea settled on a place not
far distant from Lewisburg, called Keeny's Knobs.
Clendening settled where Mr. Ballard Smith now lives,

* They were 80 miles from any inhabitants.

within two miles of Lewisburg. Yokum settled Muddy Creek. These came in the year 1763, and were soon followed by others. Greenbriar, at that time, held out many allurements to adventurers; the land was fertile, the forest abounded with game, fine range for cattle, wild horses in abundance,* sugar maple, fine mill-streams, and the best water in the world. It was not long, however, before the happiness of these adventurers was interrupted by an enemy common at that period to the frontiers of all the colonies, I mean the Indians. The second year the whole settlement was cut off by the Shawanese, the whole being either killed or made 'prisoners. Mrs. Clendening, her three children, and her brother, were among the latter—though she escaped before she was taken far. The particulars of her capture, her escape, and her subsequent sufferings, are truly interesting, and might form the subject of a novel. I had the relation from her daughter, Mrs. Maiz, who now lives near this place, which is likewise confirmed by several others. Her relation begins as follows :—

"These settlers had been occasionally visited by the Shawanese, who inhabited the place where Chilicothe is now built. They were often among the whites, appeared friendly, and were received without suspicion. One day, however, they began the work of death on Muddy Creek: they killed Yokum and several others, captured the women and children, plundered the houses and burnt them to ashes. After this, they came to Clendening's, who had heard nothing of this hostility. When they came into the house, they asked for something to eat; but Mrs. Clendening was suspicious of them, from the circumstance of their being painted different from what she had ever seen them : she expressed her fears to her husband in a low voice, but he replied "No danger." Clendening employed much of his time in hunting. He killed great numbers of buffalo, deer, elk, &c : he would cut the meat from the bones and salt it away by itself. The bones, Mrs. Clendening would collect into a large kettle and boil them, for present use : this was done

---

* I was told by an old gentleman, that those horses, (many of which he had caught,) were easily taken, but of very little service when tamed.

under a shed or scaffold, constructed near the house, for
that purpose; and at that time she had a quantity of
these bones boiling in the kettle. She therefore gave
her infant to her husband, and taking a large pewter
dish and flesh-fork in her hand, repaired thither to bring
some for the Indians.   But just as she turned the
corner of the house, she heard Clendening exclaim
"Lord have mercy on me." She dropped the dish and
fork, and turning back, saw an Indian with the scalp of
her husband in his hand; he held it by the long hair,
and was shaking the blood from it. She rushed upon
him, and in a fit of phrenzy, requested him to kill her,
likewise, spitting in his face to provoke him to do so.
He raised his tomahawk to kill her, when her brother,
John Ewing, who was present, said to the Indian "Oh,
never mind her, she is a foolish woman:" "Yes," said
the Indian, desisting, "she damn fool, too." They then
plundered the house, set fire to it, and departed, taking
Mrs. Clendening, her three children, and Ewing, with
them.   Ewing has since said that Clendening might
have saved his life, had he not been encumbered with
the child; he started to run, and was making an effort to
cross a fence that was near the door, which separated
the house from a field of Indian corn, which, had he
gained, he would have eluded the pursuit of the Indians;
it being in the month of June, the corn was high enough
to have concealed him, but he was killed while in the
act of rising the fence; he fell on one side and the child
on the other.   The Indians proceeded on to Muddy
Creek and joined another party, who were guarding the
prisoners captured the preceding day. As they passed
by the settlement of Cea and Yokum, Mrs. Clendening
discovered that they were likewise killed, and their
wives and children among the prisoners.
   On the following day, the Indians, except one old
man, left them in camp, leaving this old man to guard
them; they took Ewing with them. They were absent
three days; during which, it came into Mrs. Clendening's head, that, if the other women would assist her,
they might kill the old Indian and make their escape.
But being narrowly watched by him, she had no oppor-

tunity to mention the subject without being overheard. She in the first place asked the Indian if he understood English, and he making no reply, she took it for granted that he did not ; and consequently made the proposal to her sister prisoners, but they refused to aid her. Scarcely had they done speaking, when their ears were saluted with the whooping of an approaching party of Indians, a number of bells, and every token of a great number, both of horses and Indians. The old Indian sprung to his feet, and after listening some time attentively, exclaimed in good English, " g—d d—n good news." Mrs. C. now expected nothing but death for plotting his destruction ; but she never heard any thing more of it. The Indians proved to be those who had left them, with another party, whom they went to meet, who were returning from Car's Creek, Rockbridge county, with a number of women and children, and a vast booty, disposed on the horses. Every horse had a bell, and every bell was open. Amongst the prisoners, was the lamented Mrs. Moore, who was afterwards cruelly burnt at their towns. They collected their prisoners and set out for their towns. Mrs. Clendening resolved, however, to effect her escape, at the risk of her life. Accordingly, when they arrived at the place called Keeny's Knobs, a favorable opportunity offered upon one of these; one of the Indians was carrying her child ; the Indians were all in the van ; the prisoners next to them ; and the horses, with their bells ringing, behind ; and one Indian behind all. When she, therefore, came to a very steep precipice on the side of the route, the Indians carelessly pursuing their way, she jumped down, and crept under a large rock. She lay still until she heard the last bell pass by : concluding they had not yet missed her, she began to hope. Sometime after the bells were out of hearing, she heard the footsteps of something approaching very heavily. It drew near the place where she was ; she was leaning down on her hands and knees, with her head bent forward to the ground ; and thus she awaited the fatal stroke ! Already she felt the deadly axe on her head, in imagination ; and for the first time feared death. She ventured, how-

ever, to raise her eyes to her foe; and behold, a large
bear was standing over her. He gave a great snort,
and ran off at full speed. The Indians missing her after some time, laid her child on the ground, would go off
from it some distance, thinking its cries would induce
her to return; they would torture and beat it, saying
"make the calf bawl and the cow will come." At length
they killed it, and went on without her. She remained
under the rock till dark, when she sought her way back.
She travelled all night, and concealed herself by day.
The second night she reached her desolate habitation.
When she came in sight of the farm, she heard (or
thought she did) wild beasts, howling in every direction;
she thought she heard voices of all sorts, and saw images
of all shapes moving through the cornfield; in short, these
sights and sounds so intimidated her, that she withdrew
to a spring in the forest, and remained there till morning.* She then approached the place, and found the
body of her husband with his eyes picked out, lying
where it was when the Indians left him. She threw a
buffalo hide over it, and vainly tried to cover it with
earth; she procured a hoe for the purpose, but her
strength was so much exhausted for want of food and
sleep, that she found herself unequal to the task. She
continued her route toward the settled part of the country, travelling at night only; in nine days she arrived at
Dickinson's, on the Cowpasture river. During all this
time, she eat nothing but a little salt, and an onion,
which she found on a shelf, in a spring house, at some of
the deserted places. She likewise found an Indian
blanket, which proved a great friend to her in the end,
as her clothes and skin were torn to pieces by the bri-
ers, she made leggings out of the blanket. When she
got as far as Howard's Creek, not more than ten miles
from where Lewisburg now is, she met several white
men. These men had heard that every soul was killed,
and were coming to drive away the cattle, and whatever
else was left by the Indians. Among these men, was
one, who was heir in-law of her family; he was much

* The effect of a disordered imagination.

displeased that she had escaped. This wretch offered her no sort of consolation, nor any relief, whatever. Some of the men gave her a piece of bread and a cold duck, but her stomach loathing it, she put it in her petticoat, and pursued her journey, thinking to eat it when she felt an appetite; but unfortunately, she lost it, without ever tasting it. At the time her husband was killed, and herself taken, they had a negro man and woman, who happened to be at work in the field. The man made his escape with all possible speed, leaving the woman, who was his wife, to shift for herself. She also took to flight, but having a young child, and fearing its cries would betray her to the Indians, she picked up courage, and killed it. They both effected their escape, and got safe to Augusta; and it was from them that these people received the news of the whole family being slain. In the mean time Mrs. Clendening arrived safe, in her old neighborhood, and in the course of a few days married a Mr. Rogers, the father of Mrs. Maiz, (from whom I had this relation,) and moved to the same place where her first husband was killed—peace being restored; and on looking about the old premises, she found the dish and flesh-fork where she dropped it, on the day her husband was killed.

Meanwhile she had two children with the Indians, a little boy and girl. Her brother, by some means, returned before the general ransom of the prisoners. He informed her, that an old Indian man and woman, who had lost all their children, adopted her little son, and was very fond of it, the child likewise being fond of them. But one day, the old man displeased with his wife, on some account, told the child, whom she was sending for water, not to go, if he did, he would kill him; the squaw said she would kill him if he did not. The child stood still, not knowing what to do; at length, the old man went out to the field, and the child, glad of an opportunity to please its mother, picked up the vessel and set off to the spring, but the old man seeing him from where he was, walked up behind him, and knocked out his brains. He related the circumstance himself, and would add, " I was obliged to approach him behind,

6*

that I might not see his face, for if I had, I could never
have had the courage to kill him." The little girl was
seven years with the Indians; when she was brought to
her mother as her child, she disowned her, saying "it
was not hers," and the child was returning, amongst
various other children, who had not as yet been claimed by their parents, and friends. After the child had
left her house some time, she called to mind a mark,
which was on some part of its body, and ran after it,
with a view to be satisfied whether it was her's or not,
and upon examination, found it to be her child; but it
was long before she felt any attachment for it. The
child grew up, and being a great heiress, rang loud in
her day; many suiters came to woo her, and many were
rejected. At length she gave her hand to a Mr. Davies, by whom she had several children. one of whom, a
daughter, married Mr. Ballard Smith, late a member of
Congress, and amongst the first lawyers in the western
country. Mrs. Davies is still living. It is only seven
years since her mother, Mrs. Rogers, died. This renowned female is represented to have been a woman of
a great mind, unequalled fortitude, and invincible courage. Besides Mrs. Maiz, who is among the most sensible women I have seen, she has a son living near this
place, of highly respectable standing.

Lewisburg.—Lewisburg takes its name fron Gen. Andrew Lewis, who commanded at the battle of the Point
already mentioned. On his way thither, he encamped
upon the ground where Lewisburg now stands, which,
at that time, was nothing more than a bleak savannah.
In the following year, Col. John Stewart, (now living)
and Mr. George Matthews, of Augusta, Va. opened a
store on this savannah; a fort was likewise built on it, to
protect them from the Indians. I am now (1824) sitting on the site where this fort once stood: not the least
vestige of it, however, remains. It is now the property of Mrs. Welsh, whose house and garden stands within the limits once occupied by this fort. From Mrs. W.
who is now in her seventieth year, I collected these particulars. She is now sitting by me, and goes on to re-

late "That she was one of the earliest permanent settlers of Greenbriar, and lived within a mile of the fort just mentioned, which was called Fort Savannah. She was then the wife of a Mr. Arbuckle, who was in the famous battle of the Point, and spent all his time in guarding the settlements. There was, besides Fort Savannah, another about eight miles north-east of it, called Donnally's Fort.

The Indians, actuated by revenge, for the treatment they met with from Gen. Lewis, and his men, meditated the destruction of this second settlement of Greenbriar, and sat off accordingly in a large body, from their towns, with this design. At that time there was a party of men stationed at Point Pleasant,* (where the battle was fought,) by government, with a view of guarding the settlement, and to watch the movements of the Indians. These men, by some means, got intelligence of their march; but who would undertake the perilous task of going to apprise those unsuspecting people of their danger! The Indians were several days on their march before they were informed of it. It was an enterprise that required the utmost courage, trust, and dispatch: a counsel was held; silence, for a long time, reigned in the terrified party. At length, two champions stepped forth, John Prior and Philip Hammond: We will go, said these brave and worthy men. No time was to be lost, they sat off that instant, travelled night and day, saw the Indians as they passed them; almost spent, and out of breath, they arrived at the settlement the third day, a few hours before the Indians.

The inhabitants flew to Donnallys's Fort, to the amount of three hundred souls. It was late in the evening before they were all fairly in, principally women and children: there were but four men besides Col. Donnally, and a negro man belonging to him, and three or four guns in the fort. The negro's name was Dick Pointer, and Dick saved the fort! On the same night the Indians drew near, old Dick (as he now is, for he is still living,) and the four men, were standing

* One hundred and fifty miles distant from the settlement, with vast mountains and rivers between.

guard.   Col. Donnally's house made a part of the fort,
the front of it forming a line with the same, the door of
the house being the door of the fort.   Near this door,
Dick and his companions were stationed, and about
midnight Dick espied, through a port-hole, something
moving, but the night was so dark, and the object
making no noise, it was long before he discovered it
to be an Indian, creeping up to the door on all fours.
The negro pointed it out to his companions, and asked
" if he might shoot ;" " no," they replied, not yet.   In
about twenty minutes after this, a large force was at the
door, thundering it to pieces with tomahawks, stones,
and whatever weapon offered.   The door being of the
stoutest sort, resisted their efforts for some time ; at
length they forced one of the planks.   Dick, (who,
from every account, is as brave as Cesar,) had charged
his musket well with old nails, pieces of iron, and buck
shot ; when the first plank dropped, he cried out to his
master, " May I shoot now, sir ?" " Not yet, Dick :"
he stood ready, with his gun cocked.   The Indians,
meanwhile, were busy, and the second plank began to
tremble.   " O master, may I shoot now ?" " Not yet,"
his master replied.   The second plank falls ; " Now
Dick," said his master ; he fired, killed three, and
wounded several ; the Indians ran into some rye, with
which their fort was surrounded, leaving the dead bodies at the door.   Shortly after this, or at least before
day, they were attacked by a large party of men, under
the command of Col. Samuel Lewis, who had, during
the while, been collecting and preparing for that purpose, and were totally routed by these men.   Mrs.
Welsh's husband, Arbuckle, was one of them.   But had
it not been for Dick Painter's well-timed shot, every
soul in the fort must have been massacred.*   I have
had the relation from several persons, and from old
Dick himself.   The poor old creature wanders about
very shabby : the country does allow him something, but
his principal support is derived from donations by gen-

* This house is still standing, and the bullet holes made in it by the
Indians when they were attacked by the whites, are still visible. Mr. A.
Rayder now lives in it.

tlemen, who visit this place and admire his character. He does not know how old he is, he thinks he was twenty-five at the attack of Donnally's Fort. His head is as white as wool, which, contrasted with his black keen eye, gives him a singular appearance. His master, some years after the signal service he rendered his country, set him free.

But to return to Mrs. Welsh, the most extraordinary woman I ever saw; she has been, and is now possessed of much personal beauty. Although this female has spent her life in the western wilds of America, often running from the Indians and cooped up in forts among people as rude as the savages themselves, yet she is eminently qualified to adorn the most polished assembly. Her pleasing and courtly manners are unequalled, and every way bewitching; with a mind unimpaired, she possesses all the gaiety and sprightliness of youth; but her predominant trait is benevolence. God knows what she must have been when in youth, for she is irresistible now. She has a daughter living here, (Mrs. Reynolds,) in every respect her counterpart. How nature managed to combine so many virtues and charms in one family is matter of great wonder. There are few people in whom we do not see something to admire; but on Mrs. R. nature has bestowed the choicest of her gifts; she has adorned her with a liberality that seldom marks her munificence to the sex.

Climate.—The climate of all these counties is the same.—If any difference obtains, Greenbriar is the coldest. Generally, there is frost in Greenbriar every month in the year, but one, which is August; and one year (1810) they had a frost in August that wholly destroyed vegetation, and nearly caused a famine. The winters are very long and cold, and leave them but a few weeks that can be called summer: the climate is therefore unfavorable for the growth of any thing except wheat, rye, oats, flax, Irish potatoes, timothy, blue grass, turnips and cabbage. Garden vegetables do not succeed well, neither does Indian corn, except on the rivers; but buckwheat is reared in great quantities. The climate

is likewise unfavourable to negroes—numbers of them
die in consequence of its intense coldness. It also affects the white inhabitants with rheumatisms, sore
throats, pleurisies, palsies, and apoplectic fits. One
thing remarkable and peculiar to these counties is, the
dissolution of old people. It is very common for old
people to drop down dead out of their seats, or walking
about in perfect health. I have seen several instances
of this since my stay in this country. A Mrs. Peebles
was sitting in her porch, spinning, in perfect health—she
was heard to fall, and the sound of the wheel to stop
suddenly : her daughter ran to see what was the matter,
as quick as possible, and found her quite dead. She
was almost seventy years of age. A Mrs. Kitchen, who
lived in Monroe, famed for keeping a house of entertainment on the public road leading from the sweet springs
to the western country, dropped dead in a second of
time. She was in her eightieth year, and was sitting
in her own room, spinning on the little wheel ; no other
person was in the room but herself, though her son and
his family lived in the same house. The old lady had
a favourite little black boy, whose business it was to
wait on her, solely—the little boy, though hardly ever
absent even for a moment, was then out of the room.
She rang the bell, and her daughter-in-law stepped
to the door to see what she wanted, but before she
came in sight of her, she heard her fall to the floor, and
when she came to her, she was dead. She never breathed afterwards ! Old Mr. Bowyer, (Mike Bowyer,) the
proprietor of the White Sulphur Springs, nine miles from
hence, died sitting upright in his chair. How long before it was discovered, no one knew, as he likewise was
alone. A man, but a few days since, of considerable
age, who lived about a mile from this place, (Lewisburg,)
walked into town for the purpose of purchasing coffee,
for breakfast, and was to have returned immediately.
The teakettle was on, the table set, and every thing ready
but the coffee. One hour passed away—the old man's
daughter set out herself to get the coffee, and see what
was the matter, when lo! she found him lying dead in
the road, and the coffee by him. He had left town in

perfect health, so far as was recollected. Many instances of these sudden deaths occur in this country, which is confined to old people, and to those amongst them who live near the Alleghany mountain. I have no doubt, but this sudden extinction of life is the effect of the climate. I should like to hear the opinion of the learned on this subject.* Although the winters are so cold, and long, yet the snow does not fall deep, though it is almost perpetually spitting snow; for a few years back, it rarely snows much till March. It rarely rains in winter; but in the spring, they have heavy, cold, and almost continual rains. The seasons are very irregular; some part of the summer they are deluged ; the remainder, perhaps, every stream will be dry; and vegetation commences.

This part of Virginia exports cattle, horses, sheep, whiskey, bacon, sugar, tobacco, cheese, wool, beeswax, feathers, tallow, poultry, hemp, ginseng. Of these articles ginseng, cattle and butter, greatly exceed the others. Greenbriar breeds great numbers of horses and cattle. These horses are remarkable both for beauty and size ; they deserve much credit for the improvement they have made within a few years past in the breed of horses. I remember when there were not a dozen horses that could be called handsome in the whole bounds. They likewise take great pains in the art of rearing cattle, to which their soil is favorable, it being better adapted to grass than grain. They furnish the Baltimore, Philadelphia and Washington markets with beef. Their land is fertile, and, though unfavorable to the growth of some things, produces from thirty to forty bushels of wheat to the acre ; the best wheat grows on the top of the Alleghany mountain. The inhabitants do not take their produce to market ; they barter it to the merchants, who (except the live stock) waggon it to Philadelphia principally. They have, however, derived little advantage from commerce ; compelled to take just what the merchants please to give them. Their peltry trade heretofore has been valuable, and ought to

* The thermometer has been as high in summer as 93, and as low in winter as 5 below zero.

have yielded an immense profit ; but from their want of commercial knowledge, they always have been and still continue the dupes of the merchants.

From every thing I have seen of this people, they lack every requisite essential for commercial purposes. They are without capital, system, or enterprise, nor do they seem ambitious of either. If their sons can get a fine horse and saddle, a fine broadcloth coat, and their daughters a fine dress and bonnet, to show out at preaching on Sunday, (which is probably attended with no better consequence,) it is the heighth of their ambition. If their wives can succeed in converting their butter, cheese, wool, and feathers (their exclusive perquisite,) into as much coffee, tea, sugar, and other frippery, as will serve them the year, the farmer is content. The most of them make sugar enough from the maple, or sugar tree, (as it is called here,) for their own consumption, and many of them make it for market.

The numerous mineral springs in these counties afford the people a good market for produce ; thousands of visitors attend these springs during the summer months. This would be a great advantage to the inhabitants, were it not for the pernicious consequences which result from it. Those who visit those watering places, are people of the first rank in the United States ; they are people of fashion and taste, as well as great wealth ; they are mostly from the sea-ports, and great towns, who escape to this pure region during the sickly season. Would these yeomanry be contented with their money, and have no more to do with them, they would still be happy, and realize the advantage. But they, forsooth, must adopt their fashions ; the young men must have just such coats, hats, and vests, they must have fine ruffled shirts, two or three per week ; the ruffle must be an eighth of a yard deep, of the finest linen cambric, because the gentlemen at the Springs have them so. They must have a fine horse and saddle, with deep plated stirrups ; they must have fine boots and spurs, whip and gloves ; though, perhaps, their father never had a glove on in his life. And what must our young fop do now ? He is too fine to work, to be sure ; what would

he do, but get on his fine horse and ride about, and
smoke cigars. And as for Miss, she must have a fine
crape dress; it must be in the fashion; it must be tuck-
ed and corded, it must be trimmed with some twelve
or fourteen yards of satin ribbon; she must have a fine
ruff, of the very finest stuff that was ever seen; she
must have a flat, trimmed in bon ton style; she must
have the "nicest, nicest" sort of shoes, they must be
" prunella ;" silk hose, and silk gloves; horse and saddle, a whip too, and now behold her dashing off with
brother Tim. With all this display, they have no fine
carriage, it is true, but then the uneveness of their country is a sufficient apology for this. They have no fine
servants, but they are fine themselves, and in that consists the essence of the thing: what would fine equipage,
what would education avail, if they were not dressed
fine! It never comes into their heads, that those people,
whose exterior they so sedulously imitate, are from the
seats of refinement, and highly polished manners, that
they are people of education, information and reflection. They never reflect that so many fine dressed people are only so many fine fools, without corresponding
manners. Such eternally is the effect of ignorance,
which always chooses the worst and rejects the best: the
ignorant always choose the tinsel, it is the bait that takes
the vacant mind. Such are the advantages, if it be good
sense, that result from the great concourse at the springs.
But this is sport for the merchants, who find their account in it, whilst they laugh in their sleeve, at these
willing sacrifices to the empire of fashion.

General Character.—The people of these counties are
remarkable for moral and inoffensive manners: there
does not exist a country, which embraces an equal extent, in which fewer crimes are committed. Murder is
almost unknown; but two instances of murder are recollected, and so of every other crime. They are very
kind and hospitable to strangers, and of all people they
are the least suspicious. Their females are very domestic, particularly the married ladies. The young ladies, however, are very affected—I mean the fashiona-

ble ones. Some of the old men, and a few of the young
ones, (if I am not mistaken,) love to drink whiskey ; this
to be sure is a growing evil, and a very serious one.—
The following anecdote may serve to illustrate the character of these people.—" Three gentlemen from East
Virginia, travelling to the springs, missed their way and
were lost in the mountains. The name of a mountain,
which neither had ever seen, made the hair rise on their
heads ; but to be lost on one was dreadful. After riding a few miles, they heard the sound of an axe. They
therefore made up to the sound, and soon discovered the
wood-cutter to be a white man, which they had expected
to find black. They told him their business and their
misfortune, and asked the favour of him to give the necessary directions for regaining the road. He looked
at them for a minute, and laying down his axe, without
speaking a word, beckoned them to follow him. His
readiness in quitting his work without a stipulated reward, alarmed them very much, for now they are to be
robbed undoubtedly—each one concluding that he could
intend no other than to betray them. They thanked
him, and said they would not trouble him so far—they
would take directions. He insisted, and set off cheerfully : as was natural to expect, he walked before, which
gave to their fears considerable relief, as they would
have the better opportunity of defending themselves, in
case of an attack from robbers, which they expected to
see jump out of the bushes every moment. They were
well armed, each having a brace of pistols, besides a
dirk. They drew out their pistols, primed them afresh,
examined the flints, and awaited their fate—when at
length they found themselves safe in the road! But
what was their astonishment, when, upon offering him a
dollar, he refused it with disdain. Thus were these sons
of courage put to the blush for their mean suspicion, by
this generous mountaineer. This trait may be applied
to the whole community : you could not offer them a
greater insult than to attempt to reward them for any
trifling service. These men related this anecdote to
me, and added, that nothing surprised them more than
his refusing their bounty ; that had they offered fifty

cents to one of their peasants, he would have received
it with demonstrations of joy, and that he would have
negotiated for his fee before he performed the service.
Finally, they are people of moderate talents, but they
set a great value upon those they have."

Face of the Country and spontaneous Productions.—
The face of the country, as heretofore observed, is very
uneven. Great part of it is covered with high and rugged mountains, some of which are nothing but barren
rocks, and others are clothed with timber and luxuriant
grass. On the north side of these mountains, some spots
of good land are found; but this is rare. The timber
on the north side differs from that on the south; that on
the north being mostly stunted black oak, poplar, birch,
and dog-wood, while that on the south is pitch-pine,
with scarcely an exception. Their general course is
from north-east to south-west, but it is difficult to tell, in
some places, what course they run, as they represent a
cross and pile figure, as though it were not only one, but
various mountains piled on each other. This being the
most mountainous part of the United States, (which may
easily be distinguished on the maps,) they have found
it impossible to give names to the whole. Most of them,
however, are comprehended under the following names,
viz.—the Alleghany, (which is by far the lowest,) the
Salt-Pond Mountain, the Cove Mountain, Herbert's
Mountain, the Great or Middle Mountain, (by some
called Price's Mountain,) the Sweet Spring Mountain,
Caldwell's Mountain, and Catawba Mountain. These
mountains take different names, in each direction, as
they recede from a given point. All this groupe lie
near to each other, and are east of the Alleghany.—
Those which lie west of it are Muddy Creek Mountain,
Bluestone Mountain, Meadow Mountain, Suel Mountain,
and Gauley Mountain. The mountains which lie east
of the Alleghany were taken up sometime since by a
company, surveyed, and sold to another company of
speculators, who disposed of them to Europeans. Millions of acres were sold to these unsuspecting people,
for considerable sums, which are not worth one cent.

Thousands of families were ruined by this shocking
fraud. B— and H—, of Botetourt county, are said to
have been the principal actors of this cruel transaction,
and Heaven (so the story goes) has taken vengeance on
the former, by a signal chastisement, in the total degen-
eracy of his children, who have turned out the veriest
vagabonds in the country.

Those parts of the country that are not mountainous,
are nevertheless very uneven, and yet the inhabitants
cultivate the land with tolerable ease. You often see
them ploughing on steep hills and sides of mountains,
where any other but those accustomed to it, would be
scarcely able to keep on his feet, and you momently expect to see both man and horse come tumbling to the
bottom. The whole country has a romantic appearance.
Sometimes you see flocks of sheep hanging upon a precipice ; sometimes you behold a drove of cattle, far beneath your feet, grazing in a deep vale ; anon you see a
herd of deer retreating before you in graceful bounds.
Again, from a deep recess, you behold with affright, a
traveller, picking his way with unconcern, on a precipice over your head ; and now, from a rock on high, you
see the silver streams, and all the vast expanse of mountains, farms and meadows, to an immense distance.—
Thus the scenery is perpetually changing.   The following catalogue comprises the principal growth of the forest, viz.—White oak, black oak, swamp oak, red oak,
chestnut, spruce, white pine, pitch pine, dog-wood, hickory, sassafras, gum-ash, linn, walnut, cherry, sugar-ma-
ple, poplar, birch, locust, cedar, mulberry, sycamore,
wild cucumber-tree, pawpaw, laurel, crab-apple, alder,
hemlock, yellow willow, and persimon. Shrubs of various kinds abound, both in the vallies and mountains,
and in no country upon the globe are to be found a
greater variety of medicinal plants ; a description of
them alone would fill a volume. The mountains are
covered with whortleberries and ivy, and the vallies
with hazel, wild gooseberry, and red wood. A shrub
called pipe-stem, grows on the savannahs. It must be
observed that those savannahs are level ; these, and a
narrow strip of land found at intervals on the margin of

the streams, is all the flat land in this country. This pipe-stem is a curiosity; it grows to the height of from three to five feet, straight as an arrow, of equal size from top to bottom, and perfectly free from branch or protuberance. It is without leaves, excepting small tufts, resembling grass, at the extremity of innumerable slender branches, which terminate the top. This pipe-stem is hollow, like a reed, and about the same size. Doct. Raglin, of the Sweet Springs, informed me, that in cutting one of these for a riding switch, he observed a small worm inclosed in the cavity of the stem, and upon examining a number of those shrubs, he found that the pith was eaten out by these worms: some had just commenced, some had eaten half way, and some were completely eaten through: those that were without worms were without pith. The worm was very small and active, of a whitish hue. As you go from the sweet springs to the salt sulphur, at Uniontown, you have this pipe-stem for miles to your left: the inhabitants use them for pipe-stems, for which they answer equal to the reed, and from whence it took its name: it grows in the coldest soil, as these savannahs are mostly upon the tops of mountains. But little white pine is found west of Greenbriar river, or the Alleghany mountain. Peach-trees and pear-trees do not flourish, but apples, plums and cherries abound.

Animals.—The tame animals have already been mentioned. The wild animals are bears, wolves, deer, panthers, wild cats, racoons, foxes, ground hogs, and oppossums, (these last are rare,) rabbits, squirrels, white and striped ground squirrels, and the skunk: all of which are numerous in the mountains, and will forever continue the proprietors of those immense wilds. The bears, wolves, panthers, and wild cats, often come down amongst the farmers, and commit great depredations, chiefly in the night, and return to their hiding places before day. Wolves have been known to attack and kill grown cattle, and even horses. There is a species of the squirrel kind in Greenbriar county which the people call the "Ferrydidle;" it is in size between the ground squirrel and gray squirrel, and nearly the color of a fox squirrel; it is very tame and active; it frequents the barns and farm-yards of the inhabitants; upon the approach of the farmer it disappears with the rapidity of lightning: it will bound from the top of the barn to the ground! Capt. Williams' lady caught one of the white ground squirrels in the winter and kept it as a pet; it was white as snow when she caught it, and its eyes were red, but in summer it turned of a brownish color with bright golden stripes, its eyes changed also from red to brown. They are frequently seen by hunters both in summer and winter, but are very shy; they never come near the farms. Pied and white deer are common, west of the Alleghanies.

Natural Curiosities.—In Greenbriar county, there is a natural bridge over a creek sixty feet wide; it is said to be from 180 to 200 feet perpendicular, which nearly equals the height of the natural bridge in Rockbridge county: this bridge is about twenty miles north-east of Lewisburg. This information I received from Capt. John Williams. These counties abound with caves; the most remarkable of which, is the Singing cave, in Monroe. This cave is three miles in length; it runs under a mountain, and from it great quantities of salt-petre have been made. It is of unequal breadth. In the same county is what is called the Hanging-rock, about six miles south-west of the road that leads from Fincastle to the sweet springs, and about ten miles from the latter place. It is on the highest part of what is called Price's, or the middle mountain, and is considerable higher than it. From the top of the sweet spring mountain, from which it is nine miles distant, it looks like a huge house hanging from a precipice. I have been on this rock: it is amazingly large. It can easily be ascended by fetching a circuit as you approach it, up the mountain, which is three miles in height from the valley below, over which it projects. The main body of the rock reclines in the bosom of the mountain, while it presents a perpendicular front, which projects to a wonderful extent clear of the mountain on the north side.

When you are on the top of this rock, you have one of the grandest views in the United States, you can see to the distance of an hundred miles, in every direction : you can see the peak of Oater east, North Carolina south, with the naked eye. You see eight counties at one view, to say nothing of the endless mass of mountains of which the globe seems made. Over this vast expanse, farms are here and there distinguished, which appear in small spots no larger than a lettuce bed ; these, and the streams that run near the ridges of the mountains, render the whole superlatively grand.* The rock itself combines enough of the awful and sublime to gratity the most enthusiastic admirer of the works of nature. Particularly that part of it which projects over the mountain. This is partly convex and partly smooth ; it may be about an hundred and fifty feet from the top to the bottom, though it is hard to ascertain, from the nature of its figure and situation. It commands, however, a view of the valley beneath it. But no one has the courage to approach the edge of this precipice. The Salt-pond, on this same mountain, is not only a great natural curiosity, but amongst the greatest phenomena of nature. The mountain just mentioned keeps a south-west course from the Hanging rock, and enlarges as it proceeds until it gains Montgomery county, Va. (adjoining Giles,) in which is the Salt-pond. This pond is on the top of the highest part of the mountain, from which, it takes the name of the " Salt-pond mountain." But what is singular, no bottom has, as yet, been discovered. It has been rising for several years : the last time I heard from it, it was from three quarters to a mile in diameter: myriads of trout and other fish live in it, and the margin used to be covered with cranberries, but lately they are overflowed by the rising of the water. Some think it will form a mighty river some day, when it can be no longer confined within its present limits. Though no visible stream issues from this pond, yet, a

---

* Under that part of the rock that projects, a vast cavern is found, where a number of bears spend the winter if they are not interrupted by the hunters, who assemble there when the snow is on the ground, and with dogs and guns have great sport in taking the bears.

very bold stream rushes out of the mountain about three miles distant from it, which might lead one to believe that it had some communication with this lake. It strikes me that the water has a brackish taste, from which it probably took its name. Not far from the Hanging rock, near a creek, called Potts's creek, there is a place called the Paint banks; I have seen these banks, they are a great curiosity. The banks rise up directly from a bold stream, called the Paint-bank run; and form a perpendicular of considerable height, and the whole of it is a reddish colored earth, as red as deep burnt bricks; from these banks, it is said, the Indians procured their paint. On the opposite side of the same mountain, there is a creek, called Sinking creek; it is large enough to turn a mill, and runs very bold for several miles, when it suddenly sinks, and no more is seen of it until within a few miles of New river, the main branch of Kenhawa. In Monroe county, near to the former residence of Maj. William Royall, the mountain, known by the name of Sweet-spring mountain, presents another phenomenon. Part of it, with the trees still standing, has moved for the distance of several yards. These mountains abound in iron ore, and the most delicious honey, and game of every sort; while the vallies below afford the richest milk; wild turkies, and pheasants, (a most exquisite delicacy,) are numerous; and in the streams are caught multitudes of trout. No lime stone is found in these mountains; they are covered with a hard blackish colored stone, impregnated with iron.* Fine springs abound throughout the whole country—very little lime stone is seen west of the Alleghany mountain—very good mill-stones are found in Greenbriar county—salt is made in small quantities on Greenbriar river.

I had the unspeakable pleasure this morning of seeing for the first time a South American. He has just left us, on his way to the sulphur springs for his health; from thence he is to go on to the eastern states, and finally to Havana, where it appears he is a temporary resi-

* Alum is found in the mountains in its pure state.

dent. He observed that he had been for some time in the western states, with which he was much pleased. But our country, he said, was too cold for him; it had given him a violent cough. From his deportment he appeared to be a person of distinction. He is about the middling height, of very delicate make, and very handsome features. His colour was that of the offspring of a white and a mulatto. His hair and eyes were deep black; but his greatest personal beauty was his eye, which sparkled like diamonds, and of all men, he had the most suasive manners. His countenance wore a continual smile; he spoke the English language with great facility, and was very communicative. He called at Mrs. Hutchinson's, where I board, for the purpose of taking breakfast, and feeding his horse. Mrs. Hutchinson very politely apprised me of his arrival, and the moment he took his seat at the breakfast table, I took a seat opposite to him, with a view of enjoying his company, and conversation. He seemed to enter very readily into my motives, and gave me all the satisfaction our short interview afforded. After taking one cup of coffee, he asked the landlady for a glass of milk; she enquired whether "he would have sweet milk or sour," (common in this country,) "sweet milk, to be sure, madam," said he, "I like nothing that is sour, I like every thing sweet, a sweet temper, a sweet voice, and sometimes even a sweetheart." He spoke in terms of the highest praise of our country, our people, and our government, but added "the climate was too cold for him:" he had some letters to write, and although it was August, he had a fire made in his room. I enquired of him "how he happened to acquire such a perfect knowledge of the English language," he replied "that he learned it at college, in Buenos Ayres," of which place he is a native. He made several judicious remarks on the English language, said it had no melody, and was of all languages the most difficult to acquire. He pronounced his native state "Boness Iris." I told him how we pronounced it; "ah," he replied, "and you spell cough c-o-u-g-h, why don't you spell it coff." He was attended by one servant only, a free black man,

whom he hired in Kentucky. When he finished his letters, he, and his servant, both got into the gig, (by
which conveyance he travelled,) he took the reins himself, telling his horse to "come abeyout here, as de yankee say," and drove off. It was with infinite regret I
saw him depart. His name is Marilla.

---•◦•---

JOURNEY TO THE ATLANTIC STATES.

BEING detained by unavoidable business in Virginia, till December, I resolved to visit the Atlantic States,
taking Richmond and Washington City in my route,
and set out accordingly, by way of Staunton and Winchester, Va.   Our party consisted of the two Mr. C.'s,
and myself, just enough to pass off the time pleasantly.
The road leading from Lewisburg to Staunton passes
through hilly, poor land, with the exception of a small
strip, bordering on Jackson's river, and Cowpasture,
until you arrive at Clover-dale, which gives name to a
large body of beautiful land, the property of General
Blackburn.*   This tract lies between two mountains,
which gives it a romantic appearance. It contains
thousands of acres, of which 1000 are under cultivation, and the whole belongs to the General, acquired by
his own industry and talents.   What is called Hodges
valley, is also good land, but you find no more, until you
arrive near Middle river, a few miles above Staunton.
Our first day's journey was much retarded by the badness of the roads, and vast droves of hogs, which succeeded in such numbers as nearly filled up the road.
We spent the first night at the celebrated stand, known
by the name of Callahans.   The old gentleman, who used to give life to the tavern, has been dead some years,
at present it is kept by his sons, two very amiable
young men. I was astonished to find these young men
genteel, very much so, and agreeable in their manners.
They are stout, well-looking men, whereas, their father
was quite diminutive in size.   Here I had a striking in-

* Uncle to the celebrated Gideon Blackburn, of Tennessee.

stance of the ravages of time. Mrs. Callahan, the widow of the old man, a low, corpulent woman, not double,
but drawn down, with not one vestige of her appearance
thirty-six years ago. I saw Mrs. Callahan in the year
1787; she was then a tall, elegant figure, with a bloom-
ing countenance. I had seated myself but a few minutes by the fire, before I inquired for Mrs. C. and shortly afterwards, a low, fat-looking old lady approached.
I asked if it was possible that she was the same lady,
she replied, " the same individual," at least six inches
lower in appearance, than when I first saw her. Mrs.
C. did not look old, but was completely metamorphosed.
No matter what pains we take, to form an idea of things
long since familiar to us, we fall short of any thing like
a correct idea of things subject to the decay of time.
This stand, which every traveller recollects, is one of
the best in the country. Four great roads meet at this
house, viz. the great road from the head of navigation,
already mentioned, the Lewisburg road, the sweet
spring road, and the Staunton road. The situation is
at the foot of a narrow vale, with a mountain in front,
quite too near the house, to add to the beauty of the
scenery: indeed, the country is so full of mountains that
they are offensive to the sight. A beautiful fountain of
the purest water flows out of a large rock, within a few
steps of the door. This, and a huge rock, which projects almost over the traveller's head, on the sweet
spring road, also near the house, and a small creek, is all
that distinguishes this place. But the long, clean, cool
piazza, which runs before the door, under which, the
weary traveller can repose upon one of the benches, and
quaff the pure water from the spring, must be one of the
greatest treats at the close of a summer-day's journey.
Add to this the best accommodation the nature of the
country affords, the company of two sprightly lasses,
and the same number of beaux, it must be delightful.

The Hot and Warm springs are so well known I pass
over them; at the latter place we spent the second
night, and here I found my old acquaintance, Mrs. Lewis, the widow of Mr. John Lewis, lately deceased, proprietor of Sweet springs. This lady from being a stout

over-grown woman, of about two hundred weight, I
found reduced to a skeleton; what has become of her
since, I have never heard. She was accompanied by
her beautiful daughter, Miss Lyn. This turned out
rather unfortunate for one of my fellow-travellers, whose
heart was stolen by this fair nymph, as he informed us.
This circumstance being one of those which occur daily, gave me no surprise, and I amused myself with mine
host, Mr. Fry, proprietor of the tavern, and uncle to the
Messrs. Frys of Kenhawa. I could not forbear a few
jests with the old gentleman, on the subject of his handsome wife, whom I at first took to be his daughter. But
what was my asonishment when she informed me she
was the mother of fourteen children, though no one
would suppose her to be more than twenty-four years
of age. Mr. Fry is not only an inn-keeper but keeps a
boarding-house for the accommodation of those strangers who visit the springs, during the summer months, for
the benefit of health; he is one of your jolly, undisguised men, who loves a joke and money at the same time,
which no one regrets to pay for the best accommodations and the most assiduous attention. When leaving
Warm springs you immediately ascend the Warm spring
mountain, which is pretty steep. After getting up the
mountain, some distance, you have a fine view of the
valley below, which comprises Hot and Warm springs,
and the adjacent farms and meadows; but this is nothing to the scenery that awaits you at the summit. This
is the Blue Ridge and an assemblage of mountains be-
twixt you and it. As much as I have seen of mountain
scenery I had never seen any thing like this. To taste
its beauties, it must be seen, as no language can convey
an accurate idea of its impression. A deep valley appears under you, on the opposite side of which " Hills
o'er hills and alps o'er alps arise," the last of which, is
Blue Ridge, which mingles amongst the clouds, and has
more the appearance of a blue cloud than a mountain.
In fact, no one who was not apprised of it, would take it
for any thing else.

The Blue Ridge pleases by its sudden appearance,
by its serenity, its color, by peeping over the other

mountains in the form of blue domes, by its great
height, by its smooth waving line, by its assuming every
attitude of waves in motion. But what puzzles the fancy to delusion, is the seeming uniformity both in height
and distance of the intervening mountain, which appears
like so many steps of equal distances one from the other,
while it is evident they are not. They appear to be
near you, even the farthest, the Blue Ridge, which
seems almost within your grasp, while it must be at
least one hundred and sixty miles distant. The thin appearance of this last, resembles any thing rather than a
mountain, in its graceful curves ; but language would fail
me, to give even a glimmering of this grand spectacle.
As we began to descend the Warm Spring mountain, the
Blue Ridge disappeared by degrees. until we lost sight
of it entirely ; nor did we see it again until we were
within a few miles of Staunton ; but it did not appear to
be the same ; it no longer retained the power to please.
The third day brought us to Hodge's, who gives name
to a fertile valley, in which he resides. Hodge is one
of your plain Augusta farmers. Here we found peace
and plenty, and by the way, another young lady ; but
whether my friend had another heart to lose, or had recovered the one he had already lost, I am unable to say.

Next morning we had to contend with another mountain ; and to add to the misfortune, it rained the whole
day. We took care, however, to fortify ourselves with
a comfortable cup of coffee and a slice of ham before
we set out. It never ceased raining, nor did we cease
travelling, until we arrived at Staunton, which was a-
bout three o'clock P. M., when a good dinner and comfortable fire restored our exhausted spirits. Besides
Jackson's river, this road crosses the Cowpasture, Calf-
pasture, and Bullpasture rivers ; all of which streams
are small, but when united, form James's river, a navigable river of Virginia, well known. From Lewisburg to Staunton, which is ninety-six miles, you cross
three mountains, viz : the Alleghany, the Warm Spring,
and North mountain. The appearance of the country
as you recede from the North mountain, is precisely the
same with that on the west side of the Alleghany moun-

8

tain at the same distance ; dark shadowy vales, lofty
hemlock, laurels and cedar, with the same rolling riv-
ulets ; in imagination, it seems as though I were transported one hundred miles in the opposite direction.   A
few miles above Staunton, we cross Middle river, which
is no more than a creek ; it has its source in the North
mountain.   The land on this river is fine, and the farms
display the wealth and independence of the farmer's
vast barns, extensive meadows covered with droves of
sleek cattle, and elegant buildings.   I have always remarked, that wealth forever accompanies good land.
This county (Augusta,) is the wealthiest county, except
two, in West Virginia.

Staunton.—Although Staunton is on Middle river, it
may be called an inland town.   The nearest navigation
is Port Tobacco, forty miles.   It is the seat of justice for
Augusta county.   The Superior Court of law and Superior Court of Chancery also hold their sessions there
twice in every year.   It is situated in a beautiful valley, between the North and South mountain, and contains two court-houses, one prison, two clerk's offices, a
fire office, one printing office, one post-office, three
churches, one for Episcopalians, one for Methodists, and
one for Presbyterians.   There are no public squares in
Staunton ; the public buildings are on the streets.
Staunton contains two hundred and forty dwelling-houses, ten stores, three Doctors, and thirteen Lawyers.

History.—Staunton was first settled by an emigrant
from Ireland, by the name of Cunningham ; who built
the first framed house where Staunton now stands, on
the land contained in Beverly's grant.   In the year
1746, there were two log cabins, a log court-house and
a log prison, on the site, when Cunningham arrived ; a
man by the name of Brown, lived in one of the cabins ;
and a woman by the name of Molly McDonald (not of
very good fame) lived in the other.   I had these particulars from Mrs. Reed, daughter of the same Cunningham.   This lady is now living in Staunton ; and, although in the eighty-fourth year of her age, she retains

her intellects in their full vigour. She hears distinctly, and converses with judgment and uncommon understanding ; although her eye sight, owing to a disorder in her eyes, is very imperfect. She never was confined by sickness in her life, she informed me, until a few days before my visit to her ; she was then in bed ; but when I spoke to her, she sat up in the bed, and conversed some time without fatigue. She was born in Ireland, and was in her seventh year when her father built the house mentioned. She said they lived there unmolested, until after her marriage with Reed ; when the Indians became troublesome, she had to escape over the Blue Ridge. The citizens built a fort for their protection, where the centre of Staunton now is, though the Indians killed none in or nearer than five miles off.

I li·ed myself near Staunton, when a child ; and was often in company with this same Mrs. Reed ; who was then an old woman, and a widow ; she had a sister, Mrs. Burnes, also a widow, whom I used to know ; and who is still alive, though she does not live in Staunton ; she is two years younger than Mrs. Reed. Mrs. Burnes when I knew her, kept a tavern, the best one in Staunton. I was likewise acquainted with Mrs. Chambers, at whose tavern I now am. It is thirty-six years since I saw Mrs. Chambers . but I did not find her so much altered by time, as Mrs. Callahan ; although she has had as many children, she had shrunk down a little, and had grown corpulent, but her stature, her eyes particularly, retained much of her former likeness. She was, when young, a very handsome woman, and is still so for her years. Of all parts of the United States, Augusta county must be the most healthy, from the longevity of its inhabitants. Besides the two instances above cited, many others exist. The mother of Mrs. Chambers, who was a very old woman (upwards of seventy) when I left Augusta, thirty-six years ago, has been dead (as her daughter informed me) only five years. She had become in every respect like an infant, for several years. The salubrity of the climate is abundantly displayed in the appearance of the inhabitants. From this cause the fertility of the soil, and numerous streams of the purest

water, may he ascribed that exuberance of nature every
where visible.   Every thing seems to be propelled beyond nature ; the people, horses, and cattle, as well as
inanimate productions, are of great size.   Even the African race are overgrown, and look as though they would
burst.   Staunton is situated in a circular hollow, or low
spot of ground, entirely surrounded by hills.   In approaching it from any direction, the traveller never sees
it till he may be said to be in the town.   No town in the
world can boast better water, or more abundant, than
Staunton.   The most beautiful springs burst out in
every part: they are found in every street, and almost
in every lot.   This contributes greatly to the health and
cleanliness of the place.   Staunton is inhabited by a
sober, industrious, and moral people; it is likewise the
seat of some refinement; some of the first men, both for
talents and erudition, have their residence in Staunton.
Among these are Major Sheffy, Judge Brown, Judge
Stewart, Major Baldwin, Mr. Peyton, and Chapman
Johnston.   Staunton, however, has not improved latterly, in proportion to that success which marked the first
twenty years of its growth.   It received a great check
by those enterprising merchants west of it, some of
whom have been mentioned in these sketches.   Previous to this, Staunton drew all the trade of the west,
which was considerable.   It has no market-house, nor
has it either watch or patrol, although it is an incorporated town.

   This town, and the whole county of Augusta, is famous in history for its courage and patriotism during the
revolutionry war : the most of the people volunteered
their services, both against the Indians and the British.
It will be recollected the Virginia legislature was drove
from place to place, during that war, until it finally took
refuge in Staunton.   While it was in session there, word
came one night, that Tarleton, with a British force, was
approaching, and that he was expected to arrive at the
Rockfish gap by ten o'clock next day.   Colonel Samuel
Lewis, (son of Gen. Lewis, already mentioned,) called
about midnight at the house of his uncle, William Lewis, late of the Sweet Springs, who then lived about a

quarter of a mile from Staunton. Mrs. Lewis (from whom I had the story) said that Samuel opened the door, and calling her, hastily asked, "Where are the boys, aunt?" (meaning her sons, who were men grown.) She replied, they were up stairs in bed. "Call them up, quick," said he, "Tarleton is coming on with his forces, and we want to stop him at the pass of the mountain," (meaning the gap.) She instantly called up her sons, who were soon equipped, and set off with their cousin Sam. In the mean time, several of the members, who boarded with Mr. Lewis, arose, calling out, "Bob, Sam, Dick," (speaking to their servants,) "saddle the horses, quick:" and here they came running down stairs, she said, as though they would overturn each other. She, and Mr. Lewis, thinking they were going to the mountain, gave them all the assistance in their power, in order to hasten their departure; but instead of going to the mountain, they steered their course toward the west, with all possible dispatch. Next morning disclosed a marvellous spectacle.—The streets of Staunton were strewed with portmanteaus, saddlebags, and bundles of clothes tied up in pocket-handkerchiefs, which the affrighted tuckahoes, (as these members were called,) had dropped in their hurry to escape. Not a member was to be found next morning. They rode with the utmost speed during the night, and continued their flight the best part of the ensuing day. One member, (a Dr. Long,) rode twenty miles without a saddle! Meantime the Cohees, as the Augusta people were called, repaired, to a man, old and young, without fear or trepidation, to the place of danger. But Tarleton, getting wind of the reception he was likely to meet with from these backwoodsmen, turned his course, nor was it clearly ascertained that he ever intended to cross the Blue Ridge.— These particulars, which I had from Mrs. Lewis, were likewise confirmed by Major William Royall, who was a member from Amelia county, in the same legislature. He proceeded with the Augusta troops, (the only low Virginian,) on his way to Charlottesville, to see Major John Archer, a relation of his, who was badly wounded

8*

in an engagement with the British.* He said it was
truly pleasing to see (when day broke upon them) old
gray headed men, and little boys, with their guns and
shot-pouches on their shoulders, marching cheerfully on
to meet the foe. " Ah," said he, " you are fine fellows
—I will disown my country, (meaning East Virginia,)
and come and live among you." He was as good as
his word, for in a few years he fixed his residence in
the west of Virginia, near the Sweet Springs, where he
died.

Staunton lies in what is called the Limestone Valley,
which commences in Botetourt county, Virginia, and
ends with Frederick and Jefferson counties, near the
junction of the Shenandoah with the Potomac. Shenandoah is formed by Middle river, South, and North rivers. Middle river takes its name, from running between
these two last; they are nearly one size, and one length.
South river is bounded by the South mountain, which
lies between it, and the main Blue ridge. North river
is bounded by the North mountain, and runs parallel
with it to its junction with South river, where it ceases,
and the united streams take the name of Shenandoah.

Having rested a few days at Staunton, I took the
stage for Washington, my companions having pursued
their journey on horseback. I dislike this travelling in
stages, on account of performing great part of the journey in the night, which deprives one of the pleasure of
seeing the country. A little after day-light, we arrived
at Peter Hanger's, where the horses are changed, and the
passengers take breakfast: and here I had the worst
breakfast in all my journey, notwithstanding the en-
comiums bestowed on the house. We had coffee, indifferent bread, and the offal of hogs fried to a cracknel,
and as black as tar. The old man, a bit of a dried up
piece of stuff, paid no attention, whatever; he left us,
the driver and myself, to the care of his son, a doctor,
and his ill-natured daughter-in-law, whose pride was only equalled by her low manners. This same Peter
Hanger has lived at this place since I can remember,

* Father of the Hon. Wm, S. Archer, now in Congress.

though it was the first (and I trust the last) time I was in his house. To compensate, however, I had a beautiful view of the Blue Ridge out of his piazza. Shortly after leaving Peter Hanger's, I began to draw near the place where I spent my childhood: and here we have the Middle River again, quite a large stream; and on the opposite shore (I can hardly hazard a look) stands a house once and still familiar to me. I had often been at that house when young, and it revived in my mind scenes long since past: it produced mingled emotions of joy and sorrow, of pleasure and regret. An absence of thirty-six years, embracing a thousand (nay, ten thousand) vicissitudes, rendered those objects melancholy pleasing. The river, the house, (Col. Anderson's,) the gate, all were familiar, and inspired feelings such as I shall ever esteem the most exquisite of my life. The stone meeting-house, too, where formerly youth and beauty, age and wealth, were alike displayed; my feelings became overcharged with a thousand tender recollections, so much so, that I dared hardly trust a glance toward the house of my infant years. I can no more.

In the course of the day, I passed the former dwelling of Col. Grattan, on north river. I spent the night at Mr. Grattan's, and often saw his daughters at balls and parties on Middle river, where I lived. But the appearance of this place had no resemblance of its former likeness, owing to the erection of new buildings. The son, I am told, resides at the old farm, and has improved in wealth. Old Mr. Grattan, the father, had a daughter married to Col. Gamble, formerly of Staunton, and latterly of Richmond, in Virginia; another daughter of his, married Col. Brown, of Greenbriar county, who was one of the first settlers of that county; he and his wife are still living, though both her and Mrs. Gamble must be very old. This day was likewise distinguished by two natural curiosities; one was a natural canal, which conveyed the waters of North river to the merchant-mills, belonging to Mr. Grattan; the road runs with it some distance. The other was a place where the road was confined by the North river, on our right, and a large creek on our left, to a narrow space which forms a precipice on each side, that would prove a lovers' leap to the unwary traveller, who might miss his track. It is frightfully sublime to look at those streams as you drive over them, upon a road but barely wide enough for the carriage.

The road to Winchester from Staunton as observed before, lies through the celebrated lime-stone valley. This valley is about two hundred miles in length from Fincastle, to the place where we cross the Shenandoah, where it ends. It is diversified with neat and beautiful villages, from one end to the other. The duke of Rochefocault passing through this valley, some years back, observed that he could not discern such beauties in it, as had been ascribed to it by travellers. This remark from him surprises us the more, knowing his taste as we do. I cannot see how it could be improved ; it is one continued effusion of rural beauties, relieved at short intervals by handsome villages. It runs between two mountains of moderate height, which, with the Shenandoah to your right, keeps pace with the traveller, who makes his way through the middle of this fertile valley, which is in a high state of cultivation, presenting endless farms, indicative at once of wealth and industry. The stage makes the trip between Staunton and Winchester in two days, one hundred miles. I stopped, however, at Newtown, a small village eight miles on the west of Winchester, and spent a day at Mr. Helm's tavern, where good cheer and the most studied attention, in some degree restored my almost dislocated limbs. The road runs over a rock of limestone the whole route. This and the rough constructed stage in which one is conveyed, goes near to take a person's life, unless they are made of iron. On the evening of the second day, I took the road again, and spent the night at Winchester. Lord Fairfax was the proprietor of Winchester, and laid out the town. Mr. M'Guire, one of the finest old men in the world, lent me a coach to go as far as the river, which is twenty five miles from Winchester. We arrived at Berry's ferry about day-light in the morning, just in time to see the Shenandoah, which we forded, though it was very wide. A family by the name of

Berry lives on the east side of the river, on the best farm on the road. Accustomed to travelling as I am, it may be supposed my opportunies of observing the character and manners of people are numerous, but as much as I have mingled in the world, I never witnessed a kinder family than Berry's. Their parents were both dead; the family consisted of several young men and women. I had but a few minutes to breakfast, which was partly ready when I arrived, but the kindness and assiduity of these people was actually painful. The weather being cold, they would not suffer me to move from the fire, but placed the table with my breakfast on it upon the hearth. My wishes were consulted on the dishes, and gratified to the utmost; and when I come to pay the bill it was only twenty-five cents! But this was nothing to what followed when I set out; I was loaded with cheese, biscuit, ham and apples, enough to have lasted me a week, and this was accompanied with a thousand smiles, and good wishes at parting: this was the last house in West Virginia.

In a few yards from Berry's we begin to ascend the Blue Ridge, which at this place is nothing but an almost imperceivable ascent of two or three miles. Now and then I could perceive, at a distance, on the right and left, a rocky spur, covered with pine, stretching down to the road in sharp points, and sometimes throwing rocks of defiance athwart the travellers course. The road passes through a gap of the mountain, which, nevertheless, produces a scanty subsistence of maize and small grain, to those few inhabitants who live on the road. On the top of the Blue Ridge you have a handsome view of East Virginia, for miles distant: another mountain, too, shows itself at a distance; the driver said it was called the Bull mountain. On the top of the mountain stands a large poplar tree, near the road, on the right of which, three counties of Virginia corner; viz: Frederic, Loudon, and Jefferson. Virginia now presents herself in a new guise, different in all respects, from what she is west of the Blue Ridge; this change is as sudden as it is complete. The face of the country, the productions, the manner of cultivating, the appearance of the people, and the live stock, are no longer the same. No more lime stone, no rich land, no bold rivers, no lusty timber, every thing dwindles to nothing. The people are small, the cattle are small, stock of all sorts are hardly worthy the name. The country no longer displays variety, no more hills and dales, no luxuriant meadows, no more bending barns, no flowing fountains; the sameness is now and then relieved by the seat of some demi-lord. The land is thin; but in its appearance, so far as respects its natural growth, and its undulating surface, it is very much like the cotton land in Alabama. It is covered with a light growth of black oak and black jack; the soil red, though with that mixture of black which distinguishes the land of Alabama, and the barrens of Kentucky; like these it is free from stones. But the idea of its poverty, compared with those lands, leaves on the mind a gloomy impression. The most prominent traits of distinction in the personal appearance of the people of East or Old Virginia, are their diminutive size, ignorance, assurance, and imbecility. They have some, a great deal of animation, the eye particularly; but this accompanied with so much impudence and effrontery as to render their presence at first sight disgusting. Persons of the same class, I mean those of the same pretensions, in the western country, form a direct contrast to these, in all respects. Tney are stout able-bodied men, modest and unassuming in their behaviour. The distinguishing trait of countenance in one, is impudence; that of the other is modesty. The same disparity is visible in their minds; nothing affords a greater proof of this than the condition of their farms and dwellings. The western people speak very slow, these speak quick; the first say little, the latter a great deal. These remarks are, however, the result of a few hours observation, but they must strike those who like myself come from the west. Even the waggoners, of the western country, are readily distinguished from those others, in acts of politeness, by giving us the road, while the eastern waggoner shows no preference but for himself.

The distance from Winchester to Alexandria is sev-

enty miles; which journey is accomplished in a day by
the stage. But, whether fortunately or otherwise, our
stage broke down about half a mile from Cob-run. The
driver, by leading the horses, made out to get it to a
tavern, kept at the Run, twenty-five miles from Alexandria; and here I had to stay from Saturday till Monday evening. The accommodation was wretched as
words can describe. The tavern was kept by one O'-
Neal, of Irish descent, as his name bespeaks; he apper-
tains to the old nobility of Ireland. But unfortunately
for him and myself, the name was all that remained of
his noble family. The house was open and cold; the
family, which was no small one, had been sick and looked like ghosts, and they had but two wretched beds in
the house, with not more furniture than ought to serve
for one; this, however, I found out by degrees. The
appearance of the house out side, was certainly the
greatest take in, in the world. It was a spacious frame
building, painted white, with a long piazza. But upon
gaining the interior I was struck with horror. The first
thing I saw was a squalid young woman, who upon our
approach, jumped into the bar, and stood with her head
thrust through a small window in the same, and with a
ghastly smile seemed to signify her business, viz: she
had whiskey to sell. O poverty, to what shifts art thou
reduced! I looked at her and shuddered! I then looked,
what was the prospect? the family, which consisted of
three other women and as many children, were sitting
by a poor fire; the room was wretchedly furnished; the
only thing in it was a large sign-board, which the wind
had blown down, with Marcus O'Neal, painted in large
letters, and entertainment for waggoners. All to my comfort, (no small one,) was the appearance of the landlady,
whose countenance bespoke every thing I wished.
She was sadly dressed indeed; but she had a sweet
countenance, and evidently showed she had seen better
days; a glance at her assured me I was safe; and I
felt as happy as though I were in a palace; the event
proved that I had not mistaken her. O'Neal was
from home, he was at a sale. I took a seat by the fire;
converted the misfortune into a subject of amusement;

though these creatures, except the old lady, were little
qualified to amuse, farther than it presented human nature in a new light. Concealing my embarrassment
with all the care I could muster, I introduced common
topics, such as weather, and how long they had lived
there, how many children, &c. ; I soon gathered her
history. She was a native of Maryland, but had lived
in Virginia for the last eight years ; and for the last
eighteen months on the place where she then lived. This
last place was a low flat situation, from which cause, as
she conjectured, her family had been sick great part of the
time. She had, besides small children, four daughters that
were grown. But alas! what a falling off : those young
people seemed no more than lumps of breathing clay.
Without their sprightliness, they possessed no more
judgment than children. Whether that apathy depicted
in their every look, and inaction exhibited in their movements, was the effect of their disorder, climate, education, or mental defect, I was unable to discover ; but its
effect on me was that of mingled disgust and horror.

To divert my feelings, I walked into the piazza, and
commenced a conversation with a traveller, a young
man, the only one about the house. He lived some distance up the country ; had been to Alexandria ; was on
foot, and was waiting for a waggon, which he expected
from Alexandria that evening, to ride on to his residence.
While conversing with this stranger, I discovered sufficient matter of amusement for the remainder of the evening. This was a bank of oyster shells, at the end of
the porch ; the first I had seen. I suspected what they
were at first sight, when it was confirmed by the young
man. These shells are very like muscle shells ; they
are, however, much longer in proportion to the
width ; much thicker, and differ from a muscle shell in
this, viz : they have a protuberance on the inside ; nor
is the cavity of the shell as deep as that of the latter.
The extremity of each end is not so pointed as that of
a muscle shell ; they differ in size from one to seven inches in length ; they are broad at one end, in the shape of
a negro child's foot. Whilst I was admiring those
shells, a waggon drove up to the door, which proved to

be the one in which the young man was to take his passage, and to my infinite delight it was loaded with oysters! Curiosity was now fully gratified. We soon had a quantity produced from the waggon and laid on the fire in the shell, which is called roasting oysters. A little time serves to make them sufficiently done ; we next had them fryed, stewed, &c. From what I had heard respecting oysters, I made up my mind, that either I would be immoderately fond of them, or dislike them altogether ; but neither these conclusions proved the result. For, although I could eat them very well. I was by no means enamoured with them ; and was at a loss to account for that enthusiastic admiration on the one hand, and that violent dislike on the other, expressed on the subject of oysters, as an article of food. That fondness which many attain, must be acquired from habit ;

have since been told, that they are esteemed for their flavor ; but I did not find it agreeable, or the contrary. I heard a great deal said about the appearance of fresh oysters, (pickled oysters are common in the west.) I had heard them compared sometimes to one thing, and sometimes to another ; and amongst other things, to a piece of fat meat ; but no comparison I had heard was a just illustration of the oyster. If it be like any thing, it is like one of those tendons, or large gristles, which are attached to beef-shins, when boiled very tender. It resembles this more than any thing else, both in color and substance ; it is flexible like the gristle, when hot ; but differs from it in this : it has a hard substance resembling a kernal towards one end ; the largest is, in size, something like a man's thumb ; but to those who have seen pickled oysters, this last is needless.

At length night arrived, and with it came O'Neal, the landlord, and likewise a troop of rough looking men, who had, like him, been at the sale. O'Neal as well as his companions, had been sacrificing to Bacchus, which rendered them rather unwelcome guests. A little while after their arrival, supper, which consisted of coffee, chickens, butter, cheese, and biscuit, was placed on the table ; (in a different room from the bar-room.) I had not the courage, however, to sup with such a savage

9

looking group : and felt no very pleasing sensations,
while I from the fire beheld the party at the table in the
same room where I was seated. Their conversation
was not absolutely without sense ; but so loud and so
mingled with oaths and horse-laughs, added to their
fierce eyes, and red faces, that it put my western courage to the test. To my infinite joy the whole group departed after they had supped; and I sat to supper myself. Before I was done, however, I was interrupted by
the entrance of waggoners, who drove up to the door,
and entered the supper room without ceremony. They
called for supper, and for leave to spend the night.
This added to my perplexity again; as it had grown
late, and I wished to lie down, but my bed being in the
same room where the waggoners must eat, I had another opportunity of exercising patience, a virtue of so
much service to us in this uncertain world. In about
an hour, the supper affair being over, I located myself
upon a pallet before the fire, and slept sound till morning. Next day I derived no little amusement from
looking at the great number of waggons which (though
Sunday) were going and returning from Alexandria ; the
road, which passed near the door, was full from morning
till long after dark. These waggons were conveying
flour to Alexandria, which affords a good market for
that article. I had met upwards of an hundred the preceding day ; and it appeared that it was to have no end.
The road from Berry's ferry to Alexandria is paved the
whole way ; which, though it facilitates the transporta-
tion of flour in these waggons, is not very pleasant to
travel on at the rate of seventy miles per day ; it is the
roughest pavement I ever was on; it would not be bad
policy to have one's life and limbs insured, before undertaking the trip. The toll I am told is very high ; but
waggons with broad tire pass free, on account of the
service they are to the road. At the end of every mile,
there is a broad stone set up near the road.

These waggons, and the history of O'Neal, helped to
beguile the time, which nevertheless was very heavy.
O'Neal is a native of North-Carolina; he is a man of
gigantic size, six feet in height, weighing about two hun-

dred, strong and muscular. His manners were blunt, but sincere ; his countenance open—his face showed intemperance ; he was forty-seven years of age, and plainly clad ; but under this disguise, I could discern something generous, something like noble independence. He had six uncles, besides his father, in the revolutionary war—two of his mother's brothers, and four of his father's! One of his uncles was wounded at the battle of the Cowpens ; as he stated, the bullet went in at his breast and came out at the point of his shoulder. He placed his back against a tree and fired his piece, which he had never let fall, and then desired some of the men to take him off the field. This man, whose family contributed so large a share in securing the independence of his country, is now, with a large and helpless family, struggling with poverty ; while others, of perhaps not half his deserts, who never contributed to the amount of one cent towards this great event, and who never saw the face of an enemy, are enjoying the benefit achieved by those worthy patriots. But this is the way with this too ungrateful world.

Productions of the Country.—The principal growth consists of black oak, black jack, hickory, sassafras, box, ash, pine, and persimon. Good wheat is reared in the counties near the Blue Ridge, in some places as high as thirty eight bushels to the acre. Some of the land brings good tobacco, maize does not succeed well, timothy succeeds well as low down as O'Neal's. Some limestone too, is found in places—good water is scarce.

On Monday evening I bid adieu to Cobrun and Marcus O'Neal, and undertook a journey of twenty-five miles about sunset, in the worst carriage I ever was in! Once more patience. One distinguishing trait in the character of these lowlanders, is a fondness for drink ; besides the evidence already mentioned, I witnessed a few in the course of the evening. When we drew near Fairfax court-house, we met numbers of gentlemanly looking men on horseback, reeling in the saddle, their red faces and bloated bodies, proved them to be old veterans of the bottle. As we passed the court-house,

where the mail had to be opened, such was the press
and clamour of the crowd, (court was sitting,) that the
mail was not opened at all! The driver (though a good
hand at the bottle himself,) was so overawed by the
crowd, which really had a formidable appearance, that
he was glad to be off, and so was I. It is much to be lamented that the blessings of liberty should arrive at such
a pass, that it is dangerous to open the mail at the seats
of justice! Alas for my country, has it come to this!
The swords of your enemies were unable to conquer
you, but like Alexander, you are vanquished by your
vices! No longer, it appears, can sober men be found
to transact public business—even in transporting the
mail, a business which demands the highest trust: from
Nashville to this place, I have seen but one driver who
would not drink! My present driver is bold in it; he
carries his bottle in the box; this is soon emptied, but
grog shops abound on the road, to these he has re-
course. Several times to-night, has he left the stage in
the road, without any one to attend it, and went, God
knows where, to buy whiskey; absent sometimes thirty
minutes. It was well the horses were sober! The risk
is not only in the mismanagement of the stage, and horses, by these drunken drivers, but in matters of much
greater consequence. Although I am not much of a
coward, I must confess, I felt rather uneasy in the stage,
while this fellow was absent, particularly in a country
where mail robbery was not unknown. A little before
ten o'clock, I arrived in Alexandria, the first town I ever set foot in, in the eastern country.

Alexandria.—Having been whirled here in the night,
I had no opportunity of seeing the city. Upon going
to the window next morning, which faces the street, and
market-square, I was shocked at a sight entirely new to
me. The street and market-square presented groups of
men, women, and children, combining every shade of
colour, from the fairest white, down to the deepest
black. White and black people I had been accustomed to see, and a few mulattoes, but such a multifarious
mixture, bursting upon the sight at once, was as novel,

as it was unexpected. Some of these were about half white, some almost white, leaving it difficult to distinguish where the one ends, and the other begins. To one unaccustomed to see human nature in this guise, it excites feelings of horror and disgust. It has something in it so contrary to nature, something which seems never to have entered into her scheme, to see a man neither black nor white, with blue eyes, and a woolly head, has something in it at which the mind recoils. It appears that these people, instead of abolishing slavery, are gradually not only becoming slaves themselves, but changing color. Strange that a nation who extol so much, who praise themselves in such unqualified terms, as possessing in the highest degree, both moral and political virtue, should afford no better proof of it than this before me! Without criticising upon that degree of credit attached to self-praise, or calling into question their moral and political virtues, we would remark, generally, that those who boast most of virtue, have the least of it. But the fact before one speaks for itself, and naturally leads to the conclusion, that the man who can entail slavery upon his offspring, a free-born American, who has tasted the sweets of liberty, who can abandon his flesh and blood to the most ignominious slavery, ought truly to sound his own trumpet. There is a measure even in crime. There is a point, beyond which the most daring will not venture. History affords us many examples, amongst the most barbarous nations, in the most barbarous ages, where the most lawless ruffians became softened at the sight of human distress,* to which they were impelled by no law, but that of common humanity. But for man in this free, and (as they say) enlightened country, to doom his own children, to a state (to say the least of it,) fraught with every species of human misery, we want no better evidence to prove, that such men must not only be void of virtue, but guilty of the most indignant crime.

* Every one remembers the humanity of the robbers to Margaret, of Aragon, Queen of Henry the sixth, of England. But we have many more instances.

The Market.—I turned from this spectacle, to observe the appearance of the citizens, who were passing to and fro, engaged in marketing, which is not, by great odds, so crowded as ours are in the western country, in proportion to the size of the town. The first object that attracted my attention, was a gentlemen of middle age and good size, walking with a slow, but dignified step, his eyes bent on the ground in thoughtful mood, his mind evidently revolving some good intent, while his mein bespeaks the benevolence of his heart. Next steps a man of portly size, declining from the centre each way, arrayed in shining black, contrasted with an elevated face of scarlet red. His hands locked behind his back, keeping his coat in rear, the better to display his graceful front, and a massy seal, which he surveys with great seeming approbation. Turning his back upon the market-house, where, perhaps his royal highness found nothing to his taste, with an important step, he seeks his way whence he came. After him steps out a dignified personage, with evident signs of displeasure, followed by a black boy, with an empty basket on his arm, whilst he can hardly keep pace with the hasty step of his master. I should like to know what has turned up with him; probably some presuming mechanic, has had the assurance to set his fancy upon some delicate morsel, which he of domineering look, designed for his own breakfast. Approaching slow, with modest step, a graceful matron, with a round-crown bonnet, and a long whitish colored cloak, appears next, and with a basket in her hand, enters the market-house, whilst by her rushes a pert black boy with a basket likewise. And now we have a country man, who has sacrificed his morning nap to pecuniary views, with dusty hat, and friend of thread-bare drab, buttoned round him, unlading his sturdy cart, Sunday morning, notwithstanding. And hence steps, with deepened front and bold independence, a group of negro men, with erect impudence ; you might perceive by their forward looks that it was Sunday. Next appears forlorn, with timid step, a female whose wo-worn mien bespeaks her friendless—may God befriend you then, I thought. To these succeeded a troop

of coloured females, (as they are termed here,) in neat
attire, with heads swathed in handkerchiefs, resembling
sugar-loaves, horizontally usurping the place of the
head, with the base in front. With these are mingled
others of the same sex and colour, with bushy neither
wool nor hair, tied in a vast round knot, and looking
like another head. Anon, a doudy drab, with soiled
clothes, rivalling her African hue, walks on as cheery as
a lark, whilst a poor old man, limping upon crutches,
comes meeting her. An inquisitive old woman comes
next, I know her by the shape of her bonnet, and "what's
this and what's that." I have always fancied that the
bonnet or hat took the tone of the wearer, and gave
some indication of the predominant disposition or quality of the mind: I have thought I could perceive cunning, pride, prodigality, wisdom, folly, taste and refinement, by the turn of the bonnet or the hat, and have
been displeased with my friends when they put on a new
one which made them appear not themselves. There
goes a little boy whose mother has proclaimed her folly
by tying a flaming red "comfort" round his neck; it
crosses and ties behind, hanging down to his heels; he
is equipt throughout with corresponding foolery, and
struts with all the importance of man grown, with his
broad white collar. What thorns his mother is planting
against her old age! how she is sowing the seeds of
pride and folly, and preparing a fund of sorrow for the
evening of her life, if God in his mercy does not disap-
point her by taking this idol to himself. Hard by, on
the step of a neighbouring door, sits a little girl with
matronly attention, arrayed in her Sunday frock—no
doubt the idol of her mother's heart, as I was once of
mine.

My attention was now attracted by a party in the
street. Two young ladies, in full dress, tripped along
the pavement with mincing step and unlocked arms, as
though they would make room for a little light fop, who
walked neither exactly behind nor yet between them;
(he has a faint heart, that is evident.) In his hand he
carries a cane of neat device, which his well turned arm
advances at every step, with studied grace, in the van

of the ladies, sticking its brazen point into the interstices
of the brick, as if to let the fair ones know " I am here."
In conscious triumph he often looks to one side, and often behind, with design, no doubt, to say to those who
see him, " am I not a happy man?" " Yes, you are a
happy man," says the downcast look of a brother dandy,
who walks with a slow melancholy air, some distance
behind, while the life-cheering smiles and brilliant eyes
of the ladies, are often bestowed upon his happy rival.
A little dabbling girl, with health in her face and plenty
in her hand, goes next, and after her a black woman,
with her apron thrown over her shoulder and a string of
fish in her hand.

The slaves of this place bear every mark of good
treatment ; they look happy and are comfortably clothed, though not half so fine or richly dressed: indeed the
white people of this place lack a great deal of being
dressed equal to the blacks of Huntsville, or Lexington.
Those of the mixed breed, some have a beautiful bloom
in their face, while others again have a sickly squalid
hue, very disgusting.   Having satisfied my curiosity, at
least for that morning, I partook of a fine breakfast alone
in my parlour, and spent the day in rest and reading.

History.—The land where Alexandria now stands was
formerly owned by the Alexander family, and the first
building erected on the site, was built by one of the Alexanders.

Alexandria was erected into a town by act of assembly, in the year 1749, at Hunting Creek ware-house,
on the lands of John and Philip Alexander, and Hugh
West, in Fairfax county, on the south side of Potomac
river, 120 miles from Chesapeake, 70 miles from Winchester, 8 from Washington.   Beginning at the mouth
of Hunting Creek up the river, sixty acres of land were
laid out into half acre lots and streets.   The Rt. Hon.
Thomas Lord Fairfax, the Hon. Wm. Fairfax, George
Fairfax, Lawrence Washington, Wm. Ramsay, John
Carlisle, John Rogers, Richard Osborn, Hugh West,
Gerard Alexander, and Philip Alexander, were appointed trustees of the town, which by act of assembly was

called Alexandria. It is a very handsome town, the streets cross each other at right angles, running north and south, east and west, the former cutting the river at right angles. There are no squares in Alexandria, except the market-square, which is very small, and enclosed or surrounded with buildings, independent of the market-house itself, which takes the form of the letter L, and makes two sides of the square. In the opposite corner of the square, stands a fish-market, the upper story of which is destined for the city guards, and called the watch house. Besides these market houses, the other public buildings are, two churches for Episcopalians, two for Presbyterians, one for Methodists, (white) one for Methodists, (black) one for Baptists (black) one for Baptists, (white) one for Friends, one for Catholics— ten in all—a court-house, a museum, a town-hall, a library, an insurance office, a theatre, and six banks, a collectors office, and a post office. There are two printing offices in Alexandria. Besides the manufactory of tin and leather, a great quantity of sugar is refined in Alexandria. Great attention seems to be paid to education : there are academies and several schools.

Manners and Appearance.—The people of Alexandria are mild and unassuming. They have not that eclat and splendor, of which many of the towns in Alabama and the western states are so vain. They are rather distant, when compared with the people of the west, tho' friendly and unreserved upon an acquaintance ; they are said to be hospitable ; but my opportunity was such, that I am unable to give an opinion. They have none of that bold assurance, that distinguishes the appearance of the people between it and the Blue Ridge. They are, on the contrary, remarkably diffident. The young people are handsome, and well formed of both sexes, particularly the young men, they have very expressive countenances, and noted for black sparkling eyes. Both young men and ladies, have beautiful complexions, but as to size, they are not to compare to the people of the west, nor are they so dressy or fashionable. Labouring men and women, however, are stouter than

those who do not work.   Married ladies look pale, and
have for the most part a bloated appearance, for want,
I suspect, of proper exercise.   Viewing Alexandria in a
relative view, it does not seem to progress much in
wealth, and so far from improving, it is losing ground.
It used to reckon twelve thousand inhabitants, whereas,
it now contains only eight thousand and eight, with the
exception, however, of two thousand houses in Fairfax
county, which, though without the limits of the district,
is a continuation of Alexandria.   Alexandria has not recovered the loss she sustained by the late war, and from
every thing I have seen respecting this town, it has seen
its most prosperous days.   It is a matter of some surprise, that with he same advantages, as to situation for
trade, it should be so far behind Baltimore, which is only two years older.   In some respects it has the advantage of Baltimore, having power to furnish all the western part of Virginia, and east Tennessee, who freight
their groceries in Philadelphia vessels to Alexandria,
which is some distance, and waggon them from thence.
Why the people of Alexandria have not seized this advantage, has been owing, perhaps, to want of capital or
system.   One great cause, I am told, is want of union
amongst themselves.   Alexandria exports little else
than flour, though heretofore, it is said, that twelve thousand weight of tobacco was shipped in one year from
that port.   Besides ware-houses, it has commodious
wharfs for the lading and unlading of vessels.   These
are built in the river on piles, differing in width, length,
and heighth, to suit vessels of all sizes.   They extend in
a right angle, from the shore to a vast distance in the river, which comprises their length, and sufficiently a-
sunder to admit vessels between them.   They are perfectly level on the top, being filled up with gravel and
earth, of such heighth as to be even with the decks of
the vessels, which draw up close to them, side by side,
and roll out the cargo, and the same, when going to lade.
The first ship I ever saw was in Alexandria, and though
a very small merchant ship, it had enough of curiosity
in it, to engage my admiration.   The greatest disappointment to me, was the heighth of the deck from the

water, and the quantity of rope. I had expected these
decks were at least five times as far from the surface of
the water, nor had I an accurate idea of the extent of a
deck, it embracing the extreme heighth of the ship, with
the exception of the masts. It is nothing more than a
flat floor, from one end of the vessel to the other, with a
balustrade on the extremity, of from two to three feet in
height: the deck is the covering of the ship.* The
mast, that is the main-mast, was another matter in which
I was extremely out, as to height and thickness, it is as
large as a common tree; and as for the rope, I should be
at a great loss myself, how to dispose of the one half of
it, my knowledge of navigation notwithstanding.   I
found only the mate on board, who, with a great deal of
patience, answered the thousand queries I put to him,
while the sailors who were hard by on the wharf, testified
at once their surprise and ridicule, by a loud peal of
laughter.

From the Alexandria side of the Potomac, you have a
fine view of the Maryland shore, which is elevated and
beautifully diversified with farms and elegant buildings.
The first sight of my much loved native state, since I left
it at three years of age, filled me with sensations, for
which language wants expression.   Nor have I indeed a
distant recollection of my feelings.   The first glimpse,
vibrated upon every fibre of my heart, and seemed to fill
that vestal void, long locked up by Polina's care.   The
ecstacy resulting from the full fruition of this new affection, absorbed every power of my mind; it was amongst
the sweetest moments I ever tasted.   Every creature
loves the place of its nativity, but those only are suscep-
tible of its highest pleasure, who have, like myself, been
long absent from it.   I would not exchange the pleasure
I felt on beholding my ever dear country, for any earthly
consideration.

Alexandria has a gradual ascent from the river back
to the utmost limits; the streets are spacious, and paved with stone, and the side-walks with brick; these
streets are kept very clean, not a particle of any sub-

* Since this was written, I have seen war ships at Boston with five
decks.

stance or rubbish whatever, is suffered to lie or be seen
in the streets; they are lighted every dark night. A
man, or perhaps more, goes round at dusk with a light
ladder in their hands, by which they ascend the lamp
post, and set fire to the lamps. These lamps are at
every corner where the streets cross. The lamp is
placed in a large glass lantern, such as taverns use;
and this is tenaciously fixed on the top of a high post,
out of reach, so that disorderly persons may not have
it in their power to extinguish them. The houses in
Alexandria are built of brick mostly, three stories high,
they are comfortable and convenient, but not very
splendid. Instead of wooden cornice, the top of the
house walls are ornamented with from one to three rows
of pointed brick, (in the form of a wedge;) these brick
project beyond the wall, and gives it a handsome appearance; most of the houses are covered with slate
and tile. The banks are very handsome buildings;
but the greatest piece of architecture is the market-
house. From the centre of the north end, arises a
splendid cupola of a hexigon figure, ornamented with a
lofty steeple. The squares of the cupola present six
faces of a single clock, which shows the hour of the day
to a vast distance. The mechanism of the clock is contained within the body of the cupola and strikes so loud
as to be heard over the town.* Alexandria is an incorporated town, under the government of a Mayor and
Aldermen; the police is under the best regulation; no
disturbance, not the least noise, interrupt the repose of
the citizens. Instead of bells, the watch is preceded
by a number of loud trumpets, which blow a tremendous peal at the hour of ten at night, when the watch
goes out. They go the rounds, crying the hour till
day. If any person, either black or white, be found in
the streets after ten, who cannot give an account of
him or herself, they are taken by the watch, and put in
the guard-house till morning, when they are taken before the Mayor, and thereupon fined; if they are not
able to pay the fine, they are sent to the work-house

* These are common in the Atlantic states, being in almost every
church.

for a certain time. The market of Alexandria is abundant and cheap, though much inferior to any in any part of the western country, except beef and fish, which are by far superior to that of the western markets. But vegetables, fowls, lamb, and veal, are very indifferent indeed. Nor is their bread equal to ours in whiteness or taste. But their exquisite fish, oysters, crabs, and foreign fruits, upon the whole, bring them upon a value with us. Besides these delicacies, they have several sorts of wild duck, the greatest luxury I found in the market. Vegetables of every description are small ; what they call cabbage, with us would not be gathered except to feed cattle ; their potatoes are large enough, but not well tasted. They have no greens in the winter, owing to the excessive cold of the climate. Their fish differ from ours, even the same species. Their cat-fish is the only sort in which we excel ; they have none that answers to our blue-cat, either in size or flavor, and nothing like our mud-cat. Their cat-fish is from ten to fifteen inches in length, with a wide mouth, like the mud-cat of the western waters ; but their cat differ from both ours in substance and color ; they are soft, pied black and white. They are principally used to make soup, which is much esteemed by the inhabitants. All their fish are small compared with ours. Besides the cat-fish, which they take in the latter part of the winter, they have the rock, winter shad, mackerel, and perch, shad and herring. The winter shad is very fine indeed. They are like our perch, but infinitely smaller. These fish are sold very low ; a large string, enough for a dozen persons, may be purchased for a few cents. No fish, however, that I have tasted, equal our trout. I often went through the market ; in doing so, I would address those who had things to sell. It was laughable enough to see with what total disregard I was treated, when they discovered my object was not to buy. Upon my first approach I was met with a smile, and " will you have a piece of nice veal this morning ?" " No sir, I am a traveller, I only call from curiosity ; I am just looking at the market : your veal is very thin sir, do you not feed them in this country ?" Not a word !

10

Another, " will you take a nice stake piece this morning, here 's a charming piece ;" thank you sir, I am
only viewing the market ; I don't keep house ; this is
really fine beef indeed, how long may it have been
fed ?" Might as well address a post. " Will you buy
some bread this morning? here's some very nice."
" How do you sell it?" " Six cents, take two ?" (handing out the bread ;) " I dont wish to buy, I only wish to
ascertain the prices ; what profit do you make ?"
Could not get another glimpse of his eye. All the information I obtained was from the buyers. The benches and stalls are kept remarkably neat and clean, being
washed every day. Market is held every day in the
week, not excepting Sunday, which accounts for its thin-
ness. The constables attend to prevent riot or distur
bance. Several attempts have been made to suppress
Sunday markets in Alexandria, by those " outrageous"
religious people, but without effect. It is alledged by
them that it is a henious sin thus to violate the Sabbath ; while those who advocate the measure, contend
that the greater crime would be to debar poor slaves
from the only opportunity they have to sell their produce, the hard acquired pittance of many a weary night's
labor.* Besides, they have a number of labourers and
mechanics, who cannot spare time to provide for Sunday. These motives operate conclusively upon the majority, to continue Sunday market. Market begins at
day-light and usually ends at ten o'clock every day, except Sunday, which is out an hour sooner. At nine o'-
clock A. M. on Sunday, you hear a small bell ring for
about a minute, this is succeeded by a peal from the
great market bell. The first is to give notice to those
in market, to pick up his or her unsold articles, and be
off; by the ring of the great bell, all who fail to do this,
forfeit what they have to the constables ; whose business it is to take those articles so forfeited, to the poor
house, for the benefit of the poor. The poor house is
supported by the corporation ; it is nothing more than
a house where cooks are employed to prepare soup and

* Many of those people own slaves, and yet make a merit of enjoin-
ing the observance of the Sabbath.

bread for those who are unable to work. They attend daily, and carry home the amount of that day's provision, and so on. Alexandria, though generally a healthy town, was visited by the yellow fever some years ago, which swept off a number of its inhabitants; since that, the corporation has been very careful and attentive to the means of health. *Fountains and Baths*. There are no springs in the city; the citizens procure good water at some expense from a fountain in the suburbs of the town; for ordinary purposes, however, they have fountains in abundance. There is an elegant bathing-house, but the price of bathing is so unreasonably high, (fifty cents,) that it is of no benefit either way; whereas if it were within bounds, it would prove a fortune to the proprietor, and tend more to the health of the citizens. There seems to prevail amongst the citizens of Alexandria, a deep rooted enmity against the Federal city; they sigh to be reunited to the state of Virginia. They are now engaged in an attempt to separate themselves from the District of Columbia, by a petition to Congress.

The merchants suffered greatly by the late war, particularly in the loss of their shipping. On the day that succeeded the capture of Washington, the British entered Alexandria; the citizens capitulated upon conditions not very favorable, for it seems the British burnt their shipping, and plundered the stores and ware-houses. The citizens, however, were not guilty of abandoning their city, as were those of Washington. It was amusing to all (except the owners,) to see with what liberality the British dealt out the sugar, coffee, flour and blankets, to the poor, and the negroes. These articles were turned out into the streets, and all who wished might come and take what they pleased. It is said that the flour taken off by the British was considerable; but the Americans attacked them after clearing the port of Alexandria, and destroyed the whole.

The Potomac at Alexandria, is rather over a mile in width; it is celebrated for its beauty. It is certainly a great blessing to this county, in supplying its inhabitants with food in the article of fish, and for commercial purposes; without it, the country would not, it could not exist, the soil being nearly good for nothing. But Potomac, the only tide river I have seen, yields greatly to the western rivers, in point of beauty. It is always turbid and rough, owing, I suspect, to the wind from the ocean, and the ebbing and flowing of the tide. The tide, I am told, extends as high as three miles above Georgetown. Notwithstanding the visible decline of Alexandria, the number of strangers who pass through it, the number of stages, carriages, waggons and drays, rattling on the pavement from morning till night, and almost from night till morning, gives to it a very lively appearance. All travellers going from north to south, or from south to north, and so of the east and west, have necessarily to pass through Alexandria.

Yesterday, 22d Feb. the militia companies turned out, preceded by a band of music. The Artillery, the Blues, and the Independent Blues, were distinguished by very handsome uniforms; the Independent Blues made a splendid appearance—as respected their equipage, they were second to none that I have seen. But in manly size, they are children compared to our men of the west. They will not do, too effeminate; otherwise they are handsome-looking men. They, with the clergy, proceeded to Christ's church, where an oration was delivered by S. Cox, Esq. They then returned to the hotel, whence they set out; after firing twenty-four rounds, preceded by the band, with banners flying, followed by the clergy and the citizens. When they arrived at the hotel, they formed in two lines; the clergy walked bare-headed through into the hotel, when they dispersed: on Monday (to-morrow) a splendid ball is to close the celebration. During Saturday, national flags were suspended from the east and west fronts of the market-house. These flags are of the richest deep blue silk. floating almost to the ground, the centre being ornamented with a white eagle, with twenty-four stars of the same. They were trimmed with a border of brilliant deep red. The celebration is over; the ball took place last evening, at the city-hotel. agreeably to arrangement. Notwithstanding a very unfavourable evening, upwards of two hundred gentlemen and ladies attended, amongst whom was the Vice-President and several other distinguished characters, from Washington City. A splendid room was prepared for Gen. Jackson, (who was expected to participate in the celebration,) but was prevented by indisposition. His destined apartment was ornamented with national flags, suspended at each end; but to our great mortification, the General was unable to witness this testimony of respect. Mr. Clagett, the proprietor of the city hotel, received great applause for his promptness and skill in providing a supper, in which taste, elegance, and profusion were displayed. The national flag floated at each end of the table, which was upwards of an hundred feet in length; this was the most superb supper I ever beheld. In Alexandria, dwells John I. L., brother of him who signed the declaration of Independence. He has nothing engaging in his countenance or appearance; on the contrary, he has a sly, cunning look. He is of middling height, about fifty years of age, sallow, spare, and thin visaged. Though much disappointed in Mr. L., I was pleased with his son, a very promising young man, upwards of twenty, of genteel manners, and very engaging figure. I should, very probably, have quitted Alexandria without having either the honour or the pleasure of knowing it contained such an august personage, but for a mere accident.

After spending some months at Alexandria, I took my departure for Richmond, Va. in the steam-boat " Mount Vernon," intending, on my return, to visit Washington City. The Mount Vernon carries the southern mail when the river is open. The boats commence running the last of March, and continue till middle of December, when the stages take up their line till the return of spring, and so on. The Mount Vernon leaves Alexandria at 2 o'clock, P. M. and arrives at Potomac creek from 6 to 8 o'clock, same day, as the wind is more or less favorable : we arrived at the creek about 8, the wind being against us. Here we quit the boat and take the stages, which wait for us on the bank of the river. The boat takes in the passengers going northwards, who arrive in the stage, and turns back without delay, going

10*

all night, she arrives at Washington City about day-light, after touching at the fort and Alexandria to put out the mail: the distance is seventy-five miles. After getting out in the river some distance, upon leaving Alexandria, you have a fine view of the capitol at Washington; it is seen as low down as Mount Vernon, eight miles from Alexandria. Notwithstanding a pretty smart gale, I remained on deck to enjoy the scenery present-ed by the Maryland and Virginia shore. The farms looked very handsome, the buildings and the fish houses, which last seemed to set in the water. But the clusters of pine and cedar, indicate the poverty of the soil. A little before you come to Mount Vernon we have the fort on the Maryland side; it appeared to be large, but no one present could tell how many guns it mounted, or what number of men it required to man her; the fort is built of brick, but as I only saw it from the boat, I could give no opinion as to its strength. Governor Bar-bour, of Virginia, and several other intelligent looking men were on board; they could give no information re-specting it, in fact, they seemed to speak of it in terms of contempt. I was very much astonished that Mr. Bar-bour, who has been a member of congress for some years, and whom we might suppose, would feel enough of in-terest in his country's means of defence, did not know more of it than he seemed to know, nor have I been able since to obtain any information on that subject. The steam-boat stops a minute or two at the fort to put out the mail, which is sent ashore in a skiff; shortly after leaving it, we were in sight of Mount Vernon: we were, however, too far from the Virginia shore on which it stands to have a satisfactory view. It appear-ed to be situated in a poor soil, so far as I could per-ceive, from the quantity of cedar by which it was sur-rounded. A number of trees, (of what sort I was una-ble to distinguish,) surrounds the house itself, which nearly precludes it from sight. It appeared, partially amidst them, to be a massy white building, of the Ionic order; but no one could inform me of the architecture; it stands near the bank of the river.

After quitting the steam-boat, we had eight miles to

Fredericksburg, where we were to lodge. The stage
was very much crowded; ten passengers and their baggage squeezed us rather close together. In consequence
of being so heavy laden, our driver went very slow;
but the tediousness was relieved by the wit and sprightliness of Gov. Barbour, who proved to be a gentleman
of very agreeable manners as well as liberal sentiments;
but shone in his ability to entertain. He related many
amusing anecdotes of former days, which served to beguile a cold and unpleasant night. One of them I shall
never forget, it was something to the following amount:
" It happened while he practised law, he appeared for
two members of the Methodist religion, who were charged with disrepect to the military authority, by which,
they incurred a serious penalty. An officer," said Mr.
B. " happening to pass through a collection of Methodists, in full uniform, inquired the way, of one of the
black brethren, (as it appeared,) the negro replied to
His Excellency in a very abrupt manner, and without
taking off his hat; this enraged the man of war—you
rascal, do you speak to me thus, and with your hat on?
I 'll teach you to respect your betters, giving him a
crack over the head; take off your hat scoundrel:
' Don't pay obedience to sinful man, brother, said a
white man, who was standing near, (a class leader in
the church,) honor is alone due to God; don't despise
the temple of the Holy Spirit by honoring that vile sin-
ner:' and d—n you, I'll down upon you like forty thousand, said the officer, laying about the fellow's ears;
' Help,' said the holy man; the negro laid hold of *forty
thousand*, and the consequence would have been serious had the by standers not interfered. The next business was to arrest the two brothers for insulting the U.
States in the person of the plaintiff. The magistrate
committed the pious brethren to jail, as they were unable to give security: meantime the brethren became
alarmed for the consequences, and deprecated the disgrace of the *church* most of all. Some of the near relations of the white offender came to me and told me a
piteous tale, representing the character of the prisoner
in the most favorable light, that he was a harmless in-

offensive man, and upright withal, begged me to appear
for him, and exert myself in his behalf, giving me a liberal fee at the same time. 1 undertook his defence ; the
trial came on in a few days. I represented the thing in
its mildest colors : in doing this, I adverted to the nature
of enthusiasm ; I said that it was a species of madness,
and that men when under its influence committed acts
that were unwarranted by reason, and that no more notice ought to be taken of their actions than the acts of
madmen. This was the surest, and, in fact, the only
successful plea I could make, and I should have come
off victorious had not the man of God, who was in court,
interrupted me, with ' I am no madman, I speak forth
the words of truth and soberness, in this sinful world ;
and I can prove it to your understanding that it is the
Spirit of God, blessed be his name, that speaks within
me. I am bold in the Lord ; but these things are fool-
ishness to the children of darkness.' O well, friend, if
you take up the cause I shall lay it down, and accordingly I sat down and remained silent. Not so, said *forty
thousand*, who was sitting upon the bench ; take him
to jail, said he, take him back and let him preach there ;
this was done. I learn no more except that the negro
was dismissed by the magistrate, with thirty-nine lash-
es." He related another of himself, when he was elected member of congress. As he drew near Washington
City, on his journey to take his seat, he was very much
embarrassed in finding his way. The road became
smaller and smaller, the nearer he approached, till at
length it dwindled into a narrow path so entangled with
others that it was impossible for him to know which
was right or was wrong ; strange, he thought, " and going to the *eternal* City, I expected to see a fine spacious
road. At length he found himself in an old field, without a single trace, and the sun was near setting ! he began to think of camping out, when he espied a man
walking before him, he spurred up to the man and asked where he might find a house of any sort to spend the
night : the man informed him that a hotel was within
two miles, which he might reach by dark. He next requested the man to put him in the road, which was no-

thing but the trace he had wandered from. Fortunately he arrived at the hotel by dark, and found a man sitting at the door, barefooted and very shabbily dressed,
and the house of the last description! It had a dirt floor,
and was almost without furniture. He began to think
he had mistaken the house; no, that was the hotel, that
is the very name, and I assure you, said the man, you
will meet with few houses where you will find better *in-
comodation!* I have plenty for your *hos'* to eat and my
wife has some coffee, and I have good old brandy too;
have you, indeed, *that's my sort,* said the governor."—
At another time he happened to be at a camp-meeting,
one of the preachers took it into his head to explain
heaven, and enumerate the different nations and kind-
reds of people, that constitute the heavenly church; he,
(the preacher,) said that the heavenly church was a vast
house, that it was built of all nations of people, there
were Jews there, Hottentots, Spaniards, Dutch, Irish,
Scotch, Danes, and even Indians, but there is not one
Frenchman. It was during the French revolution, and
we may suppose by this conclusion that the preacher
was no friend to the measure.

By means of a few faint rays of the moon, I had a
glimpse of the country through which we passed. It
was entirely deserted by its inhabitants, who were unable to subsist upon it. It consisted of old fields, grown
over with stunted pine and broom sedge. I was told,
however, that the land about Fredericksburg was fertile,
it being on the Rappahannock, a navigable river.

Fredericksburg.—Fredericksburg has been represented as a flourishing town; but, whatever it might have
been heretofore, it is far from having a flourishing appearance at present. Every thing wears a gloomy aspect, very little business doing in any part of the town.
It is a handsome little town, on the south bank of the
Rappahannock, one hundred and ten miles from the
Chesapeake. It possesses two great advantages, viz:
that of a rich and fertile soil, which extends some distance on both sides of the river; and secondly, the advantages of navigation; vessels of one hundred and

thirty tons ascend to the town. The amount of exports annually, is estimated at four millions of dollars. The surrounding country is in a high state of cultivation, and exceeded by none in fertility or beauty; I never expected to see such a country as this in the worn-out east. But the soil here, from the nature of its situation, will last forever. It produces corn, wheat, tobacco, and almost every thing necessary for man. The police of the town are very lax in their duty; the streets are not kept clean, and a want of neatness is every where visible. The houses are mostly of brick, and some of them are handsome and commodious. There are two bridges over the river. It is an incorporated town; contains four churches, one for Presbyterians, one for Methodists, one for Baptists, and one for Episcopalians; a court-house, jail, collectors office, a post-office, an academy, and about 4000 inhabitants.

For several miles after leaving Fredericksburg, you pass through a country of unequalled beauty; the scenery is beyond description, rich and picturesque. Handsome buildings, and highly cultivated farms are in constant view. I was the more surprised at this, having never heard it mentioned by any traveller. In going to Richmond from Fredericksburg, you cross at right angles three small rivers; in the western country they would be called creeks. These rivers are called by the following names, viz :—Pamunky, Chickahominy, and Mattaponi.* These rivers resemble the waters of the western states much more than the Rappahannock. They flow in a smooth and silent stream, and have scarcely any banks, by which they overflow the adjacent lands, enriching them to a degree equal to any land

* Morse is guilty of an error in the orthography of this river, which took its name from the following circumstance :—This river was discovered by a party of Indians and white people, who were on a hunting party. According to custom they left one to watch the camp (on the bank of the stream) while the rest pursued the game. It so happened that the party absented themselves during the whole of one night. In the course of the night a deep snow had fallen ; upon coming to the camp next morning, one of the white men asked the Indian whom they left at camp, " how he came on with respect to the snow ;" he replied " that he put matt upon I," meaning that instead of sleeping on the matt, he covered himself with it, and hence the river took its name.

in the west. The grape-vine is seen as large as it is on the great Kenhawa. I had no idea of this, having heard so much of the poverty of the soil. I am told that this rich soil continues near the mouths of those rivers, when they unite and the single stream takes the name of York river. Eleven miles from the mouth of York river, stands Yorktown, famous in American history for the capture of Cornwallis. It is said to be the best harbor in Virginia. Although the land on these rivers is equal if not superior to that on Rappahannock, the country is by no means as handsome. Between the rivers the land is thin, covered with pines and old fields, not worth one cent. The farmers, (or planters I believe they are called,) from the great scarcity of timber enclose their fields principally with ditches. The great number of hands in proportion to the quantity of land has ruined Virginia. Their slaves, in the end, instead of being a benefit, has proved a very serious injury. But for them, old Virginia at this day would have been worth perhaps, one hundred per cent. more than she is. The great and wealthy Virginia has overshot the mark; she has killed the goose that laid the golden egg; I see evident proofs of this in their deserted worn out fields. This renowned State seems to have lost sight of posterity, and to have acted upon an unnatural plan, or rather no plan at all. They have secured nothing to their children but poverty, whilst they have reared those children up, not to industry, but with high notions, which will only serve to render them more sensible of their misfortune. Influenced by a more than foolish pride, they neglect to encourage useful arts; their lordly souls, could not brook the indignity of teaching their sons to earn their bread by their own labor. They could not stoop so low as to teach them the mechanic arts, by which they might have gained a decent and comfortable support. Virginia from these causes lags behind. New-York has gained upon her in point of numbers, since 1790, 714,936. Virginia, one of the first states in the Union in many respects, is now only the third in population, the eighth in commerce, the fifth in tonnage, the fourth in manufactures, the first only in agriculture;

the population is 605,613 whites, 425,153 slaves, 34,600 free blacks. This hasty sketch I took from Morse's Geography, which lay in my room.

Richmond.—The stage leaves Fredericksburg at two o'clock, A. M. and arrives at Richmond at three o'clock, P. M.　I was much disappointed upon seeing Richmond —I had heard it praised for its beauty, but it far exceeded my utmost expectation.　Great part of the city is spread out upon an elevation called Shockoe Hill ;—this part of the town overlooks the lower part, which lies upon James River.　In approaching the town from Fredericksburg, you enter it on the north side, while the river is on the south : the river, however, was much smaller than I expected to find it : after leaving the lordly Potomac, James River sinks into nothing.　I saw the basin, I saw the canal, and the little vessels, nothing to compare to our boats—I expected to be transported with these things, but I failed even to be pleased.　In Richmond, however, much business is done—it is all alive, every thing is in motion, the streets and shops display great activity, and a profusion of goods and wares.　Richmond is the seat of government of Virginia, and the largest town in the state, having 12,067 inhabitants, whereas Norfolk, the next largest, has only 8,478.　Its exports amount to $8,000,000 annually.—Few towns have increased so rapidly as Richmond ;—in 1783 the population was less than two thousand.　People are flocking to Richmond from all parts, for commercial and other purposes.　Many of the citizens of Alexandria have quit that city and come to this place, with a view of bettering their fortunes.　In short, Richmond bids fair to be one of the first commercial towns in the eastern country.　Its public buildings are, a state house, a penitentiary, an armory, two churcnes for Episcopalians, two for Methodists, one for Presbyterians, one for Baptists, one for Friends, and one for Jews—two banks, four printing offices, and a post office.

Amongst other disappointments, to me the capitol was one : it was not half so large or splendid as I had anticipated ; but some of the private buildings are superb.

Richmond is celebrated for its hospitality, but of this I had no opportunity to judge; I saw very little of it—indeed, I should give it quite a contrary character; nor did I find it so refined as it is represented. It would be unfair, however, for me to say any thing positively on this head, as the few days I tarried there were principally spent in my room. I saw but one of the *nabobs*, Dr. T. He was a man of vulgar manners, with his " yes mawm," and " no mawm." If this be a specimen of the refinement of Richmond, they have great room to improve. A servant (I mean a genteel one) in the western states, would have spoken with more propriety. Here too you have the " paw and maw," (pa and ma,) and " tote," with a long train of their kindred. I happened to see a turn-out of the volunteer companies of Richmond, while there. They were much better looking men than those of Alexandria; they were stout, and had a martial appearance. Their music was exquisite, and their uniform gay and splendid. But even these lack a great deal, in point of size and manly appearance, compared to our heroes of the west. The men of Richmond are very much burnt with the sun, though the ladies are fair, have beautiful features, fine figures, and much vivacity of countenance. The men have more expression than those more northerly.

History.—The land where Richmond now stands was originally owned by a man whose name was Sherror. His grand-daughter, Mrs. Doctor Dow, is now living in Richmond; she states that he was a German by birth. No vessel of any size can come to Richmond; the large vessels stop at City Point, about twenty miles below the city. Richmond is an incorporated town.

Much interest is excited in this place, as well as all others where I have been since I crossed the Blue Ridge, respecting the approaching election of President. It is amusing enough to observe the straits into which each party is driven. It is impossible to learn the truth, either from the parties or the papers. It must be a matter of serious grief to all lovers of their country, to witness the low means by which electioneering is conduct-

ed, particularly in this country, where the lower order
of the people are so grossly ignorant that they are incapable of judging for themselves. They are mere tools
in the hands of designing sycophants, who practice on
their credulity in the most shameful and barefaced
manner. The following anecdotes may give an idea of
that duplicity resorted to in this part of the Union. On
my way to the east, between Winchester and Alexandria, for the sake of amusement, (no other person being
in the stage,) I entered into conversation with the driver ; " and who do the people speak of for President in
this part of the country?" said I; " why Crawford, to be
sure," said the man, " he is sure to be our next President ;" " are there no other candidates?" " why yes,
he believed there was, but he could not think of their
names ;" " have you never heard of Adams, Jackson,
Calhoun, &c. ; have they no supporters in this country ;"
" no, d——n such men as Adams and Jackson, any man
that would vote for them ought to be hung ; do you think
we would vote for a murderer ?" " and which of those
men is the murderer, my friend ? I never heard of it before ;" " why Jackson ;" " and where did he commit
the murder ? and whom did he kill ?" " he did 'nt know
who he did kill, or where it was done, but he was tried
for his life at Washington city !" " ah!" said I, in affected astonishment, " and was he acquitted ?" " yes, I
suppose he was acquitted then;" " and what then, is he to
have another trial ;" " he could not tell how they managed it ;" " can you not tell where he killed the man ?"
" the man," said the driver " he killed three or four
men out somewhere where he lives, and he was brought
here for trial ;" " must be some mistake in this friend ;
if he committed the murder in that part of the country
at all, he could not by our laws be brought here for trial,
every state claims the right secured to them by the Constitution, of exercising exclusive privileges in disposing
of their citizens. For instance, if you were to kill a
man in this state, you could not by our laws, be tried for
it in another; so from this view of the matter there must
be some mistake ;" " no mistake at all ;" he did not know
where the murder was committed, but this much he was

certain, Jackson took his trial in Washington, and was within a hair's breadth of being hung; "you must be for Jackson," said he, "but before he should be President I'd kill him, if there was no other man in the world; no no, we want no murderer for our President;" "you appear to be a man of courage," said I, "by your manner of speaking; where were you when the British captured Washington, and Alexandria?" This seemed to check his mettle; he was at a loss what to answer; in short, it cost me a long argument and much address to convince this poor ignorant man how much he had been imposed on. In doing this, however, in the first place, I had to demonstrate what was true, that I was no ways interested in the election. He had been made to believe that Adams was the same that passed the alien and sedition law; and that Clay was a gambler. After an absence of some years from my old neighborhood in West Virginia, upon my return, I inquired of an old friend of the Jeffersonian class, how politics stood in that country; "you must by this time have your eye on some one for the Presidency;" this was in 1822. He replied "that Crawford was the favorite candidate of Virginia;" "and who opposes him," I said; he seemed astonished at the question, as it implied a total indifference on that subject, which grows more warm as you approach more near the seat of government; and but for want of courage, would bring the parties by the ears. I informed him of the truth, that nothing had been expressed on the subject in the country from whence I came, that the people there never meddled with politics, being all of one mind, and were wholly engrossed by other objects. He seemed thunderstruck at the news, and asked whom I preferred; I told him I did not know who were the candidates, and that I was perfectly uninterested since parties were done away. That I had heard John Q. Adams spoken of as a very proper person to succeed Monroe; "oh we will not have him," said my friend, "we are doing every thing in our power for Crawford; he mentioned Calhoun and Clay, and observed that some spoke of Gen. Jackson, but he thought the old *fellow* was over fond of fighting. I replied (without ever having heard the General mentioned as a candidate,) that " I thought he was the very man, and that had he been President the last war the British would not have captured the seat of government ; are all these firm republicans," I asked, " that you have mentioned ;" " yes," he answered ; " and what difference does it make which of them is President, provided their abilities and virtues are equal ;" " ah," but said he, " don't you know Crawford is a Virginian, although he lives in Georgia ;" " well, what of that, you have furnished Presidents long enough ;" " softly my dear friend, don't you know that the President has many lucrative offices at his disposal ; don't you know that he has all the appointments, officers of the navy, army, &c. in his gift." It may be easily imagined how much I was hurt at this declaration of my friend. It showed his principles in the clearest light. In other respects he was a correct upright man ; had been a member of Congress, and was esteemed for his republican principles. I was much shocked at this palpable want of probity and patriotism, which went far enough to show that no matter what party rules, or what the form of government, corruption, that noxious weed, will spring up in all civil compacts. This misfortune may be deplored, but no provision can secure us from the evil, whilst the fabric of government is composed of frail man ; he cannot resist the temptation to enrich himself, though at the expense of patriotism and moral obligation. This is the rock upon which the ark of American liberty is to be wrecked some day ; so be it : what is to be, will be. When men of the first talents and information, as we find many of these party leaders, descend so low, so far beneath the character of gentlemen, as to aid in blinding and misleading the honest and unsuspecting yeoman of his country, by fashioning him into a tool to vote as they please, to help a set of needy unprincipled men into office, it is time for the people to think for themselves—no matter what party rules, office seems to be the watchword of the old states. As I have once observed, it is ludicrous enough to see the difficulties into which the parties are plunged, particularly when it hap-

pens, as it sometimes does, that some veteran chief shat-
ters their flimsy webs to pieces at a blow. Like a hive
of bees that have been despoiled of their year's labor,
they set to work again with redoubled industry. From
the great deal that is said of Crawford, I should suspect
that all was not right, but for no other reason. He may
be worthy of the trust, but if he really be so, why make
such a din about him ; let his character speak for itself,
when any thing is praised over much, it creates suspicion.

This part of Virginia, I mean all that lies on this side
the Blue Ridge, presents another feature in that State,
which it obtains to its eastern limits : it is distinguished
from all that part west by the number of negroes and
mulattoes, by the gross ignorance of the lower class of
its citizens, by the sprightliness both of men and women ; and above all, by the beautiful form of the latter. The females greatly exceed the West Virginia ladies in well turned persons and features, though they
must yield to those in complexion. From the Blue
Ridge to the Alleghany mountain, a distinct country
obtains, differing morally and physically from the former. Next comes my Grayson republic, already described ; to the left of it, in the same parallel, lies the
great wealthy counties, of Montgomery, Wythe, Washington, &c. &c. : to the right, lies Pendleton, Harrison,
Bath, &c. &c. ; and beyond all, to the west, lie the
counties bordering on the Ohio. All these divisions of
Virginia differ more widely than so many States.

Virginia begins to awake from her lethargy, in respect to roads and canals. I saw a report from Isaac
Briggs, Esq. of Maryland, directed to the Virginia Assembly. The report embraces a survey of the Potomac river from Cumberland to tide water. This survey was made at the united instance of Virginia and
Maryland, with a view to ascertain the expense of an
independent canal along the Potomac valley. Mr. B.
makes the distance 182 miles, and estimates the cost at
$8,544 average rate per mile, total $1575,074. I was
not able to get a view of the sentiments of the Legislature on the report, or the opinion of the Board of public

11*

works; to whom all business of this nature is referred, in the first instance. A large fund is appropriated by the State for internal improvements, under the direction of a Board of public works. The members of this Board are selected from different parts of the State, thereby giving to each part an equal weight in what relates to the advantage of the people at large. Education, likewise, begins to engage the attention of Virginia in a manner worthy that renowned State. The university which is soon to go into operation is located in Albemarle county, at Charlottesville, a small village in the healthiest part of Virginia. It has been built under the direction of the Hon. Thomas Jefferson, ex-president of the United States. The plan contemplates ten professors. The buildings consist of ten pavilions, one for each professor; five hotels for dieting the students, six for the proctor, with one hundred and four dormitories, sufficient to lodge two hundred and eight students. The whole is of uncommon beauty and elegance. The sums expended upon the building have consumed the revenue allotted for its support for seven years to come. There are three colleges in Virginia, besides several academies and schools.

My visit to Richmond was limited to three or four days only, and accordingly I left it for Washington, in the stage, with three other very respectable passengers. The party consisted of a Mr. Warrick, a merchant, and the young man who drew the $100,000 prize, Gillespie's lottery. He was going to Washington City to break up the corporation, which report says has made itself liable for the whole amount. It is well that this minion of fortune is neither a son of Mars nor Minerva. He is what we, in the west, would call a soft young man. It is quite amusing to see his languishing airs, and how he tries to look big. This man is young, about twenty-three, of very pleasing countenance. But the $100,000 will not mend all defects, when he gets it. Having disposed of the $100,000, little remains to be said of the rest.—The merchant was a jolly, talkative soul, all life and humor; he was going on to New-York to purchase goods; but the flower of the party was Mr. Warrick, a man of erudition and elegant manners—had made the tour of Europe, where he had travelled three years; our time, therefore, passed off very pleasantly during the journey. A circumstance occurred during our ride, which proved that men of genius and general science, are, for the most part, deficient in the common affairs of life: we stopped to dine; when dinner was over I handed the man of the house twenty-five cents, and stepped into the stage-coach. The others soon followed, one of them observed he should like to know how I happened to come off in the affair of the dinner upon so much better terms than they, as each had to pay seventy-five cents. I told him that all licensed taverns in this State are compelled, by law, under pain of a heavy fine, to have the rates of fare nailed up in the public room or in some public place, so as to be seen by travellers the moment they enter the house. If the tavern-keeper fails to do this, it is option-ary with the traveller to pay or not. Finding no rates, I determined not to be swindled; probably the owner suspected the truth, as he took the quarter without ut-terring a word. None of the party, though all Vir-ginians, and had travelled a great deal, knew that such a law existed! For want of other matter I must amuse the reader with one or two anecdotes, of the same na-ture, which will pass off the time till we arrive at the boat, where I shall bid him good night and betake my-self to rest in one of those delicious alcoves in the Mount Vernon.

Travelling in company with some gentlemen in the west, it so happened when we called for dinner, that, not feeling over well, one of the party requested the land-lady to make him a cup of tea; she was one of your *very* important ladies, and called to Jinny to tell Peggy to go to the spring and tell Betsey to come home and put on the tea-kettle: the gentleman, provoked at this round about way of doing business, " Madam," said he, " if you will tell me where the kettle is, I will put it on myself." She took the hint, and got up, as I suspect, to put on the kettle herself, but just as she stepped out of the door she was met by her husband and communi-cated to him the substance, and the manner she had been addressed, &c.; she spoke in a low voice, which, nevertheless, I overheard that she rather exceeded the truth. The tea was made, dinner, &c. over, and our bills presented: he charged us four shillings for dinner and oats more than the rate of the county. The knight of the tea-kettle exclaimed, "Where is your rates, sir!" He was a magistrate, and happened to know the law: "Oh," said he of the tavern, in a style of the greatest importance, mixed with contempt, the law says that you shall have the rates nailed to the ceiling, but there is no ceiling here to nail them to." "The intent and meaning of the law, sir," said the other, "is, that you shall have the rates, and without them you have no right to charge; that you shall not only have them, but it is your duty to have them in the most public part of your house, so that a traveller, the moment he enters, may see what he has to pay, and be regulated accordingly. Put up your money gentlemen, said he, you have no right to pay him a cent, I shall report you, sir, for this;" addressing the landlord, and departed. The strangers laughed at the incident; and after exchanging a look between each other, one of them threw the amount of what we had, on the table, leaving monsieur, the landlord, not quite so easy in his mind. This happened in West Virginia.

But this was a rare instance; it is seldom that travellers are imposed upon in any part of the west, indeed; the fare is extremely low, every where in the western country. But we pay for this in the east, at least in old Virginia, particularly those who travel in stages. In coming on last winter, I was initiated into the secret by degrees; they began to broach the subject to me, at Newmarket, Limestone Valley, Va. thro' an old man by the name of Gray, (for the benefit of other travellers.) Being fatigued when I arrived, I went to bed without supper. Next morning we were called as usual, about 3 o'clock, to set out. The old man was up, I called for my bill. What was my astonishment to find it fifty cents. "Where are your rates sir?" said I. "They were in the next room," he said. I picked up the candle, telling him to show them. "Oh d——n it," said he, "what a fuss you make; d'ye think I am a going to get up before day, and keep fires for stage passengers without making them pay." I walked on, nevertheless, to see the rates, but looked for them in vain; the fact was that he had none in the house, which he fairly acknowledged, and in this way are strangers fleeced in this country, which is, indeed, their own fault. The reason they assign for this exorbitant exaction, is the very reason why they should make their charges low, which is that of our being stage passengers; of course they get the more custom. The stage mostly stops at some post-town, where there are more taverns than one. It is altogether a matter of courtesy in the traveller, to give any one tavern the preference. There were two young ladies of our party, that same night, they declared to me, that they had paid fifty cents for lodging heretofore at that same inn. They were entirely ignorant of the restrictions to which a tavern-keeper is subject, until they heard the altercation between the old man and myself. I threw him a quarter and (I repent it yet) departed. When I arrived at Woodstock, where we stopped to breakfast, which is the seat of justice, I inquired of the inn-keeper what the rate was for lodging; he replied twelve and a half cents! This old v———n, therefore, run the risk of losing his license and his soul, (if he had any) for lying and fraud. Thus do these highway robbers, for they are no better, fleece the traveller. I never saw one of this description thrive in any country; they are always a poor, needy set: God in his wisdom has put his fiat against them, they never will nor ever ought to arrive to any thing. And here is the steam-boat. I promised the reader good night, intending to go to rest. Accordingly I took possession of a good bed, and would soon have resigned myself to Morpheus, but for a strange adventure on board. Several ladies were passengers, some of these came with us from F. some we met at the river. One of those who seemed to rank with the better sort, observed that "the room below was too warm; she must go upon deck for air," and in the course of the night, my companion came to bed, having kept me awake during the time. How was I surprised, to hear that the lady before named,

was still on deck in company with the C. All this was
nothing to me, and probably shall not think of it in the
course of a few minutes. What pleasant opportunities
to sleep on board these steam-boats, the murmuring of
the water, the rocking of the boat, and the sound of the
wheels, which keep regular time to the motion of the
boat, the neatness of the chambers and beds, all invite
to sweet repose.

Washington City.—As I before observed, the conveyance from Richmond to Washington, by way of Fredericksburg, is partly by land and partly by water. The
steam-boat which takes you in at Potomac Creek, at 8
o'clock, P. M. lands at Washington about day-light—by
which means we lost the pleasure of an approaching
view of the city, which the river commands. When the
steam-boat lands her passengers on the shore of the Potomac, they are a mile, at least, from the inhabited part
of the city, with the exception of a few scattered dwellings. To remedy this inconvenience, the proprietors
of the line have provided a large vehicle, something
like a stage coach; it is called a carry-all, and would
carry twenty persons. This vehicle soon brought us in
view of the "mighty city," which is nothing more than
distinct groups of houses, scattered over a vast surface,
and has more the appearance of so many villages, than
a city.

It was not long before the towering dome of the capitol met my eye : its massy columns and walls of glittering white. The next object that strikes the eye of a
stranger, is the President's house, on the left, while the
capitol is on the right, as you advance in an eastern direction. Another object of admiration is the bridge
over the Potomac. The capitol, however, which may
aptly be called the eighth wonder of the world, eclipses
the whole. This stupenduous fabric, when seen at a
distance, is remarkable for its magnitude, its vast dome
rising out of the centre, and its exquisite whiteness.—
The President's house, like the capitol, rivals the snow
in whitness. It is easily distinguished from the surrounding edifices, inasmuch as they are of brick. Their

red walls and black, elevated roofs, form a striking contrast to the former, which is not only much larger, but perfectly white, and flat on the top. From the point just mentioned, it has the appearance of a quadrangular; it displays its gorgeous columns at all points, looking down upon the neighboring buildings in silent and stately grandeur. The War Office, Navy Office, the Treasury department, the Department of State, the General Post Office, and the City Hall are all enormous edifices. These edifices, the elevated site of the city; its undulating surface, partially covered with very handsome buildings; the majestic Potomac, with its ponderous bridge, and gliding sails; the eastern branch with its lordly ships; swelling hills which surround the city; the spacious squares and streets, and avenues adorned with rows of flourishing trees, and all this visible at once; it is not in the power of imagination to conceive a scene so replete with every species of beauty.

History.—The following is from Watterton's history of the District of Columbia:—" The District of Columbia was originally inhabited by a tribe of Indians called the Manahoaes, who, according to Smith, were at constant war with the Pohatans, of Virginia. Their history is but imperfectly known. The war, the small pox, and the introduction of spiritous liquors thinned the population rapidly. In 1669 a census was taken, and it was found that in sixty-two, one third of their numbers were wanting. They are said to have migrated westwardly, and to have become blended with the Tuskaroras.* This District was ceded by Virginia and Maryland 1791, and became the permanent seat of the general government in 1800.

At the time of its cession, the principal proprietors on the eastern side of the Potomac, were D. Carrol, N. Young, and D. Burns, who cultivated corn, tobacco,

* Warden, in his description of the District of Columbia, says " that the origin of Washington, like that of several ancient cities, is already wrapped in fable. The story is that a few families in it had lived there in rural solitude, for nearly a century, of which one was established on the borders of the Columbia Creek, from whom it received the name of Tiber, and the place of residence was called Rome. History may hereafter record the belief that this simple farmer, endowed with prophetic powers, foretold the destinies of the Columbian Territory.

and wheat, where the city of Washington now stands."
It is hardly necessary to mention what every one has
heard, viz. that the District of Columbia is ten miles
square, and includes within its limits, Georgetown and
Alexandria, and is under the immediate government of
Congress. The city of Washington is situated on the
Potomac, on the Maryland side, at the confluence of
the eastern branch with this river. The eastern branch
was formerly known by the name of Annacasta;—it
stands in lat. 38° 55' N., and in long. 76° 33' from
Greenwich. Washington is distant from

Philadelphia,	143
Baltimore,	43
Richmond,	132
Annapolis,	40
Monticello,	124

It is three miles in length from north to south, viz.
from Greenleaf's point south, to Rock creek north,
which separates it from Georgetown. Its breadth is
about two miles. The city is laid out into regular
squares—all the streets crossing each other at right angles, north and south, east and west. At present (1824)
it may be said to be built out the whole length—the
buildings extending up to Rock creek, although it might
contain tripple the number of houses. Besides the
streets already mentioned, there are several avenues
which lead to the different public offices. These avenues are very wide, and run in arbitrary directions.

The city is distinguished by whimsical names by the
citizens, such as the Navy yard, Greenleaf's Point, (or
the Fort,) Capitol Hill, Pennsylvania Avenue, F. Street,
the Twenty Buildings, the Ten Buildings, the Seven
Buildings, the Six Buildings, Howardstown, Frogtown,
and the Wharf. Besides these, the capitol, the president's house, and the different bulky public offices,
form each a town within themselves. The greatest
number of houses in all those groups, is on the Pennsylvania Avenue, between the capitol and the president's house. The Six Buildings are very near Georgetown, then we have the Seven Buildings, between the
Six Buildings and the President's house. Proceeding on

in the same direction, (south,) we have the President's
house, the War Office, the Navy Office, Treasury Department, and Department of State, on the right, while
F Street, the Post-Office, the City Hall, the Poor-house,
and the Prison, are on the left. Proceeding on in the
same direction, viz. down the Pennsylvania Avenue,
with the Potomac about a mile on our right, we come
to the Capitol. Leaving the Capitol, same direction, we
come to the Ten Buildings; further on, the Twenty
Buildings, and finally Greenleaf's Point, which is on the
point of land formed by the Potomac and the eastern
branch. The Navy yard, which is a considerable town,
and the Marine Barracks, are on the eastern branch, a
mile distant from the point, and the same from the capitol. Capitol Hill lies east of the capitol, and comprises
no inconsiderable part of the city: Howardstown is
nothing more than a continuation of Capitol Hill, eastwardly in the direction of Bladensburg. Frogtown lies
on the Potomac, where the steam-boats stop, below the
bridge. Pennsylvania Avenue alone, is denominated
" the city," by those living in the other parts just mentioned; when they would visit that part of the city,
they say " we are going to the city."

The Capitol.—I am almost deterred from attempting
to give even a sketch of the exterior of this vast edifice.
It stands on an elevation of eighty feet above the tidewater of the Potomac, and covers nearly two acres of
ground. It stands north and south, presenting an east
and west front. The ascent to it is on the west, nearly
a perpendicular, and parallel to its whole length; whilst
the ground on the east front is perfectly horizontal. On
the east principally lies the capitol square, enclosed
with iron railing. The following are the outlines taken
by Mr. Bulfinch, the present architect. Dimensions of
the capitol of the United States.

Length of the front,	- - - -	350 feet.
Depth of wings,	- - - -	120
East projection and steps,	- - -	95
West projection do.	- - -	83
Covering one and one half acre and		1826

12

Height of wings to top of balustrade   -   70 feet.
Height of centre dome   -   -   -   120
Representatives' Hall, greatest length,   -   95
Representatives' Hall, greatest height   -   60
Senate Chamber, greatest length   -   -   74
Senate Chamber, greatest height   -   42
Great central rotunda, 96 feet in diameter and 96 feet high.
The basement story   -   -   -   -   20
The entablement   -   -   -   -   -   7
The parapet   -   -   -   -   -   6 1-2
The centre of the building from the east to the west portico is in depth   -   -   -   -   240

The east front will (for it is not yet finished,) present a colonade of one hundred and sixty feet, consisting of twenty-five Corinthian columns, twenty-five feet in height. The ceiling is vaulted, and the whole edifice is of solid masonry, of hewn free stone, of the Corinthian order. Both the inside and out is painted white, and reflects a lustre dazzling to the eyes. All the steps, stairs and floors are stone, with the exception only of the Senate chamber and Congress hall. No wood is found in any part of the building but the doors, sash, and railing, which last is mahogany. The covering is of copper; the domes are also of copper. The great centre dome in shape resembles an inverted wash-bowl; only magnify a wash-bowl to the size of ninety six feet in diameter, and you will have correct idea of its figure. What would be the rim of the top, is of solid stone. The rim of the bottom which is a balustrade is of wood; this encircles the sky-lights; the great body of the dome is copper, with steps leading from the bottom to the top, from which you have one of the grandest views in nature. The two wings are likewise ornamented with domes and sky-lights; they are low compared to that of the centre. The sky-lights of these last are finished in a style of inimitable taste and beauty; their snowy graces charm and attract the eye of every beholder.

It is not in the power of language, to express anything to equal the interior of those domes, for richness

and beauty ; flowers and wreaths, in profusion, decorate
their inside as white as alabaster.   The marble columns, the richness and splendor of the drapery, carpeting and mahogany furniture, which adorn and almost
fill Congress Hall and Senate Chamber, are likewise
objects of admiration. The seat of the Speaker, I should
fall short of the truth, were I to attempt to describe it.
I had no idea of its figure or furniture.

The Representative Hall is in the form of a semi-cir-
cle ; upon the middle of the segment stands the chair of
the Speaker, considerably elevated.   Over the chair is
a canopy of the richest crimson silk, trimmed with
fringe equally rich ; the canopy is supported by four upright posts, higher than the tallest man's head.*   From
the top of these, the canopy drops to the bottom in copious folds of the same brilliant material.   This would
completely conceal the Speaker from view, were it not
gracefully festooned on each side, and even then, he
can only be seen in front.   Precisely in front of the
chair, stands the Clerk's table, also elevated above the
floor of the Hall, but much lower than the chair, so as
not to intercept the view between it and the members.
At this table sits the Clerk and his assistants, with their
backs to the chair, and so near to it, that the Speaker
by looking over can read the documents.

On the right and left of the chair sit the members, (a
goodly number,) in semi-circular rows, one behind another, extending from the chair to the door of entrance,
leaving a straight line open from one to the other.   The
members are encompassed by the bar of the *house* ;
behind the bar is a lobby quite round the hall.   The
sergeant-at-arms stands outside the bar, and the door-
keepers outside of the door of Congress Hall.   In as-
cending to the gallery you do not enter Congress Hall,
but proceed through the lobby fronting the door up a
stair case, (no ordinary height,) which lands you at
the gallery.   The galleries are conveniently adapted
to the purpose intended, consisting of different rows of
seats, one above another, resembling an amphitheatre.
From these seats you look down upon the members,

* The top of the canopy resembles an umbrella spread.

who are commodiously seated in mahogany chairs, of
the richest fashion; each one has a chair to himself,
and before him is a mahogany table with drawers and
places for pen, ink, and paper; these seats are arranged in regular rows.   The Hall is heated by furnaces; I
saw two fire places only.

The Senate Chamber is similar to the Hall, and
furnished in like manner also, with the exception of the
President's chair, which is quite plain, compared with
that of the Speaker's.   I attended a few times to hear
the debates, but was unable to hear, at least, distinctly,
owing to the noise made in the galleries, lobbies, and
that made by the slaming of the doors.   I was greatly
surprised that so little order was maintained; such running to and fro, both by visitors and members; and from
the nature of the great centre dome, the slightest tread
is echoed by it for several seconds.   Although I could
not accurately hear the members, I could easily distinguish the shrill, clear voice of the Speaker, Mr. Clay.
There is something peculiarly sweet and harmonious in
the tone of his voice; and he was always necessarily
saying something.   He has to put the question; he has
to call for the ayes and nays; and that very often.—
When a member rises, Mr. Speaker announces it as follows: "the gentleman from Maryland," or as the case
may be; several will rise in the course of a few minutes, which keeps him incessantly proclaiming to the
House.   When a motion is made, the Speaker repeats
it to the House, and calls for the ayes and noes, thus;
" those gentlemen who are in favor of ——, say aye,
and those who are against it, say no;" all the members
answer immediately; some saying "aye," and some
saying " no," at the same instant.   If the Speaker be
satisfied from the sound, which has the majority, he pro-
nounces aloud, " the noes have it," or as the case may
be. But if the Speaker cannot distinguish by the sound,
he says " we cannot distinguish by the sound, the noes
will rise;" when they all rise from their seats, and he
counts them to himself, pointing to each member with
his finger.   He will sometimes then be at a loss, and call
upon the ayes to rise.   When any member calls for the

yeas and nays, as they do very often, the clerk calls upon every member by name, the person answering "aye"
or "no," while the clerk, with a pen in his hand, sets
down the vote.

I have in vain attempted to come at the minutia of the
architecture of the capitol : either those to whom I applied were unwilling to furnish the plan, or have lost it.
Although it would fill a volume of itself, it would have
been pleasing to me to have added this to the work, and
such is the nature and number of its eternal intricacies,
that no one unskilled in architecture, could give any
description that would be satisfactory.   The first story,
which is that under Congress Hall and Senate Chamber, with the exception of an apartment assigned to the
Supreme and District Courts, is nothing but an assemblage of small apartments, committee rooms, vaulted
galleries, and lobbies, where no honest person ought to
be seen.*   The second story comprises Congress Hall,
the Senate Chamber, clerk's offices, and post offices for
both Houses, the great Rotunda, rooms for the President, rooms for the heads of Departments, and apartments for Foreign Ministers, a library, and a room
appropriated to paintings.   Above this story are two
others, all laid off into small apartments, designed perhaps for committee rooms.   It appears that those who
planned the capitol committed a great oversight by an
useless waste of room.   Taking from the whole length
of the edifice, the length of the Senate Chamber, Congress Hall, and the Rotunda, it leaves eighty five feet.
Had this surplus been divided between Congress Hall
and the Rotunda, it would have rendered them more
convenient.   They had to enlarge the Hall the last
census, and will probably have to do so after the next ;
and as to the Rotunda, which is designed for the inauguration of the President, and other public occasions ;
it will be found inadequate for the accommodation of
such numbers as may wish to attend.   But as respects
the beauty, grandeur and durability of the workmanship,

* Under all is a cellar filled with choice hickory wood for the use of
Congress

this edifice is not surpassed, perhaps, by any other in the world.

It has already been observed, that the capitol presents an east and west front. The east front commands a view of the capitol square, that part of the city called the capitol hill, the navy yard, and the Eastern branch. The west front commands the Potomac, the bridge, the canal, (which is to bring the waters of the Potomac and the Eastern branch through the city,) the president's house, the city hall, the public offices, the Pennsylvania and Maryland avenues. The Pennsylvania and Maryland avenues meet at the west front of the capitol, in the form of the letter V. The ground lying between these avenues is sacredly reserved as an ornament, and commands an extensive view of the surrounding country, as well as the Potomac, and the canal already mentioned. The Pennsylvania avenue, which is the right side of the V, is planted with four rows of trees, and the best private buildings in the city; while the Maryland avenue, (which is the left side of the V) as yet remains undistinguished among the commons, which gives to its fellow an odd appearance, by throwing it into an obtuse angle with the capitol. Was the Maryland avenue even planted with trees, it would add greatly to the prospect, and show the design.

Those planners for eternity have been guilty of another oversight, a blunder which ought never to be forgiven. Instead of setting the President's house (which terminates Pennsylvania avenue) at the end of it, which was evidently intended, they have placed it on the right, without its area; and, although the avenue commands a view of the house, its relative position gives to it an awkward appearance.

President's House.—The President's house is one mile and seven-eighths from the capitol, and is likewise built of free-stone, but built according to the Ionic proportion. It is two stories high, 170 feet in length, and 85 in breadth. It has a large square of ground attached to it, planted with beautiful and flourishing trees. In the midst of this square, which is enclosed with a wall, upon an elevated situation, sits the queen of the city, enrobed

in snowy white. Before entering upon a description of
the other public establishments, it may be as well to notice the capitol square, one of the principal ornaments of
the city.

Capitol Square.—The principal part of the capitol
square lies on the east of the capitol, extending no further to the west than just to take in the brow of the
hill upon which the capitol stands. The ground within
the iron railing contains twenty acres and one-eighth.—
The foot-walk outside of the railing is three-fourths of a
mile and 180 feet in length. It is planted with trees and
shrubbery, consisting of the spontaneous growth of the
surrounding country, with the exception of the horse-
chesnut. They have procured the elm from Massachusetts, and the fir and spruce from Maine. Those trees
are planted in the form of a border round the square,
without order or regularity, and by far too thick for their
well being : there are a few scattering ones throughout
the square. Had the projectors of this plan been less
prodigal of attention to this part of the square, and
spared a few more for the remaining part, it would have
added much to the convenience, if not to the beauty, of
the design. As yet this shrubbery is in its infancy. A
man is kept continually at work amongst those trees, with
a view of keeping them free from grass, or whatever else
may impede their growth. On the outside of the railing is a single row of trees, between which and the railing is a convenient walk for the citizens. The railing,
in mechanism, may vie with any thing of the sort, both
for beauty and strength. It consists of slender palisades of iron, about an inch square and four feet high.—
These palisades are placed upright, the lower end being
inserted into a solid stone, and soldered with lead. The
tops of these palisades terminate in a point, are about
four inches asunder, and are firmly confined with a double plate of iron, through which the points are inserted.
The stone which confines the lower end of the palisade
is about two feet wide, and completely protects a stone
wall, of about two feet high, from the weather. This
wall supports the whole fabric. Every sixteenth is a

triple palisade, which is to be ornamented with a cap
of brass.

The other Public Buildings.—The war office and the
navy office are vast buildings of brick; they are on the
left of the President's house, and not far distant from it.
The treasury office, and office of the department of
state, are likewise large brick buildings; they stand on
the right of the President's house, and about the same
distance from it as the former. Another large building
of brick is occupied by the general post-office, the city
post-office, the patent office, and the Washington library.
But the largest building in the city, excepting the capitol, is the city hall: it is 200 feet in length, and high in
proportion. In it the mayor holds his court, and here
all city business is transacted. The whole of these
great edifices are divided into numerous rooms and a-
partments, and swarm with clerks and other subordinate
officers of government. The city hall and the general
post-office occupy the highest ground in the city, and the
scenery from this point is by far the richest ground view
within it. Near the city hall is the prison; it is a large
building, surrounded with a high brick wall. The other
public buildings are, a poor-house, an orphan asylum,
two churches for Roman Catholics, three for Presbyterians, three for Methodists, two for Baptists, two for
Protestants, one for Friends, one for Unitarians, two
masonic halls, four banks, four market houses, a theatre,
a circus, a fort, a ware-house, and a magazine. Besides
these there is the navy yard, with its work-shops and offices, and barracks sufficient to contain one thousand
men.

Navy Yard.—The navy yard is a complete work-shop,
where every naval article is manufactured: it contains
twenty-two forges, five furnaces, and a steam-engine.—
The shops are large and convenient; they are built of
brick and covered with copper to secure them from
fire. Steel is prepared here with great facility. The
number of hands employed vary; at present there are
about 200. A ship-wright has $2,50 per day, out of
which he maintains his wife and family if he have any.
Generally wages are very low for all manner of work; a

common labourer gets but 75 cents per day, and finds
himself. The whole interior of the yard exhibits one
continual thundering of hammers, axes, saws, and bellows, sending forth such a variety of sounds and smells,
from the profusion of coal burnt in the furnaces, that it
requires the strongest nerves to sustain the annoyance.
The workmen are as black as negroes, and the heat of
the furnaces at this season of the year, (June,) is insupportable to one not accustomed to it. The whole is one
scene of activity, not one is idle.

After amusing myself with those sons of thunder, I
was gratified with a sight equally new to me;—this was
an inspection of a forty-four gun frigate. It was lying
up, under cover, completely out of water. This was
really a curiosity to me, having never seen a ship of any
sort, with the exception of a small merchant ship, at Alexandria. Its amazing length, its great height from the
bottom to the top, afforded sufficient matter of wonder.
I had a very indistinct idea of a ship, till seeing this;
but I lost half the pleasure, in the total absence of the
rigging, as they were unable to draw her under cover,
without divesting her of this incumbrance. The greatest disappointment to me was the width: I had expected
to find those vessels not so narrow in proportion to the
length; but until I can see one properly rigged for sea,
I shall never have an accurate idea of a ship of war.—
I saw one more on the stocks, at which men were at
work. I found in the yard three hundred cannon, thir-
ty-four and forty-two pounders, with two brass pieces;
and was told there was a large quantity of arms in the
armory, which were kept in excellent order. After
several unsuccessful attempts, I was unable to get into it.
Of them, therefore, I can say nothing.

The navy-yard is enclosed with a very high wall, and
no one can be admitted without the permission of the
commandant: I found some difficulty, although furnished with a letter, through the politeness of Mr. Seaton,
editor of the National Intelligencer. The interior is
guarded by a centinel, who parades before the gate, day
and night, with his gun erect in his arms. Besides himself, a large eagle, cut out of solid stone, guards the

outside: it looks down from the top of a magnificent
gate, which opens for the admission of strangers, as well
as the workmen who may have occasion to pass. While
beholding this eagle, I could not help upbraiding him
for his cowardice, in suffering the British to pass unmolested under him, and his ostensible bunch of arrows,
telling him, at the same time, that he deserved to be
disfranchised for this dastardly conduct of his.

Directly fronting the gate, on the inside, stands the
monument erected to perpetuate the memory of the
brave men who fell at Tripoli. This monument, which
is of marble, was executed in Italy, by eminent artists.
It is a small Doric column, embellished with suitable emblems, crowned with an eagle in the act of flying. The
pillar rests on a base, sculptured in basso relievo, representing Tripoli, its fortress, the Mediterranean, and
our fleet, in the fore ground. On each corner stands an
appropriate figure, elegantly executed; one representing Columbia directing the attention of her children to
History, who is recording the daring and intrepid actions of the American heroes. The third represents
Fame, with a wreath of laurel in one hand, and a pen in
the other. The fourth represents Mercury, or the god
of Commerce, with his cornucopia and caduceses.
This is all the trophy Potomac can boast. Besides
this part of the navy-yard which is enclosed, there are
a great number of houses on the outside, which likewise take the name of the " navy-yard." These contain stores, shops, and private families. In the midst of
them stand the barracks.

Barracks.—The barracks are enclosed by a handsome brick wall, 400 feet in length, 50 wide, and 20 in
height; the ground within is level, and neatly gravel-
led, while the apartments for the marines, line the wall;
the Colonel's house stands at the head of the barracks,
surrounded with a neat shrubbery, and a handsome spot
of ground in which he keeps the marines at work, when
not on duty. These men are mustered twice in the
day, accompanied by an elegant band. Col. Henderson,
the present commandant, waited upon me through the
establishment, ordered the men to parade, and the band

to play. He is of middling age, and a man of genteel manners.

The Poor-House.—This wretched establishment only exists to disgrace Washington. I found several wretched children in this dreary and comfortless asylum, without one cheering voice, or hand of kindness to comfort or cherish them. Some were stretched on straw, unable to rise, others were bedecked with crocus, (I think they call it) the coarsest stuff I ever saw. The whole group had a squalid appearance, which filled me with disgust, and the smell of the place was insupportable. I asked one of the unfortunate women whose business it was to attend to these sufferers, what made the rooms smell so ill; but she was too simple to understand me. The intendant and his wife are Irish; he appeared to me to be wholly unfit for the place, and his wife a perfect she dragon. It is much to be lamented, that in such cases care is not taken to select persons of humanity, who are capable of administering comfort and consolation to affliction. The house is large and beautiful, and in the finest situation in the city, but death would be mercy compared to the situation of the unfortunate inmates. I was told that a part of the house was appropriated to a work-house, for the punishment of disorderly persons, but I had neither the courage nor the inclination to see more of a place so replete with human wo! and with an aching heart I turned my back upon those cheerless, friendless sufferers.* Three thousand dollars are appropriated annually for the support of this establishment!

The Prison.—I found the prison of Washington under very different regulations from that of the poor house. Here I found health, cleanliness, and plenty of wholesome food ; the prisoners cheerful and happy. I examined every cell that contained a criminal, which was twenty-four, and found neither desponcency nor complaint. They were severally laughing, talking, and singing ; and but for reality it would not appear that they were confined. The debtors apartments are spa-

* Warden, speaking of this, says. "No friendly shade appears to support the feeble convalescent."

cious and airy ; and in no part of the prison did I witness any thing but the greatest tenderness and humanity toward those unfortunate beings. Much credit is
due to the keeper, whoever he be, who thus does honor
to himself, and to human nature. The prison is supported by the county, whereas the poor-house is supported by the corporation.

 Orphan Asylum.—But the glory of Washington is
the Orphan Asylum. This Asylum, which reflects
the highest honor upon its promoters, is supported by
private contribution, under the care and direction of a
number of ladies. It is truly interesting to see those
destitute and forlorn little creatures amply supplied
with every comfort. I found fifteen female children in
the asylum, from five to twelve years of age, who bear
every mark of the tenderest treatment ; they were neat,
and well clad, and had a healthy appearance. They
were furnished with clean and comfortable bedding,
disposed in suitable chambers. The Intendant, (Mrs
M'Kenny,) is a lady, apparently well calculated to fulfil the high trust committed to her care. Unlike the ti-
gress of the poor-house, she is mild, sweet, and com-
passionate. To these amiable qualities, she joins a
highly cultivated mind, which enables her to teach those
little orphans the rudiments of useful instruction. They
are taught reading, writing, and needle-work. No
male children are admitted. When they arrive at an
age sufficient to procure a livelihood, they are discharged. Of all institutions which ennobles human nature,
those which have for their object the alleviation of human misery, are certainly the most so ; but no institution combines in one such a number of distinguished
and laudable objects, or affords a greater instance of
enlarged kindness and charity, than those established
for the benefit of orphans. To cherish and protect their
infant state ; to sweeten their cup of sorrow; to sow
the seeds of virtue, and " teach the young idea how to
shoot," to draw out those hidden beauties of the mind,
which gain our admiration, and fit them for the various
duties of life, are certainly the most god-like acts of
which our nature is capable. This establishment might

be rendered more convenient by enlarging the building; but as it is, it is the brightest ornament of Washington.

The Bridge.—The Potomac bridge, at Washington, is a mile in length, and wholly constructed of wood. It contains draw-bridges for the passage of vessels; these bridges are raised by a pulley, and by a single individual. This bridge cost ninety-six thousand dollars, and belongs to a company. At the end of sixty years the company is to be dissolved, and the bridge becomes the property of the United States. The profit of this bridge is nothing, except when the river is frozen, as the toll is abominably high. The numerous boats which ply the river, save the people a vast expense in travelling, and this among the rest. Besides this bridge, there are two others over the Eastern branch; opposite to one of these stands the magazine, on the Eastern branch, upwards of a mile from its mouth; and still higher up the river is the public burying-ground.

Public Grave-Yard.—The grave-yard is among the principal ornaments of Washington: it is two miles from the capitol, and makes a very handsome appearance. It is seen at a great distance. The white points of those beautiful monuments glitter in the sunbeams with refulgent brightness. It is enclosed with a wall, which you enter by a stile; we (the party who accompanied me) found a number of tombs and monuments scattered over the ground, which, however, bear no proportion to those interred in simple graves. These tombs (the first I had ever seen) are of solid freestone, and consist of five parts, viz. the top, the two ends, and sides—the whole adheres closely together, resembling a huge chest. They are about three feet in height, the lid or top projecting about one inch over the whole. On the top of these tombs are written or cut, whatever the friends of the deceased think proper, with the age, &c. The monuments differ very widely from the tombs, inasmuch as they are square at the bottom, high, and terminate in a pyramid. The most conspicuous are those erected to the memory of George Clinton and Elbridge Gerry, late vice-presidents of the United States. That erected in honour of

13

Mr. Gerry, is truly magnificent: it consists of solid marble, of the purest white, ornamented with an urn, of the same material, on the top. It is about twelve feet high, and greatly excels, both in symmetry and design. The monument erected to Capt. Gamble, is also very handsome, though made of freestone. Those erected to members of congress are quite low and plain : there are fourteen of these, with the name and age written on them, in large letters, with black ink, or paint, which retains the colour in all its freshness. Besides this, there are several private burying-grounds in the city.

After walking to and fro amongst the tombs until my curiosity was satisfied, we sat down upon the grass under the shade of those monuments, to enjoy the cooling breeze from the river, and the scenery of the surrounding country, which is beautiful beyond description. You can see up and down the Eastern branch to a vast distance. The farms upon the opposite shore, rising in amphitheatres, skirted with wood of the most luxuriant foliage, render the scene most enchanting. Whilst reposing in this manner, four ladies, gaily attired, entered the grave-yard, attended by a very shabby looking beau. They passed near the place where we were sitting, and seemed to examine us with what I should call an arrogant assurance. In one respect, however, we stood upon equal ground—they indulged their curiosity, we did the same. In a short time after they passed by, three other ladies entered, unattended : they were clad in sable dresses, and accompanied by several children. These last had the appearance of genteel females, who no doubt had come to breathe a sigh over some departed friend. I could not, however, approve their taste in choosing that hour of the day, in their costume.

The Fishery.—Great quantities of herring and shad are taken in these waters during the fishing season, which commences in March, and lasts about ten weeks. As many as 160,000 are said to be caught at one haul.— When the season commences no time is to be lost, not even Sunday. Although I am not one of those that make no scruple of breaking the Sabbath, yet, Sunday as it was, I was anxious to see a process which I had never witnessed—I mean that of taking fish with a seine —there being no such thing in the western country. It is very natural for one to form an opinion of some sort respecting things they have never seen; but the idea I had formed of the method of fishing with a seine was far from a correct one. In the first place, about fifteen or twenty men, and very often an hundred, repair to the place where the fish are to be taken, with a seine and a skiff. This skiff, however, must be large enough to contain the net and three men—two to row, and one to let out the net. These nets, or seines, are of different sizes, say from two to three hundred fathom in length, and from three to four fathom wide. On one edge are fastened pieces of cork-wood, as large as a man's fist, about two feet asunder; and on the opposite edge are fastened pieces of lead, about the same distance—the lead is intended to keep the lower end of the seine close to the bottom of the river. The width of the seine is adapted to the depth of the river, so that the corks just appear on its surface, otherwise the lead would draw the top of the seine under water, and the fish would escape over the top. All this being understood, and the seine and rowers in the boat, they give one end of the seine to a party of men on the shore, who are to hold it fast.— Those in the boat then row off from the shore, letting out the seine as they go; they advance in a straight line towards the opposite shore, until they gain the middle of the river, when they proceed down the stream, until the net is all out of the boat except just sufficient to reach the shore from whence they set out, to which they immediately proceed. Here an equal number of men take hold of the net with those at the other end, and both parties commence drawing it towards the shore. As they draw, they advance towards each other, until they finally meet; and now comes the most pleasing part of the business. It is amusing enough to see what a spattering the fish make when they find themselves completely foiled: they raise the water in a perfect shower, and wet every one that stands within their reach. I ought to have mentioned, that when the fish begin to draw near the shore, one or two men step into the water, on each side of the net, and hold it close to the bottom of the the channel, otherwise the fish would escape underneath. All this being accomplished, the fishermen proceed to take out the fish in greater or less numbers, as they are more or less fortunate. These fishermen make a wretched appearance, they certainly do bring up the rear of the human race. They were scarcely covered with clothes, were mostly drunk, and had the looks of the veriest sots upon earth. Some were lying down on the grass, drunk, resembling any thing but human beings.

Eastern Branch.—Whilst detailing subjects connected with the Eastern branch, I shall drop some remarks on this extraordinary river. The Eastern branch, though deep enough at the navy yard for the largest ships of war to ride in, and wide in proportion, yet at Bladensburg, which is only five miles distant, it is nothing more than a common creek! It forks at Bladensburg; one branch is called Paint, which has its source near this place, the other is called West Paint. Formerly, shipping used to ascend the Eastern branch as high as Bladensburg; but now, boats only can ascend with difficulty.

Canals, Fountains and Baths.—Previous to my visit to Washington, I had heard much of the canal and Tyber creek. How was I surprised to find the mighty canal, a little, dirty, dribling pool of fœted water, only a few inches deep; and as for Tyber creek, a man can easily jump across it, when the tide is down. The citizens are now engaged in cutting another canal, upon a much better plan: this canal is to bring the waters of the Eastern branch and the Potomac through the city, which will add much to its beauty. Much credit is due the corporation, for its attention to public fountains, which abound in every part of the city: you find them at short intervals, in every street and avenue where houses are built; and the water is exceeded by none in the world. Independent of these, there are a number of springs, of pure and never failing water. There is but one public bath in the city; the price of bathing once is fifty cents!

The Market.—Every article of food is much higher in Washington than either in Alexandria or Georgetown. While beef sells from 4 1-2 to 6 cents in the two latter,

it sells from 8 to 12 in Washington: all descriptions of
meat are in the same proportion. Vegetables, however,
are low when compared to meats; you cannot buy one
pound of veal or lamb for less than ten cents, and that
so poor, that it would not be eaten in the western country. Bread-stuffs at this time are low; flour sells from
five to six dollars and fifty cents per bbl.; corn-meal, fifty cents per bush.; bacon, twelve and a half cents per
pound; butter, from twenty to twenty-five cents; the
butter is very indifferent; eggs are eighteen cents per
dozen; wood in winter, is six dollars and fifty cents; in
summer, three dollars per cord; coal, thirty cents per
bushel. Fish is abundant, and cheap at all seasons;
shad is three dollars per hundred; herrings, one dollar
per thousand; a milch cow (common,) twelve dollars.
Every article is much lower in market during summer
than winter, owing to the absence of congress: in general, vegetables are very fine.

Commerce and Manufactures.—At present, commerce
is confined to the retail of commodities of daily consumption; coffee sells at twenty five cents, brown sugar
from ten to twelve cents. All descriptions of groceries
and dry goods are low; good substantial calico can be
bought for twenty-five cents. Manufactures are confined to those of glass, tin, and leather, besides the naval
articles already mentioned.

Public Libraries.—With the exception of the library
which belongs to government, Washington claims but
one only; this is called the " Washington Library;"
it contains about seven hundred volumes. That which
belongs to government, contains two thousand volumes,
most of which were purchased from Thomas Jefferson,
Esq. It is said to be a choice collection of the best au-
thors. Any citizen or stranger has liberty to go to the
library and read as often as they choose, but none except
the members of congress, are permitted to take any out.
Apprentices' libraries, which yield such a fund of amusement and instruction in almost every town in the United
States, are wholly unknown in Washington.

Societies—There are five societies in Washington,
viz. the " Columbian Institute," the " Colonization So-
13*

ciety," the "Benevolent Society," the "Typographical Society," and a "Medical Society."

Education.—From the limited opportunity afforded me, I am unable to affirm any thing positively, respecting the encouragement given to learning. From all accounts, education is in its infancy. There are no academies, no grammar schools, and but two free schools, for the exclusive benefit of the poor: these are supported by the corporation. A number of other schools are kept by indifferent teachers, where little children are taught to read, write, and "*cipher!*" I have seen girls of fourteen years, learning to cipher, who did not understand a word of grammar. This gives the best idea of the sort of instruction bestowed on the youth of Washington. The Columbian college, however, in some measure atones for the deficiency in other respects. It is a magnificent edifice, and well endowed.

The proximity of the Georgetown college, and a well-regulated female seminary at the same place, has hitherto superseded the necessity of literary institutions at Federal city. Notwithstanding these anterior advantages, the dissemination of knowledge does not appear to have received that encouragement which we would expect in the first city of the nation.

Literary Men.—It appears that Washington has produced one man of letters: George Watterston, Esq. He proves to be the author of Glencairn. Besides this celebrated novel, he has written several other works; two only of which I have seen, viz: "Letters from Washington," and the "L. Family, or a winter in the Metropolis." He writes with ease, and as one familiar with Belleslettres. The letters are a short analysis of the laws and constitution of the United States; sketches of the heads of department, and some of the most distinguished members of Congress. These letters exhibit many strokes of original beauty, energy of thought, and purity of style; his judgment marked with accuracy, perspicuity, and great deference. The L. Family is a work of his own fancy; it abounds with humour, incident and good sense. It is nothing more than a mirror, held up to reflect the follies of human life. In this

last, however, he departs from nature, than which nothing is more easily detected. The L. Family set out
from —— upon a visit to Washington, where they spend
the winter. He introduces them as a people but a
small degree removed from rusticity; and while he
exhibits them under this character, the novel (or whatever it be,) is truly amusing; but in getting on he exhibits them in a different light; the same persons on a
sudden become refined, and surprise us by their judicious remarks, and a display of elegant manners, which,
though nevertheless pleasing, is a distortion of nature.
Besides these works, he is the author of several plays;
and one other work of some merit; which last I have
seen. His style is very much improved since he wrote
Glencairn, at which time he must have been quite
young indeed, as he does not appear to be over twenty-
five at this time, (1824.) But in none of these works
appears that simplicity which some admire in a writer,
and which so eminently distinguishes Glencairn. Mr.
Watterston is however a good writer, inferior to few in
the United States. He is librarian of the public library of Congress, for which he receives fifteen hundred
dollars per annum. Previous to my knowledge of him
as a writer, I visited the library, and was much struck
with his gentlemanly appearance and manners; I mentioned the circumstance to some who knew him, when
I learned his claims to literary fame. On my next visit
to the library, I ventured an indirect compliment to
him as the author of "Glencairn;" he blushed deep,
and asked where I had seen it. Mr. W. is a man of
good size, neither spare nor robust; he is a fine figure,
and possessed of some personal beauty; his complexion fair, his countenance striking, shows genius and
deep penetration, marked with gravity, though manly
and commanding. A sweet serenity diffuses itself over
his countenance, which no accident can ruffle; and under the veil of retiring modesty, discovers his blushing
honors thick upon him. No mental pleasure is equal
to that which we feel in beholding an author, particularly one whose works we have read, without the small-
es idea of ever seeing the writer; there is something

which we cannot express, arising from mingled feelings
produced by this intellectual feast.   Besides Mr. Watterston, whom Washington may almost claim as her
son,* the city reckons two other literary men, viz :—
Doctor Ewell and Doctor Watkins.   The former is the
author of a medical work which bears his name, and
which is in the hands of almost every physician in the
western country.   Doctor Ewell is a native of Virginia,
and supports the character of an able physician and an
eminent surgeon ; he is a man of plain and simple manners, a true indication of science and sense.   He is easy of access, and condescending in his address ; Socra-
tes himself was not more artless in his common deportment.   He is rather low of stature, inclined to corpu-
lence, and somewhere about fifty years of age.   He has
a most engaging countenance ; his fine, full, hazle eye,
beaming with all the intelligence and vigour of youth.
His features still retain the marks of beauty ; his face is
round, full, and perfectly free from wrinkles.

Doctor Watkins is in size very near the proportion
of Doctor Ewell ; perhaps taller, and not so corpulent ;
nor is he so old as the latter ; he appeared to me about
forty years of age.   To the advantages of a very engaging person, Doctor Watkins unites the most captivating manners, in which grace and dignity are equally
blended ; his complexion fair ; his face oval and full ;
his brilliant blue eye bespeaks genius and quick discernment ; his countenance open and benevolent ; in
short, he appears to be of the first order of gentlemen.
He is said to possess some talents as a writer, though
I have never seen any of his works.   He is a native of
Maryland, and secretary to the commissioners for settling Spanish claims under the treaty of Ghent.   I am
sorry my opportunity of doing justice to this amiable
man, is by no means adequate to the task, having been
in his company but a few minutes.   In delineating character and personal appearance, a thorough acquaintance and close observation are indispensable ; but such
has been the nature of my situation and engagements

* He was born at sea, of Scottish parents, but reared and educated
in Federal city.

since my residence in Washington, as to put it out of my power to avail myself either of the one or the other. A brief sketch, therefore, is all that I aim at ; were I even competent to do justice to a subject of all others the most difficult.

Since the nature of these observations has led to the mention of literary men, it may not be unwelcome to the reader to add one more remark respecting two men, eminent for their public services ; I mean Messrs. Gales and Seaton, editors of the National Intelligencer. It will, no doubt, be pleasing to many to hear even a slight outline of two gentlemen who have been so long before the public ; but it will be no more than a hasty sketch.   Mr. Gales is of middle age, and quite a small man ; his complexion dark, his face pale, and of an oval figure, with a keen black eye.   In his manners he is affable and easy, in short, he seems to have dwelt all his life among the graces.   On the score of politeness, he is a perfect model.   In his conduct he is just, generous, and humane.   In attention to business, indefatigable.   Mr. S. yields greatly to Mr. G. in point of graceful and easy manners, he is a young looking man, not more than thirty years of age.   He has, however, much the advantage of Mr. G. in personal appearance, he is an elegant figure, tall, stout, and well made, his complexion fair, his face round, his features regular and handsome, with a penetrative blue eye.   His countenance very manly and dignified, his conversation marked with decision.   Both those gentlemen evince a general knowledge of men and manners, and demean themselves with all the rectitude and correctness of honest and respectable citizens.   They have for several years edited the celebrated paper in Washington, called the " National Intelligencer."   Mr. Force, the editor of the " National Journal," is a man of mild and unassuming pretensions, steady in his principles, deliberate in his actions, modest in his deportment, and humanity itself. Mr. F. is a man of good size, rather spare, his face oval, his complexion dark, his eye a soft hazle, his countenance calm and serene, with much expression.   He is about twenty-six years of age, a partner with Davis, of

New-York, in an extensive firm, as publisher and bookseller. He is a member of the City Council of Washington. Besides the " National Journal," and " National Intelligencer," there is a third paper published in
Washington, called the " Washington Gazette," published by Mr. Elliot, a paper of unlimited circulation.

Washington City is laid off into six wards, each of
which has one alderman, one constable, and more or
less common council-men. The corporation is governed
by a mayor, who is elected by the citizens annually.—
These constables are the most hateful of their species;
they are ferocious in their appearance, and the most important men (if they deserve the name,) in all the city.
They execute the duties of their office without pity or
feeling, and take the most nefarious measures with those
victims who may be so unfortunate as to fall into their
clutches. It would be a great alleviation of human misery, if men of feeling were selected for an office which
has so much to do with it. I have all my life remarked,
that constables have less humanity than any of the human
race. Whilst speaking on this subject, it is with the
most heart-felt pleasure I advert to an act of Congress
exempting females from prosecution for debt in the District of Columbia. This magnanimous and humane act
in favor of the tender sex, has done them immortal honor,
and ought to obliterate all their faults, were they as numerous as the sand on the shore. It is to be hoped that
every state and city in the Union will imitate their noble
example, and blot out for ever this foul stain upon the
American character. The shameful practice of impris-
oning men, is worthy only the most despotic governments, (I was going to say the Inquisition;) but to subject females to cruel confinement, is highly disgraceful
to a free people;—it is high time this misguided imitation of European policy should be discarded from our
shores.

Gardens, &c.—There are no public gardens in Washington, nor do the private ones deserve the name. The
citizens yield greatly to those of Alexandria in their attention to gardens, in which neither taste nor utility appears. A very handsome public garden is laid out near

the capitol, but suffered to remain in a state of nature. Neither watch or patrol is kept in the federal city, and although there are lamps in all the streets and avenues, they are never lighted except in winter.

Manners and appearance.—With respect to the manners and appearance, no description can be given that would yield satisfaction. Perhaps no body of people can be found equal to the number, in which there is less similarity than in Washington. In their appearance scarcely any resemblance can be traced, and so of their manners. The cause of this is to be found in the nature of its population, which is derived from every part of the world. The inducements held out to all classes of people to settle the metropolis were many and lucrative. Here was much work to do, of all descriptions; a number of buildings to be erected, which required artificers of all sorts. These artificers were to be victualed and attended, which drew another species of emigrants. Anon, the Congress and a long train of public officers are to be furnished with accommodations, and foreign ambassadors and ministers swell the demand.— These allurements, added to the eager desire of government to sell the lots donated to it by the proprietors of the city lands, produced a flood of emigration to the metropolis from all parts, both of Europe and the United States. These people brought with them different habits, religions, and customs; most of them, however, were from Ireland, and principally of the humblest class of citizens. This age must pass away before any thing like assimilation of manners or characteristic traits can be assigned to the citizens of Washington.

The population of Washington may be said to consist of four distinct classes of people, whose pursuits, interests and manners, differ as widely as though they lived on opposite sides of the globe, viz. those who keep congress boarders and their mutual friends, the subordinate officers of government; these resemble in every respect and ought never to be separated; secondly, the labouring class; thirdly, what may be called the better sort; and fourthly, the free negroes. It may be observed briefly, that the first mentioned class are proud, ignorant;

and many of them insolent. The labouring class (of which there are a great number employed, both at the capitol and the navy yard, and improving the city,) are mostly very dissipated, and spend their earnings as fast as they obtain it. And as to that class which may justly claim the appellation of the first citizens, unfortunately, they form but a small minority. In justice to Washington, however, it must be observed, that amongst these are to be found many men of worth, whose virtues and talents may justly rank them with the first men in the United States. The ladies of Washington are very handsome, they have delicate features, and much expression of countenance, and excel in the beauty and symmetry of their persons*; but (excepting the higher class, who are females of education,) are, withal, most detestably proud. As to the appearance of the men, as observed above, it is impossible to say what it is, differing so much as they do.

Dialect.—The dialect of Washington, exclusive of the foreigners, is the most correct and pure of any part of the United States I have ever yet been in. It is very rare that you hear an improper word, even amongst the common people. A few words are, however, peculiar to them, such as the following, " you're right, he (or she) did,' tautamount to an affirmative." A negative is signified by " could ever," which means " I will not ;" as well as a general negative. Another phrase is " my dear," used by all sexes and ages, and upon all occasions : " my dear, when we saw the cloud, we ran the balance of the way."

General Remarks.—No conception can be more fallacious, or any idea more wide of the truth, than that entertained by one who has never seen this city. Our hearts swell with national pride at the mention of its name—Washington! Washington city is repeated with a sort of holy enthusiasm ; nothing evil or low mingles with the sound ; it conveys sentiments at once the most elevated, the most pleasing. But how are we disappointed upon coming to this Idol of America! In every

---

* This can only be said of the natives, as the foreigners are very coarse and ill shaped.

other country, in every other town or city, some semblance is maintained in that attention which is due to the poor and to the rich. But if you are poor, you have no business in Washington, and unless you are well dressed, you will have good luck if you be not kicked out of doors by the servants, should you attempt to enter a house. These servants, which are nothing more than so many bullies, swarm in every boarding house, and so much do they and the proprietor resemble, differing only in slight shade of colour, that it would be difficult for one (if he were much frightened) to distinguish one from the other. In point of politeness, the advantage is often on the side of the former. In short, ignorance, impudence and pride, are decided traits in the bulk of the citizens of Washington, particularly those mutual friends before mentioned. One is astonished upon going into the shops and stores, which are spacious buildings, to meet with the most unpolished, uncouth looking people, particularly the Irish women. They are certainly the most disgusting in their appearance and manners, of any females I have seen ; they have a fierce, savage countenance, quite appalling to those unaccustomed to foreigners ; though the Irish men are generous and humane, very much so. I have known them in a few minutes make a handsome collection for some indigent traveller, (who might happen to pass the work-shops) whom they had never seen before, and perhaps might never see again!

Warden, in his history of Columbia, extols every thing with servile minuteness, a remuneration, no doubt, for the kindness lavished on him by the great. But a writer of more independence will not give Washington so high a colouring. True, respecting the beauty of the place, and the surrounding scenery, too much cannot be said ; it far exceeds whatsoever can be sung or said. Nature and art seem to vie with each other for the victory in decorating this spot. Warden says " the inhabitants of Columbia are social and hospitable," he does not say they are polite, and had he said so, of the citizens of Washington generally, he would have said it at the hazard of truth. The same writer observes, " at Wash-

14

ington, respectable strangers, after the slightest introduction, are invited to dinners, tea and evening parties." To one the least acquainted with the extent of
the opulence and refinement of the persons he alludes
to, this remark might excite a smile. Either he must
have overlooked the general character, or they must
have underwent a most wonderful change since his day.
Perhaps he meant the heads of Department. As respects their hospitality, for myself I cannot boast much
of it, and from the opportunity afforded me of judging,
were I to express an opinion, I should say that the
number able to appreciate the society of respectable
strangers, is very limited. Speaking of the ladies of
Washington, he says " they have been accused of sacrificing too much to the empire of fashion." He does
not, however, confirm the accusation. Whatever Washington has been heretofore, I am unable to say, but at
present, it yields even to Lexington, Kentucky, in point
of taste and fashionable elegance. This will readily be
admitted by those who have seen both places. After
paying a high-wrought compliment to the ladies, Warden remarks, " with all our predilection for the Columbian fair, we have seen with regret, among the ladies of
Washington a fondness for play, that bewitching passion
which extinguishes the very best sentiments of the heart,
and creates a dislike for every useful or pleasant occu-
pation. When indulged from motives of gain, the vio-
olence of fear, and other worse passions, changes the
very features, in effacing that divine impression of the
female countenance, which is so often irresistable."
Gambling, and play of every description, is almost
wholly exploded in Washington at present, and (I am
sorry to add) I wish I could say the same of other vices.

It is certainly not to be expected, that the Metropolis of the United States should be exempt from evils
common to every large city, but I will venture to say
that no city of the same age has kept pace with it in
vice and dissolute manners. And what is still more astonishing, is, that it should erect its empire in the very
capitol itself. In the first place, there are about two
hundred hands engaged at work, on that part of it which

remains to be finished, and out of the whole number, there are perhaps not half a dozen sober men.* They do however work during the day, but when their day's work is ended, they hie to the grog-shops and taverns, and usually spend their day's wages, sitting up to a late hour, and often committing broils in the streets, to the great annoyance of the citizens.

Besides these there are a number of strangers who flock to Washington during the sessions of Congress, with a view of begging money from the members ; and so great is the infatuation of those unfortunate creatures, that they will implore even a cent in the most emphatic language. They will sell the coat off of their backs and hat off their heads to purchase drink. The lady with whom I boarded relates several anecdotes of a man, her next neighbor, who, to obtain spirits, will step into a house and ask for a cup to procure a drink from some neighboring pump ; and upon receiving the cup, will step into another house and sell it for a few cents, which he will instantly lay out in drink. Before she was aware of his character, he came to her house one day with an axe, which he offered to sell to her for a trifle. While he was speaking, a young lady happened to step in, and exclaimed "don't buy it Madam, he has just stole it from Mr. ——." In the mean time, the owner suspecting the truth, followed him and recovered the axe. But the evil does not stop here. The M..... of C..... are accused of indulging the practice, and (it is said) their C..... cannot steady the pen in their hands, till they have swallowed a draught of their beloved beverage. And for the mutual accommodation of all parties, spirituous liquors are permitted to be retailed in the capitol! Can we blame those of inferior rank for want of discretion, when their superiors set

---

* The means they use to elude the vigilance of the overseers, is conclusive evidence that those who are fond of drink, will not be restrained from indulging the habit. One of them will place a bottle or jug in a pail, put it on his head, and set off to the spring for water ; on his way he fills the bottle with *scute*, (as they call whiskey) and when he procures his water, he plunges the bottle into the pail, and returns to his shop, which with many others stands near the capitol.

them the example?* But of all sights that ever disgraced a city, a house of Legislation I mean, and one which most astonishes a stranger, is the number of abandoned females, which swarm in every room and nook in the capitol, even in day-light.   One would think that, within the precincts of a legislative body, supposed to comprise all the wisdom and talent of the nation, at least some regard would be paid to decorum.   I have seen these females with brazen fronts, seated in the galleries listening to the debates.   They used (I have been told) to mix promiscuously with the respectable class of females, until Mr. Clay (the Speaker,) assigned them a place by themselves.   Mr. Clay certainly does deserve much credit for this public homage to virtue, as does Mr. ——, for submitting a resolution for banishing those retailers of spirituous liquors from the capitol : the fate of this resolution will hardly be credited ; it was lost.

What would the saviour of his country think, were he to arise from his tomb; what would he say were he to witness the daily scenes exhibited in the capitol of the city which bears his name!   In his last injunction, we have the following words : " Of all the dispositions and habits which lead to political prosperity, religion and morality are indispensable supports. In vain would that man claim the tribute of patriotism who should labour to subvert these great pillars of human happiness, those firmest props of the duties of men and citizens."   I should suspect that man of sound principles, who boldly, in the face of noon-day, in the face of the world, in the face of virtue, religion and common decency, sets such examples of immorality as are to be met with in the capitol of the United States.

Near to the very door of the Representatives Hall, immediately fronting it, is a temple (as Mr. W. calls it,) dedicated to one of those females; it is a circular apart-

* I ventured one day to expostulate with one of those mechanics (a very promising young man) upon the subject of his intemperance. After saying all that I could to convince him of the fatal tendency of a practice, so disgraceful to the character of men ; he burst into a laugh in my face, and replied, " why, the very heads of Congress do the same thing !"

ment, lighted with sky-lights. The opening fronting the Hall is always displayed; and no matter who comes or who goes, president, foreign minister, respectable citizen or stranger, this *Hortensis* proclaims the frightful progress of vice! She commands the pass to the gallery and the hall; and all who pass from the latter to the Senate chamber, or from thence to the hall, must necessarily pass through this temple; here she stands or sits in her chair of state, with a table spread with accommodation, and a maid to attend her. I have seen her surrounded by her smiling votaries in dozens; I have seen the representatives of a great people cringing around this C . . . . ; yes I have seen this! while me thought the genius of Columbia dropped a tear! In short, the bold strides of licentiousness seems to threaten the total overthrow of virtue! It is a maxim universally acknowledged, that virtue is the basis of all republican governments; it is the ultimate security of the people; this once gone, farewell to freedom! One of the members informed me, that when an effort was made to expel those retailers of spiritous liquors, &c. from the capitol, it was alleged " that it was a place of general privilege, over which Congress had no control." It would be an useless waste of words to say what this argument would lead to; the inference is plain. But the municipal laws of every petty corporation contradict this principle. They cannot pretend to say the constitution denies the right.

Before my visit to the metropolis I had heard much of the insolence of the subordinate officers of government;* within a few years past. I had heard them stigmatised with every opprobrious epithet, such as " insolent mob, rabble, aristocracy," and many other harsh names; that it was almost unsafe for any one to venture in Washington, who was not a prince, a foreign ambas-

* A good story enough is related of General Jackson, which happened upon his first visit to Washington after the victory of New-Orleans. The general came on to settle his accounts, and those upstarts who are in the habit of quizzing strangers, by sending them from one room to another, tried the game with him, not knowing who he was. It may be supposed that the general soon discovered the scheme, and drawing his sword, said he would go no farther; adding, that his name was Jackson, that he came to settle his accounts, which must be done instantly.

14*

sador, or a member of Congress. No one, however,
ought to credit report, least of all reports of this nature,
which too often have their origin in envy. Nor ought
we to expect any government, in which the infirmities of
frail man are unavoidably blended, to be infallible ; but
that it should at once blunder upon such an assemblage
of ignorance, is matter of singular surprise! In extenuation it may be alleged that prudence became sacrificed
to zeal in extending relief to poverty, but it is a maxim
that holds good, exalt ignorance and it immediately becomes insolent. Go to any of the public departments,
and you are sure to meet with some indignity from those
upstarts, which swarm in every part of them. Of such
I am told (or at least the major part) are the officers of
the legislative department. Even at the President's
house, a pack of the most insolent miscreants, in the
character of his domestics, guard the avenues to his
presence. One would think that civility, at least, might
be expected at the door of the first man in the nation,
but I never met with more vulgarity or less polished servants. I would by no means however, be understood
to say that these remarks are without exception ; many
of those clerks being men of desert and refinement.

I am far from saying that poverty ought to exclude
men from any gift in the government, on the contrary,
they are the very men upon whom they ought to be con-
ferred. But I do contend that ignorance ought to be an
eternal objection, because it strikes at the vitals of our
government, not only by its dangerous tendency to encourage vice, but to arrest the progress of knowledge, one of the surest props of its existence. It is absurd to expect that men will respect rights, which they
do not understand, or that learning can flourish when it
has no incentive ; what encouragement for aspiring genius when illiteral men are promoted over its head? Besides, it is casting pearls before swine, their growling
souls are incapable of gratitude or estimation, they
know nothing but to value themselves, and under-value
every one else. I have seen men of worth and learning leave Washington for want of employment, who
would have sacrificed their talents for $100, while a pet-

ty door-keeper receives $1500 per annum, though not
employed more than six months of that time.

It is amusing enough to see the inturns, intrigue
and cunning, those leeches resort to, when they happen
to be rivals for office.   They are always upon the lookout, and when a vacancy happens, they observe the utmost secrecy on the subject, even with their bosom
friends, and repair to their respective patrons without
loss of time, and it often happens, that the candidate
least qualified proves successful.   An instance of this,
occurred under my eye, during my residence in the city.
The commissioners of Ghent, for settling the Spanish
claims, held their sittings in the old capitol, adjacent to
the room I occupied.   It happened in the time, that a
messenger in this service died; several candidates
stood for the office, and amongst them, a respectable
young man, who boards at the same house with myself,
whose talents were worthy of a more respectable office.
But a man by the name of F. bringing a letter from the
P. obtained the place; the most abandoned miscreant
in existence!   The board dissolved in a few days, and
the building was assigned to the commissioners of the
board of St. Petersburg; those last, transacting their
business principally in their boarding houses, were seldom in the building.   During this time, the house is left
to the care of Monsieur F. who is constantly drunk; taking droves of lewd women and worthless characters into
the house, which is furnished in the richest manner, (fine
carpets, tables, chairs, and desks,) by government; here
he feasts his guests upon oysters, drink, &c. at untimely
hours.   Sometimes he comes in drunk, throws himself
on the floor, without sense or motion, leaving the door
open all night, and the property exposed to fire and
theft.   At another time you see him in broad day-light,
in the wide street, staggering after a black woman, in a
manner shocking to decency!   This fellow is one of
those who insulted me, at the house of the P. where he
acted as porter, and used to usher in Secretaries and
foreign Ministers!   Now one of these men receives as
much per annum as a New England governor.

Whilst Col. L. acted as commissioner for the public

building, (some years back) I am told by several of the
workmen, that a mason whose wages were $2,50* per
day, would spend a whole day in faceing a stone, the
next day, another mason in placing the stone on the
building, would hit it a blow with the sledge and split it
to atoms! Col. L. (so says report) used to put his hand
into the treasury as often as he pleased, for much of
which he has never accounted. The money is known
to have been drawn from the treasury by him, but what
then? Col. L. is dead, and government may get the
money as it can. Thus much for the public *purse.*

Here an important question might be asked, where a
man of sound principles is promoted to office, does he
not eventually become corrupt? In many instances I
should think he does. And why may he not be as vir-
tuous as before? Because the same incentives no longer exist. Before his promotion, his all depended upon
his reputation, neither had he the means or temptation.
After his elevation, he has much money (that bane of
virtue,) to spend, little work to do, and that not his own,
he asks no favours, his fortune is made, he sits down
and enjoys himself with his friends, whilst he is doing
this, his fellow hireling is doing the same thing, of course
they stand mutually pledged to each other in ———. If
this be the case in the best choice that human wisdom
can make, how dangerous then is patronage to liberty!
hence it is that corruption is winding itself into the executive department, which is loaded with officers who
fatten upon the people. These remarks have insensibly
led to the source of the evil, I mean the great patronage
of the President, and proves the impropriety of eleva-
ting the same man for a longer term than four years.
Hence it is that the executive has drawn an aristocracy
(not of nobles by the way) around it. These are the
men who have rendered Washington city so obnoxious
abroad. On the other hand, it must be acknowledged,
that there is a vast deal of business to transact in the executive department which requires a great number of
hands; the whole business of the United States, it may

* It is now reduced to $1 25.

be supposed, is enormous ; nor do the people expect this business to be transacted for nothing, but they expect civil treatment from men in their service.[*]

It often happened while in Washington, that I met with "uncle Sam's" men, as they call themselves. Walking in the capitol square one day, I stepped up to a man whom I found there at work, and asked him whom he worked for, (meaning his employer, from whom I wished to obtain some information,) "me," said the fellow, "I work for uncle Sam," in a tone of unequalled impudence. No matter where you meet those understrappers you may distinguish them by their unparalleled effrontery.

Heads of Departments.—In order, I ought to have noticed these before the subordinate officers, and hope I shall be pardoned for the omission. The truth is, these gentlemen have been so often and so ably described, and so long before the public, that I had intended to confine my remarks to those objects less known. Besides, what can I say of them, that has not been said a thousand times ; yet, as it may argue a want of respect, in a general view, wholly to overlook men who have been so eminently distinguished by their country, I hazard a brief sketch of their persons ; to attempt any thing more, would be a great piece of arrogance, even did I possess the talents, which I do not.

To begin then with the President, I never saw him but once, and that in his carriage at some distance, I had merely a glimpse at his features, he looked very old and venerable. I went to his house for the purpose of seeing him, but was repulsed by his domestics, of him therefore, I can say no more. The next great man I called on, was the attorney general. I promised myself much pleasure upon seeing the author of the Spy, and waited for him at his office, with no little enthusiasm, but was never more disappointed. He received me with a smile, to be sure, but it was rather a sarcastic one. Mr. W. is a good figure, being tall, straight, and well form-

---

* In justice to these clerks, I must observe, that they pay the strictest attention to their duty; in going through the various departments, I found every man at his post. The hours of business are from 10 to 3.

ed, though somewhat corpulent. He walks erect, and with haughty air, in short, he has the remains of much personal beauty, for he is far advanced in years. His complexion is fair, his face wan, though round and full, with a vacant blue eye. In his countenance there is nothing striking, no dignity, no in dependence, or expression; it is neither grave nor austere, but marked with an unmeaning smile. I mentioned my disappointment to a gentlemen of this city; his reply was, "that had Mr. W. died when he wrote the Spy, he would have rendered his name immortal." Taking leave of Mr. W. I called upon Mr. Adams, Secretary of State. It being his hour of business, I found him in the State department. Mr. A. received me with that ease of manner, which bespeaks him what he really is, the profound scholar, and the consummate gentleman: he saluted me in softest accents, and bid me be seated. I had heard much of Mr. Adams. I had admired him as a writer, and applauded him as a statesman. I was now in his presence. While beholding this truly great man, I was at a loss how to reconcile such rare endowments with the meek condescension of the being before me. He neither smiled nor frowned, but regarding me with a calmness peculiar to him, awaited my business. Mr. A. appears to be about fifty years of age, middling stature, robust make, and every indication of a vigorous constitution. His complexion is fair, his face round and full, but what most distinguishes his features, is his eye, which is black; it is not a sparkling eye, nor yet dull, but one of such keenness that it pierces the beholder. Every feature in his face shows genius, every gesture is that of a great man, his countenance is serene and dignified, he has the steadiest look I ever witnessed, he never smiled whilst I was in his company, it is a question with me whether he ever laughed in his life, and of all men I ever saw, he has the least of what is called pride, both in his manners and dress.

Mr. Calhoun is quite a young man compared to Mr. A. and possessed of much personal beauty: he is tall and finely made, neither spare nor robust : his movements are light and graceful, his complexion (if I do not mis-

take) is dark, his features handsome and animated, with
a brilliant black eye; in his countenance all the manly
virtues are displayed, overcast with shining benevolence.
In his manners he is frank and courteous.   In Washington, as well as elsewhere, Mr. Calhoun is held as a model of perfection.   He is secretary of War.   The secretary of the navy, *Mr. Southard,* I never had the pleasure to see; be unfortunately was absent.   Fame speaks
of him in the highest terms.   I was told that I missed a
great treat in not seeing him.   *Mr. Crawford,* secretary
of the treasury department, was confined by indisposition during the whole of my stay in Washington, of
course I did not see him.   *Mr. M'Lean,* the post master general, is apparently older than Mr. Calhoun; in
his person he is tall and spare, his complexion fair, his
countenance mild and pleasing, his fine blue eye beaming with good nature, reveals the benevolence of his
heart.   His manners are those of an accomplished gentleman.   The chief clerks, auditors, and comptrollers,
are said to be men of standing integrity and talents,
whose worth are equally entitled to notice, but their
number is too great for the limits of this work.   Gen.
Brown, General in chief of the U. S. army, Judge Thurs-
ton, Gen. Van Ness, the Messrs. Brents and Carrols,
(all of whom are gentlemen of wealth and distinction)
have their residence in Washington.

Corporation.—Too much praise cannot be bestowed
upon the corporation of the city.   To its zeal and indefatigable industry may be ascribed the rapid improvement of Washington.   Perhaps there never was an instance of so *much* being done in so *short* a time, and by
such *limited* means.   The vast number of houses, the
beauty and size of the buildings, streets and avenues, is
highly honourable to that body.

Yesterday the *fourth of July* was celebrated in a
style of magnificence never before witnessed in this city; it was ushered in by a round of twenty-four cannon.
Much pains was previously taken to render the day
splendid and interesting.   It certainly was the grandest
spectacle I ever beheld.   The design, which was the
first attempt, had a very imposing effect; this was the

appearance of the different mechanics in the procession,
at work ; the freemasons in full uniform ; the marines
in theirs ; beside these, there were no uniform companies in the procession, which much surprised me.   The
President, heads of department, foreign ministers, and
citizens, joined the procession, which formed on a plain
south of the President's house, and moved thence to the
capitol in the following order :—1. Music in front, performed by the marine band.   2. Marines in full uniform,
four deep.   3. Masons in full uniform, two and two.   4.
Washington Benevolent Society, two and two.   5. Typographical Society, preceded by a carriage containing
a press, at which men appeared at work throwing off
copies of the declaration of independence, two and two.
6. Stone cutters, with aprons on, preceded by a carriage in which the craft were at work, two and two.   7.
Painters, which were also at work, followed as above.
8. Blacksmiths, preceded by a carriage with forge and
bellows, the sparks of fire flying, and the sound of hammers heard on the anvil, two and two.   10. Four marshals, in uniform, mounted on white chargers, distinguished by red plumes and sashes.   11. President in a
plain chariot.   12. Secretaries of the different departments, in carriages.   13. Foreign ministers, in carriages.
14. Twenty-four young ladies, representing the twenty
four states.   15. Pupils of the different schools preceded by their respective teachers on foot, two and two.
Each party had a banner with appropriate emblems, and
the procession lacked nothing to render it grand and
beautiful, but a complete band of music, which they
have not.   The ladies, by invitation, repaired to the
capitol, and took their seats in congress hall, no gentleman being allowed to enter the hall until the procession
arrived.   The capitol, from its situation and size, afforded a fine opportunity for every one to witness the display.   About one o'clock the procession reached the
capitol, down Pennsylvania avenue.   The hall and galleries were crowded to suffocation, nor could half the
people get in   Gen. Stewart, an old revolutionary officer, read the declaration of independence, and an oration was delivered by —— I know not who.

Peculiar Traits.—Every house of any distinction in the city, has a bell, distinguished by a brass knob on the side of the front door,* and whoever may be so unfortunate as to have business with the proprietor or any boarder. pulls the brass horizontally, this rings the bell, which brings an insolent free negro to the door. This negro opens the door with great caution, something as we used to do in the Indian wars, and if he finds you are not a member of congress, head of department, or foreign minister, he thrusts his body directly in the entrance, taking all possible precaution to keep you out, by holding fast the door, and thus to the general question, is the master or mistress at home? you receive the same answer ninety-nine times out of an hundred, which is that " he is not," although he is then listening to the negro, who slams the door in your face. It sometimes happens that they are at home ; in that case the negro leaves you standing on the steps of the door, like another servant, while he walks up stairs at his leisure, and returns at the same gait ; and after some negociation in this manner, the master or mistress walks down stairs, or from whence they are, with a countenance something like a hyena ; and lest they might be contaminated by your breath, they stop at a *disrespectful* distance to hear your business, without inviting you to walk in, or showing you the least politeness, though you were dropping with fatigue, or drenched with rain. It is, however, due to the respectable portion of the citizens to say, that they form a decided exception ; they are at all times easy of access. Generally you find them on the lower floor, and a ready admittance, particularly at Secretary Adams' ; no respect of persons is shown there ; the rich and the poor meet with a cordial welcome ; and more,† you do not have to stand and wait,

---

* This is the case in all the Atlantic towns.

†Mrs. Adams is represented to be one of the most charitable females in this or any other country ; the distressed are ever sure to meet a friend in her. She is not so old as Mr. Adams ; perhaps about forty years of age : in her person she is tall, slender, and elegantly formed ; her features are regular and handsome for her years : in her manners she is affable, and by far the most accomplished American lady I have seen ; her countenance is suffused with ineffable sweetness ; in short

and knock till you are weary; you are ushered in at
once.   But those who keep the Congress boarders,
even the females, are a savage, fierce looking people,
and the most detestable in their manners of any to be
found, either black, white, or red ; the Cherokees and
Choctaws are a polished people compared with them.
To account for this peculiar trait, it must be explained,
that the most of the houses in the city belong to the
banks ; in consequence of their having advanced the
money to erect them, the builders being unable to re-
fund the money, the houses became the property of the
banks.   These houses they rent out to needy adventurers, who purchase a carpet, two or three dozen tables and chairs, hire a score of free negroes, and take
in members of Congress as boarders.   This enables
them to pay for their furniture and servants, and go to
market.   Thus they are no more than a chief cook and
butler, whose insolence to strangers is only equalled by
their servility to their boarders.   They live like princes
during the winter, but have pinching times all summer.
   The first house erected on the land where Washington is built, is still standing ; it is the property of a Mrs.
Prout, by whose father it was erected.   I called on the
old lady to see this sacred relic of antiquity, which has
stood an hundred years !   Mrs. Prout waited on me to
the house with no little enthusiasm.   The frame, (which
is rudely formed by the axe,) the joints and rafters, are
still sound and entire ; also a great part of the weather
boarding : this last has a very primitive appearance, and
recalled to my mind the structures built by the first settlers of the western country, consisting of what we
call clap-boards.   Without molesting a particle of the
original, the old lady has had it recently enclosed with
new plank, to shield it from the weather, which she informed me was the second time ; the interior is tinged
black with smoke.   Mrs. P. has turned it into a stable
for her favorite horse, who was then standing in it, and

the virtues and the graces seem to have taken up their abode in her
fair form.   Perhaps the best eulogium that could be bestowed upon
this example of worth and excellence would be to say, that she is worthy
of such a husband.

appeared to participate in our pleasure, as he regaled himself at his ease on the most delicious hay. This house stands near the navy yard. Her father's name was Slater.

Whilst I remained at Washington, I often rallied the citizens upon their want of courage and conduct in defending the city, when invaded by the British. This was differently received by the different classes to whom it was directed: the humbler rank repelled the charge with spirit, laying the blame on their superiors, particularly Armstrong, the secretary of war, in unqualified terms, expressly charging him with treachery. "Oh," said they, "the city was sold, no doubt of it, because when application was made to him to put the city in a posture of defence, and arm the militia, he replied, no danger, the British will never come here." Some had it, "that Gen. Cockburn was in the city in disguise, several days before the invasion; that he was seen sitting in the garb of an old woman, upon the steps of the war office." The more thinking part of the citizens, allege that it was unavoidable, in consequence of the blockade of the Chesapeake by the British, which confined Commodore Barney in the Patuxent, and fairly acknowledged that they sought their safety in flight. I had the particulars of the disaster from one of the citizens as follows:—"That several weeks before the invasion, all the money and records were sent out of the city, to a place of safety: that the first intelligence of the approach of the British, was, that they had landed, and were on their march towards Washington, and Gen. Winder was endeavouring to arrest their progress, by hanging on their rear. This being the state of affairs, and the British expected every minute, a man on horseback kept a constant lookout; he would advance in the direction of the enemy, and after reconnoitering, would gallop back and report the result to the citizens. This was kept up about three days: meantime, all that were able and willing to bear arms, repaired to the scene of danger, under Gen. Winder. Commodore Barney having travelled by land, joined the army.

At length the direful day arrived, and the roaring of

cannon announced the battle of Bladensburg. The
British, however, met with a warm reception from Commodore Barney, until his horse was killed under him,
and he severely wounded. All was then over; Gen.
Winder then ordered the men to " retreat to a better position." No sooner was the word given than the
whole of the militia betook themselves to flight, making for the heights of Georgetown. Many of them
never stopped running, until they arrived at Montgomery court-house. They ran with such swiftness, that
they never stopped to comfort their wives and children,
but left them exposed to the mercy of the British and the
negroes. Not a man was to be found in the city, with
the exception of a few old men who were unable to run
away. It was not long after the cannon ceased firing
at Bladensburg, before the British made their appearance in Washington! Here was a scene of terror and
dismay. The women and children, frightened out of
their wits, ran to and fro, expecting to be massacred or
some worse thing, and not a man to protect them. In
the height of this dilemma, Gen. Ross rode through the
city, intreating the women not to be alarmed, that no
harm was intended to them ; " Stay in your houses ladies," said he, " and no one shall molest you." He
was as good as his word ; not a female was insulted or
molested in the slightest manner by the army. Meantime they fired the capitol, the President's house, and all
the public buildings. Commodore Tingey, who had the
care of the navy yard, put his family in a boat, and after
rowing them off from the shore, set fire to the navy-yard
himself, to save the British the trouble. Amongst the
property consumed was a valuable ship of war, just finished. The citizens set fire to the bridge themselves,
(a wise action) to prevent the British from going to Alexandria. The smoke from these fires, and the dust
raised by such numbers, filled the city with such a cloud
of darkness as nearly excluded the light of day.

But the best of the story is that part of it which relates
to the magazine. A party of the British were dispatched with orders to blow it up. Near to the magazine was
a dry well, in which was a large quantity of powder con-

cealed. After laying the train for the magazine, one of the men, who was standing over the well, twisted off a part of the match which he still held in his hand, and threw it down into the well. This, which was the actual magazine, blew the unconscious man, with about fifty of his companions into the air, the most of whom were torn to atoms: some were never seen afterwards, some fell into the Potomac, and some were lodged in trees—one, in particular, was lodged in a peach-tree without receiving much injury, and is now living in the city.

The day that succeeded the invasion, was equally hostile to the peace of the inhabitants. It was distinguished by the most tremendous storm ever witnessed in the memory of man: trees were torn up by the roots, houses unroofed and overturned, and the people tossed to and fro. The British, who were still in the city, became alarmed and embarked precipitately. The lady from whom I had the relation, said she was walking out on the morning after the destruction, and fell in with a party of the British officers before she was aware, when one of them accosted her with "Good morning, madam —dreadful times." "Yes, sir," said she, and passed on. During the storm, some of the officers took shelter in her house, and one of them observed to the other, "that the wind had like to have blown him to h—l."— Here, as well as at Alexandria, they turned out the coffee and the sugar into the streets, for the benefit of the poor and the negroes, taking no more than they wanted for their immediate use. They killed a number of cows, pigs, poultry, &c.—One of the officers making a false pass at an old gander, whose head he aimed to cut off with his sword, told a little drummer, who was standing near, to put down his drum and catch the gander: the woman to whom the gander belonged, ran up to him, saying, "you little son of a b——h, if you touch it I'll break your drum over your head." The drummer, however, was obliged to obey his superior, and pursued the gander; the woman set off likewise, and the race was a tight one; the woman, however, prevailed, and rescued the gander, to the great amusement of the officers.

15*

A number of ludicrous anecdotes are related of our men, when retreating before the British, after the battle of Bladensburgh. A man of high repute (the door-keeper) ran with such speed that the bushes took off the skirt of his coat. Then comes Mr. H. in a hack, mortally wounded—"heavens! where, where?"—"in the thigh!"—while some as resolutely affirmed it was in the leg! "Poor man, what is to become of his wife and children?" A surgeon examines him, when lo! he is not touched!—not a drop of blood, nor the smell of powder upon him! Another man, in loading a gun with canister, put in the cartridge which contained the shot first, and in his efforts to correct the mistake, dismounted the gun, and had to leave it behind. The President, (whom our western boys cursed so heartily,) did go into the ranks like a man, and remained with the army some minutes, at least, until some of his friends advised him to take better care of himself, which he did. The memory of Gen. Ross is much respected in Washington, on account of his gentlemanly conduct toward the females. The property destroyed by the British was estimated at $1,031,541.

The citizens of Washington look forward with pleasing anticipation to the accomplishment of the Ohio and Chesapeake canal, and much interest seems to be staked upon its success. It is thought by some, that ten years at most, will bring about this happy event.

The capital lacks a great deal of being finished; although a number of hands (200) are constantly at work upon it, it is thought it will take twenty years to complete it. It would astonish any one to see the immensity of stone lying about it, (one would think enough to build another capitol,) which remains to be put somewhere, but it would puzzle Apollo to tell where. They are now at work upon the Library, which when finished will be the most splendid apartment in the capitol. I confess it is not in my power to do justice to this part of the edifice; the artist appears to have reserved the ultimatum of his skill for this repository of the literati: he seems to have exhausted the treasury of taste in decorating it with wreaths and flowers of the finest stucco.

The west colonade is finished in a style of unrivalled beauty ; it consists of ten vast columns.   But the columns which are to form the colonade for the east portico, are objects of great admiration.   They are brought by water from a quarry of freestone about thirty miles below the city, and are very large, weighing eighteen tons each.   They are brought from the wharf by the workmen, without the aid of horses, upon a strong carriage, made for the purpose—and an hundred men pull one with ease.   This is quite a frolic for the men ; and sometimes the members of congress will turn out in the evening to assist in pulling " the big waggon," as it is called, and join in all the pleasantry to which the novelty of the thing gives rise.   When the column arrives at the capitol, it is cheered by loud huzzas from an hundred voices.   The cost of the two wings destroyed by the British, was $290,000.   The centre building, which comprises the rotunda and the great centre dome, will cost $400,000.   The rotunda is supported by forty-four columns.

When congress adjourns* for the session, one half the city goes into mourning, and the other half shout for joy.   The first, it will naturally be guessed, comprise my old friends who board the members, (and perhaps a few of the fair sex,)—the latter are those who are relieved from a most oppressive market.

Gen. La Fayette.—I cannot take leave of Washington, without bestowing a few remarks upon our illustrious guest, whose visit took place while I was there. His arrival in the United States, so soon as it was known in Washington, was announced by the artillery of the navy yard, and the whole city rung with acclamations of joy.   Meantime the citizens were divided into companies, distinguished by different uniforms, and kept in continual training, with a view of receiving the General with military honours.   The newspapers furnished daily accounts of his movements, and long before he arrived we

* I omitted to state, in the proper place, that when Congress assembles in the morning for business, the national flag is hoisted over the capitol, and remains so till they adjourn in the evening, when the flag is taken down—and so on through the session.

had the La Fayette ribbons, La Fayette waistcoats, La Fayette feathers, hats, caps, &c. ; every thing was honored by his image and superscription—even the gingercakes were impressed with his name, and nothing was heard, either in the streets or in the houses, but La Fayette ! La Fayette !

At length we were gratified with his presence ; crowds of men, women and children, flocked from the country, from Alexandria, from Georgetown—the houses in the city were left empty—every one hastened, at an early hour of the day, either to meet the General, or to secure some convenient place from whence they might behold him. The capitol was crowded to overflowing, and the capitol square, large as it is, was covered with a countless multitude. I, with several others, seated myself in the third story of the old capitol, near the street through which he was to pass, and in full view of the whole fete. Twenty-five young ladies, dressed in white, each with a flag in her hand, took their stations near the arch which had been erected for the occasion, at the east entrance of the square. Twenty-four of these represented the twenty-four states, and the twenty-fifth the district of Columbia. Besides these young ladies, the pupils of the different schools formed a line from the arch to the capitol, through which the General was to pass.

An elegant carriage, drawn by six horses, was dispatched to meet him, while the military, and a vast number of citizens, repaired to the toll-gate, a mile from the city, to await his arrival. As soon as he passed through the gate, a federal salute was fired by the artillery, and shortly afterwards a cloud of dust proclaimed the General's approach ; but so great was the throng around him, that I only saw the necks of the horses that drew his carriage : his horses were led by six gentlemen on foot, distinguished by red sashes. The crowd, particularly those on horseback, who were from the country, rudely pressed upon the General, to the hazard of his safety, until the marshals drew their swords and dispersed them. His arrival at the market-house, (which had been adorned for the occasion, and upon which a living eagle was perching,) was proclaimed by loud cheers from a thou-

sand voices.   Here the General alighted from his carriage, passed through the market-house, thence through
the arch, where he was addressed by the daughter of
Mr. Waterston, a little girl of ten years old, who represented the district.   She addressed him in prose, expressing briefly the prosperity of the United States since
his first visit to America, the deep sense they retained of
his services, and the joy his present visit afforded them.
The General bent an earnest ear to what she was saying,
took her affectionately by the hand, and passed on to
the capitol.   As he proceeded, the young ladies waved
their flags over his head, and showered flowers and jew-
els upon him.   At the capitol he was received under the
tent of Gen. Washington, and a federal salute proclaimed his arrival.   He was covered with dust, and the
warmth of the day, with the fatigue he had undergone,
nearly overpowered him.   He asked for water, when
Mr. Dorset hastened to procure it; but so great was the
throng, that it was impossible to get near him, until the
civil authorities interfered, and even then the gentlemen
were obliged to hand the water from one to another over
each other's heads.   After receiving a welcome address,
delivered by the mayor, the troops passed in review before him, accompanied by a number of fine bands, provided for the occasion.   The appearance of the troops
was in every respect worthy the first city of the Union.
From the capitol the General was escorted to his quarters, (Franklin-house,) by the Washington Guards, the
city authorities, and committee of arrangements; on his
way he was saluted by the different companies of artillery; and at 5 o'clock he sat down to a splendid dinner,
(prepared by Mr. Gadsby,) in company with the President of the United States, the heads of department, foreign ministers, officers of the army and navy, and other
distinguished officers of the government, besides a great
number of private citizens.   The day was one of the
finest I ever saw, not a cloud was to be seen.   In short, I
could fill a volume with the honours paid to this illustrious hero at Washington alone, to say nothing of his
splendid reception in Georgetown and Alexandria.
    It must be observed, however, in justice to the citi-

zens of Alexandria, that they greatly surpassed us, particularly in good order ; the crowd was kept at a respectful distance ; the shops and stores were ordered by the Mayor to be shut up, also the grog shops ; no carriage was suffered in the streets ; and business of every sort was suspended. Nor did their attention to the General end here ; a centinel was placed at his door during the night, that his slumber might not be interrupted ; and total silence enjoined throughout the city.

In 1820 Washington contained 13,474 inhabitants, and 2,141 houses.

Georgetown.—Georgetown is situated on the Potomac river, above Washington city, and north of it. (the river running north and south.) It is also on the Maryland side, and separated from Washington by a large creek, called Rock Creek, over which are thrown three bridges.   Georgetown has a romantic appearance, being built mostly on hills. It rises up from the water's edge and spreads out in all directions. The streets, which are few and narrow, are paved with stone.

On the top of the hill, at the extremity of the town, stands the Georgetown College, two stately buildings of brick. It has a handsome square in front, planted with trees, and commands an extensive view of the Potomac, Washington, and the surrounding country. I found the Rev. Mr. Baxter, President of the college, playing at ball with the students ; he seemed to enter into all the glee and innocence of their juvenile mirth. Mr. Baxter is a man of middle age, good size, and handsome person, and captivating manners. He very politely conducted me through the college, and gave me all the information I could wish on the subject. It has a library attached to it containing 9000 volumes. Whilst we were in the library, I looked through a window which overhung one of the finest kitchen gardens in the country. " You take a few of the good things of this life then," said I, pointing to the garden ; " to be sure," said he, " why not ?"   I was struck with his reply— " why not ;" and why not truly. This college was founded in 1799, and richly endowed ; it is called " the

Roman Catholic College ;" and contains from 100 to 150 students. Every branch of education is taught here ; all the professors are Roman Catholics.

Besides the college, they have an academy, and a seminary for young ladies, which is also under the dominion of Roman Catholics ; and wholly under the direction of the convent ; the pupils being taught by the nuns. All denominations send their children to this seminary, which is much celebrated for its salutary regulations.

Convent of the Visitation.—From the college I went to the convent ; my curiosity was wrought up to the highest pitch as I traced the uneven streets leading from the college to the convent. I felt what Addison said, viz : " every thing new or uncommon raises pleasure." I had often heard and read of nuns and convents ; but now I was to be gratified in full. It is no great ways from college hill ; Mr. Baxter pointed it out to me, and keeping my eye upon the steeple, a few minutes brought me to the door of the convent, at the west end of the town. Here, as directed, I opened the door without knocking, and entering a small passage pulled a bell, which brought a nun to the inside door, when I informed her of my business ; she directed me to step into a small room on my left, which she called the " *speaking room*." After waiting here a few minutes two other nuns approached, on the opposite side of an iron grate, which separated them from the world and me ! I had however a full view of them ; they drew up close to the bars, saluted and conversed in terms of the utmost sweetness and condescension. Amongst other things, I asked them "if they were happy ;" they both replied " very happy, would not exchange their present situation for any earthly treasure ;" and they looked so.

Having heard that Catholics look upon all other sects as heretics, I asked them if it were true ; " no," they answered, " God forbid that we should think so ; we believe there are many good people who are not of our religion." One of them had been in the convent eleven years, the other eight ; and in all that time they would not have left it if they could ; they have the option in two years. They were dressed in coarse black stuff gowns, with wide sleeves, resembling those of a clergyman's gown. Their heads were first bound with a black cloth, which came low down on the forehead; over this a white cloth, and over all a hood; this hood is of the same stuff as the dress, and like "a slouch bonnet." Take the pasteboard out of one of those bonnets, fold a few inches of the front back, and you will have an idea of these hoods. They wear a small square white handkerchief, hardly sufficient to cover the bosom; this is hollowed out under the neck so as to extend up to the ears on each side; on their breasts they wear a silver cross; this they informed me was the uniform dress of the convent. I expressed a wish to get into the building; but they said they dare not admit me without the consent of the mother superior, and she could not be seen at that time, not even by the nuns themselves; she was gone into *retirement*, which means that she secludes herself day and night in some part of the convent *for* several weeks. This ceremony she performs once a year, which time she spends in fasting and prayer. I would have given much to have seen her, as she was the sister of a respected friend of mine.

For the same reason I could obtain no information respecting the establishment; they told me, however, to call on the father superior, and how to find him, and I bid them adieu. These nuns dare not converse with strangers unless there be two present. I never beheld that simplicity and innocence, that humble demeanour which distinguishes these nuns, in any of the sex; they have a most heavenly expression in their looks; they are humanity itself, and well they may; they have no earthly care, and spend their time in continual devotion. They attend prayers regularly three times a day, and some of them are almost constantly in the chapel.

At the upper end of the building, I found the father superior, Rev. J. P. De Clorviere, who is a French nobleman; he is about sixty years of age, of middling height, and spare make, and dressed in the simplest manner. I found him very affable and communicative: he took me into the chapel, (which is a part of the same building,) stepping in, he before me, and I close at his heels, he turned around and told me in a whisper, that "I must not speak loud." He proceeded on until he came opposite to the altar, here he stopped short, and dropped on his knees, where he remained in silence some minutes, he then arose and stepping on tip-toe to that part of the chapel which separates it from a long room, appropriated exclusively as a place of worship for the nuns, he raised a green baize curtain, and peeping through another iron grate, he beckoned me to approach. When I drew near, he whispered " that he had used this precaution lest he might have disutrbed some of the sisters, who often retire there in the intervals to worship." He permitted me to look through the bars; the room was dark and gloomy, and several books were scattered upon the long plain seats which filled the room. Here the nuns sit and chaunt the sweetest music, whenever service is performed; and here they can hear distinctly what is said in the chapel. The seminary is very large, enclosed (together with the convent and a large piece of ground,) with a high wall, the front of the convent answering for part of the wall. The ground within the inclosure is cultivated as a garden, and adorned with trees, walks, and summer-houses. Here the nuns walk about and amuse themselves, when they choose. They have to cross this garden in going to the seminary, which forms another part of the wall. This seminary embraces every branch of female education, and the strictest attention is paid to the morals of the pupils. By an article of the institution, the pupils must conform to a uniform dress, which is a brown frock and black apron in school, and a white dress on Sunday. The other public buildings are 1 church for Roman Catholics, 2 for Episcopalians, 2 for Methodists, 1 for Presbyterians, 1 for Quakers, and 3 banks.

Manners and Appearance.—The people of Georgetown are polite and hospitable; they form a striking contrast to their neighbours of Washington, their minds being more generally cultivated. It is hardly possible to conceive, how towns so near each other, should differ so widely as they do. One cannot behold the people of

16

Georgetown, without being struck with the disparity. Their appearance is much like those I have seen east of the Blue ridge.

Mr. Millegen, who walked with me over the town, very politely pointed out the objects worthy of notice, and amongst other things, he showed me the spot of ground upon which Braddock landed, when he arrived in America to fight the French : we both stood on the spot for some minutes. He showed me too, the first house (which is still standing,) built in Georgetown.

The Potomac, which is over a mile in width at Greenleaf's point, suddenly narrows at Georgetown to about two hundred and fifty yards. It is, however, deep enough for vessels of moderate size, to ascend to Georgetown, which is a port town. The population, last census, was 7,400.

History.—Georgetown was erected into a town by the lord proprietor, the governour and house of assembly, May session, 1751, upon sixty acres of ground, the property of Messrs. George Gorden and George Beall, (this last pronounced Bell,) in Frederick county. An inspection house had been built by Beall, at the mouth of Rock creek, some years previous ; and at this place Georgetown stands : many additions have been made to it since. It was incorporated in 1789, and governed by a mayor and aldermen.

I cannot omit a circumstance which excited my astonishment, and one highly honourable to this town. As Mr. M. accompanied me through the market-house, I observed a great quantity of fresh meat hanging in the market, which the owners being unable to sell in the morning, had retired to their homes without the least apprehension of its being stolen. Mr. M. accompanied me over the bridge, and I parted with him with great reluctance, and a great debt of gratitude.

How much have I heard said about these Roman Catholics ! I have heard them stigmatized by every harsh name, and accounted little better than heretics. But I must confess, I never was amongst people more liberal, more affable, condescending, or courteous, than the citizens of Georgetown. I could have spent my days with this endearing people.

Journey to Baltimore.—After spending six months in Washington, I took my leave one bright morning, for Baltimore, in the stage-*coach*, drawn by four sprightly grays. I was the last passenger taken up—found four persons in the stage, one lady and three gentlemen. To the homeless traveller, no pleasure is equal to that which he feels, when, after paying his fare to a certain place, he takes his seat in the stage. Here at least, he is at home. The thought that he is for the time being, sole proprietor of the small space he occupies, gives him an independence which he feels no where else. The lady by her dress I took to be a Quakeress, an old maid by the way, very coy and very sensible, as most old maids are. She and I had the back seat to ourselves. She seemingly drew up to her own side of the stage, and I, not willing to infringe my neighbor's rights, as cautiously adhered to mine. She need not, however, have taken this precaution as it respected myself, for I would not have hurt a hair of her head had it been in my power, which it was not. She now and then addressed a young man who sat before her on the next seat, who proved to be her nephew, also a Quaker. Upon further observation, I found that one of the other gentlemen was a Quaker, so that it was something like a Quaker meeting. The fourth was a French gentleman. The Quakers, one was from Massachusetts with the lady, and the other a merchant from Georgetown, a Virginian by birth and education. They were all lively and sensible, particularly the Frenchman; he was very facetious, and though his hair was touched by the frost of time, or (most likely) the frost of untoward fortune, yet his countenance retained all the animation of youth. He had been in America some years, spoke the English language with fluency and grace, and was a friend, if not an officer of the departed Buonaparte. He amused us with a number of interesting anecdotes, which he told with admirable humour, and while his thread-bare coat bespoke his situation too plain, yet his manners revealed a highly improved and polished mind. I endeavoured to recollect one of his stories, but it is impossible to give to it that expression of countenance and gesture peculiar to

Frenchmen. It was, however, something like the following.

"When he was a youth at college, he and his messmates were stinted in their daily allowance of food. They bore it patiently some time, but at length they repaired in a body to the principal of the College, (who was a priest of course,) and stated their grievance. The priest listened to their complaint with great courtesy, but being (as they afterwards discovered) leagued in the plot of starving, he endeavored to soothe them into submission. My children, said he, it is not wholesome for you to indulge your appetite, it will protract your progress very much, you ought to live very obstemiously, it is best both for your health and your studies. See me, I fast one, two, three days in the week, I drink only water,"—here if you had seen him mimicking the sanctity of the priest,—"and feed on the most sparing diet. Finally the students withdrew without success. But suspecting the priest's veracity, and concluding from his portly size, that he fared sumptuously every day, they resolved to watch him; but such was his precaution, that they were completely baffled. At length they got it all out of a domestic, whom they bribed to leave the door open upon a certain time agreed upon. "Here" said the Frenchman, ve vas very much to de loss vat excuse to make to get into de house, some say von ting, some say de oder ting; I say, me vill say de fire, de fire, and run to de priest for de safety. You see, ve all run, say fire, fire, and rush upon him and four or five of his friends dat eat wis him, da have all rish savory meat, de table full de wine, de champaign, de madeira, de burgundy. He say, vere de fire. Me, I say, I would be glad to have so good abstemious dinner like you sare, me dont wish better den you have. He say you too cunning rogue for me, you shall have more liberal usage in future. "Oh," he added "dem priests will cheat you to your face."

The two Quaker gentlemen however relieved him, by descanting upon the approaching presidential election. The Georgetown man was in favour of Mr. Crawford, and the yankee of course was in favour of Mr. Adams.

The Georgetown was a man of pleasing manners, but the other, though a perfect boor, had the best of the argument. The first praised the talents, the long and faithful services of Mr. Crawford; the yankee opposed the sound judgment, the head to contrive, the skill to direct, and tried experience of Mr. Adams, and gained a complete victory over his opponent. The Frenchman took no part in the discussion, but sat with his arms folded upon his breast. The lady and myself exchanged a few remarks upon the appearance of the country: she was a handsome female, but had a sting in her countenance withal. These Quakers, it seems, were going to a great Quaker meeting, which was to be held at Baltimore the ensuing week.

The day was fine, and the road excellent, being a turnpike the whole way. Our way lay through Bladensburg, rendered famous in history by the battle fought there between the British and Americans. I passed over the battle ground, which lies on that side of Bladensburg next to Washington, upon a perfect plane. Bladensburg, one of the oldest towns in Maryland, is nothing but a small village, going to decay. It lies on the Eastern Branch, which, as already observed, is only a small creek at this place, which we crossed by a bridge, below which we saw a few small schooners. The land is generally level, but very poor, being mostly worn out and abandoned to the pine and sedge-grass, resembling the old fields of Virginia. We saw, however, a few well looking country seats during the journey. My fellow-travellers observed that the road lay through the poorest part of the country, and that there was excellent land in many parts of the state.

We dined at a tavern on the road, called Waterloo— and here the Virginian (alias Georgetown) and myself were gratified with a dinner to our taste—I mean ham and greens. There was, besides, a savoury turkey and a pair of ducks, which the Frenchman seemed to relish better. The yankee gentleman tasted a bit of the turkey, and the lady dined principally upon bread and butter: she remarked that "she seldom dined upon any thing else."—What odd creatures old maids are! Be-

16*

sides these, we had a variety of excellent vegetables;
over and above, there was another article on the table,
which the waiter affirmed to be cheese, but no one
would have known it as such from the appearance; it
resembled ginger-bread crumbled fine.   The poor waiter, I felt for him, his feelings must have been wounded
by the sarcasms of the company, all but the Frenchman
and myself.   One said it was saw-dust, another said it
was potash: at length the Virginian made us all laugh,
by saying, " O yes, I recollect now, it is cheese—it is
the identical cheese I dined upon seven years ago, on
my way to Washington!"   Having dined, I asked the
waiter what was to pay ?   " Three quarters of a dollar,"
quoth he.   The other passengers threw down the cash,
but I sought the landlord: " and what do I owe you, sir ?"
" Three quarters."   " Where is your rates ?" said I.—
" We fix our own rates," said mine host.   " So then we
stand on even ground, you fix your rates, so do I," and
handing him fifty cents, I stept into the stage—not another word passed between us.   My fellow travellers, however, appeared mortified that they did not, like myself,
save the odd quarter.   It is nothing but an act of justice to society, to treat these pickpockets in this manner
—common sense must point out to the lowest understanding, that the traveller has the same right to refuse, that
the publican has to exact an exorbitant bill, unless the
rates are fixed by law, and placed in public view, which
ought to be the case throughout every civilized country,
changing them with the rise and fall of the market.   It
tickled the Frenchman exceedingly, my behaviour to the
landlord.   As he was the last to quit the house, one of
the party asked him what the landlord said.   " He say
not a word, he look like one statue, he tunderstruck, he
stand, he look astonishment after de coach, he say not-
ing."

A pleasant anecdote is related of Gen. La Fayette, as
he travelled from Baltimore to Washington.   Being told
he was to dine at Waterloo, he refused to do so, disgust-
ed with the name, and actually pushed on to his quarters without stopping.   This warning hint has determined the landlord to change the name of his inn—so

says report. It must have been a great disappointment
to him, as he doubtless had made great preparation,
knowing too that a large escort would accompany the
general.

In the course of the day we crossed the Patapsco and
Patuxent rivers, which, to my astonishment, are quite
ordinary streams, being narrow, shallow, and unnavigable. No house or farm distinguish their solitary course
—they flow through a poor hilly country. Towards
evening we came in sight of Baltimore, some miles before
we reached it! The towering spires and white monuments first appeared, then the city, and here the Patapsco again, spread out into a vast sheet. This river forms
what is called a bason, at this place, sufficient for ships,
which led to the idea of a commercial town.

From the time we got out of the stage to this day, I
have never laid eyes on my fellow travellers. What a
difference! In the western country, we are not only
more sociable while travelling, but constitute one family during the route, at all times and places. From the
mutual dangers, the pleasantries, accidents, and priva-
tions, incident to travellers, an attachment takes place
which is not dissolved, perhaps ever. But here in the
east, they jump out of the stage, and each one sets out to
his quarters with perfect indifference, and even without
taking leave. This difference, is no doubt owing to
their superior numbers, to their journey's being shorter,
and the numerous impostors, who are constantly on the
wing seeking for prey, and flying from one seaport to
another. Admitting these causes however, in their wi-
dest sense, I cannot reconcile that unsociable deportment, which wears such obvious marks of groundless
suspicion.

Baltimore.—I just arrived time enough in the evening to have a view of this (to me) great city. A host
of wonders bursted upon me at once, the vast number,
heighth and density of the houses, the massy public buildings, the Washington monument, the Baltimore monument, the great expanse of water, the quantity of shipping, the number of well dressed people in the streets.

overwhelmed me with astonishment. I have not the
least doubt but this remark may excite a smile, particularly in those who were never out of a populous town,
but they must remember that till now I was never in one,
and that those things which are matter of so much indifference to them, are as gratifying to me, as our long,
deep, smooth-flowing rivers, our endless prairies, our
solemn forests, our wild mountains and deep caverns,
our flowery plains, rude hamlets and fertile fields of bending corn, would be to them. It is natural for one to desire to see whatever is new or uncommon, and next to
this, a description of them; but that person to whom they
are new, will be more likely to point out their distinguishing traits, than one who has spent his life amongst
them. One who has spent his days in a great city, sees
it without emotion, because it is familiar to him. I begin too late to discover, that I have fell very short in describing the western states, from having always resided
there. Dropping this digression, however, I shall en-
deavor to convey my own impressions, as best calculated
to give satisfaction to those who like myself have always lived in the back country.

Had an awkward back woods country person, myself
for instance, been taken up and dropped down in this
world of houses, I should have been afraid to budge, lest
those formidable carts and waggons might have settled
the question with me for ever; and as for entering one of
those splendid houses, it would be the last thing I should
think of. I should have been afraid the lord of the mansion would look me out of existence. But I had been in
Alexandria, I had been in Washington, and had, it is true,
seen a few fashionable people, and some splendid houses in the western states, but not so many by half. If
such be Baltimore, thought I, what must be Philadelphia
and New-York. I put up at the same house where
Gen. La Fayette lodged, and saw the room which the
General occupied, just as he left it, the furniture had not
been disturbed, out of respect to him.

Baltimore lies on the north side of the Patapsco river,
18 miles from the Chesapeake. It stands upon an elevated situation, with a gentle descent to the harbour.

The city is divided into the old town, and Fell's Point, by a creek called Jones's creek, (called by the citizens the falls.) This creek strikes the harbour at a right angle, and divides the town into east and west. The east is Fell's Point, which projects some distance into the basin, and gives the city the form of a bow. Large ships come up to Fell's Point, whilst none but the smallest size come to the west part of the town. I had been told that Fell's Point was low and unhealthy; it is so represented by geographers; what was my astonishment to find it no ways inferior to the other part of the town, either for beauty or situation; if any thing, it is the most desirable part of the city. Elegant buildings, fine paved streets, and splendid churches distinguish Fell's Point. It is called the Point simply by the citizens. Half a dozen bridges at least, are thrown over the creek mentioned, and so close do the houses come to it, that the creek is hardly perceptible. It is walled up with stone on each side for a considerable distance above the mouth.

Baltimore is two miles in length, and of different widths. The streets are paved and lighted; the houses, though well built, do not look so handsome as those of Washington, because they are older, they have not that fresh appearance. The houses of Washington too, standing so far asunder, have not the same chance of being tinged with smoke.

Public Buildings.—The public buildings of Baltimore are a town hall, a court-house, an exchange, a library, a prison, an alms-house, a hospital, a penitentiary, a masonic hall, a circus, a theatre, 3 market houses, 2 coffee houses, 2 colleges, 18 churches, viz.—4 for Roman Catholics, 1 for Scots Presbyterians, 1 for Swedenbourgians, 1 for Swedish Lutherans, 2 for Universalists, 1 for Unitarians, 4 for the Evangelical Society, 1 Prison Chapel, 1 Orphans Asylum, 1 Widows Asylum, 1 Magdalen Asylum.

Of these, the exchange and the Roman Catholic cathedral are by far the most conspicuous. The exchange is a beautiful structure of white freestone, 360 feet by 140!—In it is transacted all commercial business. The cathedral is celebrated as being the most superb church

in the United States.   It certainly is superior to any
thing I have seen, except the capitol of the United States
and the President's house.   It is of the same architecture with the capitol, and like it was planned by Latrobe.
It is a massy building, of freestone, in the form of a
cross : the sexton, who lives near the spot, showed it to
us, but he was unable to tell the dimensions.   It has four
fronts, and a portion of scripture cut in large letters on
each.   It has a dome similar to that of the capitol, and ornamented in like manner with wreaths and flowers in stucco ; but the capitol is of the purest white, whilst the cathedral is of a grayish colour, and the stucco has a reddish
hue.   The interior of the church is remarkable for a superb altar, and a painting representing our Saviour, just
taken down from the cross : the piece is said to excel
any thing of the sort in the union ; it was presented to
the church by Louis the XVI. of France.   The body of
our Saviour is represented with a white cloth round the
waist ; he is lying on the ground, with his head and
shoulders in his mother's lap, who is also sitting on the
ground.   She is represented as fainting away ; her eyes
are closed, and the beloved disciple leaning over her :
Joseph of Arimathea is standing near the body and looking upon it ; also Mary Magdalen and Nicodemus.   Mary
of Salome is standing up, with her eyes and hands raised
to heaven : the Roman guards are likewise standing near,
with fierce aspects.   The whole is painted to the life, and
looks as though they were living beings.   The crown
of thorns has just fallen off, and actually looks as though
one might go and take it up : the blood is issuing from the
wounds inflicted by the thorns, from the temples of our
Saviour, also from his side and his feet.   Our Saviour
is represented in different paintings in the cathedral,
from infancy to the time of ascension into heaven.   I
am told it is subject to a ground rent of $2000 per an-
num.
    The Unitarian church stands nearly opposite to the
cathedral, and wants but little of being equal to it in size
and magnificence.   Having heard nothing of this last,
and being struck with its singular beauty, I asked a gen-

tleman standing near, " what church that was ?" He
smiled, and replied, " that is the line of opposition ;"
alluding to the opposition lines of stages and steam-
boats. But of all the splendid buildings in Baltimore,
or any where else, the masonic hall is the most so ; language would fail me, were I to attempt a description of
it ; (the interior I mean,) the beauty and richness of the
furniture is not exceeded by that of congress hall itself.
The rich drapery, superb tables and chairs, and an hundred things which decorate the G. Master's chair of state,
the candlesticks, the finest carpets, and the great size of
the hall, filled me with amazement : it was hung in
mourning for Mr. Pinckney, whose death has long since
been noticed, who belonged to the fraternity.

The Baltimoreans seem to be taking the lead in the
fine arts. Besides those specimens of taste and public
spirit already mentioned, the Washington monument,
and that erected to the memory of those brave men who
fell in the battle of Baltimore, in the late war, command
both admiration and applause. The Washington monument is a plain marble pillar, 150 feet high from the
ground ; it is 50 feet square at the bottom, and 14 at the
top, and white as alabaster—upon the top of this, the
figure of Washington is to be placed. This beautiful
monument is seen from every part of the city.

The monument erected to perpetuate the battle of
North Point, was executed by Maximilian Godfrey, Esq.
in 1815. It is 16 feet each front ; each of those fronts
have a door of black marble, which are four in number.
Above this arises a circular *facis*, of symbolical union,
on the fillets of which are inscribed the names of those to
whose memory the monument is consecrated. Above
the cornice, and at the four angles *socle* of the facis, are
four marble griffins ; the base of the facis is ornamented
with two basso-relievos, representing the battle of North
Point, and the bombardment of Fort M'Henry. Two
lachrymal urns are placed in the intervals. The top of
the facis is bound with two crowns, demi-relief. The
facis is surmounted with a socle, bearing a statue of Baltimore, formed from the representation of Juno Cybele,
holding a crown in one hand, and an antique helm in the

other, with the United States' eagle, and a bomb alongside; the whole is of marble, and fifty-four feet high. Laying the corner stone of this monument, for pomp and military eclat, constitutes an era in the history of Baltimore.

Hospital.—The hospital is seated upon a lofty eminence at the east end of the city, a mile from thence, and has more the appearance (in idea) of a princely palace, than the abode of pain and disease. It consists of two great buildings, to which are attached a spacious yard, which is walled in; this is overgrown with luxuriant grass, and planted with trees; the whole architecture is of brick. The gate is locked day and night, and a man duly stationed on the inside, to open it for those who apply for admittance, for which you pay him 12 1-2 cents, you then have liberty to visit the whole establishment. The keeper, who is a plain, honest, obliging Quaker, very readily conducted me through the apartments. The buildings have a long gallery running through them from end to end, on each side of which are handsome apartments for the sick and insane. Those apartments (except the insane) are lighted with large windows, and furnished with bedding, chairs and tables, the whole exquisitely neat, and even splendid. It is against the rules of the institution to suffer strangers to see the insane; this prohibition proceeds from motives of delicacy towards the friends and relations of the afflicted, who do not wish them exposed. The doors of their cells are secured with bars of iron, and heated by furnaces placed in the outside of the wall, one to every room, which conveys the heat to the patient. I looked into some of these cells, which were vacant; they were similar to those occupied by the sick, excepting the bedsteads, which were of iron, and without chairs or tables. Though I could not see these unfortunate beings, I could hear them utter the most shocking oaths! Those patients who are not so ill as to be confined, are permitted to walk about the yard, and amuse themselves in the public parts of the building, the managers taking care to guard against them by having the seats and tables in their dining room fastened to the floor. Their food is the best the marke affords, particularly the bread, which is of the finest sort. There were no sick worth naming in the hospital, except sailors ; one portion of the hospital is appropriated for the exclusive reception of sick sailors, being one entire room, in which I found about thirty of those brave sons of Neptune, laid low enough! They were crowded to suffocation, and made a wretched appearance : some of the poor fellows, however, seemed to have nearly completed the voyage of this boisterous life! I cannot applaud that rigid adherence to established rule, which in this case excludes these sailors from any other part of the building than that alotted to them. There were empty rooms in the hospital at this time, sufficient to hold 200 persons, and humanity, I should think, ought to overrule an illiberal provision, by allowing those unhappy sufferers to be disposed of in a manner more consistent with their situation.

After visiting the different parts within the buildings, the keeper conducted me through the roof aloft, upon the top. From the situation of the hospital alone, which, as already noticed, stands upon a high hill, and the height we had then attained, the beauty and extent of the prospect may easily be conceived. The whole city of Baltimore, with its grand edifices, the wharfs crowded with the busy multitude, the wide spreading Patapsco, visible for miles, the shipping, and the adjacent country seats, present to the eye one of the finest pictures imaginable. The site of Baltimore somewhat resembles that of Washington, but the adjacent country, in point of beauty, does not equal the latter. Those beautiful rising grounds, spotted with farms and superb buildings, intermingled with the richest foliage, which encompass Washington, rising up one behind another, gives it the advantage in regard to scenery. My conductor pointed out to me North Point, and Fort McHenry, where the battle was fought between the Americans and British, during the late war. The day on which this engagement took place, must have been one of deep excitement to the citizens of Baltimore. Brave men! How richly you deserve the admiration of succeeding ages, which will be yours.

17

As I descended from the top of the hospital with my
friend, in passing through one of the galleries, my attention was attracted by a man who was crouched close
to the wall.   He wore a smile of mischievous cunning;
and seemed meditating some plan of attacking us.   He
clenched his fists as we drew near, and bent his eye on
me; I drew up close to my conductor, taking care to
keep him between me and the lunatic, for such I took
him to be.   When we came opposite to him, he seemed
upon the point of springing upon me; my friend without speaking a word, raised a cane which he carried in
his hand, and we passed him in safety; but the moment
we passed him, he rushed forward in the opposite direction, and flew down stairs with surprising swiftness.
Whilst we followed him with our eyes lingering on the
spot without uttering a word, a gentleman of good appearance, well dressed, and of a genteel air, walked de-
liberately by us.   As he had nothing uncommon in his
behaviour, I concluded he must be one of the attending
physicians; what was my surprise when the keeper informed me that he also was one of the convalescent lu-
natics!   I should not court a residence amongst these
convalescents; they might in some unguarded moment
rise upon me as Sampson did upon the Philistines, and
crush me before I had time to call for assistance.

Prison.—From the hospital I went to the prison,
which is also in the suburbs of the city; it is likewise a
large building of brick, several stories high, and has an
extensive yard attached to it, enclosed by a wall of considerable height.   At the opposite end of this wall stands
the penitentiary, also a fine brick building.   The prison
is secured by a double gate, and huge bars of iron; the
opening of which takes up no little time.   I found thirty
prisoners, including the debtors; which last are kept
separate from the criminals.   The apartments were not
large, and several were confined in one room; all have
the privilege of walking in the yard at certain hours of
the day.   They looked cheerful, and bore the appearance of kind treatment, though they were all destitute of
bedding, except those that were able to furnish it themselves.   The apartments are warmed by stoves.   But

my feelings were much shocked upon finding amongst
the prisoners, six females confined for debt,* and without
even a blanket to repose on, or a seat of any description.
I offered a few words of consolation to these unfortunate
females, at which several of them burst into tears, and
cast on me a look which I shall never forget, as I hastened abruptly from the scene ! The keeper happened to
say in the presence of the male prisoners, " that I was
going to write their history ;" one of them (a criminal)
spoke out, laughing at the same time, that " he hoped
I would say something clever about him." I was unable to get into the penitentiary, though I saw the prisoners at work from the walls ; they were clean and neat
in their dress, and looked well. The keepers both of
the prison and penitentiary were men of much apparent
humanity and mildness, as well as experience and education ; such as ought always to be selected for such places ; a brutal keeper, such as I have seen, has it too much
in his power to exercise cruelty toward his fellow creatures ; why it is the case is not material, but certain it
is, give an ignorant man power over the liberty of his
fellow men, and he will exercise it without mercy.
Much credit is due to the constituted authorities of Maryland, whoever they may be, for giving such obvious proofs of humanity and attention toward their fellow men.

Colleges.—I met with a total defeat on the subject of
the colleges : the president, or principals, were absent,
except in that restricted (as I was told,) to the education of priests. I found only a French priest, who
could speak hardly a word of English, and withal appeared rather averse to giving me any information. He
had on a woollen night-cap, and the rest of his dress
accorded therewith. His face was wrinkled with
age, or ill humor ; and in short he looked more like something broke loose from bedlam than any thing else.
Upon making my business known to him, he jabbered
something which I could not understand, and wheeled
to the right about, and marched off without more ceremo-

* Since writing the above, Maryland has abolished the law for im-
prisoning females.

ny! But my misfortune did not end here; I entered the
other part of the college, which was within a few steps,
where the boys are taught, but found no person whatever. I went through such of the apartments as were open,
and found them not in that condition we would expect:
neither of these buildings are any thing to boast of. Baffled in my endeavours, I made one more attempt; seeing
a number of boys engaged at play near the college, I
walked towards them, and enquired for their teacher:
they pointed to a man who was walking towards us, in
a shabby great coat. When he drew near I apprized
him of my business, but what was my astonishment to
find in him another foreigner! This last was an Irishman. who spoke worse English if possible than the other,
and the most uncouth being I ever saw. I turned from
him in disgust; not however without condemning my
countrymen, who could invest such men with the control of a matter of the first importance. I addressed several of the students (who were the youths just mentioned) with such questions as "what studies they pursued?
how many classes? the number of professors?" but from
them I received such replies as reflect little honor upon
the institution. The Irishman, who was standing by, was
brought to blush at their behaviour, shook his head at
them, and seemed no little concerned at their rudeness.
The medical college is also called a university; it has
six professors, and is said to be in a flourishing condition. Besides these three colleges, there are said to be
many schools and academies. A great storm of wind
and rain prevented my seeing the alms-house.

Markets.—Nothing pleased me more than the markets
—here I found ample scope for my curiosity; never had
I before seen any thing to equal it, either for variety or
abundance, and every thing much cheaper than I had
expected—vegetables of all sorts, fruit, meat and fish,
both fresh and salt—in short, every thing that was to be
eaten. Here an old woman sitting with a table spread
with nice bread and butter, veal cutlet, sausages and
coffee; there another, with a table bending under the
weight of candy, sweet cakes, oranges and apples; another with choice vegetables; another with fowls, as fat

as corn could make them. These take their stations at each end of the market-houses, and form a perfect phalanx. The market houses are in the streets, long and narrow.

Manners and Appearance.—The people of Baltimore are polite and affable in their manners, liberal, brave, and hospitable; they are active, enterprising, and attentive to business. The men, generally speaking, dress plain; but the ladies dress gay, and even fantastical.—Both sexes walk as though they were walking for a wager; the streets are full from morning till night. The constant buz of the multitude, with that of carts, waggons and coaches, nearly distracted me. Both men and women, in stature, are much like those already described, east of the mountains: the men are small, but well shaped, and both sexes are very sprightly. Their complexion is dark, with black eyes; their features are very delicate, but regular and handsome, with much expression of countenance. Baltimore is the third commercial city in the Union; it has several manufactories of glass, tin and leather, and contains 62,738 inhabitants.

History.—Baltimore was located, in the year 1730, on the north side of Patapsco river, upon the land called Cole's harbour, or Todd's range: sixty acres were laid out into sixty lots, by an act of the legislature. Major Thomas Tolly, Wm. Hamilton, Wm. Buckney, Dr. Geo. Walker, Richard Ghrist, Dr. Geo. Buchanan, and Wm. Hammond, were appointed commissioners for carrying said act into execution. The history of Maryland is very imperfectly known; it was a mere accident that I happened to meet with the foregoing act, and a few other sketches of the history of Maryland. As we are fond of tracing things to their source, it may afford some gratification to add, with respect to Baltimore city, that at the time it was erected into a town, a man by the name of Fleming, (a tenant of Mr. Carrol,) resided in a house (the only one in the place) called the Quarter, which stood on the north bank of Usher's run, near the house of Gen. Striker, in Charles-street. All we know of Baltimore since, is, that it has advanced in wealth and com-

17*

merce, at a career unparalleled by any other city, until within a few years back.

Maryland, it is well known, was settled by Lord Baltimore, who was a Roman Catholic in religion.* The Catholics being oppressed by the British government, a number of gentlemen of rank and distinction, with Lord Baltimore at their head, set sail from Cowes, in the Isle of Wight, and arrived in the Chesapeake, at Old Point Comfort, in Virginia, in 1634. He sailed up the Potomac, thirteen leagues, and came to an Indian town, called Potomack, from whence this river took its name.—The Indians received Lord Baltimore with great hospitality, and after some conversation with them, he asked the chief, " If he was willing to let him and his companions stay in the country ?" to which the chief replied, " I do not bid you go, nor bid you stay ; use your own discretion." The governor (as Lord Baltimore was now called,) not willing to hazard a settlement amongst these Indians, sailed back again, and proceeded up a smaller stream, where he found other Indians, called Yoamancos. He landed here, and gave it the name of St. Mary's, after having purchased the land of the natives. The first thing he did after landing, was to build a guard-house and a store house. This place is still known in Maryland by the name of St. Mary's. A singular anecdote is related of Lord Baltimore and these Indians. Shortly after the governor landed, a number of them came to visit him, and amongst others the king of Patuxent, who had formerly been a prisoner of the English in Virginia. To please these people, the governor made an entertainment on board the ship, then at anchor. The king of Patuxent was placed at table between the governor of Maryland and the governor of Virginia, (Sir John Harvey, then on a visit to Lord Baltimore,) in great state. All was mirth and glee, and mutual good humour overspread every countenance. But an incident happened which had like to have destroyed the pleasure of the feast :—A Patuxent Indian coming on board, while they were at dinner, and seeing his king thus seated, started

* Bosman's History of Maryland.

back and refused to enter the cabin, supposing that his
king was confined there as a captive, and would have
leaped overboard, had not the king himself interposed,
and satisfied him that he was in no danger.   These Indians lived amicably with this colony: they went to
hunt, every day, with the new comers, killing and fetching home deer and turkies.   Meantime the colony cultivated the soil, planting corn on the land formerly cleared by the Indians, with such success that the next year,
or the year following, they exported 10,000 bushels, and
the utmost harmony for many years subsisted between
them and the Indians.   The first assembly met in 1638,
the governor taking the chair as speaker of the house ;
but it was long before the king of England could be
brought to sanction any of their laws.

Having written some dramatic pieces while in Washington, I waited on Messrs. W. and W. proprietors of
the theatre in this city, to whom I had a letter of introduction.   The first of these (though I had claims of a
sacred nature upon him, which it is needless to mention
in this place,) received me with a snarling growl, not unlike that of a surly, ill-natured dog, when another of his
species enters his tenement.   Had I been a highway
robber, monsieur could not have treated me with less
ceremony; he brushed by me, as though he would have
overset me, without uttering more than one short sentence, which as near as I could distinguish, was "that he
wished to have no concern with me."   I am fond of seeing human nature in all its variety, and taking every
thing into view, I must say, this was one new, as it was
unexpected.   I stood a few moments, thunderstruck as
it were, and summoning my resolution I waited on the
other W.   He was as polite and affable, as the other
was vulgar and abrupt.   He received me with an air
worthy of Chesterfield himself, but when he understood
that the piece I wished him to patronize was my own
production, " oh," said he, " that is out of the question,
we play no American pieces at all, you must excuse me
nor give yourself further trouble."   This last, I found
was the chief of the band, and if he objected the matter
was at an end.   Thus those foreigners, (for I am told

they are both Englishmen,) who are so generously patronized by us, and live on the fat of the land, refuse us
their patronage in turn. No wonder the English cry
down American works when they find their account in it.
And here I cannot help lamenting the taste of my own
country, which leads it to prefer foreign works. As to
the persons alluded to, they are too contemptible to be
brought into question, although they have the impudence
to laugh at the credulity of the generous sons of Columbia, who save them from starving. Yet it would be
pleasing to us, could we awaken a spirit of encouragement in favour of our own literature. We are sorry to
find the American character, so praise-worthy in other
respects, should fall short in one by which it is ultimately to rise of fall. It may be said of nations as of individuals as that man must be blind indeed, who would
sacrifice his personal interest to the aggrandizement of
another, so that nation must be blind to its interest which
enriches another by means that impoverish itself. I
would by no means exclude foreign literature, but I
condemn that rage for it, which hurries us beyond reason, beyond interest, and beyond national pride. I have
now a letter before me, from a noted bookseller in Philadelphia, wherein he says " that American works do not
pay the expense of publishing, owing to the rage of the
American people for foreign productions." Another
says, " such flimsy stuff is unworthy of support." We
might as well say that because a mechanic spoils a piece
of cloth, or a shoemaker should make a flimsy pair of
shoes, we will not encourage domestic manufactures, we
will revoke the tariff, and let them shift for themselves,
we will rather encourage the manufactures of others
than our own. We aspire to great actions, we pride
ourselves upon being a great nation ; will we then neglect the growing genius of our country, is it alone unworthy our regard? It is labour in vain to contend for
schools and colleges, for expensive establishments to ed-
ucate our sons and daughters, when all the advantages
derived from these would not keep them from the poor-
house! For if they were to write a book, they would
find no purchaser, because the writer lived on this side

of the Atlantic. Away with such policy. I shall only further observe, that all our efforts ought to go hand in hand, to the grand design of national excellence. Instead of that, we are in effect pulling down with one hand, what we put up with the other.

My visit to Baltimore being limited to ten days, I prepared to leave it for Philadelphia.* I cannot, however, depart without one more remark, which forms a link in the long chain of human depravity ; and proves, that as men become refined in the arts and sciences, they also become refined (if I may be allowed the expression,) in knavery. The circumstance alluded to, is a fraud committed against myself, in the purchase of a piece of silk, from one of the merchants. The clerk, either willingly or through mistake, kept back part of the silk. Discovering the default, I requested the silk or the money. He, putting on a sarcastic grin, refused to do either ; I applied for justice to the proprietor in the counting-room ; but from him I received nothing but the most wanton, the most brutal insults ! Being in haste to leave the city, and withal unwilling to swear to a man I never saw but once, I quit them so. Taking the whole into consideration, the insults, and the manner by which I obtained the money to make the purchase, viz. a donation from the —— of Baltimore, I must say, the man who would be guilty of such an act, would rob the dead. Respect and gratitude for the citizens of Baltimore, compel me to apologise to them for exposing the turpitude of those men, not meaning to say, but they would be as unwilling to screen such an action. " It is not one diamond which gives lustre to another, it is the rough stone compared with it which proves its genuine value ;" so the conduct of these men serve to cast a bright lustre on that of their fellow citizens, whose memory will ever live in my heart.

* An execution of a negro took place the day before I left Baltimore. Next to the appalling event, I was shocked a: the eagerness of many of the citizens, (and even of the softer sex,) to witness the tragical scene ! Of what materials can that being be formed, who is said to have a soul at all, who can calmly stand by, and view the struggles of a fellow mortal in the pangs of such an exit Even the sight of a gibbet, which I happened to see once by the road side, filled me with sensations of which I have not yet recovered.

Journey to Philadelphia.—We left Baltimore about
sun-down, and arrived in Philadelphia about sun-rise
next morning, (Nov. 15;) the distance between ninety
and an hundred miles; fare $4. This journey is perfor-
med partly by steam-boats and partly by stages. You
leave Baltimore in a steam-boat, and sailing down Patapsco, land at Frenchtown. Here you take the stage
to Newcastle, (Delaware,) and then take the steam-boat
again, and sailing up the Delaware, arrive at Philadelphia. It is very unpleasant to those who wish to see
the country, to make this journey in the night : to me, it
was provoking; nor can I see through the policy of such
a plan, which deprives the traveller of so much pleasure.
The night was dark and dismal, so much so, that it pre-
cluded the view of every object.

The steam-boats in these waters, are elegantly furnished with every article of convenience, particularly in
the articles of meat and drink, (though gentlemen and ladies breakfast, dine, and sup together;) yet they are
greatly inferior in size, to the steam-boats in the western
rivers : the ball-room in the General Green is fully as
long as most of the boats in these rivers. Nor is the furniture equal to ours; I have seen no satin spreads, or
gold fringe in any of them as yet, which are common in
our boats, although we are looked upon as little more
than savages, by many of the people in these large cities. Here, as well as there, you must choose your birth,
and have it registered, or go without, as was the case
with many of us to night, the passengers exceeding the
number of births. I richly deserved my fate, as I was
the first on board, and neglecting to engage one, had to
sit up. One of the ladies who had a birth, bore us company from pure politeness; she lived with a friend in
Baltimore, though formerly of Philadelphia, and was
then going to the latter, to meet her only son, who had
just returned from a long voyage at sea. She was a
woman of elegant manners, and highly improved mind;
delighted with her company, time flew fast, nor did I envy my companions their better fortune.

Amongst the party who sat up, I discovered a Miss
Alexander, a cousin of the Alexanders in Monroe, Va.

This gave rise to some very interesting conversation, respecting old times; although this lady, it appears, was never farther south than Baltimore, where she resides. She is a native of Ireland, handsome and genteel. She is a milliner, and was then on a journey to New-York, to lay in a stock. We laughed, and beguiled both time and care with pleasant stories, and had the good fortune to get a short nap before we arrived at the landing.

About midnight we came to shore, and here was pulling, hauling, settling bills and fare. An hundred people were in motion, men, women, children, and parrots. Here was every one running to get their ticket; "I want my ticket, give me my ticket;" they overset me several times. In short, being at a loss to comprehend the meaning of the ticket, and thinking I might in some way be concerned, I brushed the dust from my clothes as well as I could, made up to my friend of Baltimore, and asked her the meaning—"Oh," she cried, "you are undone if you don't get one." "Are they lottery tickets?" I asked; "Lottery tickets indeed! no, they are tickets to entitle you to a seat in the stage; if you don't get one you will be left behind." A sense of my danger inspired me with courage, and flying through the crowd, oversetting some in my turn, I gained the table where the ticket man sat, and demanded one. He gave me a bit of a card an inch square, No. 5. I hunted my friend once more to inquire what next? "Hold fast your ticket till you arrive at the stages, and call for the No. on your card; upon looking at my ticket, she said I must call for No. 5; and that after all the passengers were in stages, a man would go round and collect the tickets." I thanked her for her friendly counsel, and was told that this was done to prevent fraud, on account of the numerous passengers. Nothing could equal the uproar and confusion which now took place; such running with porters, band-boxes, trunks, and portmanteaus, flying in all directions; such pushing, elbowing, and trampling on one's toes; it was emphatically every one for himself. And what made the matter worse, we had but one lantern! For my part, I went by guess; seriously, I never saw a worse managed piece of business, neither order

nor light.   After encountering a number of disasters, we
were seated in the stage, and the man came round for
our tickets, but it would have been the easiest thing in
life to have cheated him, it being so dark, that one could
not see their hand before them.   The cavalcade now set
forward, in a solemn walk, without one lamp amongst
seven or eight, perhaps ten stages, whilst we prayed
heartily for an opposition line.   All the amusement I
had, was the chattering of a poll-parrot, who found great
fault with the jolting of the stage, and would ask its mistress, if it was not breakfast time.   It seemed an age before we arrived at Newcastle, and here we had to get out
in the dark, and grope our way to the steam-boat, which
we did not quit till we landed at Philadelphia.

Porters are attached to all those lines, for the purpose
of conveying the baggage of the passengers from one vehicle to another, or to your quarters, when you have
completed your journey.

Newcastle.—I only saw a few houses in Newcastle, as
the people were in bed, no doubt.   I never was more
out of humor to think I had traversed a whole state, without seeing a single tree in it!   Newcastle is in the state
of Delaware, 35 miles below Philadelphia, on the bank
of Delaware river.   It was settled by the Swedes, in
1627, and called Stockholm:—it was afterwards taken
by the Dutch, and called New-Amsterdam—it next fell
into the hands of the British, and was called by its present name.   It is the oldest town on the Delaware river,
but it is going to decay.   I am unable to tell any thing
of its trade, population, or the number of houses.   It is
quite a small town.

I had a fine view of Philadelphia, just in sight, as the
sun was rising.   The sky was clear—the Jersey state
on my right—Pennsylvania on my left,—and the noble
Delaware on all sides.   This river is as large as the
Ohio, but not so handsome, being rough and turbid.—
The constant ebbing and flowing of the tide, (I know no
other cause.) always keep those Atlantic rivers rough
and muddy; so near the ocean, too, they are visited by
the breezes from thence.   Pennsylvania, at this place,

is very low and flat, the shore being but little elevated above the river: the Jersey shore is much higher, but the land looked thin in both, though in a high state of cultivation.

Nothing could equal the pleasure I felt, at seeing a country of which I had heard so much; the islands, the handsome dwellings, the river covered with vessels, and Philadelphia in full view:—it was a feast, indeed. My eye, however, rested principally on Jersey shore. I thought of Washington—I thought of his toils, his dangers, and the soul-trying scenes he underwent, whilst retreating through that state, before the enemies of his country. Matchless man! what greatness of soul! what an example of human excellence hast thou set to an admiring world! But to describe and to feel, are two very different things. Proud America! well mayest thou boast, since thou hast given birth to Washington, the greatest among the great of human beings!

Philadelphia.—My friend of Baltimore, and myself, landed together, and this charming woman understanding I was a stranger in the city, conducted me to the house of an acquaintance of her's, and after introducing me to the family, she left me. The accommodation was just such as I desired, and after taking a cup of coffee, I retired to refresh myself with sleep, before venturing on my pleasing expedition. Philadelphia, I hardly know which end to begin with, though it was in appearance as I had set it down in my mind—the long, straight streets, stretching beyond the ken of human eye, the stately, plain buildings, many of which are full an eighth of a mile in length, under the same roof, same in all respects, as to size and outward appearance, but divided into different apartments, appropriated to different purposes, and owned, no doubt, by different persons. The only disappointment I met with, lay in that facility with which I found my way through the city, and the ease with which I could step off a mile or two upon the smooth pavements, which are as level as a house-floor.

It had often been a subject of my thoughts, many years since, and up to this time, what was meant by

"South Second-street," and "North Second-street"—
the jumbling of so many sounds, and streets, and names
confounded me. Why, I thought, have so many "second streets;" and should I ever visit Philadelphia, I
should never be able to find my way through the eternity
of streets. I asked those who had often been in the
city, but received no satisfactory explanation. But the
whole mystery vanishes after coming to see the city in
reality, and that which I looked upon as the most intri-
cate and puzzling, proved quite the reverse, and instead
of retarding one's progress, is the means of quickening
our speed. In the first place, Market-street is the index
of Philadelphia : take Market-street away, and total
anarchy would ensue—it runs from east to west, quite
through the city, that is, from Delaware river to the
Schuylkill, precisely two miles ; this is called the width
of Philadelphia. It is equidistant from the northern and
southern extremities of the town, and cuts it into two
equal parts, so that Market-street holds the balance of
Philadelphia, on this as well as some other accounts.—
Beside Market-street, a number of others, running parallel with it, at equal distances on each side of it, constitute the length of Philadelphia, and make it upwards
of three miles. All these streets, with Market-street,
(we must not forget that,) run as was said, from the Delaware on the east, to the Schuylkill on the west. These
streets are crossed by others, which run from north to
south, precisely at right angles, which lays the city out
into exact squares, eight squares to a mile. These last
streets run parallel with both rivers. Beginning at the
Delaware, we have first Front-street, then second, third,
fourth, and so on to what is called the centre square.
The streets then commence at the Schuylkill in the same
manner, first, second, third, and so on to the centre
square. That part of Second street therefore, which lies
north of Market-street, is called north second, and that
part which lies south, is called south second, or third, or
whatever it be, though it is nothing but a continuation of
the same street. These distinctions, with those living
east and west of the centre square, are all that are used.
Those streets running parallel with Market-street, are

called after the names of the trees which grew there when the city was laid out, such as Chesnut-street, Pine, Walnut, Spruce, &c. Of all these streets, Market-street is the most interesting to a stranger, as in it is the greatest market in the United States. The market-house, which is nothing more than a roof supported by pillars and quite open on each side, begins on the bank of the Delaware, and runs one mile, that is, eight squares in length ! It must be understood, however, that the market house stops at the edge of every square, (so as not to interfere with the cross streets,) and begins on the next square, and so on, leaving an interval for every street: but on market days, of which there two in the week, a strong chain is drawn quite across the street, at each end of the market-house, and no horse or carriage is permitted to pass—these intervals, as well as the whole market, are then occupied by both buyers and sellers, to a degree beyond belief. No one, who has not seen it, can form an idea either of the variety, abundance, or neatness, of the Philadelphia market. That of Baltimore was plentiful indeed, so far as it went, but yields greatly to Philadelphia, both in neatness and abundance. Nothing can exceed the whiteness of the benches and stalls; the meat, which consists of every sort, is exquisitely neat, cut with the greatest care, smooth, and disposed upon tables, on cloths as white as the whitest cambric. The butchers wear a white linen frock, which might vie with a lady's wedding dress. The vegetables excel in neatness and perfection, and consist of the whole vegetable kingdom ; fruit of all sorts, and fish of every kind, besides a variety of game, butter, cheese and milk. Here, for the first time, I saw milk brought to market in churns. These churns differ in size, but are as white as a curd— they are uniformly bound with copper hoops, as bright as sand and hands can make them. Every one who comes to sell, has one particular place assigned him or her in the market, from which they never move. The butcher stands at his table, the woman sits in her stall; no moving except that of the citizens, who are coming and going continually, from early in the morning till nine o'clock at night. The whole of this mighty scene is conducted

with perfect order; no contention, no strife or noise—
presenting one of the most interesting sights perhaps in
the world. Imagine a double row of the finest looking
vegetables, a mile in length, viz. on both sides of the
market-house, with every thing else that can be named
for the table; and then the butchers' meat, filling the
whole length of space between; the multitude passing
to and fro; and you may form some idea of the market
of Philadelphia. Although there are but two days in
the week which are styled market-days, yet there is market every day except Sunday; but this is trifling, compared with the set days—indeed there is a market on
Sunday morning, for milk only. Market-street is so wide
as to afford a passage for carriages on each side, independent of the footway. Besides this market, there is
one called New-market, in the south part of the town,
which is very considerable, and every thing, I should
say, is cheap. Towards the close of the day, you may
buy good veal for four cents per lb. and often cheaper.
   Having disposed of Market-street, I shall drop a few
remarks upon the city generally. The most business, as
well as most fashion and opulence, is found in Chesnut-
street, next to Market-street, south, and parallel with it.
The ware-houses are principally upon the Delaware river. Very large vessels can come up to Philadelphia;
these ascend the Delaware—very few are able to
ascend the Schuylkill, it being much smaller than the
former. That part of the city adjacent to the Schuylkill is very thinly settled, and the streets near it are mostly unpaved: all the others are paved with stone, and the
side-walks are neatly paved with brick, are wide and
well lighted. The profusion of merchandize which lines
the streets and windows is incredible. Dry goods are
strewed along the side-walks, near the store doors; flan-
nels, cloths, muslins, silks and calicoes, are hung up over
the doors in whole pieces, hanging down on each side to
the pavement; others are placed in rolls, side by side,
on boxes standing each side of the door; barrels of sugar, coffee, raisins and fruit, stand out of doors. These
are intermingled with shoe-shops, book-stores, merchant
tailors, where clothes are ready made; add to these jew-

eller's shops, china-shops, saddlery, tin, iron and copper ware, to say nothing of millineries, upholsteries and groceries. The windows are low, large, and project into the streets some distance. These windows (or the most of them,) are from eight to eleven or twelve feet wide, and from four to six feet high. Some are filled with the most splendid plate, glass and china ware; some with caps, ruffs, bonnets and ribbons; others with liquid medicine, contained in vast glass bottles of every colour, and look exceedingly beautiful at night. The windows have different rows of shelves on the inside, from the bottom to the top, and upon these shelves the articles are disposed. But it is at night that the wealth and splendor of Philadelphia appears to the best advantage; the windows being lighted with numerous lamps and gas-lights, which, with the lamps in the streets, and the lustre of the glittering wares in the windows, present a scene of astonishing beauty.—The houses are principally of brick; large, well built, and many of them elegant.

Churches.—There are in Philadelphia 74 places for religious worship, viz.—8 for Baptists, 1 for Bible Christians, 1 for Covenanters, 10 for Episcopalians, 5 for Quakers, 1 for Free Quakers, 5 for German Lutherans, 2 for German Reformed, 2 for Jews, 4 for Catholics, 1 for Menonists, 1 Mariners Church, 13 for Methodists, 1 for Moravians, 1 for Mount Zion, 17 for Presbyterians, two for Reformed Dutch.—Besides the markets and churches already mentioned, there are, in Philadelphia, a university, 2 colleges, 4 academies, a city court-house, a county court-house, a carpenters' hall, a philosophical hall, a dispensary, an hospital and offices, an almshouse, an orphans' asylum, a museum, (formerly the state-house,) a masonic hall, 16 literary institutions, an institution for the deaf and dumb, 10 banks, a house of correction, a dramatic theatre, a medical theatre, a public observatory, a public prison, a fish market, a customhouse and offices, a post-office, 13 insurance offices, 15 breweries, 16 taverns, 74 boarding houses, and 4 public baths, 27 charitable institutions, 26 societies for the promotion of religion and morality. The Philadelphia library alone contains 24,000 volumes; the total number
18*

in all libraries is 65,000 ; 7 weekly papers, 11 daily papers, besides quarterly and monthly journals ; 5000 looms, 30 cotton factories, 3000 females employed in the tailoring business.* Besides these there are numerous articles manufactured in Philadelphia; in short, every thing that is either useful or ornamental. To describe them would fill a large volume. But the glory of the city is the water-works.

Fair Mount Water Works.—What is called the water works, are two reservoirs on the top of a hill, which supply the city with water. This scheme unites both beauty and utility, and is one that none but Philadelphians would have thought of. In 1819, the sum of $350,000 was voted, to carry the plan into effect, and was undertaken by A. Coley, Esq., who died when he had nearly completed the work. In the first place, a dam is thrown across the Schuylkill, in a diagonal line. By the power of this water, several wheels are put in motion, which, by the aid of double force pumps, is conveyed upon the top of a vast hill, into two reservoirs, which communicate with each other. From these reservoirs, the water is conveyed by leaden pipes under ground, to every part of the city, by means of hydrants. The reservoir nearest the Schuylkill is 316 feet by 139, 12 feet deep, and contains 3,000,000 gallons. The other (divided only by a few feet,) is nearly as large. The city uses one million gallons per day. These reservoirs, in shape, have the appearance of a square, so smooth, so limpid, so large, and, overlooking the whole of the city, the Delaware, the Schuylkill and the surrounding country, to which we may add two beautiful bridges over the Schuylkill, yields a most delightful prospect. The plan of supplying the city of Philadelphia with good water, has at different times engaged the talents of Drs. Franklin, Rush, and Muhlenberg. The present plan was suggested by Latrobe, though the necessity was perceived by Dr. Franklin. Previous to this, the city was watered by means of steam, also a contrivance of Latrobe's, but this mode proving ineffectual, was abandoned. I saw the old water-works ; they were at the centre square of the city ;

Taken from the picture of Philadelphia published by Cary & Lea.

nothing remains of them but a romantic edifice, resembling a temple; it occupies a whole square itself. It is the only building on the square, which is enclosed, planted with trees, and forms one of the many ornaments of the city. It is seen from every point.

Museum.—It may readily be supposed, that the idea of seeing a place so celebrated as the museum of Philadelphia, inspired me with no common curiosity: that, and the market, to me, were objects of the first interest, which I had long and ardently wished to see. The museum is in Chesnut-street, near the corner of South fourth-street. I soon discovered it by a sign, and after crossing a gallery, came to a stair-case, wide enough to admit a waggon and team. I made but a few steps, before one of them springing under my feet, rung a bell, to my great surprise, and upon gaining the stairs, I was met by a man whose business it is to receive the money paid, which is twenty-five cents. The first object of my inquiry, was the mammoth skeleton, but I was greatly disappointed in its appearance. The skeleton is indeed as large as is represented, but it had not that formidable, dread-inspiring aspect which my romantic turn led me to expect, and with which I expected to be overwhelmed: I beheld it without surprise or emotion. It is standing upon its feet in a small room, which is lighted by a large window, enclosed with a rail as high as one's breast, and presenting its side foremost. I could not forbear smiling at a gentleman, who, like myself, had formed extravagant notions of the mammoth. He stooped under the rail in order to examine it minutely, and scraping a part of the skeleton with his pen-knife, swore " it was nothing but wood," saying to his friend, that he was cheated out of his money; they both retired displeased. It has indeed the appearance of old smoky-looking hard white oak, and might impose upon wiser-looking people than Monsieur or myself. The whole has a very dark appearance, and in many parts it is quite black. In some instances the bone is as hard as iron, while other parts seem to be in a mouldering condition. If any thing, the head appears the most amazing; but I haste to describe it.

Mammoth Skeleton.—Height over the shoulders, 11 feet; do. over the hips, 9 feet; length from the rump to the chine, 15 feet; length from the tusks to the end of the tail, following the curve of the back bone, 31 feet; width of the hips, 5 feet 8 inches; length of the skeleton, in a straight line, 17 feet 6 inches; width of the head, 3 feet 2 inches; circumference of the thigh bone, 1 foot 6 inches; length of the longest rib, 4 feet 7 inches; circumference of the grinder, 1 foot 6 1-2 inches; weight of the skeleton, 1000 pounds. The skeleton is entire, except two of the ribs, which are made of wood. The back is curved, something like what is called a roach-backed horse; the head is shaped very much like that of the elephant, wide at the top, and tapering off suddenly at the chin; the hind part is much lower than the shoulders, as may be seen.

This skeleton was found by accident, in Ulster county, N. Y. on a farm belonging to Mr. John Mastin, as he was digging for marl. It was in a morass, and the water flowed in so fast upon him that he was forced to desist from digging. In 1801, Mr. C. W. Peale, of Philadelphia, purchased the right of digging for the skeleton, and after six weeks of intense labour, his efforts were crowned with success. He obtained the skeleton perfect, except what has been mentioned. These particulars I transcribed, from a printed account kept in the museum, which was furnished me through the politeness of Mr. Peale the younger. Although I was not thrown into hysterics at the sight of the mammoth skeleton, I found enough of the marvellous in the museum to remunerate for the disappointment. Amongst these were the sea-lion, the skeleton of a horse, which, when living, measured 20 hands in height, with a human figure on its back! a sheep weighing 214 lbs. (*ovis aris,*) the devil-fish—in short, ten thousand things wonderful and pleasing. What Mr. Jefferson said of the natural bridge, might with as much propriety be said of Peale's museum, viz. that it was worth a trip across the Atlantic. Here are 1100 birds of different kinds, 250 quadrupeds, 3,450 insects, fish, wax figures, and what was very pleasing to me, 200 portraits of our most distinguished men. The quadru-

peds, birds, and sea-animals, are stuffed, (that is, their
skins,) the hair, and even the gloss on the feathers, are
perfect, and all standing upon their feet, in full size. I
shall notice a few of them, and of the principal curiosities, of which there are not a few.

The most remarkable is the sea lion; what surprised
me is the eye, which is of glass, very large, full, fierce,
and as natural as though it were living; even the eye lash
was entire. The animal in size is enormous, greater
than the largest ox: then there is the elephant seal, which
is still larger! It lies flat on the floor, and has four feet,
or rather claws, stuck on its sides, with a tail resembling
that of a fish. These animals are covered with hair like
that of a thrifty horse, of a bright brown; the elephant
seal, much the lightest color: they are singular curiosities as to size. The devil fish is twelve feet in length,
and fifteen round the body, weighing upwards of 2000
pounds! And then a cow with six feet, or legs rather, two
of them are on her shoulders, doubled up, as cattle do
when lying down; she was a full grown cow. The
sheep is very large indeed, the sight of it alone was
worth ten dollars; the wool is abundant and long; it is
remarkable for great length of body, for the shortness of
its legs, and a huge flat tail. Next there was a camel-
eopard, of which I had often read; this has a very slender body, and in appearance between a deer and a horse:
its lean long fore legs contrasted with the shortness of
the hind legs, gave it an unnatural and awkward appearance; it resembles a horse whe nin the act of rising, with
his fore feet stretched out and his hinder parts on the
ground. A great Missouri bear and the largest Buffalo
bull, an old buck elk, with his tremendous horns on his
head, and the whole family of the deer kind. All those
animals and many others, are standing on their feet, facing each other, and as near as possible, presenting something like a furious combat of the most awful looking
wild beasts, amongst which the tiger, and the lion, which
last with his dreadful jaws extended, seems to threaten
the whole affair of them with instant destruction. Besides those which are on the floor, the apartment appropriated to wild beasts is lined with large shelves from

bottom to top, which are filled with the smaller species
of animals ; amongst these I was gratified to find the hyena, such as it is described, with fury and vengeance in
its countenance, and under it a famished wolf standing
over a lamb which he had just killed, and was in the
act of tearing to pieces. This was the most natural
representation of the whole ; the bowels of the sheep
looked as though they had that instant been torn out of
the body, and the blood besmeared upon the wool seemed yet warm. On these shelves stand on their feet, look
ing you in the face, the whole tribe of small quadrupeds ;
amongst these is the whole generation of monkeys, a subject of much amusement to the country people, particularly two of those human-looking animals who are dressed in clothes, sitting on stools engaged at shoe-making :
it is surprising how the mischief and cunning peculiar
to the countenance of these animals can be so perfectly
retained. One of them had his shoe, (about an inch
long,) on his knee, fastened with a strap, under his foot,
while he is boring with the awl, the ends in his hands
ready to thrust through the hole, with all the eagerness
of a person in a great hurry.

From the wild beasts I went to that part of the museum where the birds are exhibited. If I found matter of
wonder and astonishment before, I now found equal
matter of pleasure and delight, mingled, however, with
the prodigious. The birds are classed and disposed in
regular order, upon shelves, in a large room, which
stretches the whole length of the building. The room is
narrow, the birds on one side and large windows on the
other, of no inconsiderable size. Upon these shelves the
birds are placed on their feet, and close shut up with
glass to preserve them from dust, and being handled by
visitors ; the name of each bird is written in large letters,
and either laid at its feet or fastened to it. Beginning
with the largest, we have first the ostrich, which may be
called the mammoth of birds ; the one in the museum,
however, was not a full grown one, although it measures
six feet from the bottom to the top of the head. They
have a body in shape something like the turkey, the neck
proportionably longer, and forms about one third of its

height; it is of a dark (but not of a black) color; the feathers are as fine as silk, differing little in texture from those worn by the ladies. This one was much injured, having had its tail pulled out. Its wings have nothing but the pinion, or wing bones, common to other fowls, covered with a sort of down. The leg bone of a full grown ostrich was standing by the other, which came up to its neck, two-thirds of its height! It was four feet in length, and as thick as a man's wrist: what then must have been the height of the ostrich! nine feet at least. There were lying by it two of the eggs; the largest was five inches in length, and four in width; they are smooth, and of a cream color. The hooping crane seems to be a candidate for size with the ostrich. It is nearly as large, similar in shape, but of a beautiful white. The oron bird, of Africa, is also very large, and exceedingly beautiful. It is of a deep shining black, with deep red cheeks, viz. turfts of feathers on each side of its head. The gaber, of Africa, is likewise large, four feet in height, it has a bill eight inches in length. But the pelican and the Patagonian penguin were to me greater curiosities. The pelican has a long bill, eight or nine inches, and from the under part hangs a pouch, extending from the tip end of the bill to the throat, the size of a beef's bladder, and looks precisely like one, being thin and transparent: It is said to carry its food in it. The Patagonian penguin is in shape like the old fashioned pudding bags, standing on its end with the pudding in it. It has neither legs or neck; its feet are stuck on one end of its misshapen body, and its head on the other. Besides these there were swans, geese, and a great variety of ducks, parrots, and a thousand others. the least remarkable of which is worthy the attention of the refined and the curious: but it was the smaller birds whose plumage astonished me most. These beauteous little creatures abound in the museum, and afford the most pleasing and rational of all entertainments. Neither language nor pencil could paint that brilliancy of tint, or that delicacy of shade, which diversify their plumage. I was completely surfeited, the eye riots in beauty. The description of those birds in books gives you scarcely any idea of them.

Amongst the curiosities, the Chinese and Persian shoes deserve attention. The shoe of a full grown Chinese lady, is about the size of a child's, of two years old! They have a plate of iron inside, but are richly embroidered on the outside with gold and silver; they are of different shapes, but are all very large at the instep, owing probably to the foot being pressed close with iron. The Persian shoes, or rather slippers, are a singular curiosity; they are made of something as hard as iron, but were so covered with gold and silver that it was impossible to tell the principal material. The slipper tapers off from the ankle to the toe, nor does it stop there; a crooked substance, of the same material, issues from the toe, and turns up to the instep, in the form of a bow. They are very heavy, and look like any thing but convenient. The Chinese hats are plaited of cane, and differ in size. One of those in the museum was two feet in the brim: those worn by the females are extremely small, and seem to be platted of fine grass—they are in shape like a tunnel. The Persian caps are made of feathers of different colours, and of the richest hue. They are made in the form of a wreath, in which is displayed great taste and elegance—these I understood were worn by men. Another great curiosity was a pair of pantaloons made of the intestines of the whale. They came from the north-west coast, where they are said to be worn by the inhabitants. And here too was a complete Spanish barge. It was remarkable for its great length in proportion to its width, something like a canoe, being very narrow: men were sitting in it, in the act of rowing; though, believe me, they made but little progress. I shall notice but two more of the cabinet; one was a work-basket, the work of a female Indian, curiously plaited of fine grass, in which both beauty and skill were eminently displayed; the other was the shoe and stocking of the Irish Giant Obrian, who measured eight feet seven inches and a half in height. They were presented to the museum by Fitzgerald, and are perfectly sound and fresh; the size may easily be imagined. I was so much exhausted going through the apartments, that I was unable to measure either, but from the looks of the stocking, his leg must have been as thick as a common woman's body, (it was of coarse silk.) It strikes me that it was a foot across the calf. The shoe was enormous, and what made it appear more so, near it lay the shoe of Simon Pap, the dwarf, who was but twenty-eight inches high. His shoe was three inches and one half in length. It is a pity they did not stuff the skin of the giant; his figure astride of the mammoth, would have capped the climax.

Of all the portraits, I was particularly struck with those of Commodore Perry, Doctor Rush, Latrobe, and Albert Gallatin. There was something peculiarly engaging in Com. Perry; his countenance was placid, steady, and thoughtful. That of Dr. Rush, was mildness itself; the face reminded me of Mary, Queen of Scots, the same benignity, blended with a different sweetness. The portrait of Latrobe, shows genius, benevolence, openness, and penetration; it has more expression than I ever witnessed. Gallatin; his dark eyes, soft, mild, and winning, his countenance diffused with that captivating modesty which ever distinguishes a great mind. How often have I hung with delight upon that overwhelming eloquence with which he lightened (without thunder) the walls of congress hall, whilst he was a member of that body, putting a host of enemies to flight. The republican party of the United States, (whether they be right or wrong,) owe much of their success to Albert Gallatin. I saw too, the misguided Meriwether Lewis, in wax-work, clothed in his Indian dress, but never having seen him, (or indeed any of those I have mentioned,) I could not judge of the likeness.

The museum was founded by Mr. Peale, in 1784; this indefatigable man has done more since that time, than one would suppose could be done by a whole nation—the collection is endless. Ores, fish, crocodiles, serpents, monsters, amphibious animals, insects, shells, marine petrifactions, and coins of the whole known world, are here exhibited daily; the sight of which is well worth ten times the money demanded. I saw in the museum a Roman coin, dated 283 years before Christ; it appeared to be of copper, and about the size of our cents; like-

19

wise, the under jaw of a whale, which was about seven
feet wide. I had not the pleasure of seeing Mr. Peale,
but was much gratified in the acquaintance of his son,
and by seeing a full length portrait of the old gentleman,
painted by himself—it stands in the museum. The
young Mr. Peale is a small man, upon whom, however,
nature and art have lavished their favours; I met with
him in the museum, and received from him those marks
of politeness and attention, which none but the learned
and the refined know how to bestow; I was charmed
with his conversation, which proves him to be, not only
a man of classical education, but of much taste and reflection—" For he is gentle born." After paying once,
you have free liberty of the museum as often as you
choose to call.

Prison.——The prison of Philadelphia is celebrated
throughout the world. I had often heard of it, and was
now within the reach of that gratification which interesting objects inspire. Having obtained a letter of admission from Mr. Bradford, one of the trustees, I waited upon the keeper, who resides in prison. The keeper, I
thought, seemed little obliged to Mr. B. for giving him
this trouble, and finally refused to admit me into some
parts of it. The prison is 500 feet in length, and 296
in width. It consists of two vast buildings, with a large
space between, which is enclosed with a high stone wall,
and open at the top. At one end of this yard is that
part of the prison designed for women, at the other,
stands that for men. The sexes are on no account permitted to mix or visit each other. In that part appropriated to women, I found 84 females, from which to
480, is the usual number, and from four to five hundred
men. The women were in a very long room, in two
lines, one on each side of the room, leaving a space between; they sat on long benches close to the wall, and
every one with a little wheel, (viz. a flax wheel) before
her, spinning as fast as though they were spinning for a
wager. One side of the room was lighted by windows,
the other side was divided into lodging rooms, where
they slept at night. These rooms were furnished with
neat and comfortable beds; they have another large

room where they eat, besides a kitchen to cook and wash in. Several of them were employed in cooking, washing, and cleaning the prison. Several black women were amongst them, and all well clothed, and cheerful: one of the blacks asked me for money; I inquired of her what was done with her when she did not perform her task? (they are all tasked so much per day;) she replied, " that they put her in a dark room, where she could see no body, and fed her on bread and water; ' But,' said she, laughing, ' I be bound da never gets me dare again.' The whole establishment was remarkably clean. These females spin, weave, and make their own clothing: they also make coarse carpeting, which is sent to the stores for sale. The men work at their respective trades. I did not visit their prison, being refused admittance by the keeper. I saw a number of them, however, at work in the yard, from the door of the female department; they were engaged in cutting and splitting stone. The whole of the prisoners eat three times a day, as follows :—" Rye coffee and bread, for breakfast; meat and soup for dinner; mush, molasses, and water, for supper." None but criminals are confined in this prison. The prisoners are overlooked with great care, by men appointed for that purpose. I was attended by one of those men through several parts of the prison; he had the principal charge of the women; this man is one of the most amiable of his sex. He appeared to possess that soft and undisguised charity, that meek-eyed philanthropy, so requisite to one in his place: he spoke to those females, not with the authority of a callous, unfeeling task-master, but with the mildness of a brother. All was peace and stillness, no strife or loud talking was heard throughout the prison.

Hospital.—Of all the benevolent institutions of Philadelphia, the hospital is the most interesting; both it and the prison are nearly in the heart of the town. There were few in it when I called; and after what has been said of the humanity and benevolence of the place, it would be needless to give a minute description of it. It is a very large building, disposed into apartments similar to that of Baltimore, but has a handsome botanical gar-

den attached to it, and like it enclosed with a wall. I
was admitted without paying any thing, and after feast-
ing my eyes with the figure of Penn in bronze, in front
of the hospital, I entered the building itself. I was conducted through the apartments by a seraph; he resembled one more than an earthly being. In the first place
he led me to a door, at which he knocked, and in a moment it was opened by a most heavenly-looking female;
" here madam," said he, (calling me by name,) " wishes
to see your part of the establishment ;" he blushed deep
as he spoke, then stepped back a few steps, and told me
in a low voice he would wait for me. This lady then
led me into a spacious parlour, where, and the adjoining
one, I beheld a sight unequalled, perhaps, in the world!
—It was the lying in hospital. I found eight females sitting at dinner; some were convalescent, and some were
soon to be confined. But the neatness of the parlour,
the furniture, the dinner, servants attending, the attention
paid to the females by the aforesaid lady, the sweet accent in which she addressed her charge, was something
altogether unexpected : but guess my astonishment, upon being told by the lady, that " those were poor women, who were unable to support themselves during
their confinement, and that they were nursed, fed, and
furnished with medical aid throughout the whole time,
gratis !" She then conducted me into another large
apartment, which might vie with a king's palace, for
comfort and beauty. Here was a number of females indeed, closely confined. But in the cradles I saw a most
interesting sight; this was the dear little infants, 4 in each
cradle. It is impossible to do justice to this establishment. I was lost in admiration to see how clean, how exquisitely neat those sweet little creatures looked; how
comfortably they lay and slept, whilst both they and their
mothers were watched with the tenderest care. Immediately beneath those apartments were two others; the
same size, appropriated to the same purpose, and attended to in like manner, by a matron and servants; it also
contained a number of females and infants. This astonished me the more, as I was wholly unprepared for such
a display of disinterested charity. I observed the finest

bread, veal, chicken, and wine on the tables, and every other article of food and drink, suited to their situation. Having seen every thing in that part of the hospital worthy of notice, I sought the young man, whom I found waiting patiently in the place where I left him. Upon joining him, his face was dressed with a most becoming blush; a mutual interchange of which was all that passed between us; and we walked through the balance of the hospital, which I need not describe, after what has been said. It may justly be supposed that the unbounded humanity, which could lead to the foregoing establishment, would stop at nothing to render the whole ample and complete. Here, as in Baltimore, strangers are prohibited from seeing the insane. After viewing the city from the top of the hospital, which presents a grand spectacle, I descended with my friend to the garden. On passing some of the rooms, he pointed out to me two objects of singular interest; one was the chair in which Penn used to sit when administering justice; the other was a clock made by Rittenhouse. The chair was sound and fresh, just as it was when Penn used it, except the seat, which has been replaced by a new one: the back is of plaited cane. I sat in it for some minutes, which was spent in pondering over that success which crowned the enterprise of its former owner. The clock is an ingenious piece of mechanism; besides the hour of the day, &c. it revolves several of the planets with regularity and order; so it is said. The garden is laid out with much taste, and contains almost every rare and useful plant, though the frost having laid the whole under contribution, there was little to be seen except in the glass or green-house, where many tropical productions are cultivated with success. Here were a thousand things which, though they are very pretty to look at, yet a description of them would be tedious and dry. The house is very small, I should think by no means calculated to extend the design to a matter of much interest; it seems, however, to gratify the curious. I saw one or two orange trees; they were little higher than my head, though they had several small ripe oranges hanging upon them.

I declined visiting West's painting, principally because I am no judge of paintings, and having heard it
extolled so highly, I expected another disappointment,
and besides, having no curiosity of my own to gratify,
and not being qualified to gratify the public, and above
all, the fear of doing injustice to the piece, I would not
see it.   The house in which it is kept, stands near the
hospital.   As we walked back, my friend pointed out
the grave of Mrs. Girard, wife of the celebrated Girard
of Philadelphia : she died in the hospital, being deranged some time previous.   Although Girard is said to be
worth $10,000,000, yet this grave is undistinguished by
the least mark of respect.

As I before remarked, a full statue of William Penn,
the founder of Philadelphia, is on the Hospital-square.
He is standing on a pedestal, with his Quaker hat on, in
full Quaker dress.   In his hand he holds a roll, on which
is written, " Toleration to all sects, equal rights and justice to all."   The statue is of brass, and as black as the
blackest negro.   It was presented to Philadelphia, by
the nephew of Penn.   It was made in England.   The
hospital has a library of 5000 volumes, and an anatomical museum.

Deaf and Dumb Institution.—I shall notice but one
more of the institutions of Philadelphia, as, to describe
them all, would be impossible in a work like this.   Besides, it would only be a repetition of the same thing; so
nearly do they resemble, that a description of one may
serve for the whole, I mean so far as benevolence and
the most exalted charity is concerned.   Having already
mentioned the number of charitable institutions, which
is twenty-seven, the institution for the deaf and dumb,
is amongst the number.   It is a place where deaf and
dumb children are taught to read, and write, in short almost every sort of literature in the English Language.
Many of these are orphans, and taught, fed, and clothed
gratis, a few only being able to pay for tuition.   Besides
literary pursuits, the females are taught all sorts of domestic work, such as sewing, knitting, but mostly the
manufacturing straw bonnets.   When I knocked at the
door, it was opened by a little girl of about twelve years

old, who I perceived was one of the pupils ; she bowed
her head gracefully, and beckoned to me to come in, and
with a second motion of her hand, invited me to follow
her, turning round often as she advanced through the
gallery, to see if I kept the right way. When she opened
the door of the sitting room, she pointed to a lady and
then to me alternately, which was in effect an introduction to the matron of the mansion. Having done this,
she betook herself to her task, which was that of plaiting
straw for bonnets. This lady-matron possessed all the
sweetness and meek-eyed charity of her sisters of the
hospital, and answered my inquiries with the most obliging condescension. Her vocation she said only extended to the care of the female pupils when out of school.
During school hours, they were under the care of their
respective teachers, but the moment school was out,
they came into her part of the building. Whilst with
her, they were employed in making and mending their
clothes, and plaiting straw for bonnets, or to whatever
their fancy led them. None, however, were allowed to
be idle. It happened to be vacation when I called, and
of course I found about twenty of the pupils in the matron's department. There were two long tables in the
room ; at one of these were seated those engaged in bon-
net-plaiting, and at the other, those who were engaged in
sewing. I drew near to those who were plaiting straw,
with a view of inspecting their work. It was truly interesting to perceive not only the skill and ingenuity, displayed in the accomplishment of their pursuit, but the
pleasure they took in my approbation of it. Each one
of the dear little creatures held up her work as I approached them, accompanied with a pleasant smile,
whilst she kept her eye fixed on my countenance, in
which she could easily discover approbation, or the contrary. I praised them all by signs, and highly commen-
ded their work, at which they were mightily pleased.
This being the first manufacture of straw I had seen, I
was curious to see how it was done, particularly that
trimming which looks so exquisite, the ingenuity of which
we so much admire. No lady, however accomplished
in the art of pleasing, could have taken more pains than

did the little girl, over whose shoulder I leaned to watch the movement of her fingers whilst she folded the straw.

One of the pupils, a full grown young lady, (a number of them are women grown,) was writing a letter. I took the pen out of her hand, with an intention of conversing with her in writing. When she discovered my design, she jumped up and brought me a slate and pencil, upon which I wrote the following sentence and handed it to her. " Did you find it hard to learn to read and write." She looked at it some time, and then handed it across the table to a girl apparently thirteen years old, pointing to the word *hard*, which it appeared she either did not know the meaning, or could not make out the hand. The little girl to whom she gave the slate, instantly un- derstood it, and explained it to her friend, by throwing her face into that contortion occasioned by lifting a heavy weight, which contracts the muscles of the face. The former then took the slate and wrote under it the follow- ing : " Yes, it was very hard." She answered several questions in the same manner. She wrote a beautiful hand, without, however, so great a mind as her younger companion. Being desirous of seeing the boys of the institution, the lady-matron sent for the principal teach- er to her room. He appeared well pleased with my vis- it, and an exhibition being to take place the next day, he very politely presented me with a ticket, referring to the exhibition, as a place better suited to my purpose and feelings. At my request, however, he repeated in a few words, the system of education, viz. 1st, they taught the pupil the thing, 2d, the name, 3d, the quality, and 4th, its use, until they have learned them the names of all things. Next day I attended at Mr. Wilson's church, which, from its amazing size, afforded a fine opportunity for the exhibition. The exhibition was to commence at a certain hour, previous to which, every thing was suita- bly arranged for the accommodation of the spectators, who, to the amount of two thousand, at least, took their seats in the pews and galleries fronting the pupils, who were all arranged at one end of the church, the boys on one side, and the girls on the other, of their teachers, who were some in the pulpit, and some on a temporary rostrum fronting it, where the pupils were to exhibit. The rostrum was elevated even with the pulpit, the seats of the pupils were also raised even with the rostrum, so that they had only to rise and advance forward. On the opposite side of the rostrum from the audience, in full view, were placed large, long slates, four feet at least in length, and about eighteen inches wide. They were placed upright against the wall, upon these slates the pupils were to exhibit. In the first place, an eloquent and feeling oration was delivered, by whom I did not understand. Here was a sight indeed! More people than I ever saw within the walls of a house, every eye bent upon the objects of their care, who from a state of wretchedness and ignorance, had become the delight of every eye. The orator; any man might have been eloquent upon an occasion like this ; but he was more than eloquent. He seized upon every efficient argument to awaken sympathy or warm the heart, he laid hold of every advantage which language affords to enforce his arguments in favour of the objects before them, who looked up to them not only for instruction, but for food and raiment. Whilst the audience, wrapped in deep attention, seemed to enter into all the pathos of his feelings, he ran briefly over the principal incidents of the institution from its commencement, setting forth the difficulties, the patience and unwearied attention of the instructors, the astonishing success of the undertaking, and the benefit resulting from it. Having concluded his speech, the pupils, from four to six at a time, stood up to exhibit. The teacher gave out a sentence, first to the audience, and then by signs to the pupils, and in an instant, they wrote it on the slates, conjugating the verbs, and declining the nouns. After the grammar class had got through, examples in arithmetic were exhibited, then ancient and modern history, several gentlemen present putting questions in each, through the teachers. Two of them held a long conversation with each other about Gen. La Fayette, the teacher interpreting their signs and gestures, as they proceeded, word for word. One of them would ask the other who La Fayette was, how he came to this country, his services to the United States, and the

whole of his movements since his last arrival, the honors
paid to him, in short, his whole history. The exhibition
took up about three hours, but they were the pleasantest
I ever spent. It must be a source of ineffable pleasure
to the citizens of Philadelphia, to think, that they have
given happiness to such a number of human beings, and
what must be the feelings of those destitute orphans toward their benefactors! They regarded the audience
with a look of calm composure: what gratitude must
have warmed their bosoms! what emotions of tenderness
and delight, must have filled the breasts of their benefactors! The female pupils, (with their matron sitting
behind them, in her simple Quaker dress,) all modest
and gentle, looked round upon the assembly, with that
steady self-possession, which bespoke conscious worth
and innocence. Of all the institutions of Philadelphia,
this sheds the brightest lustre on its citizens. Great people! They must be emphatically such, who make the
misfortunes of others their own.

My time being short in Philadelphia, I determined to
employ it in seeing every thing worth seeing in the city;
and amongst the rest, the form of worship used by different sects, of which I had hitherto never had an opportunity. Accordingly, I attended the Jews' Synagogue one
Saturday, which is their Sabbath. Here I found about
twenty men, and not one female. They all had their
hats on, and were standing, although there were seats
convenient. Over their shoulders they wore a long lin-
en scarf, in shape and size similar to those worn by ladies; it came down before, and each end was slung o-
ver the arm, as ladies wear them in summer. The service was begun when I entered; but one of them walked up to me and pointed out a place on the opposite side
of the house where I could be seated. The service was
nothing more than one of them dressed like the others
standing at a desk, with a large Hebrew book open; out
of which he read aloud as fast as his tongue could go,
with a singing tone; and turning the leaves over with
surprising rapidity; during all the time he was bowing
his head up and down with such rapidity, that it kept
pace with his tongue, or kept time with his song rather.

Whilst he was thus engaged, the audience were walking to and fro, bowing in the same manner; now and then they would sing out right; but such singing! I never heard any that had less melody. In the course of about three quarters of an hour he shut up the book, and walked to a closet, (I should call it,) opened the doors, and shut them instantly; walked about, and bowed, and sung awhile, and then approached the same place as before, and repeated the same ceremony. But what was contained in the place, I was (from the distance) unable to see. The service now broke up; and the party dispersed; and here ends the 1st chapter of the Jews.

Next day being Sunday, I went to hear the Quakers or Friends, as they are called. Here was a direct contrast to the preceding; nought but silence reigned; not a word was said; all was solemn as midnight. Amongst them were a number of the most fashionable people of Philadelphia, between whom and the Friends, appears to exist the greatest harmony. I had been at Quaker meetings before; in fact, I was reared a Quaker myself, but never saw such a display of beauty and dress. Nothing could exceed the richness and neatness of that of the young Quaker ladies. The richest silks and satins, so uniform, and made so exquisitely neat, mostly white; their plain small round crowned bonnets; their neat square handkerchiefs, of the finest muslin, gave them a celestial appearance, and fairly eclipsed their more fashionable neighbors. The church was amazingly large, and yet it was filled to overflowing; the men, that is the Quakers, all wear their hats. The elderly men and women sat at one end of the building upon elevated seats, and during the meeting seemed deeply engaged in thought. Their countenances bespoke minds wholly withdrawn from outward objects. After sitting in this manner nearly two hours, two of the old men shook hands, the signal for breaking up; the noise which succeeded the signal, resembling distant thunder.

Besides these I heard one of the Episcopalians; and though disappointed in the oratorical powers of the preacher, I was abundantly compensated by the sound of the organ, the second I ever heard. The first of my hearing those instruments was in Baltimore, which I forgot to remark. I have often heard the organ applauded, and as often condemned, with that heat and violence which unfortunately distinguish religious disputes. Without any attempt to settle the point between them, I can only speak for myself, that it is the most heaven inspiring sound I ever heard ; its soft, solemn, sweetly flowing melody, lifts the soul from earth to heaven ; it for the moment shuts out every earthly thought, and is at once the most rational and pleasing of all devotions. The instrument consists of a number of brass pipes, or hollow tubes, from ten to twelve feet in length ; the sound is conveyed through these by means of a bellows, which is worked by keys. It fronts the pulpit, on the opposite end of the church from the parson, upon a level with the first row of galleries, (the churches in these towns have double galleries.) The organ is accompanied by a choir of singers. both male and female, who make occasional pauses, which are filled by the sweet swelling sound of the organ.

Manners and Appearance.—Respecting the manners and appearance of the people of Philadelphia, I can give but a very imperfect sketch, owing to the shortness of my visit, and the abridged opportunity I had of mixing in society ; my observations being entirely limited to meeting them in the streets, and a very few calls upon business. They have been accused of distance and reserve towards strangers. As respects the common acts of politeness I cannot concur in this particular. When accosted, the Philadelphians are polite and condescending, whether abroad or at home. I found them very easy of access, and always a ready admittance into their houses, as much so as in Baltimore, and much more so than in Washington. But in acts of benevolence (and I might add charity,) toward strangers, they are greatly behind either. In answer to a remark on this contradistinguishing trait in their character, I received the following reply :—" That when they became thoroughly acquainted, they were very kind to strangers." This is a pitiful subterfuge for their want of charity and hospitality to strangers, one of the brightest of christian virtues,

particularly when thousands of dollars are spent here
annually by strangers; it is an ungrateful exception to
the example of a few warm-hearted *yankees*. In their
appearance, they are rather taller than those of Baltimore, well made, and of delicate conformation; nor are
they so active in their movements as the people farther
south. Both men and women are very handsomely fea-
tured and have fair complexions. The ladies of Philadelphia are celebrated by travellers for their beauty.
I would, however, make very little difference between
them and those of Baltimore; the latter are not so fair,
but they have more expression of countenance. As to
dress and fashion, if I were to give an opinion at all, I
should give it in favor of Baltimore. Baltimore has
more splendor, Philadelphia more taste; but there is
little difference; the difference as respects moral appearance was this, that there were more idlers, more
blacks, and more trifling looking people, and more
swearing in Baltimore than in Philadelphia, particularly
on the wharves. These remarks are, however, the result of a few hasty observations.

Respecting the literati of Philadelphia, it is not in
my power to say a word. Nothing would have been
more gratifying to me than to have seen some, at least,
of those eminent men, though, perhaps, I saw the greatest man in the city; I mean Mr. Cary. From the very
limited opportunity I had of judging, I am inclined to
think education does not receive that attention we might
expect, in a city so devoted to the public good. The
dialect of the citizens, particularly of the children, gave
rise to this opinion; it is very defective, and the young
misses are detestably affected in their manners, dress and
dialect. I questioned a few on the subject of grammar,
geography, and history, who were said to be engaged
in these studies, and found them wretchedly defective. They have, withal, a whining tone in their
speech, extremely disgusting; though the higher classes
pronounce the English language with purity and even
elegance.

Having mentioned Mr. Cary, that giant of the pen deserves some notice. Being slightly acquainted with his
20

son, H. Cary, I gently reproached him for not introducing me to his father; he stepped into an adjoining room,
and the elder Mr. C. soon made his appearance ; " what
is your business with me," said he rather abruptly ; " only to say that I have seen Mr. Cary," I replied. He
immediately scanned my motives, blushed, and said,
" come this way, I have something for you ;" and leading me into the same room from which he came out, made
me a present of his last works ; but his engagements calling him away, I to my great disappointment, exchanged
but a few words with him before he departed. Mr. C.
is about the middle height, and robust make. He appeared upwards of fifty years of age, black hair and eyes,
his face round and full ; his countenance grave, but
manly, dignified and striking, marked with lines of deep
thinking, but the keenest eye, and the blackest I remember to have seen ; his looks are so penetrating as to dis-
compose the beholder. Upon seeing him, I thought of
his Olive Branch, which was so eagerly read, and so
highly esteemed, even to adoration in the western states ;
a work which no American ought to be without ; I have
known it to sell as high as five dollars per copy. The
works he gave me were *Hamilton*, and some addresses
to the people, which need no comment. Admirable
man! what majesty of genius! what powers of mind!
and how laudably devoted !

History.—The place where Philadelphia now stands,
in 1681 was a forest, inhabited by wild men and savage
beasts. In 1678, a ship from Stockholm, commanded by
Shields, was the first that sailed so high up the Delaware.
She approached so near where the city now stands that
she run her bowsprit among the trees that lined the bank.
The ship was laden with passengers, destined for Burlington, still a small village, to which they gave that
name. They remarked the advantageous site as they
sailed along, little thinking, (the historian says,) and still
less foreseeing the contrast between the city afterwards
built on it, and their still humble village to which they
were bound. The place where Philadelphia now stands
was called by the name of " Coaquannock." This was
an Indian town, which stood near the place now called

the Bake-house. William Penn, whom the greatest men of Europe have ranked with the Solons and the Numas of Greece and Rome, was born in 1644. His father was Sir William Penn, of Penn, Vice Admiral in the time of Cromwell, and afterwards knighted by king Charles II. William, the son, joining the sect called Quakers, incurred not only the displeasure of his father, who turned him out of doors, but of the government, who imprisoned him in the Tower.

These persecutions, principally levelled at the Quakers, led Penn to seek a place in the new world, where they might worship God in peace ; and, obtaining a grant from king Charles, he with a number of his followers set sail for America, where he landed in 1699 ; and, purchasing the soil of the natives, laid out the city upon its present plan. Previous to Penn's arrival, some of his party having preceded him, built themselves bark huts ; others lived in caves on the banks of the Delaware, which they dug themselves. In one of those rude caves was born the first native Philadelphian, John Key, who reached the age of eighty-five. He was born in a cave afterwards known by the name of " penny pot," on the bank near Race street. This man, when eighty years of age, walked from Kennet to Philadelphia, a distance of thirty miles, in a day ! Another man, Edward Drinker, born in a cave, lived till independence was declared. The first house erected in Philadelphia was a low wooden house, east side of Front street. It stood in what was called Bud's row, a little north of the inlet, now oc cupied by Dock street. This inlet flowed as far to the north as Chesnut and Third street. The owner kept it as a tavern for many years ; it was called the Blue Anchor. The first brick house built in Philadelphia, was standing recently ; it stood north side of Chesnut street, opposite Carpenter's Court. In Letitia Court, east of South Second street, still survives the town-house of William Penn, built a few years after his arrival. The last of the original trees, a walnut, stood in front of the state-house, Chesnut street.

I have been on the spot where the first citizen was born ; I surveyed the place where lived mine host of the

Blue Anchor—now a street; but chiefly, I sought
with eagerness the ancient dwelling of the venerable
Penn. Letitia Court, which is nothing but a narrow alley,
leading out of Market street near the Delaware, soon
brought me to the venerable pile. It is a low two story
brick house, and though of so long standing, it has not
that ancient appearance we would expect. It is built of
brick, and enclosed with an entire new wall of the same
material. It is laid off into small rooms and occupied as
a tavern. I sat in that used by Penn as a chamber, with
feelings which may easily be imagined. Upon men-
tioning to some one, my motives for visiting the house,
a voice exclaimed, " what, are you writing a book ?"
I turned round, and regarding the man (for it was a man
who spoke,) with silence ; " pardon me," he cried, " my
name is Darby, author of the Emigrant's Guide." This
was an unexpected pleasure ; I had seen the Emigrant's
Guide, but had never seen the author till then. Darby
is a small man, about forty years of age ; sensible, and
possessed of much general information ; he was the only gentleman in Philadelphia who invited me to his
house. His countenance bespoke him a man of feeling
and generosity ; and I am sorry that it was not in my
power to accept the invitation, as from him I should
probably have obtained that information, which, from my
peculiar circumstances, I found rather difficult. I found,
however, a very obliging friend in Mr. Lea, of the firm
of Carey & Lea. He is a son-in-law of M. Carey, and
a most consummate gentleman. To him and Mr. Bradford I am much indebted ; particularly to the former.
But, to return ; William Penn, after laying off the city
of Philadelphia, drew up a code of laws for the government of the colony. The foundation of these laws was
" that every one who believed in one Almighty God,
should not be compelled to worship contrary to his own
opinion; granted free toleration to all sects ; equal right
and justice to all men." This may be considered (says
the historian,) as the foundation stone upon which the
sublime edifice of free toleration has since been built
throughout these United States. Philadelphia is situated in 39 deg. 55 min. north, upon the west bank of the

Delaware, which is here nearly a mile in width ; it is
126 miles from the Atlantic, and six miles above the
confluence of the Schuylkill, which gives room for nearly
a square.   The northern and southern liberties are nothing but a continuation of the city, though both are out of
the corporation.   These lengthen it to a mile longer
than it is wide.   The site is a perfect level, excepting a
slight elevation at the southern end ; this, and the streets,
which are wide and straight, to mathematical nicety,
and the numerous squares, adorned with handsome trees,
gives to Philadelphia that beauty, so much admired by
travellers.   Besides the streets, it has numerous courts
and allies, (a court is like an alley, but is only open at
one end,) which cross about the middle of each square ;
the latter run from street to street.   These are wide
enough for a cart or waggon to pass, and have neat side
walks.   The streets are swept every day, and the pavements washed ; nothing can be neater.   The city was
called the town of Philadelphia till 1701, when it was
incorporated and took the name of a city.   It was the
seat of government till 1801 ; the public mint is still in
Philadelphia.   It contained 108,000 inhabitants the last
census.   It may be called a manufacturing rather than a
commercial city ; and although it is said to exceed every part of the United States in the beauty, quantity and
excellence of its manufactures, yet it is a great way behind Baltimore in architecture.   The new Bank, planned by Latrobe, is, however, a fine edifice of marble,
in imitation of the temple of Minerva.   I was quite provoked with them for pulling down the dwelling-house of
Dr. Franklin, which they have done, and erected a public Library upon the spot where it stood.   This Library
was founded by the Doctor himself, and a few of his
friends ; the oldest in Philadelphia.   A full length statue of the Doctor, in an old fashioned dress, is placed
over the door of the Library, on the out side, and seems
to invite the traveller to walk in.
   Amongst the ornaments of the city, may be reckoned
the celebrated " Pratt's Gardens," but I did not visit
them ; albeit I must not forget the two bridges over the
Schuylkill, the noblest structures of architecture belong-

ing to the city; when viewed in a distant line with the river they are truly magnificent. The churches are very plain, being mostly without steeples.

From Alexandria to this place, rye coffee is drank by a great portion of the inhabitants, also black tea. Rye is regularly toasted, ground, sold in the markets, and mixed with coffee at the best boarding houses! (except in Washington.) Many of the citizens drink it in its present state; this they do for their health, being told by the physicians that it is better for the lungs. Black tea I never heard of, till asking the waiter for a cup of tea, between Baltimore and Philadelphia, he asked me whether I chose black tea or green, whilst I was at a loss what answer to make. This, however, is fair, because you have the option to drink it or not; but you are completely taken in by the coffee. Black tea is very fashionable in Philadelphia, being also recommended as more healthy than green, which I believe to be true, it is certainly not so injurious to the nerves; but I never could be reconciled to the rye coffee: yet they live well in Philadelphia, and boarding is cheap, though they excel us in none of their cities in any thing but beef and fish; their lamb, veal and fowls are not equal to those sold in the Lexington market, of Ky. by a great deal, or in that of Cincinnati, or Chilicothe; indeed, their best beef comes from Greenbriar, west of the Alleghany, and from the South Branch, west of the Blue ridge.

The lady of the house, (in many instances,) instead of taking the head of the table, sits at the side, about midway, (supposing the table to be long and narrow,) with her tea equipage before her, and, without the aid of her servants, with great facility helps every one at the table.

Journey to New-York.—After spending two weeks to a day in Philadelphia, I entered my name on the waybill, paid my passage over night, and set off for New-York in the steam-boat next morning, sailing up the Delaware in a north-east direction. Day was dawning as we put off from the shore; I remained on deck to eatch a parting view of the city, and the fast receding objects. I never left a place with less regret; not that

I was displeased with Philadelphia, I was pleased that I had seen it, I was pleased with it for its own sake, and above all I was pleased with an evidence of what human nature is capable, and the effects of that capacity verified to a degree which ranks Philadelphia amongst the first cities of the world, either ancient or modern, in acts of beneficence towards the human race; but in it I found but few of those courtesies which fasten upon the heart of the stranger.

The sky was overcast with clouds, which, added to the gloom of the season, was ill calculated to restore my flagging spirits, exhausted from incessant toil in traversing the streets and public places of Philadelphia, which kept me on my feet from morning till night each day. Here again we have New-Jersey on our right, and Pennsylvania on the left; the land on both sides appears poor, though fine buildings, good orchards and meadows, diversify the borders of the river, the land being flat as far as the eye can see. A short time brought us to Burlington, already mentioned; it is a poor village, on the Jersey shore, shows age and decay: it has two small wharfs, and a few small vessels anchored near them. This town is older than Philadelphia. Whilst I was absorbed in thought, upon the political changes which had taken place in the country before me, since its first settlement, and the never to be forgotten sons of New-Jersey, who clung to our Washington when almost forsaken by every one else, * I was interrupted by the captain of the boat, who walked up to me and asked for my fare; thunderstruck at his request, it was some time before I could answer that I paid it in Philadelphia; " Where is

* " New-Jersey signalized herself during the revolution—as a state, she suffered more from the ravages of war, than any state in the union. It was the seat of war for several years, during our contest with Great Britain, and her losses both of men and property, in proportion to her population, was greater, infinitely greater than any of the thirteen states. Her militia, always obedient, for a long time composed the strength of the army. Nearly every town in the state has been rendered famous for some signal exploit. Trenton, Princeton, and Monmouth will forever be held in veneration by all the friends of liberty. The success of her arms, and the various achievments of her soldiers, gives New-Jersey a title to the first rank amongst her sister states." I have often marked her sons in the western country, for their bold and independent spirit

your receipt ?" " I am not in the habit of taking re-
ceipts." He coolly replied, " you must go ashore at
Bristol, (a village in sight,) you have taken the wrong
boat." " It is the wrong boat which has taken me," I
replied ; you, or some of your men told me this was the
boat : at this instant one of the passengers pointed to the
steam-boat which I ought to have taken ; it was but a
few rods behind, and I gladly exchanged. I had taken
the opposition, it appeared ; the fare which used to be
six, is now only two dollars in each ! nearly 100 miles.
Had my boat been ahead, the consequence might have
been serious.   To guard against similar mistakes, I advise all those who may come after, by water or by land,
either not to pay in advance, or take a receipt with the
name of the line, boat, &c.   Mutual congratulations
were interchanged between myself and the captain, who
testified much pleasure that it turned out no worse ; after
which I went down to enjoy the comforts of the stove-
room for the first time that day, although it was freezing !
I found about fifty strange faces below, independent of
those on deck—ladies and gentlemen all in one large
room.   I took a seat in silence amongst them, admiring
the republican simplicity of their manners.   The ladies, unembarrassed, modest, and discreet, conversing
familiarly with the gentlemen, all mingled together, leaving it difficult to tell who were, or who were not their
husbands.   In this respect they differ greatly from their
more southern neighbours, who would have taken it as an
insult, were they reduced to sit in the same room with
gentlemen, particularly where men of all classes are passengers.   Here was no silly affectation amongst the females, no impertinent frowardness amongst the men ;
they cracked their nuts and eat their apples very much
at their ease ; these I thought must be New-Yorkers,
which proved to be the case.   Here, society appeared
in a new light, presenting a medium between those ex-
tremes under which I had been accustomed to view it,
equally removed from impudent rusticity on the one
hand, and repelling hauteur on the other.   None seemed greater than his fellow, presenting one of the most
pleasing proofs of our salutary government I had hither-

to seen: amonst the pleasures (and the pains too) which
a stranger enjoys, it is not the least that he is one.   To
sit amidst such vast crowds wholly unnoticed and unknown, left at perfect liberty to observe their manners,
conversation, and physiognomies, is truly a mental luxury.   I have often wondered at the desire which many
people betray, to become acquainted with strangers,
whilst all my pleasure arises rrom being unknown.   My
meditations, however, were soon interrupted by a call
upon the passengers to come and receive their tickets,
as it appeared we had to leave the Delaware, take stages and proceed by land across the country, to the Raritan river, (New-Jersey,) where we take the steam-boat
again.   But here the porters understand their business
much better than those of the Baltimore and Philadelphia line.

So soon as the tickets are distributed, the porters ask
you for the number of your stage, and to show them
your baggage ; they then proceed to label your baggage
with the number to which it belongs, setting the baggage
of each stage by itself : every stage has its porter, and
the moment the boat lands, every one to his business.
I was astonished at the dispatch used in transferring the
contents of the boat within the stages.   Every one, even
the passengers seemed to testify the most eager desire to
beat the other line, whose passengers had just left the
shore in their stages as we arrived.   They kept a small
distance ahead of us in the Delaware, but our hope of
success was founded upon the mettle of our horses, and
the advantage of our second boat, which was the best
sailer.

Being in favour with the captain, I got No. 1, the foremost stage, upon the fore seat of which is always seated
one of the proprietors, for the purpose of regulating the
speed of their horses, repairing accidents, &c.   It was
our good luck to have an Irish gentleman in our party,
of great vivacity, who enlivened the conversation which
took place in the stage, with effusions of wit and humor.
We were nine in all, three ladies and six gentlemen.
They dipped occasionally into polite literature, but the
appearance of the country through which we were passing

engaged too much of my attention to profit by the conversation, particularly a stately edifice to the left of us,
not far from the road; upon inquiry I was told it was
Joseph Bonaparte's dwelling, the first time I heard that
he resided in the U. States! Upon the whole, I repent-
ed that I had not taken the other line, as it passed through
Princeton, where I might have been gratified by at least
an exterior view of Princeton College; but the lines taking separate roads upon leaving the Delaware, I missed
that pleasure. New-Jersey is a broken, uneven country, and poor soil, at least that part of it through which
we passed; the natural growth is white oak, hickory,
chesnut, and pine; some meadows appear at intervals,
and fine orchards of cherry, apple, and pear trees. But
the diminutive stalks of maize in the adjoining fields, surprised me. It produces wheat, rye, barley, buckwheat,
and flax, and has a number of iron manufactories from
ore, within the state. It is likewise watered by a number of streams, which prove beneficial to the inhabitants,
by enabling them to realize the advantage they possess
over that of any other state in the union, both in the
quantity and quality of its ore, which is said to be sufficient to supply the United States.

New-Jersey was settled by the Dutch, at Bergen, in
1618. It was granted to the Duke of York in 1664, by
Charles II. and erected into a distinct government.
There are no large towns in New-Jersey: it trades with
New-York, which lies on the one side of it, and Philadelphia, which lies on the other. Trenton is the seat of government; it is seated on the Delaware, thirty miles a-
bove Philadelphia, and contained 4,000 inhabitants in
1820. The falls of Delaware lie near this town, above
which it is unnavigable. This river divides New-Jersey from Pennsylvania on the west, and Hudson river
divides it from New-York on the east. It is the only
state in the union where females are allowed to vote,
though the men exercise the privilege.

When we began to draw near the Raritan, we had a
view of the other line, and it is probable they had a view
of us, from the rate they were driving. Each line was
running on elevated ground, in view of each other, du-

ring some miles; but all in vain, we got to the river first, and I was almost carried to the boat by the porters, in their eagerness to conquer the other line. The foremost stage of the opposition made two desperate attempts to pass us within a few yards of the Raritan; they came so near effecting their purpose that the fore-wheel struck the hind wheel of ours, the one I was in, and nothing but the narrowness of the pass prevented their success. These opposition lines are certainly an advantage to travellers, and a great one too, but it is one of great hazard. We take water at New-Brunswick. New-Brunswick has a college, and contains 6,764 inhabitants.

No sooner were we in the boats, (which was almost at the same instant,) than the steam was liberally plied to the wheels, and a race between the "Legislator" and the "Olive Branch," commenced for New-York. The former was our heroine, and a stately boat she was; but although she seized upon the middle of the channel, her rival drew up alongside somewhat boldly, and sometimes had the presumption to run ahead, which her ability to sail in shoal water enabled her to do; often, however, she lagged behind. It was quite an interesting sight to see such vast machines, in all their majesty, flying as it were, their decks covered with well-dressed people, face, to face, so near to each other as to be able to converse. It is well calculated to amuse the traveller, were it not for a lurking fear that we might burst the boilers. I confess for one, I would rather lose the race than win it, (which we did,) under such circumstances.*

The Raritan is what I should call a common, though a handsome river; it is about the width of New river, or Big Sandy, in Virginia. With a smooth, gentle current, it flows through the Jersey state, and enters Arthur Kill Sound, one of the finest harbours in the world, which lies open to Sandy Hook. The land, as you sail down the river, is thin, as most of the lands in those states are. The farms are small, and so are the houses. Orchards

* Shortly after this, the Legislator did burst her boiler, by which some lives were lost, and others were much injured. A boy saved himself by jumping into a chest.

and meadows continue, though the hand of winter sits
heavy on them. Cold as the day was, nothing but a
heavy fall of rain could have forced me below. The
clouds, which had been lowering all day, burst into a torrent about 4 o'clock, and with great reluctance I had to
give up my speculations.

Without noticing or being noticed, I took a seat by the
stove, with true republican independence; ladies and
gentlemen all mingled promiscuously together—some
sitting, some walking about, some lying down on the settees, as their leisure served. Two gentlemen sat upon
the same seat which I had taken, engaged in conversation upon the approaching presidential election. One
(as I took it) was of New-Jersey, the other of New-
York. He of New-York expressed some surprise at
the result of the New-Jersey election. "I was led to
believe," said he, "that your state would have supported Mr. Adams."—the vote, it appeared, was in favour
of Gen. Jackson. "Do you think," replied he of N. J.
warmly, "that we would vote for a man who does'nt believe in the Christian religion? No sir, we are not come
to that yet, and I hope never will." "Not believe in
the Christian religion!" answered N. Y. "why how is
that? I don't understand you." "I mean," said N. J.
"that John Q. Adams is a Unitarian." What can he
mean? thought I; surely a Jew, Turk, or Algerine—it
was the first time I ever heard the tenets of the sect.—
"He may be a Unitarian, said the other, but that does'nt
prove him not a Christian. But tell me, friend, if that
be all your objection to Mr. Adams." "Yes, he would
have got the vote of the state, had it not been proved to
their satisfaction that he was no Christian—we had made
up our minds once to vote him." "I should like to
know, sir, how you make it appear that Unitarians are
not Christians; I am a Unitarian myself, and believe in
Christ; I believe that he died to save sinners, in the re-
mission of sins, that we are justified through Christ. We
believe that love to God and love to man constitutes a
Christian." "Yes, but you deny that Christ is the Son
of God, and you wont admit of total depravity."—
When they had proceeded thus far, several old ladies

came forward to partake of the warmth of the stove, and the gentlemen arose to give them room. This was provoking, just as I was upon the point of being enlightened upon the two great subjects of religion and government. I think it was Sir Isaac Newton who said "he would have discovered longitude had it not been for an old woman."

The boat now began to rock and pitch from side to side, with such violence that I was unable to keep my feet, and was forced to remain not only sitting, but clung to the back of the seat to keep myself steady, and my head became dizzy, attended with slight faintness. I asked one of the passengers the cause of this rocking, and was told the boat was in the bay. Here I was again unfortunate, as by this time, and long before, it was as dark as Egypt, by which I lost perhaps the most interesting view in my whole travels!

New-York City.—We landed in the city of New-York about 8 o'clock, (Nov. 15th,) and I took up my lodgings in Front-street, at the house of Mr. Jacques, to which place I had been directed by the captain of the Legislator. If I was pleased with the independent manners of the passengers in the boat, I was much more so with the company I found at the house of Mr. Jacques. On entering a large room, I found an assembly of ladies and gentlemen sitting before a blazing fire, (no unwelcome sight.) The old men were smoking their pipes, and the younger ones were amusing the ladies with anecdotes, perfectly regardless of the copious draughts of tobacco smoke. To diversify the picture, one of the young ladies sat down to her piano forte! Never did I witness such independence of manners, even in the land of Jackson; our western heroes, when it comes to smoking, withdraw from the company of the ladies. It is not in the power of a mere reader to form an accurate idea of mankind. Without meaning any irreverence either to books or writers, I honestly confess, no description of New-York, which ever fell in my way, led me to expect such a picture as the one before me. "Free trade and sailor's rights," truly; I never found myself more at

21

home in my life.   The company was composed of persons above the common order, most of them people of
intelligence and business.   The ladies were sensible and
handsome, plain in their dress and manners.   Mine host
seemed to be a man who had seen better days ; his countenance was calm and serene, and he welcomed me with
a smile which at once bespoke kindness and hospitality.
It was nothing more than a boarding-house, which seemed to be sufficiently filled, yet this good man showed no
disposition to refuse me a night's lodging.   After a comfortable supper I retired to my chamber, with no unfavourable impressions of New-York.
   Next day, after breakfast, I bent my course toward the
far famed Broadway ; which exceeds any street in Philadelphia, except Market street, in width, the first being
80 and the latter 100 feet wide ; it is four miles long,*
and the side walks paved with flag, (the middle of the
street in all the towns and cities in this country are paved with common round stone.)   Broadway in other respects exceeds any street in Philadelphia, both for beauty and business.   It extends from the Battery through
the heart of the city.   Next to Broadway, in point of
beauty, is Hudson, Washington, Greenwich, and the
Bowery ; this last runs in a diagonal line, and joins
Broadway.   Besides these, there are 250 streets and allies, without reckoning those recently laid off.   Pearl
street, with many others first laid out, are narrow and
crooked ; there are, however, many handsome streets
which cross at right angles, viz : Market, Grand, and Canal streets.   Of all these streets, Pearl street does the most
business, being the principal mart of the merchants.
Wall street is also a place of much business ; in it are
the banking houses, exchange, brokers, insurance, auc-
tioneers, and custom house offices ; in short, all commercial business is transacted there.   Nothing can exceed the throng of gentlemen in Wall street ; particularly when their merchant ships arrive ; on such occasions it is dangerous to walk in Wall street ; here the

*Since the above was written, Broadway has been extended to eight
miles ; the whole length is laid off into lots, streets and avenues, but
not yet built on.

commercial papers are read, and ship news detailed. This street alone, may give a stranger an idea of the business and trade of New-York. Broadway, on the other hand, is distinguished for the fashionable, the gay, and the idle, as Pearl street and Wall street are for men of business. It is likewise the seat of much business; the lower stories of most of the houses being occupied by retail shops, and book stores, for upwards of two miles; the principal booksellers are in this street. The broad windows are filled with china and glass ware, plate, millinery, fruit, confectionary; in short, every thing, and much more abundant than in Philadelphia. But shops, furniture, superb buildings with their marble fronts, are completely eclipsed by the teeming fair ones, from morning till ten o'clock at night. It is impossible to give even an idea of the beauty and fashion displayed in Broadway on a fine day; the number of females, the richness and variety of dress, comprising all that can be conceived of wealth or skill, mocks description; the throng resembles a dense multitude issuing from the door of a church. In Philadelphia business is confined to one or two streets principally; in New York, Broadway, Chatham, Pearl and Division streets, Maiden-lane and the Bowery are literally strewed with every article of ornament and use, which, with the thrice told multitude, not only fills the western stranger with amazement, but is the wonder of foreigners. Here the feminine graces meet you at every step; they thrust their lovely faces into yours, and shoulder you on all sides, without even stopping to apologize. Here the earnest merchant steps, there the gay cook and merry chamber-maid, with some scores of honest tars, hucksters, rude boys, and chimney sweeps, with the rolling coaches, and the rattling carts, may give some idea of this life-inspiring city. But all this is only a drop in the bucket compared to that on the wharves or slips, (as they are called here,) the warehouses, docks, ship-yards, and auction stores, which occupy South, Front, and Water streets, pouring a flood of human beings. Here the sound of axes, saws, and hammers, from a thousand hands; there the ringing of the blacksmith's anvil; hard by the jolly tar with his heavo :

the whole city surrounded with masts; the Hudson, East. river, and the bay covered with vessels, some going out and some coming in, to say nothing of the steam-boats; in short, imagine upwards of an hundred thousand people, all engaged in business; add to these some thousand. strangers which swarm in the streets and public houses; such is New-York. This is, however, only a running glance; the result of my first ramble through the city. I shall compose myself, and give something more like a description.

New-York is on Manhattan Island; it is upwards of four miles in length, and from three quarters to one mile and a half in width, nearly in the form of a triangle. It has Hudson river on one side and East river on the other, which unite at the southern end, and form a beautiful bay of nine miles in length, and four broad, which, with the several islands it embosoms, and the fortifications, affords a delightful prospect. Its public buildings are a city hall, a hospital, an alms-house, a state prison, 2 city prisons, a penitentiary, 2 colleges, 2 theatres, an orphans asylum, a magdalen asylum, an asylum for the deaf and dumb, a masonic hall, the New York institute, 11 banks, between 80 and 90 churches,* 32 charitable and benevolent societies, 13 missionary societies, 10 bible societies, three tract societies, 8 societies for promoting education, 16 manufacturing companies, 8 insurance companies, 12 daily papers, 13 weekly and semi-weekly papers, besides a great number of journals and magazines, 6 market houses, 2 circuses, vauxhall garden, the park, the battery, and bowling green. There are eight great hotels in New-York, besides boarding and eating houses which abound throughout the city, to which we might add some hundred oyster cellars. Besides the colleges already named, there are 6 free schools, the New-York high school, several academies, and private schools.

City Hall.—The City Hall stands nearly in the centre of the city, fronting the harbor; it is said to be the most beautiful edifice in the United States. Although

* The number of churches cannot be ascertained, as there are new ones building every day

the front is of native marble, yet, I cannot agree that it is as handsome as the capitol of the United States, or the President's house ; it certainly is not so showy, and as to the architecture I am no judge. I should think it too low for its size. It is, however, a beautiful building, 216 feet long, and 105 in width, and, including the attic story, 56 feet high ; with a handsome colonnade and cupola. The ends are of marble as high as the basement. Thirteen different courts hold their sessions, (some of them every day,) in the Hall. It cost 500,000 dollars ; it stands in the park, which contains four acres of ground, planted with trees, and enclosed with an iron railing.

Hospital.—The New-York Hospital was founded in 1771. It is under the direction of twenty six governors, a president, vice president, treasurer, secretary, visiting committee, committee of repairs, committee of inspection, superintendant, and matron. Besides these there is a society of gentlemen, consisting of 151 members, together with the mayor, aldermen, recorder, and twelve of the first clergymen in the city, which constitute the corporation, and have the control of all pecuniary matters. These are incorporated by the name of the " Society of the New-York Hospital." This society is subject to the 26 governors, who meet on the first Tuesday in every month, at the Hospital. The governors are elected once in every year by the society. The governors choose their officers by ballot, viz : president, vice president, treasurer, secretary, &c. All the respectable physicians and surgeons in New-York, take it by turns to visit the hospital daily ; their number must not, however, be less than twelve each day. Every gentleman connected with the institution is of the first learning and talents ; and all, excepting the subordinate officers, devote their services GRATIS ! Physicians included. The building stands near Broadway and Duane street ; it is built of gray stone in the Doric style, 124 feet long, 50 feet deep in the centre, and 86 in the wings ; four stories high, including the basement. The building is divided into 16 wards, besides a lying in ward (which last is greatly inferior to that of Philadelphia,) and a surgical theatre. These wards are divided into sixty

21*

rooms. The edifice is crowned with a handsome cupola, from which you have a fine view of the city, the harbor and the Hudson. The state allows the Hospital the sum of $12,500 annually, chargeable upon the duties on sales at public auction, in the city of New-York. The greatest number of patients at any one time on record, in the Hospital, is 2,000! As high as 1,725 have been admitted in one year, (including U. S. seamen;) of this number 1,185 were paupers! Out of the whole, 1,320 were cured : 527 of the patients were Irish. There is a library to the Hospital of 4,800 volumes ; containing some of the most rare and most valuable works in medical science in the world.

By a law of the United States, every seaman in the merchant service pays 20 cents per month (deducted out of their wages,) for their support, if sick or disabled. This not being sufficient for the support of all who applied for hospital relief, the governers have admitted 1,649 more than what has been yearly paid for by the United States ; the cost of which amounts to $15,141 28, which Congress as yet refuses to pay: so says report.

The Asylum for the Insane stands near the Hospital, and is included in the institution, and both are kept equal to those of Baltimore and Philadelphia, excepting only the lying in ward. Clinical lectures, both medical and surgical, are delivered here by the professors of both colleges, viz : Columbia college, and the medical college ; being physicians of the Hospital, they use the Surgical Theatre for this purpose. There are usually an hundred students, medical and surgical, who attend those lectures ; they were first introduced by Dr. Bard. Besides this hospital, there is one on Staten Island, three miles below the city, where quarantine laws are enforced at certain seasons of the year. This hospital receives all that are afflicted with epidemic diseases ; it is one of the finest buildings in the United States. A board of health sits at this place.

Columbia College.—Columbia college was founded in

* The annual expence of the Hospital is $40,000. No domestic or officer of the Hospital is allowed to receive any present or bequest from any patient.

1754 ; it stands near Park place, and consists of one
great building of gray stone, three stories, and contains
twelve apartments in each story. It also contains a
Chapel, Hall, Museum, Anatomical Theatre, a Laboratory, a Philosophical apparatus, and a library of 5.000
volumes. The annual revenue is upwards of $4.000 ;
it has a President, and five Professors. The average
number of students is 200. It is governed by Trustees,
but their number I was not able to ascertain ; the President, when I called, being very much indisposed. The
Elgin Botanical Garden, formerly the property of Dr.
D. Hosack, was purchased trom him by the state, and
conveyed to this college, (under very rigid restrictions ;)
it contains twenty 20 acres of ground, and upwards of
2,000 valuable plants.

Medical College.—The medical college stands in Bar-
clay-street ; it was incorporated finally in 1813. by the
legislature ; the regents of the university, previous to
this, granted them a charter, but the institution did not
prosper until 1813 : it is now in a flourishing condition,
and a number of young men have graduated at this college. The medical department, which formerly belonged to Columbia college, has been transferred to this,
which is better known by the name of " the College of
Physicians and Surgeons." The course of lectures embraces " the theory and practice of physic, obstetrics, and
diseases of women and children, chemistry, and materia
medica, anatomy, physiology and surgery, natural history, the clinical practice of medicine, the principles and
practice of surgery, and the institutes of medicine, and
medical jurisprudence."

Being insensibly led to mention the university of N.
York, it becomes necessary to explain, that the regents
of the university are nothing more than a literary society, of twenty-one gentlemen, whose duty it is to distri-
bute the money designed for all literary institutions
throughout the state ; also to visit all the colleges, academies, and schools, within the same ; to inspect the system of education in each, and make report thereof to the
legislature. They appoint presidents and principals of
academies ; incorporate colleges and academies, &c. and

confer degrees by diplomas of a higher order than master of arts and medical degrees. The governor and lieut. governor are members *ex officio*; the regents are appointed by the legislature, and choose a chancellor and vice chancellor of the university from their own body. They are prohibited from requiring any religious test of any president or principal of an academy or college, and no regent can be a president, trustee, or principal, of any seminary or college in this state.

State Prison.—The state prison of New-York, stands on the Hudson river, in Greenwich-street. It is built of free stone, in the Doric style; it has two stories, each 15 feet in height, besides the basement, and is 204 feet in length; it has four wings extending back; the buildings and yard cover four acres of ground; the whole is enclosed with a stone wall, 23 feet next the river and 14 in front. It contains 54 rooms for the prisoners, rooms for the keeper and agents, a chapel, an hospital, a dining hall for the prisoners, with kitchens, and cells for solitary confinement. In the yard are the work-shops of the prisoners, and the whole is well supplied with water. These prisoners do not work out of doors as at Philadelphia; the most of them are kept at weaving; the first stocking-loom I ever saw was in this prison, but such was the intricacy of the thing that I am unable to describe it. Besides weavers, there are turners, brush-makers, coopers, blacksmiths, tailors, painters, shoemakers, carpenters, and many card and spin; they eat three times a day, mush and molasses for supper, cocoa sweetened with molasses, with bread, for breakfast, beef shins, made into soup, thickened with beans or rice, for dinner, and once a week they have a pork dinner, and always plenty of potatoes; some instances of industry are rewarded by a pint of beer. Good behaviour generally shortens the term of confinement; the young and the old, who are illiterate, are carefully instructed. The prison is warmed by stoves; they have pumps and fire-engines in the yard.

No convict, sentenced for a less term than three years, can be put in this prison : when a convict arrives, he is stripped, washed clean, and dressed in new clothes, and after taking a description of his person, which is entered in the prison-book, he is put to work. In the summer, they work from 6 o'clock A. M. till 6 P. M.: on beat of drum, at 9 o'clock, in the summer, and 8 in the winter, they retire to their beds, which are neat and comfortable. There were 500 in when I called; amongst these were very few women; many of them were fine looking men, one of them in particular, (as I was leaning over the loom to examine his work,) in reply to an observation I dropped, that people of their inoffensive looks should be guilty of crimes, "ah," said he, "many of the people you see here are put in for very little."— A sentinel parades on the wall during the day with fixed bayonet, but at night fifty men stand guard. Many instances occur of the same person being put in the second, third, fourth, and even the fifth time! a number are put in for life; the crimes which subject a convict for life, are, rape, robbery, burglary, sodomy, maiming, house-breaking, forging proof of deeds, or public securities, and counterfeiting gold or silver. Until very lately they received no compensation for their labor! The supreme judges and the attorney general of the state, regulate the laws of the institution, which, with all deference to them, are very rigid. A physician and surgeon reside in the prison, and others visit there daily from the city, none of which receive compensation.

Alms-House.—The alms house is a plain stone building, with a cupola, situated on the bank of East river, two miles from the city hall; it is the largest building in the city, being 320 feet long and 50 feet wide. Including the penitentiary, work-house, and other buildings connected with this institution, the expense was 418,791 dollars. As many as 1,487 paupers were in the alms-house at one time; there were upwards of 600 when I visited it, a great number of whom were children. The alms-house is well regulated, and no gentleman's parlour looks neater, the floor being scrubbed with sand daily. The paupers looked plump and hearty, and were comfortably clothed; most of their beds were of feathers. I conversed with several of them (not in the presence of the keeper,) on the subject of their treatment; they eager-

ly replied that they never lived better, nor had a wish
ungratified. I saw an exception in the cruelty of an
Irish woman toward some of the children. The managers are highly censurable for placing these Irish women over the children—I would as soon put them under
the care of a tiger. I am the more surprised at this, as
these savages are sometimes brought before the police for
their cruelty to their own children. My feelings have
been torn to pieces since my visit to the Atlantic states,
by the cries of children under the lash of these Irish
hyenas. But to return : This establishment might be
improved. by removing the children to a separate asylum. There are too many children in one house, even
were there no grown persons. I do not know whether
any one has made the remark which I have, viz. that a
great number of living beings, whether of the human
species or the brute creation, will not be healthy for any
length of time, when crowded together.

Work-House.—The work-house stands in rear of the
alms-house, and is used for the employment of the poor.
It is built of brick, 200 feet by 25 ; it contains a hospital for males, and one for females.

Penitentiary.—The penitentiary, likewise, stands in
the rear of the alms-house ; it is a stone building, 150
feet long, and 50 in width. In this prison, all convicts
are confined, whose sentence to be imprisoned falls under the degree which subjects to confinement in the
state prison, and those only can be confined in the penitentiary whose offences have been committed within the
city or county of New-York. The average number of
convicts in the penitentiary, is 250 ; these are kept at
work. The whole of those buildings are enclosed, together with six acres of ground, with a wall of 7 feet
high ; on the outside is a school for the poor children,
called a free school : also a garden, where those of the
paupers who are able, cultivate culinary plants. A
physician, surgeon, and apothecary reside in the alms-
house, and attend to the sick of the whole establishment ; for which they receive a salary ; it has, also, a
visiting physician, and surgeon, whose attention is honorary ; they receive no compensation.

Bridewell and the Jail.—Bridewell and the jail are in the park, near the city hall; and two black, dismal looking edifices they are; one stands at one end of the hall, and the other at the other end : they are both built of stone, and painted black. Bridewell is a small building; in-it are confined all those who are committed for trial, also those under sentence of death ; likewise the higher class of convicts : besides these, are a number of poor, constantly in bridewell, who are picked up daily by the watch and constables in the streets, and put in here until they can be sent to the alms-house ; I saw about 15 of these, whom the keeper told me were brought in that morning! It appears to be the pride of New-York, to have no poor seen in the streets. It contains a hospital, which is regularly attended by a physician, who also attends the jail. Although the sessions are held monthly, they cannot empty bridewell : 170 prisoners are arraigned on an average, and often 200 tried. I found about 200 in this abode of wretchedness, white and black, male and female, about one half of whom were females. The males presented nothing in their appearance different from their equals in the streets ; indeed, I was struck with the innocence and modesty of their looks and behaviour : pointing to one of them, I asked the keeper " if it were possible that one of his interesting appearance, could be guilty of a crime ?" his reply was, that he was charged with forgery. But the tender sex, I am sorry for them ; in all matters where they and misfortune are concerned, nothing affects our nature so forcibly. To see a friendless female in a gloomy prison, locked in with massy iron doors and grated windows, the mind that can think, and the heart that can feel, must be shocked at the sight, however just it may be, and however necessary for the good of society. But never did I, till now, feel that degree of compassion for the sex, which the sight of those females called up. Here was a lamentable proof of depravity, of which I thought human nature incapable! There were about forty females in bridewell, for crimes, no doubt, and in the whole of them there is not more prudence, virtue, or modesty, than one ought to possess. They were the most abandoned, vicious, impudent; they were audacity itself, without one particle of aught besides. Alas! once more for human nature—alas! for frail woman. Lost to the blush of shame, no compunction, not one trace of contrition ventures to oppose that double headed monster, vice. They laughed, they romped, they gigled, and saluted me with the familiarity of an old acquaintance! asked " if I came to keep them company?" I would have suffered the guillotine first. And is this woman? I asked, mentally; can lovely, generous, heaven-inspiring woman, become such a callous, I was going to say brute, but I will not insult the brute creation by the comparison. And this is the effect of great cities! But what a poor piece of the creation is woman! man, when he comes finally to take leave of virtue, he pauses, he hesitates, he proceeds by degrees; but woman makes one plunge, and is gone forever. Here is an instance before me; some of these females are quite young, not more than fourteen or fifteen years of age. But what most astonishes me is, that vice should be able so completely to erase the loves and the graces from the female countenance, and change them into perfect demons, while the same vices have not the same effect on man. Here are men who are said to be guilty of the blackest crimes, even murder, and yet they have some traces of grace left.

The Jail.—None but debtors are confined in the jail, but it was at this time vacant!

Museum.—The collection in the museum of New-York, is nearly similar to that of Philadelphia, so far as it goes; in some things it exceeds it, in others falls short of it. The birds I think are better preserved, and in a neater condition. They have a huge white Greenland bear; but I saw no portraits. I am told it belongs to a Mr. S——, whom I had not the honour to see; but with deference to him, he is as far behind Mr. P. in his catalogue, as he is in his title to patronage. I called one day and paid my entrance, but not being sufficiently at leisure then, I returned next day to examine the collection at my leisure; when the fellow whom he employs to keep it, demanded another quarter; I paid it, however, without endeavouring to convince him that the visit would perhaps, be as much for his interest as mine. It is kept in the " New-York Institution," a large building of brick, 260 feet by 44, three stories; it stands in the rear of the city hall, in the park, facing Chamber-street. Besides the museum, it contains halls for the literary and philosophical society, historical society, the academy of fine arts, the lyceum of natural history, the asylum for the deaf and dumb, and a dispensary. The literary and philosophical society consists of gentlemen of the first learning and talents, under a president, 3 vice presidents, 12 counsellors, 2 recording secretaries, 2 corresponding secretaries, a treasurer, and curator : the funds are limited to $5,000 per annum. They are divided into four classes, viz.—1st. Belles-lettres, civil history, antiquities, moral and political science—2d. Medicine, chemistry, natural philosophy, and natural history—3d. Mathematics, astronomy, navigation, and geography—4th. Husbandry, manufactures, and the useful arts. They meet monthly, when all communications are referred to the counsellors. Gentlemen of all countries are admitted as members. The historical society is divided into two branches, the civil branch, and the natural branch. It consists of a society of literary gentlemen, under a president, secretary, committee, and special committee. The object of the first, is to collect books, MSS., medals, maps, prints, paintings, pamphlets, gazettes, busts, coins, and every thing calculated to illustrate the civil history of the United States. The natural branch devote their talents to the study and investigation of zoology, geology, botany, mineralogy, and vegetable physiology ; procuring specimens and illustrations on these subjects, from every part of the world, the whole constituting a complete school of nature. It is richly endowed by the state, and the collection already acquired, amounts to $40,000.

The Academy of Fine Arts was founded by chancellor Livingston. It contains a great number of rare specimens in printing, statues, busts, bass-reliefs, and books, which last consists of views, designs, and drawings, chiefly relating to antique subjects, amongst which, are

22

24 superb volumes, presented to the academy by Napoleon Bonaparte. The academicians and associates must be artists by profession; the former must be 24 years of age, and within one year after his election every academician must deposit a specimen of his talents in the academy, to become its property, otherwise he forfeits his election. Associates must be 21 years of age.

The Lyceum of Natural History is a society formed for the express purpose of cultivating natural history, their researches extending to the whole terraqueous globe; they have already made considerable advances in this laudable undertaking, having travelling committees out, who are men of enterprise and talents, in pursuit of the various productions of nature.

The Asylum for the Deaf and Dumb.—This institution resembles that of Philadelphia, the pupils mostly being instructed gratuitously as well as fed and clothed. They learn in the same way, but their number is small compared with that of Philadelphia, the funds not being sufficient to extend the design to any magnitude; the funds are limited by charter to $5,000 per annum. It is supported partly by the state and partly by private contribution; several of the pupils exhibited before me with surprising facility; their teacher making known to them my name, business, and place of residence, they, in an instant of time, wrote it in a fair hand, upon their slates, and even pointed out the state on the map. Mr. Loofborrow, the principal, is a gentleman of education, and seems to possess an amiable disposition, of mild and conciliating manners, combining every requisite for his arduous employment. He is assisted by Miss Stansbury, a lady from Philadelphia, who appears to possess all the sweetness and meek-eyed charity of her native city. Two of the deaf and dumb mutes are likewise assistants. The pupils are fond of their teachers, even to adoration. Mr. L. favored me with a number of their specimens in composition, of which, I have only room for the following :—
" When I was a little boy in ignorance, the world and all things that are created, were unknown to me. I observed the numerous beautiful stars, and thought they were placed in the heaven by a great man to adorn it,

and were like the candle. I believed the fire of the sun moved around the plain earth, which was fixed. I supposed men might be inside of the sky, in which there was a large circular iron wall and very thick door; I thought many inhabitants were cruel who belonged to it. When I looked at the moon, I saw a resemblance of a man's face, and imagined that he was watching the world. I did not wish him to see me; I was afraid of him, for I expected to be caught suddenly through the moon to burn me. How foolish I was because of my imagination! but I have been taught in school, now I know the Lord God has created the earth and stars, which are planets.   JOHN H. GAZLAY."

Free Schools and Academies.—It would require the constitution of Sampson, to visit all the public institutions of New York, and to do justice to them is impossible in a book of this size. The liberality of this state towards the encouragement of schools, stands pre-eminent. The funds for supporting free schools throughout the state, consists " of the proceeds of half a million acres of land! of all surplus monies received into the treasury, from the several clerks of the supreme court for the fees, perquisites, and emoluments of their respective offices, and of certain sums of money directed to be paid into the treasury, by the bank of America, and the City Bank, which, in one year alone produced half a million of dollars, giving a revenue of $36,000!"—" These sums have given rise to a vast number of free schools in the state; six of these are in New-York city, all of which I visited. One of these is at the alms-house, the others are in different parts of the city. The whole of them are conducted upon the Lancasterian plan, that is, a monitor attending each desk; it being understood that those school rooms are much longer than wide. The teacher sits upon an elevated seat, at one end of the room, from whence he can see the whole at a glance, the pupils facing him : these sit on long benches, one behind another, gradually ascending to the last, from the teacher, which is the highest. Each row of benches has a desk before it the whole length, upon which the pupils have their sand, books, and slates. The juniors, that is

those learning their letters, have sand; the monitor
takes hold of the fore finger of the pupil, and guides it in
forming the letter.   After a few lessons in this manner,
the pupil, by the aid of a machine which contains the
letters of the alphabet in large print, proceeds alone by
keeping his eye on the letter before him.   When they
are perfect in the alphabet, they are removed to the
next desk, where they have words of two letters; these
are pasted on boards which hang before the pupil : when
he is perfect in this, he is removed to the next desk, and
so on.   When they read or spell, they rise from their
desks and stand within a circle marked on the floor, each
class under its respective monitor, whose business it is
to correct them ; the teacher and his assistants walking
through the lines during the time.   The female children
of each school are under an assistant female teacher, in
a separate room ; besides reading, writing, geography,
grammar, and arithmetic, the females are taught needle-
work.

These schools are by far the most interesting objects to
a stranger in the city ; to see such a vast number of children, from four to eight hundred in one house, governed
by a word, a nod, or even a glance of their teacher, is
truly astonishing.   The best disciplined army is not
more regular or obedient ; at a signal they are hushed
as death ; at another they proceed in their lessons, with
that instantaneous order and alacrity which wants a
name.   Mechanics, and any who choose, have the liberty
of sending to these schools gratis !   They are open
to all classes of citizens.   The teachers are gentlemen
of talents, temper, and ability, whose system and labors
reflect the highest honor upon those by whom they were
appointed,   I spent many hours daily in these schools,
which were the most pleasing to me of any I spent in the
city.

I only visited three of the academies, viz : Union Hall,
and La Fayette academy, and one kept by Miss Orem.
They were likewise crowded with children, youths and
young ladies ; and in which every branch of literature
is taught.   The pupils in each are regularly classed
under their respective tutors, who, with the principals,

appear well qualified for the trust, as the progress and proficiency of the pupils in their various branches, pre-eminently prove and entitle them to the highest applause.

New-York High School.—The New-York High School is quite a recent institution, similar to the high school of Edinburgh ; being designed for the education of gentle-men's sons, who pay for their tuition. It is formed upon the monitorial plan, under a president, vice president, and twenty-four trustees ; these again, are under a socie-ty of the first gentlemen in the city, who have the su-preme control. In this school, the classics, as well as the rudiments of education are taught. Lectures on chemistry, history, and natural philosophy, are deliv-ered. The pupil is fitted for college in this school, or may complete his education here, at the option of the parent. The High School is divided into three classes in distinct departments, viz : Introductory, Junior, and Senior classes. The first pay $3, the second $5, and the third $7 per session. The capital stock for supporting the school is $30,000. Six hundred and fifty pupils were present when I visited the school ; four hundred of these were very small, called the introductory class, all in one room ; the handsomest children, as to beauty and stature, I ever beheld. Indeed, all the children of those schools are the very picture of health. To return, corporal punishment is strictly forbidden except in ex-treme cases. Another rule is, that " the exercise of each department commences with reading a chapter in the Bible ; but no catechism, or instruction in the tenets of any religious denomination shall be introduced, or used in the school." This rule is rigidly enforced.

The Fire Department.—The Fire Company is at once, the most respectable and useful society in the city ; but I can only afford a brief remark on this establishment. The Fire Department is " a Body Corporate and Pol-itic," consisting of Fire Companies in every Ward, un-der the control of one *chief* Engineer.

Engineers and Fire Wardens.—The common council carry a wand, with a gilded flame at the top. The en-gineers wear a leathern cap, painted white, with a gild-ed front, and a fire engine blazoned thereon, and carry a

21*

speaking trumpet, painted black, with the words " engine, No. 1," (or as the case may be,) in white, painted on their caps. The fire wardens wear a hat, the brim black, and the crown white, with the city arms blazoned on the front, and carry speaking trumpets, painted white, with the word " warden," in black: the firemen also have badges. When a building takes fire in the night, the watchmen cry " Fire," the bells are set to ringing; the companies attend as above described, with all possible dispatch, with their engines, which are pulled by the firemen running at full speed; the constables and marshals of the city attend with their staves of office, and obey the corporation under the penalty of a heavy fine. Every man, even the mayor of the city are under the control of the fire corporation, during a fire. They use no buckets, or at least rarely, the rivers being so near, and their hose* extending from one engine to another, and finally to the river, it is conveyed through them to the fire. The engineers, chief engineers, and fire wardens only direct; they are constantly running to and fro, directing the firemen. The firemen when they are fixed each in his station, stand still and play the engine; their superiors speaking to them through the trumpets, calling to each engine, to " play away No. 2, No. 3," or whatever it may be; for the noise and crackling of the fire, and that of the multitude which gather, would effectually drown their voice. None but the fire companies join in extinguishing fires; the citizens which gather in crowds, are kept at a distance by the city officers. The engines are the most superb piece of mechanism in the city, most of them being richly gilded, and the fire companies consist wholly of reputable men. The membership is deemed one of honour, but it is one dearly bought; the smoke from the fires, as near as they are obliged to approach, would strangle any one else. Very little damage has accrued from fire, since the department has been organized upon its present plan.

The Gas Company, Manhattan Company, and New-York Dying and Printing Establishment, are not only

---

* A leathern pipe, from four to five inches in circumference, of great length.

respectable, but important companies to the city. The
first supplies it with light, and the second with water ;
each are incorporated ; the Gas Company with $100,-
000, and the Manhattan with a capital of $2,050,000.
The New-York Dying and Printing, with a capital of
$200,000. This grand establishment is in William-
street, where all kinds of dying and printing is done in a
superior style. The printing on silks, cotton, and woollen is astonishing, particularly to back woods people ;
the brilliancy of tint, and delicacy of shade, is not exceeded by any in Europe. Old faded silks and satins
are restored to their original beauty. But I must stop.

Markets.—The Markets, taking the whole together,
would, perhaps, exceed that of Philadelphia in abundance and variety, but it is greatly behind it in neatness
and order ; there are no stalls for vegetables ; these are
found promiscuously scattered about near the market
houses. The Fulton Market is said to equal any in the
world for abundance, variety, and quality ; no article
formed by art, or produced by nature, but may be purchased in Fulton Market ; and yet it would hardly make
one square of Philadelphia market-house. Consequently it is over-crowded.

Manners and Appearance.—It is difficult for a stranger to decide upon the manners and appearance of any
city or town, for this reason, at least one half of the people he meets in the streets and public places, are strangers. These are from the country, from other towns,
other states, or as it may happen ; this is what makes a
city. To build a number of houses and fill them with
people and merchandize goes but half way towards forming a city. The system of cities, the motives to their
existence, is to furnish the surrounding countries with
such articles as they need, receiving their produce in
exchance. The advantage which New-York has over
almost any other city, attracts a vast number of strangers presenting a multifarious mixture, in which no likeness can be traced. The native citizens of New-York
are about the middling size, more stout than those of
Philadelphia, differing little in complexion, a slight
shade darker ; black hair and a full black eye are pe-

culiar characteristics ; they lay no claims to taste or refinement ; their attention to business, which pours in upon them like a flood, leaves them no time to cultivate the
graces.   They have, however, a sort of untaught nobility in their countenance, and all their movements. They
are mild, courteous, and benevolent ; and above all
people they have the least pride.   That curse of the human family, if it exists at all in New-York, is found
amongst the lower order of her citizens ; it is banished
the houses of the great and the opulent : their manners
are truly republican; no eclat, hauteur, or repelling
stiffness ; much of which exists in Philadelphia, and the
boasted hospitality of the more southern towns.   These
are hospitable, it is true, but the poor man is made to
feel the difference between him and his hospitable en-
tertainer.   Not so, New-York, as respects that sort of
homage exacted from a fellow man ; all are upon a level.
    Owing no doubt, to the unparalleled increase of com-
merce, too little attention, too little time, has been
left for improvement in literature.   Yet this great people, fertile in resources, decisive in action, liberal and
unanimous, can do much in a short time; doubtless a
people so renowned for devotion to the public good, will
not neglect a matter of so much importance.   I perceive
there is a great want of grammar schools amongst
them.   But although New-York is censured for her neglect of education, yet she is not destitute of genius. She
can boast of her Clintons, her Livingstons, her Mur-
rays,* her Irvings, her Hamiltons, her Pauldings, her
Mitchills, her Hosacks, her Coopers, her Sedgwicks, and
a long string of poets.
    The ladies of New-York, like the gentlemen, are affa-
ble, modest, and domestic ; the better sort are easy in
their manners, plain in their equippage and dress, and are
seldom seen in the streets.   Upon inquiry whether those
ladies who are daily on parade, in Broadway, were of
the first distinction, I was told they were not, and that
the first ladies, from motives of delicacy, were never seen
in the streets on foot, that they always took a carriage

* Lindley Murray was born on Long Island; so also was Dr. S. L.
Mitchell.

be the distance ever so small. Every one, however, can not afford a carriage, and though I never inquired into the cause of this concourse of females in Broadway, it is natural to suppose, from the population, that exercise or indispensable business forces them abroad. I must suppose this, for I never saw more industry, or more general application to business of every description, than in this city. Turn which way you will, mechanics, carvers, carpenters, bricklayers, ship-carpenters, cartmen, all is one continual bustle, from morning till ten o'clock at night. I have known young ladies, (those who have no dependence but their industry,) since I have been in the city, sit up till twelve o'clock at night, to complete a suit of clothes, the proceeds of which was to purchase a fine cap, or a plume of feathers, to deck herself for church. Hundreds of those females thus maintain themselves in a style of splendor; no ladies in the city dress finer, a ten dollar hat, a thirty dollar shawl, with silk and lace, is common amongst the poorer class of females. This keeps them employed; industry promotes virtue, and virtue promotes happiness. No wonder New-York outstrips all her rivals! Her Clinton at her head, her Hudson and canals at her back, the Atlantic before her, covered with the wealth of nations, her citizens industrious, generous and enterprising, her whole system elevated and grand, she must succeed. Whilst others are debating the question of right and wrong, New-York is acting. Meantime, her hospitality holds out a hearty welcome alike to the oppressed,* and to the opulent. This is not only the effect of good policy, but good feeling and good nature.

History.—The various efforts of Europe to discover a north-west passage to India, led to the discovery of the place where New York city now stands. Henry Hudson, an experienced seaman, and an Englishman by birth, having made two unsuccessful attempts at this discovery, quit the service of England, and went over to Holland, where he was well received by the Dutch East-India Company, who took him into their service. Nothing is known of the birth, education, or early history of Hudson.

* In no city in the world, does the distressed stranger meet with that relief and kindness which he does in New-York.

He set sail from Amsterdam, on the 25th of March, 1609, in the Half-moon, which was navigated by twenty Dutchmen; his object still being that of finding a passage to India. After coasting backwards and forwards, in different directions, he came to anchor in a fine harbor, in latitude 40 deg. 30 min.—the present Sandy-Hook, on the 4th of September. On the 6th, he sent a boat to survey what appeared to be the mouth of a river. This is the strait between Long-Island and Staten-Island. Here was fine depth of water; within was a large opening, and a narrow river on the west; the channel between Bergen-neck and Staten-Island.* As the boat was returning, it was attacked by some of the Natives, in two canoes. One man (John Coleman) was killed: he was buried on a point of land, which has since been called Coleman's point. On the 11th they sailed through the narrows, and found a good harbor, secure from winds.

The next day they turned against a north-west wind, into the mouth of a river, which now bears the name of Hudson, and came to anchor two leagues within it.—Here they spent two days: during these two days, says the author, we were visited by the Indians, who brought us Indian corn, beans, and other vegetables. They then sailed up the river as high as where Albany now stands.

Hudson then returned to Holland, and making a favorable report of the country, the Dutch sent over a company in 1610, for the purpose of trading with the natives. In 1614, the States General having granted a patent to sundry merchants, for an exclusive trade on the Hudson river, they built a fort to protect the company from the natives on the west side of the river, where Albany now stands. The command of this fort was given to Henry Cristiæns, who was the first permanent settler, not only of Albany, but of the state of New-York. The fort was called Fort Orange. They also built a church. About the same time, a trading-house was established on the south-west point of Manhattan-island, where New-York city now stands, and called New-Amsterdam: the whole colony was called New-Netherlands—the aborigines were called Manhattoes.

* Belknap.

Amongst the first settlers of this colony, were the Tenbroeks, Beekmans, Van Rensselaers, Carterrets, Livingstons, Delancys; all of whose descendants distinguished themselves in the revolution, either as patriots or loyalists. Those gentlemen bore the marks of respectability about them, such as family plate, family portraits, &c. The first man, however, who settled the spot where the city now stands, was *Van Twiller.* The colony built a fort where the battery now is, whence it took its name. About this time the Hudson river was settled with numerous and powerful Indians, consisting of wandering families, but the Dutch purchased the land of them for a trifle, (so says the historian,) being unable to cope with them in the field. The renowned Five Nations lived on the Mohawk; they were an ingenious people, and cultivated maize and beans.

In a few years the tranquility of the colony was disturbed by the English of Massachusetts Bay, who laid claim to the colony, and finally the disputes between them and the Dutch assumed a serious appearance. The new and old England combining, the New-Netherlands were invaded by an armed force, and threatened with an attack if they did not immediately surrender. The Dutch therefore capitulated, and upon very favourable terms; every thing was to remain as it was, only they acknowledging the British sovereignty. Fort Amsterdam (where the battery now is) and Fort Orange were delivered up to the British; the first took the name of " New-York," after the Duke of York, and the latter that of " Albany," another of his titles.* This change of masters took place in 1664, old style. Albany, before this, was called " Oranienburgh," (rather a hard name.) At this time, New-York consisted of several small streets, which had been laid out in 1656, and was not inconsiderable for the number of houses. To this day the Dutch hate the British, and are the truest whigs I have met with yet, the Tennesseeans not excepted.

Richard Nichols, a man of great prudence and moderation, now took the government upon himself, under the

* Smith's History of New-York.

style of "Deputy-governor, under his royal highness the
Duke of York, of all his territories in America." The
first object of Gov. Nichols's attention, was the gradual
introduction of the English language; and in 1665, on
the 12th day of June, he incorporated the inhabitants of
New-York under the care of a mayor, five aldermen, and
a sheriff. Till this time, the city of New-York was governed by *scout, burgo-masters and chepens.*

When Smith wrote his history of New-York, the city
(he says) contained about 2,500 buildings, was a mile in
length, and half a mile in breadth. How many inhabitants the city contained at that period, Smith does not
say; but the population of the whole colony, consisting
of ten counties, (including the city,) only amounted to
100,000. These were assessed at £10,000,000, and
taxed at £45,000. The city of New York alone at this
time greatly exceeds this number. The small state of
Connecticut, at the time just referred to, contained 133,000
inhabitants. This great increase of New-York, is to be
ascribed not only to its natural advantages, which exceed
all calculation, but to the character of its citizens.

Literary Men.—It is well known that New-York has
produced her share of literary men; my business, however, is simply to notice those who are at present esteemed men of letters. Of these perhaps Washington
Irving is the first—next, Paulding, Cooper, Dr. Mitchill,
and Dr. Hosack; of these, Paulding has ever been my
favourite. Very little time, therefore, was lost, after my
arrival in the city, before I paid my respects to this celebrated man. If I admired him as a writer, I was charmed with his appearance and manners, which perfectly
correspond with the idea we are led to form of him from
his writings. Mr. P. is in height about five feet ten inches, his figure is light, and he moves with ease and
grace, being spare, but well formed. His complexion is
dark, his hair the deepest black, his eyes what is usually
termed black, of the middling shade, and uncommonly
brilliant. His face is oval, his features delicate, but regular, and what may be called handsome; his raven
locks fall over his neck and forehead in ringlets of ineffable
beauty. His countenance comprises all that can be con-

ceived of benignity and diffidence, a little dashed with
the facetious. His language is simple, his voice soft and
harmonious. In his manners he is frank, generous, and
gentle as the dove. He is a man of quick discernment,
and is said to be humane to a fault. Mr. P. lives in
princely style, and his house is the abode of hospitality.
He is said to appertain to the same family of the high-
minded soldier of that name, who captured Major Andre.
He appears to be upwards of 40 years of age.

Dr. S. L. Mitchill, the distinguished philosopher, is
celebrated throughout the world, as a man of great natural and acquired abilities. His mind enriched with science and experimental philosophy, he is at the head of
every literary and scientific institution in New-York, as
well as honorary member of many in other countries.—
Dr. M. appears to be somewhere about sixty years of
age, about the common height, a good figure, and heavy
make; his complexion is fair and ruddy, his face oval,
with a high forehead, and small blue eye, which is almost
closed when he laughs or smiles. His hair is white, but
whether from age or not, I could not distinguish; but his
countenance, for benevolence and good nature, is unequalled. I should take him to be one of the best tem-
pered men in the world, and no man's temper, perhaps,
is put to a greater trial; his house is constantly filled
with strangers who honour him with calls; it is a perfect
levee, each taking his turn to be admitted. In his manners he is familiar and condescending, without any parade
of learning. In short, he is one of the most agreeable
and pleasant men I ever met; his conversation is marked with that unconscious simplicity common to children.
He has a little daughter, about four years of age, already
treading in the steps of her father; she had a number of
fossils and shells ranged before her, and seemed eagerly
engaged in the study of natural philosphy; he has one
more daughter, and no son.

Dr. Hosack is quite a young man, compared with Dr.
M. He is in the prime of life, a gentleman of immense
wealth, and one of the greatest botanists of the age; to
his labour and indefatigable industry may be ascribed the
success of that study in New-York. He is also a man of
23

general science, and devotes much of his time, talents
and fortune, for the advancement of knowledge. He is,
besides, a member of many of the most respectable institutions of the state.   Dr. H. is of the common height,
and portly size; his complexion is dark, his hair and
eyes of the deepest black; his face is oval, with a high
retreating forehead, of the finest polish. His countenance is open, manly and dignified, with an eye of the
deepest penetration. In his manners he is affable and
engaging, and as a scholar, a physician, and a gentleman,
he ranks amongst the first of great men.

I have little to say of Mr. Cooper, having formed no
acquaintance with him.   I never saw him but once, which
happened in a bookstore, where he was sitting reading a
newspaper, from which he never took his eyes, whilst I
remained in the store.   As he sat, he appeared to be a
man of good size, about 30 years of age, fair complexion, and full oval face; his features are neither handsome nor the contrary, with a morose countenance. It
is, however, impossible to delineate countenance without seeing the eye, which his authorship never deigned
to lift on me. He notwithstanding had something genteel in his appearance.   The author of the Pioneers, &c.
would neither gain nor lose by any thing I could possibly say of him—his fame having placed him far beyond
the range of my strictures.

Miss Sedgwick, also a native of New-York, is an authoress of some reputation ; she is the author of New-
England Tales, and Redwood. I had the pleasure of
seeing her once, but formed no acquaintance. She is
about 30 years of age, of good stature and fine figure ;
she is of spare make, with an oval face and thin visage ;
her complexion wan, with a gray eye, her features well
proportioned, her countenance rather austere.

Besides these, there are a number of literary gentlemen and ladies, and no small share of poets in New-
York. Mr. Carter, editor of the Statesman. is said to
be a handsome writer.   Mr. Woodworth, the poet, is
well known ; he is an amiable man, struggling hard
with poverty and a large family.—It is abominable in us
to neglect the genius of our country as we do. Mrs.

Weare likewise deserves to be noticed as a poetess, tho'
she does not wish to be known as such; yet she has written several pieces of the finest poetry.

New-York seems to have burst the chains of ignorance, and promises a rich harvest of literary honours.
Many young men of promising appearance have taken
up the pen. Several of these were pointed out to me,
amongst whom I was particularly struck by the editor of
the New-York Mirror, Mr. Morris, a young man of no
ordinary endowments, of pleasing manners and disinterested generosity. Mr. M. will pardon this public homage to virtues which deserve the patronage of every
generous and enlightened mind.

Fortifications.—The city of New-York is strongly
fortified, being defended by twelve well mounted forts,
including the one at Sandy-Hook, 27 miles below the
city.

Amusements.—I have already devoted so many pages
to New-York, that it would be doing injustice to other
places, to dwell longer upon it. The principal amusement of the citizens is the Theatre; in winter, that and
sleighing constitute the sum. In summer, the gardens,
the circus, the park, and the battery, draw vast crowds
together. These gardens are neatly fitted up, with accommodations, booths and boxes, and tables are spread
with every delicacy of refreshment. The gardens are
brilliantly illuminated with fire works, to which we may
add the finest music, while the citizens regale themselves
with ice-creams, wine, fruit, and confectionaries. The
park is quite too small to afford much amusement, and
much too warm in summer. But the battery is the pride
of New-York; it is a large green lawn, handsomely paled
in, and planted with trees. It lies on the point of the
island, and commands a view of the bay, the shipping,
adjacent islands, the numerous fortifications, and the Jersey shore. It is refreshed by the breezes from the sea,
and would be the most delightful spot on earth, on a sultry day, if it was provided with seats.

The first regular play I ever saw performed, was in
New-York, at the Chatham Garden Theatre; the play
was " the Saw-Mill, or Yankee Trick," a native produc-

tion. Mr. Barraree, the proprietor, deserves much credit for his liberality in patronising the genius of his adopted country. He is a Frenchman by birth, and a gentleman of an amiable disposition, and great generosity of
heart. Mr. Price, proprietor of the Park Theatre, is an
Englishman; but since the Baltimore affair, I am shy of
the English. I am told, however, he is a morose man in
his manners, and rejects all American plays. In this he
acts perfectly right; a people who have no more national pride, ought to be treated with this sort of contempt.
Mr. Simpson, his manager, is a man of very genteel manners. A new theatre is in agitation, which is to excel
any thing in London.

A word on the *dialect* of the New-Yorkers. A few
words are peculiar to them, such as *stoop*, by which they
mean a platform, or piazza, before a door; and *how*, a
substitute for sir, or madam, when they do not hear distinctly—you hear nothing but " how, how," all over the
city. They have a few more words, in common with the
low yankees, for instance, the *guess*, and the *be*—" be
you going," &c.

The Water of New-York is very unpleasant to a stranger, though it abounds in every part of the city. The
corporation are adopting measures to supply the city with
good water, which will be attended with an immense expense; but after what they have done, we may suppose
they will not be discouraged at any thing.

The Houses are principally of brick, covered with tile
and slate, three, and many of them four stories high.—
Those in Broadway are large and splendid, several of
them having marble fronts. There are but few wooden
houses in the city, and the fire is thinning them every
day. A law of the corporation prohibits the erection of
wooden houses in the city.

Trinity and St. Paul's churches are vast buildings of
stone, and have lofty steeples, the latter 234 feet high—
they are both situated in Broadway, and are seen several
miles distant. In 1818, the remains of Gen. Montgomery, who fell in the attack on Quebec, in 1775, was conveyed from thence and deposited in St. Paul's church,
with great pomp and solemnity.

In 1820, the city contained 123,706 inhabitants, and it has greatly increased since. The revenue of the customs will be found at the end of the volume.

New-York was once the asylum of a respectable body of French Huganots ; they built a church in Cedar-street, and aided greatly in improving the society : some of the first families in the city are descended from them, of whom the Governeur family is one. About one third of the citizens are yankees, and their descendants.

Brooklyn.—Brooklyn lies S. E. of New-York, on Long-Island, and only separated from it by East river, which is three quarters of a mile wide, and deep enough for the largest ships. Brooklyn, though called a village, has 8,475 inhabitants, 6 churches, and a bank. The town is upwards of a mile square.

The United States have a navy-yard at Brooklyn, at the head of which I found the hero of Lake Ontario, Commodore Chauncey, one of the finest looking men I have seen ; and quite a young looking man to have commanded at the lake. He is a man of good size, and engaging manners. The navy-yard comprises 40 acres of ground, encompassed with a wall, and strictly guarded. It is, moreover well stored with death-dealing weapons, (to use one of Knickerbocker's expressions,) " breathing gunpowder, and defiance to the world!" Here I saw the celebrated steam frigate, a huge machine, but is only used to muster and discipline the marines for the service of the navy. The deck is remarkable for being the largest in the known world!

The first settlers of Brooklyn, were a family by the name of Remsens, who came from Holland ; the first house built in it is still standing. I find no date of its history ; it is said to be older than the city of N. York. This place was originally inhabited by the Canarsee Indians, who were subject to the Mohawks. Brooklyn is increasing rapidly ; 143 dwelling houses were erected the last year! It is also inhabited by wealthy and fashionable people. Gen. Swift, one of the most accomplished gentlemen I have met with in my travels, has his residence in Brooklyn ; though he, as well as Com. Chaun-

cey, are natives of Massachusetts. Through the politeness of Mr. J. Sands, I received much interesting information on the subject of the revolution, for which I la-
ment I have not room.

Journey to Albany.—After spending better than two
months in New-York, I took the advantage of a tolerable snow, of sleighing to Albany. The Hudson river,
which affords a speedy and delightful conveyance to that
city, was at this time fast locked up with ice; we, therefore, took the stage body from the wheels, and placing it
upon a sleigh, took our departure at three o'clock, one
clear cold morning. This was the first time I ever rode
in a sleigh; it is very pleasant where the road is smooth,
but this in many instances was not the case. Although
I was unable, from the darkness within the carriage, to
obtain a glimpse of my fellow passengers, yet by the aid
of the moon, I caught a flying view of the barracks,
erected at Flatbush, for our soldiers in the late war. A
number of them are standing, though in a state of decay,
and many have fallen quite down.

In a few hours, day-light disclosed the surrounding
country, and the faces of my fellow travellers, in which
I found nothing very interesting; seven gentlemen and
two females—I made the tenth passenger. The females
appeared to be rather under par, as did some of the other sex; but we were soon rid of the fair ones, the driver
sitting them down about mid day, by the way. I dislike
travelling with ladies in a carriage, they keep such a
chattering, and forsooth must be shut up so close, that
one cannot enjoy either the conversation or the appearance of the country. One gentleman belonged to the
town of Hudson, two were of Albany, one, with a boy, belonged to Troy, an Irishman, and a Virginian. The Albany gentleman and the one of Hudson were quite entertaining, and very politely pointed out to me the villages, with their names, as well as the numerous country
seats, and answered a variety of questions respecting the
country, and the customs of the inhabitants. Peekskill,
Cattskill, Fishkill, Hudson, and Poughkeepsie, all lie on
the Hudson river; some of them are towns of considera-

ble size, and have much trade. Hudson river is navigable for large ships to the town of Hudson.

Our road lay through that part of the country, the scenery of which is so much extolled by travellers; even at this dreary season it is not without its charms. The snow resting on the icy bosom of the sleeping Hudson, which is hardly ever out of sight, the eye, aided by the absence of vegetation, can see this noble river for several miles each way at once; it stretches itself directly north, in an unbroken line; in this it differs from all other rivers, which constitutes its superior beauty. This, added to the capricious figures of the swelling hills on the opposite shore, sometimes rounding off into domes, suddenly sinking into a curve, now running in a smooth, unbroken line, all clothed in one uniform dress of lucid white, seems to compensate the traveller for the absence of summer. A voyage on the Hudson in summer must be delightful, diversified as its borders are with hill and dale, farms, towns, and country seats, mingled with wild rocks and mountains, added to the numerous vessels, which pass up and down the river, it must be one of the greatest treats to the admirer of landscape. Of all the towns, Hudson is the handsomest: it sits on a plane on the river, while you approach it from a lofty eminence which overlooks the town; it is built of brick, which are painted deep red. The vivid tints of the houses, contrasted with the snowy plain, gave it a romantic appearance. It is 30 miles below Albany, and contains about 6000 inhabitants. We spent the night (the only one we spent on the road) at Poughkeepsie, where I found the best accommodation I have met with, during my travels! I never sat down to a better supper in any country. We had oysters, chickens, game, and fish, cooked in various ways; beef steak, veal, hash, all sorts of pies and sweetmeats, with the best tea, coffee, cream, and butter: what was my astonishment upon taking my seat at the table, to find myself joined by two persons only! The northern and southern stages both met there that night: there could not have been less than twenty travellers in the house. Some went out to the eating houses, and eat their suppers for a trifle, others had the meanness to go

out, purchase cheese and crackers, and made a meal of
it before our faces!—I was truly sorry for the landlady,
who had put herself to so much trouble ; she remarked
" that it was mostly the case with oppositions, that the
meanest people travelled in them ; but she never (she
said,) had seen them behave so mean before." If it
took the last cent I had in the world, I would not have
acted as they did ; nor did I ever see a house more worthy of patronage : my bill next morning was only 75
cents !—If people were to do so in the western country,
they would be put in the papers.

Owing to the present situation of the country, I had no
opportunity of forming an opinion of the quality of the
soil ; nor would it be material, as what I should call indifferent land, would be called good by the people of
these states. I was told that Dutchess county, through
which we passed, was the richest in land in the state.
Much of the tillable land I have seen, resembles the
meadows in Greenbriar, Va. though it is impossible to
be any thing like correct. The Livingstons have seated themselves along the banks of the Hudson, presenting
to the eye of the traveller (particularly by water,) some
of the finest specimens of taste and industry, in the elegance of their houses, and the management of their farms.

On my way to Albany, I had an opportunity of seeing many Dutch families, for the first time : what are
called Dutch where I came from, are from Germany,
and form a distinct people from the Hollanders : they
are as remarkable for sluttishness, as the Hollanders are
for neatness. This I had heard, but now I had occular
proof. Every utensil in their house, even the stoves
shine like silver ; their apparel and furniture correspond
with these in neatness. These country Dutch are mild
and simple in their manners, particularly the young females ; these have a sweetness and innocence in their
countenance which is peculiar. Both men and women
are slow in their movements ; the females are better shaped than the men ; a broad face is common in both, and
a middling complexion. When we arrived at Albany,
(at least in the neighbourhood,) we have the Hudson to
cross, it being on the opposite side from N. Y. city.

Some doubts were suggested as to the strength of the ice, and to be upon the safe side, the passengers got out of the stage, and walked over the river on the ice, leaving the Trojan and I, to sink or swim together; being a man of unwieldy size, the other passengers insisted very hard upon him to join them, lest his weight might cause the stage to break through; but no entreaty could prevail with cuffy, and finally he and the driver mutually growled at each other, during the drive over the river.

Upon gaining the western shore of the Hudson, you are in Albany. A few paces brought us to Palmer's, where a comfortable stove, a good supper, and a kind landlady, added to the thoughts of seeing one of the greatest men of the age, De Witt Clinton, together with the legislature, then sitting, consoled me for the fatigue and cold I underwent during my journey.

Albany.—Albany stands on the west side of the Hudson, 150 miles from New-York city. The compact part of the city lies on two principal streets, viz. Market and State-streets, which, in relation to Hudson river, takes the form of the capital letter T, reversed thus. ⊥. The base is Market-sreet, near the shore of the Hudson, and the perpendicular is State-street. Market-street is handsome, and two miles in length; State-street is quite short, and terminates at the capitol: it is, however, a beautiful street, as wide as any of the avenues in Washington.— These streets are crossed by others at right angles, but the main body of the town lies on these, and one which leads back from the capitol. Market-street is on a level, and runs parallel with the Hudson, but from this, the city rises up till it gains the top of a considerable eminence, upon which stands the capitol, precisely at the end of State-street. The capitol, from whatever point you view it, is strikingly handsome, being one of the finest edifices in the United States. But the view *from* the capitol, for beauty of scenery, baffles all description. You have the whole city, the Hudson, the grand canal, the basin, the villages on the opposite shore, with the gently swelling hills, peeping up behind them, the Catskill, and the distant mountains of Vermont, all under your eye at once! Between Market-street and the river, there is another street running the same way, called Dock-street; Pearl-street is also considerable, and runs the same way above. Albany, though it does much business, falls far behind New-York, in bustle and activity—not a fourth so many people in the streets—it is handsomely built, mostly of brick, and covered with slate and tile. Many of the houses, either for size or beauty, are not inferior to any in New-York, take away the marble fronts. It is the seat of government for the state of New-York, and the principal officers of the government, with the governor, reside in Albany. Its public buildings are a capitol, a state-house, a prison, an alms-house and hospital, an arsenal, 2 theatres, a museum, an academy, a city powder-house, a chamber of commerce, a lancasterian school, a library, 4 banks, Knickerbocker hall, a mechanics' hall, a Uranian hall, a post-office, and 2 market-houses: it also contains 12 places for public worship, viz. 3 Presbyterian, 1 Baptist, 1 Methodist, 1 Lutheran, 1 Apostolic, 1 Cameronian, 2 Dutch Calvinists, 1 Roman Catholic, 1 African. The capitol stands upon an elevation of 130 feet above the level of the Hudson; it is built of stone, and has a portico on the east front, facing the Hudson, of the Ionic style, *tetrastile*, adorned with stucco. The east front is 90 feet in length, the north front 115; the wall is 50 feet high; the whole is finished in a style of the first architecture; it cost $120,000. It has a large square of ground in front, which is neatly enclosed and planted with trees. The judiciary and the mayor of the city, as well as the legislature, hold their sittings in the capitol, the building being laid off into suitable halls, lobbies, and offices, The representative hall is a splendid apartment, yielding nothing to congress hall in the richness of the furniture and drapery; it is nearly the same, excepting only the size, marble columns, and the speaker's chair. Their clerks stand up at a superb desk, on the left of the speaker. The hall is heated by fire places, one on the right and the other on the left of the speaker, called north and south. When the speaker takes the chair, which he never does till after prayers, he cries with an audible voice, " the gentlemen of the north will please take their seats, those of the south will," &c.

I attended the debates toward the close of the session, and was much surprised at the facility and dispatch manifested in their proceedings, although worn out by their long session. I never saw finer looking men, as to appearance, stout, well made, and fine complexions; they appeared to be all nerve, some were far advanced in life, as their gray hairs bespoke; most of them, however, were in the prime of manhood. But my attention was attracted from them to the Hon. speaker, Clarkson Crolius, a most interesting man, modest, dignified and manly; he strove to rally his broken spirits, exhausted by his long and arduous duties—serene and unmoved amidst the tumult of an 130 members, (besides the officers of the house,) all in commotion and disorder, about to take their seats, yet each unwilling to forego the liberty of the present moment. Loath to interpose his prerogative, the speaker, in accents of the most winning sweetness, conjures them to be seated; "Gentlemen, the day is far advanced and we have much to do, take your seats, and let the house come to order." But his voice is drowned by the mingled sound of doors, foot-steps, and the hum of human voices. He strikes the desk with his mace and allures them by looks of anxious solicitude to come to order.

The senate chamber is a small apartment, though very handsomely ornamented; here I found a very thin house, not more than a dozen members present; they were men of mature age, differing little, in other respects, from the representives. I waited some time in each house, to hear a specimen or their abilities, as speakers, but was very sadly disappointed, their proceedings being confined to examining bills and matters no way interesting.

State-House.—The state-house is a large three story brick building in State-street; occupying a place in common with the other buildings near the capitol. In it the Secretary of State, the Surveyor General, the Attorney General, and other officers of the government have their offices; the records of the state are also kept in the state-house.

Prison.—The prison of Albany is in the city, upon the same elevation with the capitol, and not far from it ; a little south.   It is a brick building of great size, though not of great strength ; kept in excellent order, the rooms clean, well aired and white-washed ; it contained 18 men and six females, all of whom were criminals ; they looked cheerful and healthy and spoke in the highest terms of the keeper.   I saw but one debtor, an English gentleman, who had sacrificed his liberty out of affection for his son, on whose account he was imprisoned.   He was (to the honour of the keeper,) admitted to great indulgencies, spending most of his time in the keeper's apartment.   Both the keeper and his wife are people of exemplary humanity.

Alms-House and Hospital.—The alms-house is nearly a mile from the city, and consists of two very indifferent wooden buildings, which are crowded with paupers. They made a wretched appearance, and looked any thing than comfortable.   And as for the hospital, which is a part of the same buildings, it is a burlesque on the name.   In short, both these establishments, and the manner they are kept, are every way unworthy the capital city of the great state of New-York.   In extenuation, however, it is but justice to explain that the great number of Irish who flock to this country for the purpose of bettering their condition, when they arrive here, become the most abandoned sots.   Their fondness for ardent spirits, and the low rate at which they can obtain it, sinks them to the lowest (and far beyond it,) grade of humanity.   The victims of poverty and disease, the poor-house becomes their final retreat.   A great number of those unfortunate creatures were employed in making the grand Canal, but from their intemperance, have become reduced to pauperism, and are now a dead weight on this city !   Such was their number, and so sudden the application, that the present buildings were found inadequate.

It is much to be lamented, that those Irish who come to this land of liberty and plenty, should so shamefully abuse their privilege by turning a blessing into a curse ! The poor-houses in all these Atlantic towns affords a deplorable proof of the justness of this remark. The annual expense is $7,883 20.

Lancasterian School.—The building in which this school is kept, stands in one of the most commanding situations in the city, upon the same elevated ground with the capitol, and remarkable both for beauty and size. From 300 to 400 children are taught in this school, which is the best organized of the sort I have seen. It is under the eye of an able board, consisting of the first gentlemen in the city, who seem to take much pride in its success. The main school-room is divided into two equal parts, by an open passage or gangway quite across the building ; from this area, the desks of the pupils rise up one behind the other in regular succession, on each side of the passage, to the height of a story, so that the whole is seen at a glance. The teachers have their desks one at each end of the passage, elevated about half way to the sealing.

The alphabet class have each a small wheel before him, with the letters of the alphabet printed on it, which shows but one letter at a time, the wheel being concealed in the desk. When the pupil is perfect in one letter he turns the wheel which brings the next letter into view.

But what they excel in is their correctness of pronunciation, cadence and emphasis in reading and spelling ; this is to be ascribed to the indefatigable labor and attention of the Principal, Mr. Tweedale. When the classes read, Mr. T. adjourns to a reading room, where one of the pupils commences by reading a paragraph alone, in which he is corrected by the other pupils, who, with the teacher, hold a book of the same sort in their hands. But neither the teacher or the pupils interrupt the reader until he has finished the paragraph ; any of the pupils, or all of them must point out the errors, either in emphasis or pronouncing ; he then reads the same over again and again, until he is perfect. After which all the pupils read the same paragraph together, with an audible voice, observing the most uniform exactness in prosody, emphasis and cadence.

Library.—Respecting the public library of Albany, I

am unable to say any thing. The Librarian, (the greatest boor except two in Albany,) would neither let me examine the books, or show me the catalogue. A gentleman who was present, however, informed me that it contained 4,000 volumes. It appears that strangers are not allowed to sit in it and read, which liberty is common in other public libraries.

Museum.—The Museum of Albany is a tolerable collection, much more so than I anticipated ; but after seeing the museum of Philadelphia, it had not enough of interest in it to amuse. The mischievous boys adverted to sundry tricks to surprise me, while passing through the apartments, by ringing bells, raising Samuel from the dead, &c.; and though they failed in their attempts to frighten me, they succeeded in the case of some gentlemen and ladies. There are a number of wax-figures in the museum ; amongst which is the execution of Louis XVI. of France. Louis, all pale and emaciated, is seated with a guard standing round him, and others on horseback. A hideous blood-thirsty figure is setting with his eye on a watch, which lies before him ; he is watching the minute-hand to ascertain the fatal moment. Robespierre is also present, out-looking vengeance itself. The scaffold upon which Louis is to suffer, stands near; both that, and the steps leading to it, are covered with black. The proprietor of the museum is justly entitled to the patronage of the public, were it only for his obliging manners, though there is sufficient matter of entertainment in the museum, even for those who have seen richer collections. Here, as at Philadelphia, you pay but once.

Kninckerbocker Hall.—Knickerbocker Hall, and the New Theatre, are alike conspicuous as specimens of taste, in size and architecture. The first is a spacious assembly room, fitted out in a style worthy the capital city of New-York. It contains a long ball-room, with a splendid orchestra, also dressing-rooms and supper apartments, all of which are superbly furnished. Assemblies are held here twice in each week, to which the fashionable and the enlightened of both sexes repair for amusement. It is under the direction of the first gentlemen in the city.

The new theatre, just finished, is one of the finest buildings in this or any other city, and promises fair to beguile the gloom of the long winter nights of this region.

Markets.—There are two market-houses in Albany, nearly in the centre of the city. Nothing is sold in market during the winter, but meats; vegetables are sold out of carts and waggons, in the streets, very cheap.

Manners and Appearance.—Albany embraces three distinct classes of people. The first class comprises the executive officers of the government, the supreme judges, the gentlemen of the bar, the physicians, and a few of the reverend clergy, with the principal merchants of the city. These constitute the first circle, take them on what ground you will; amongst them are the Clintons, the Van Rensselaers, the Taylors, the Lansings, the Spencers, the Woodworths, the Laceys, the Chesters, the Ludlows, and the celebrated De Witt family, with many others, whose talents may rank them with the first men of any country. The second class comprises shop-keepers, mechanics, clerks, &c. &c. This, the middle class, constitute the religioso of the place, and are people of moderate pretensions on the score of philosophy and learning. Between these and the better sort, the line of distinction is strongly marked the one, as remarkable for intelligence, affability, and liberality of sentiment, as the other is for bigotry, harsh and uncourtly manners.— In those you find cheerfulness, hospitality, and highly polished manners; in these a grim, cold, contracted deportment, in all they say or do. This is not the effect of religion, but the want of it. The reign of bigotry, however, is short in Albany; that attention which is bestowed on education, will, in a few years, compel it to fly to some other region—it is a monster that cannot endure the light. In all the towns I have visited, I have not found education in a more flourishing condition than in Albany. Guess my astonishment at seeing little boys, and even little girls with Euclid in their hands. The last and third class of citizens, are mostly foreigners, who rank with blacks and sailors; having little commerce with the respectable citizens.

The churches of Albany are very splendid indeed,

particularly the north Dutch ; it is second to none I have seen in my travels ; its glittering domes are the greatest ornaments of the city. The south Dutch is also a splendid building ; the furniture is superb in all, and the music fine. Their clergy rank high in theology, being men of the first literary attainment. Being no respecter of sect or party, I went to hear them all, and was much disappointed at the display of eloquence. Amongst their first preachers stands the Rev. Dr. C. Rev. L. Lacey, and Ferris. Dr. C. is an orator of the first class. But of all their clergy, I was most pleased with the Rev. Mr. Lacey, of the Episcopal church ; a man of the most captivating manners ; his modesty and christian meekness, incontestibly proves his devotion to his divine master.

History.—In tracing the history of Albany to its origin, we discover the commencement of the state, as the first permanent settlement was effected at this place. Albany was settled by the Hollanders, in 1614 ; they built a fort, a store-house, and a church, the commencement of the present city. The name of the commander was "Christiæns," which has been mentioned. It is matter of much regret that the history of New-York is very imperfectly known, the original account being kept in Holland, in the Dutch language ; by the change of masters which took place, and through the most unpardonable neglect on all hands, much of the most interesting history of New-York is lost. In Mrs. Grant's letters I found a few particulars relating to Albany, and its primitive inhabitants. She mentions this fort, as being at one time occupied by an independent company, commanded by Captain Massy, the father of Mrs. Lennox, the celebrated protege of Doctor Johnson. She also makes mention of Colonel Philip Schuyler, a most enlightened gentleman, who first settled what is called the Flats,* where he displayed great power of mind in maintaining peace and harmony with the Indians. She likewise makes honourable mention of the principal families who settled this part of the state, many of whose

* Now Utica.

descendants are still in possession of their ancient patri-
mony. Amongst these is the respectable family of the
Van Rensselaers. They possessed, by patent, large
tracts of land which they leased out to the poor; they
were called patroons, which means landlord; they still go
by that name. The present patroon of Albany is Gen.
Stephen Van Rensselaer, one of the most worthy of the
human race. But to return to Mrs. G.—"There was one
wide street in Albany which run parallel with the river.
The space between the street and the river was laid out
into gardens. There was another street which run east
and west, (now called State-street,) this street was
still wider than the other. In the middle of this street
stood all their public buildings. In the centre of the
town rose a steep hill; this last street passed over the
hill and descended rapidly towards the river; at the
bottom of this descent, stood the old low Dutch church.*
In the winter season the young people used to amuse
themselves by sleighing (so they do now,) down this
hill, the sleigh being pulled by themselves instead of horses. I have enjoyed much pleasure in standing near
(continues Mrs. Grant,) and contemplating this patri-
archal city; these primitive beings were dispersed in
porches, grouped according to similarity of years and
inclination; at one door young matrons, at another the
elders of the people; at a third, the youths and maidens,
gaily chatting or singing together; while the children
played around the trees, or waited by the cows (who
wore little tingling bells,) for the chief ingredient of
their supper, which they generally ate sitting on steps,
in the open air." "In my time," (continues the same
author,) "one of those vallies was inhabited by a
Frenchman; his residence was called a hermitage. The
Albanians respected him as something supernatural;
they imagined that he had retired to that sequestered
spot from having committed some deed in his life time;

* This, the oldest church in the Union, has very recently been pulled
down as a nuisance; it was scarcely one story high, with painted glass
in the windows. This painted glass was thus described to me by a lady
of Albany:—Every member of the church, that is, the heads of families,
had the escutcheon of his family, or his diploma, if a professional man,
painted on a pane of glass, with his name, &c.

24*

they considered him, however, in the light of an idola-
ter, because he had an image of the Virgin Mary.
There was always a governor, a few troops, and a small
court in Albany."

Albany is in latitude 42 deg. 38 min. N., at the head of
tide water. Besides the public buildings already noticed, it contains 2,000 houses and 17,000 inhabitants. It
is governed by a Mayor, Recorder, and ten Aldermen.
The streets are paved and lighted. It is the oldest city
in the United States, next to Jamestown in Virginia.

Secretary Yates and Mr. Moulton are now engaged in
writing a complete history of this state. From the ability and talents of these gentlemen, and their indefatigable researches we may expect the best compilation that
has ever been published. Mr. Yates, the present Secretary of State of New-York, is said to be a gentleman of
high literary attainments ; and, from his appearance,
I would suppose him justly entitled to the character. He
is apparently about thirty years of age, middling stature,
and fine figure ; his manners very suasive, his countenance mild and pleasing. Mr. Moulton is also a gentleman of very interesting manners. But of all the gentlemen I met with in Albany, I was most pleased with Gen.
Van Rensselaer, the present member of Congress, and
Mr. Southwick, the poet. Of Gen. Van Renselaer little may be said, his actions speak his praise wherever
he is known, and even where he is not. He lives at the
northern extremity of Market-street, quite out of the city. His house fronts the end of the street, and stands
near the Hudson. It is the finest building in the vicinity ; the ground, shrubberies, gardens and walks attached
to it are laid out in a style of taste, and elegance worthy
its generous owner. The ancestor of this great and good
man owned twelve miles square adjoining Albany, granted to him by the states of Holland. He leased those
lands out, " while water ran, or grass grew," exacting
the tenth sheaf of grain the land produced. He reserved to himself a large demesne, which has descended to
the present patroon. as the general is called. He is in
every respect worthy his princely fortune ; being one of
'hose rare few who may truly be said to lay up treasure

in heaven. Perhaps no man of the present age can equal
him in acts of charity and benevolence. His house is
the resort of the poor and the distressed, both strangers
and citizens. His purse and his heart are alike open to
all, he turns none empty away. When he is absent,
which is a great part of the year, his strict orders to his
steward are to relieve the poor. He has a great number
of tenants, many of whom often fall short of their rent,
and relate their inability to pay; when he has heard
their story, he, like Henry the fourth of France, pulls out
his purse and divides the contents with them. In short,
he is the idol of the poor, and the admiration of all who
know his worth. This amiable man is advanced in
years. In his person he is tall, slender, and perfectly
shaped, his eye a deep hazel, his countenance what his
actions bespeak, the very milk of human kindness.* Mr.
Southwick though not possessed of a princely fortune,
has a princely heart, and "though his portion is but
scant, he gives it with good will." Mr. S. once a man
of independence, has suffered shipwreck, and in the decline of life has to struggle with untoward fortune, encumbered with a numerous family. He is one of your
warm hearted yankees, though long a resident of this
place, the victim of a too generous heart. His misfortunes it is thought, drew from him that beautiful poem,
" the pleasures of poverty." He is at present vending
lottery tickets, in a passage scarcely wide enough to turn
about in. He laughs at the incident, (speaking very
fast,) and says he must be going to heaven; " I am in
the straight and narrow way." He has nine (if not
more) sons, the handsomest youths I ever saw, and he
himself is the handsomest man I have seen in this state.

Amongst the great men of Albany, it will be expected,
particularly by my western friends, that I am not to overlook one whose fame is held in veneration by them; I
mean Governor Clinton. His Excellency De Witt Clinton, the present governor of New-York, is about fifty
years of age; he is six feet (at least) in height, robust,
and a little inclined to corpulency; he is straight and

* Mr. V. R. seems to consider himself as nothing more than a steward,
put here for the benefit of others.

well made ; he walks erect with much ease and dignity ;
his complexion is fair, his face round and full, with a soft
dark gray eye, his countenance mild and yielding; he
regards you in silence, with a calm winning condescension, equally removed from servility and arrogance,
while it inspires the beholder with admiration and respect.   His whole deportment is dignified and commanding, with all the ease and grace of an accomplished
gentleman.   Like all men of sense, he uses few words.
I had two interviews with him, during which I never saw
him smile, nor did he speak half a dozen words ; in short,
the predominant traits in his countenance, are benignity,
and modesty, lighted by genius.   To a mind highly endowed by nature, he has added a rich store of practical
and theoretical knowledge : in few words, Governor
Clinton is a man of great size, great soul, great mind,
and a great heart.   To him may be applied that line of
Thomson; " serene, yet warm ; humane, yet firm his
mind."—Perhaps his best eulogium is " The Governor
of New-York."   De Witt Clinton, Jun. about twenty-
five years of age, promises fair to rival his father, in those
qualities which constitute a great man.   Fame begins to
whisper his growing merit, and predicts the natural result of genius, improved by education.   He is tall, and
comely in his person, fair complexion, his features regular and handsome, his visage thin, his countenance soft,
though luminous and pleasing.   In his manners he is still
more fascinating than his father.   The ancestors of this
distinguished family, were originally of Ireland ; we
hear of them, from their first arrival down to this day,
filling the first offices of their country.   Besides Mr. S.
I met with many yankees in Albany, whose generosity
and benevolence overwhelms a stranger with obligation
and delight.   Amongst these, I cannot forego a remark
on O. Kane, Esq. His magnificent mansion and pleasure-
grounds, may well be styled an earthly paradise.   He
lives at the southern extremity of the city, in a most superb building, which stands upon an eminence, with an
extensive shrubbery in front, descending towards the
Hudson.   This shrubbery is enclosed by a parapet, and
communicates with Market-street by an avenue leading

from the front of the building. In the rear of the mansion are the gardens : the beauty and magnificence of the
whole plan taken together, of this delightful spot, is only
equalled by its generous and hospitable owner.

It was my design to enliven these sketches with anecdotes, and detached incidents of daily occurrence, such
as the gossip of the day, &c., but the principal subjects
have so increased upon my hands, that I find it impossible. I cannot, however, resist an anecdote of two countrymen at the theatre. They were in the same box with
myself, and it appeared from their conversation, they
had never witnessed a stage performance before. They
were both well dressed, the one a young, the other a
midlde aged man. The young man assumed a knowledge of the world, and explained to his friend the meaning of the wonders before them. " What is all them
there things for, that's upon the doors, or whatever they
are, that looks like they are painted, but I suppose that's
the play," says the elderly man to his friend : " O no,
that's jest, I don't know what it's done for, but it isn't
the play," replied the friend : " You'll see live people
a playing, and running about like mad, and making love,
and making speeches, and the most funnyest things that
ever you saw ; John Steward says it will make you split
your sides with laughing." " What's all them people
doing down there ?" (pointing to the pit,) said the first,
" O they're the players, you'll see um begin presently ;
(looking at his watch) it's most time." Thus the one
continued to inquire, and the other to explain, until their
patience became exhausted : the commencement of the
play, being from some cause protracted nearly an hour
beyond the time mentioned in their bills, they in a violent passion, at being cheated out of their money by a
set of lazy fellows, that just made fun of them, were actually about to quit the box, when the bell rang, and I
informed them the players were coming on the stage ;
at this moment the curtain flew up, and our fascinated
strangers were amply compensated for the delay. It
was amusing enough to hear them during the performance, " that's a tarnation pretty gall, is'nt she," all
aloud. When the actress (as was sometimes the case,)

would seem to shrink back as though afraid, the young
one would rise up and eagerly exclaim, (beckoning to
her at the same time,) " come out, come out, let's look at
you, don't be afraid." The house was in one continued
roar: of all things, they disliked the clapping and the
drop of the curtain.

Troy.—Before my visit to the New-England states, I
took a ride up the Hudson as far as Troy, to see the canal. The distance from Albany to Troy is six miles,
and the road lies on the margin of the canal. The canal is 40 feet wide, 4 feet deep, and very straight; this,
and its symmetry, constitute its°beauty: it is upwards of
300 miles in length—cost rising of $4,000,000, and ter-
minates in Albany, by a basin. From a bridge which is
thrown across it, on our way to Troy, we had an extensive view of it both ways. Nothing can be handsomer.
But language fails me in describing this wonder-working
state. Besides this canal, they have, at their last session,
appropriated $1,000,000 for public uses! this speaks the
character of the people more emphatically than volumes
of news-papers and books. Troy is at the head of sloop
navigation, and has considerable trade: it is a very handsome city, built chiefly of brick, and some of the houses
on the bank of the Hudson are five stories high, having
double ware-houses, so that when the river is high, the
goods can be taken in at the second story, the first being wholly under water. From these houses which hang
over the Hudson, you have one of the finest prospects in
the country A female seminary of high repute is kept
at Troy, by Mrs. Willard, who has nothing very remarkable in her appearance, excepting her masculine size.—
She appeared to be about thirty years of age, of a fair
compexion, and regular, though coarse features. Her
countenance and carriage are very majestic and striking.
She is said to be the best qualified female teacher in the
state. Here, too, I had an interview with the celebrated
Mrs. French, one of the handsomest females of the age:
her beauty, however, is her least recommendation, being possessed of every accomplishment which adorns her
sex, or renders them interesting. To my no small pleas-

ure, I met with Miss D——s, with whom I had become
acquainted in the course of the winter, in Albany. We
rallied each other on the total defeat of our anticipated
pleasure in visiting Troy, turning out as it did, one of
the most tempestuous days I had witnessed since my visit
to the state. The two ladies just mentioned were not
only among the first, but the most amiable females I have
met with in the eastern states. Troy contains a
court-house 2 banks, 5 churches, and 5,264 inhabitants.
It lies on the opposite side of the Hudson, from Albany.
Mr. Boardman, of Huntsville, editor of the "Alabama
Republican," went from this city, and his mother lives
here now. Also Mr. Adams, who prints for Mr. Boardman. He and his lady I have often seen in Huntsville.
Troy is also the residence of Mr. Holley, brother of the
president of the University of Lexington. He edits the
"Troy Sentinel"—a paper of no small merit. Mr. Holley is said to be eminent for his literary acquirements,
both in poetry and prose. He is possessed of surprising
personal advantages, being one of the finest looking men
in the United States! I saw him in company with his
counter-part, Mr. G——, son of the ex-post-master general. These men bid fair to figure in the affairs of their
country. They are nearly of the same age and size, being about twenty-four years of age, and want a little of
six feet in height, stout, able-bodied men. of perfect symmetry. Mr. H. has blue eyes, of the *softest* lustre—his
complexion fair, his face oval, and finely proportioned.
Mr. G. has black eyes, fine, full, and expressive; his
face round and beautiful, with a countenance at once noble, open, and captivating, with the manners of the first
order of gentlemen, and every requisite accomplishment.
We may expcet he and his friend will, one day, if I am
not mistaken, share the honors and confidence of their
country.

On my return to Albany, I called at the Watervliet
U. S. arsenal, which is on the same side of the Hudson
with Albany. The armory consists of a vast building in
length, filled from the bottom to the top, with arms, as
thick as they could stand, one by the side of another.
There were 35,251 muskets, 1,835 rifles, 11,500 pistols,

9,853 swords, in complete order. The swords, by some
legerdemain contrivance, are formed into flowers and
figures, which stick to the ceiling over head, as if by
magic. The pistols are likewise suspended in bunches
from the cross-beams which support the ceiling; the
space between each beam being filled up with the swords,
which are fastened with straps of leather to their places.
The muskets, each with a bayonet, are placed on their
ends, in one solid column, from one end of the building
to the other, and confined to their places by strips of
wood, leaving a narrow space between each column, to
pass, that no room may be lost. The side walls of the
building are garnished with swords, in a style of studied
elegance. The cartridges are all boxed up, and the
whole in complete marching order, at a moment's warning. One cannot help shivering at the sight of such an
immense pile of deadly weapons. Among the cannon
I saw three brass pieces, which were taken from the
British, at Saratoga. The gun carriages lie a little west
of the arsenal, under long, low sheds, which protects
them from the weather; and near these, in rows, are the
awful cannon. The commandant, Maj. G. Talcott, is a
man of accomplishments, and very gentlemanly appearance : I found him at his post, and received from him a
very polite reception.

Journey to Springfield, (*Mass*.)—On the second day of
April, 1825, I bid adieu to Albany at 3 o'clock A. M.,
and set off in the stage for Boston, taking Springfield
in my way. It was a clear star-light morning, but the
absence of the moon deprived me of the pleasure of seeing the country until day-light, when I found we were in
a broken uneven soil, consisting of rugged hills, and
narrow vales, which are watered by bright streams of
running water. Along those vales, are strips of meadow, covered with cows, calves, and a few shabby colts ;
amongst which, you see some sorry sheep, and young
bleating lambs. It is amusing enough to observe the
low Dutch houses sitting down upon the lowest spot they
can select, and around mynheer, in close array, stands his
cow-house, his stable, and barns, so that he has but a

step to make from his warm stove-room to feed his stock.
Their houses are small and void of ornaments, with cam
el-backed roofs, (I think they are called,) and universally painted red, a color to which the Dutch seem partial.
The Dutch are greatly behind the Germans in farming.
That comfort, ease, and opulence which distinguishes the
farm of the industrious, thorough-going German, bears
no comparison with the former. The country is almost
destitute of timber, it having been long since cut down
and appropriated to ordinary uses. A stunted growth
has succeeded the first which is very unpromising. Our
course lay directly east from Albany. The Catskill, the
Green mountains of Vermont, the hills bordering the
Hudson, all capt with snow, resembling so many magnificent domes, the silent streams winding their way
through those heights, seen to a great distance from the
road, the cherry-cheeked Dutch girl milking her cow,
the whistling boy staring at our coach, and chopping his
wood alternately, and a hundred things beside, present
to the traveller one of the richest prospects imaginable.
The vales become wider and the streams larger as you
proceed, the hills gradually diminish, the Dutch houses
disappear, and you find yourself in a rich soil, in high
cultivation, which continues to Springfield, on the Connecticut river. My fellow-travellers consisted of two
young gentlemen from Boston, and four others, who were
citizens of Massachusetts; some of whom were men of
information, and enlivened the time with pleasant and
amusing stories. Going to Boston, I attached myself to
the two Bostonians, whose lively manners and liberality
of thinking, began to change my opinion of their city.
Night overtook us long before we reached Springfield:
the air was cold and piercing, and not even a star was
to be seen.—To complete our misfortune, the stage
broke down within eight miles of the town. Here we
were in a dreadful predicament; over a mile from any
house, and not a particle of light by which we might ascertain the extent of our disaster: one thing, however, was unanimously agreed upon, which was, that we
should all get out of the stage, and by putting our wits
together. see whether the misfortune could be remedied.
25

After a long groping about the stage, it was pronounced
unfit to carry us; the body being completely unhinged
from the wheels; otherwise it was unhurt.   The passengers had now no alternative but to stay where they were,
in the dark, or travel on foot, therefore they resolved to
walk to town.   On occasions like this, a little common
sense is worth all the philosophy in the world.   One of
our party, whom we may suppose was no friend to walking, observing some fence-rails lying by the road-side,
asked the driver if he had any leather straps, old lines or
ropes of any sort: being answered in the affismative, it
was proposed to raise the body of the stage, and lay on
a couple of rails under it, which all being mutually fastened together with a pair of old lines, it made out to carry us to Springfield, though in a slow walk, where we arrived at half past ten o'clock at night, cold and hungry.
I suffered from cold, this day, for the first time since my
arrival in the Atlantic states ; the wind from the snow-
covered mountains being chilly and piercing to a degree
hardly to be borne.   The inn-keeper, who expected us,
of course, had kept up a glowing fire, which in a few
minutes so overcame me with drowsiness, that I was
compelled to go supperless to bed.

Springfield.—Springfield is distant from Albany about 65
miles, and from Boston 87 miles.   It is situated on the
Connecticut river, in a rich soil, and is the handsomest
town I have seen yet ; it lies partly upon an eminence,
and partly on a low, flat situation, precisely like Albany.
It consists principally of one street, upwards of a mile in
length along the Connecticut, one of the handsomest rivers in the United States.   This street is very wide, and
lined on each side with rows of large elm trees, from one
end to the other, which, contrasted with the white houses, gives it that rural appearance, which is so delightful.
This street is crossed by others at right angles with the
river, and ascends the eminence just mentioned, upon
which a considerable part of the town lies.   But what
renders Springfield an interesting object to travellers, is
the U. S. Armory.   At Springfield is the principal manufactory of arms in the United States : it is also a milita-

ry post. The site of the armory contains 102 acres. The number of buildings are, for work-shops, 34; arsenals and magazine, 9; dwellings attached to the establishment, 29; making in all, 72 buildings. It was established in 1795. The number of arms made since that time, is 237,411. The number now made, is from 14,-000 to 15,000, annually. The number now deposited in the arsenals there, is 95,000. The water-shops are situated on Mill river, about one mile south of the armory, 9 work-shops, 28 forges, 12 trip hammers, and 20 water wheels; 250 workmen are employed in the establishment, who complete, on an average, 50 muskets per day. The arsenal and magazine are at the extremity of the elevated part of the town, from whence you have an extensive prospect of the surrounding country, while the main body of the town with the majestic Connecticut river lies far beneath you. I spent two days in going through the different shops, admiring the ingenuity of the machinery, and the skill of the workmen. The whole of the gun, polishing and all, is done by water power, the workman only applying that part of the gun which is assigned to him to the mechanical instrument, which is turned by water. The arms in the arsenal are kept differently from those of New-York, being packed away in wooden boxes. Colonel Lee, the superintendant, one of the most gentlemanly men I have met with, took all imaginable pains to furnish me with information on the various matters of this grand establishment; and though he was very unwell, I found him at his post, engaged in the duties of his office, a trust which he seems to fulfil with the strictest integrity. Much honor is due to this amiable man for his unparallelled labors in behalf of the United States, I have not found in her a more faithful servant!

Springfield likewise contains an extensive manufacturing establishment of paper, upon a newly improved plan. It is on the same stream with the work-shops, and owned by Messrs. Ameses, one of the most distinguished families of Massachusetts. The improvement consists in fabricating the paper in one long piece of several yards in length; and this is performed wholly

without manual labor. It is wound upon a short cylin-
der, (which is turned slowly by the water,) like cloth
upon a weaver's beam, and then taken off and cut into
sheets.   The paper is of a superior quality, and the improvement is the effect of Mr. Ames' own fertile genius.
Springfield is principally built of wood, contains four
churches, and 3914 inhabitants, and 17 public schools !
The whole state of Massachusetts is laid off into districts;
every district is compelled by law to support a certain
number of grammar schools.   This town is inhabited by
people of considerable wealth, and is a place of much
fashion and hospitality.   Col. Trask, one of the wealthiest men in the state resides here.   He spends one part
of the year in Natchez, where he has large possessions.
In his house and equipage he displays great taste and
elegance.   But of all the citizens of Springfield, I was
most pleased with the Rev. W. O. Peabody, the most a-
miable and interesting human being I ever met with in
any country, the centre of every grace and every virtue;
whether we regard him for the beauty of his person, the
elegance of his manners, or the virtues of his mind.   His
wife equals if she does not surpass him in every human
perfection.   To her may be applied what Milton says of
Eve.   She is a niece of Judge White, of Salem.   They
spread their hospitable board with every dainty, and
" pressed and smiled, and pressed again," I could not
eat ; wine was brought, that was refused ; beer and porter, I could partake of neither.   I never shall forget the
expression, in the goodness of his heart, he exclaimed
sorrowfully, (calling me by name,) " will you neither eat
nor drink with me ?"   " Yes, sir," I replied, " I will
drink a glass of water with you ;" he waited on me himself although a servant was present.   It was the sweetest drink I ever quaffed.   Amiable pair may they meet
their reward.*

*Mr. Peabody has a twin brother, named O. W., a lawyer, who resembles
him so nearly that it is difficult to distinguish one from the other.   A lady of Boston related to me the following anecdote of these extraordinary brothers, viz : " That they learned at the same school, took their degrees at the same time, and both fell in love with the same lady, (this is
the least of the wonder,) but the lawyer generously resigned her to the
parson. They are both poets, and resemble each other in every respect "

Manners and Appearance.—The manners of the citizens of Springfield may be gathered from what has been said. They are polite and hospitable, beyond any thing I have seen in the Atlantic country—and these are yankees! How differently have they been represented; but I shall suspend further remarks till I have seen more of the country. In their appearance they are about the same as in New-York, with fairer complexions; the children and females are uncommonly beautiful. I have often stopped in the streets to admire the children as they returned from school, nor could I resist the curiosity of ascertaining the progress and nature of their pursuits, which proved honourable to them and to their teachers.

History.—In 1636 a company of men from Roxbury, (Mass.) under William Pynchon, Esq. traversed the wilderness all the way from Boston, and settled Springfield. The first house built in Springfield is still standing; it is of brick, looks quite fresh for its age, and is tenanted. It was built by Mr. Pynchon himself, and was used as a fortification to defend them from the Indians. It stands on Main-street, and not far distant from it dwells the grandson of Mr. Pynchon, a man of considerable wealth and respectability. His uncle is still living: I should have called on him, but was told it was troublesome to converse with him, on account of his deafness; he is very old. The Connecticut river is the handsomest river of its size, I have seen in the Atlantic states. It is nearly as large at Springfield as the great Kenhawa. It is fully as wide as the Kenhawa, but not so deep. It flows with a smooth gentle current. No vessels come to Springfield, the river not being navigable above Hartford, Conn. Over the river is a very handsome bridge. The land on Connecticut river, is rich alluvial bottom, and of considerable width. No land is better, not excepting the Kenhawa and Ohio bottom. This is the country represented to us of the west, as an impoverished soil, producing nothing but beans and pumpkins! Finer meadows and finer cattle are not to be seen in the United States. But Doctor M—— informed me that " the lands on Connecticut river are fine ;" true, but

25*

Dr. M— was a yankee and few people believed him ; besides he praised his own country too much, and others too little.

Journey to Hartford, Conn.—After amusing myself three or four days at Springfield, I sat out (in the stage again,) for Hartford, being told that it was only 18 miles, or such a matter out of the way ; and that a ride down the Connecticut river, through one of the handsomest countries in the world, would richly repay me for my pains.   This was enough ; and with a stage full of full-blooded yankees, I set out for Hartford, keeping a south course.   Nothing worth naming, occurred during the journey, which we performed in a few hours.   My fellow passengers, some were ladies and some gentlemen. The conversation was desultory ; banks, roads, bridges, and mercantile concerns engrossed us by turns.   My attention, however, was principally engrossed by the country, in which I was not disappointed.   Our course lay down the Connecticut river, which, in fertility resembles the lands on the Sciota and Miami, in the state of Ohio, rich, level, and extensive bottoms.   The river appearing at intervals ; the extensive meadows, orchards and corn fields extending on both sides of the river beyond the reach of sight.   The villages, the lofty white steeples of the churches, peeping up through the trees, perhaps three, four, or five miles distant, may give some idea of the scenery.   We arrived at Hartford long before night, by which means we had a full prospect of the city, which mostly lies high, and presents a fine appearance as we approach it.

Hartford.—Hartford is a port town, in the state of Connecticut.   Its form is not regular, though the streets cross each other at right angles.   It lies upon the Connecticut river, and does much commercial business ; the river being navigable for sloops.   Every article almost is manufactured in this city ; there are iron and copper foundries, gold leaf, chords, looking-glasses, stone-ware, and various other articles manufactured in Hartford. It contains a state-house, jail, circus, poor-house, work-house, retreat for the insane, American asylum for the deaf and dumb, market-house, Washington College, 3 banks, 2 fire insurance companies, 1 marine company, 1 bridge over Connecticut river, 1 bridge over a small river in the middle of the town, 4 Congregational churches, 1 Episcopal, 1 Baptist, 1 Universalist, 1 Quaker, 4 public schools, 14 charitable and other societies, and 6,901 inhabitants, the last census. Hartford is principally built of brick. It is governed by a mayor, four aldermen, and eight common council men. The streets are paved with stone, the side-walks with flag; the streets are not lighted.

The State-House, in which the Legislature of the state hold their sessions is a very handsome plain building. The representatives' apartments are entirely void of ornament, representing one of the most striking pictures of republican simplicity. The plain seat of the speaker, the silent solemnity which reigned throughout the edifice, reminds one of the august palace of Marcus Aurelius.

Washington College is a recent establishment, not yet thoroughly in operation. It has a president, four professors, and one tutor; several other professors are contemplated. The Rt. Rev. Thomas C. Brownell, D. D. LL. D. of Hartford, is the present president. Bishop Brownell is said to be one of the most distinguished men in New-England, in whatever light he may be considered. I attended at the college, one forenoon, to hear the students recite, and was equally surprised at their proficiency and modest deportment. The public schools of Hartford are the best regulated institutions I have seen. They are not only under able teachers, who are qualified in every branch of literature, but are under the eye of a visiting committee, who are composed of vigilant, enlightened men, whom they would find it difficult to deceive.

Poor-House.—The poor-house of Hartford is situated nearly at the extremity of the city. It is a large building, containing 48 paupers and a few refractory citizens. The keeper, Mr ——, one of the most benevolent of his species, and his wife, (one of my angels,) the most feel-

ing, angelic, transcendently kind and charitable females,
I cannot find names in our poor language, adequate to
her deserts ; well may the poor call her *blessed.* It is
needless to consume time in describing the poor-house,
after what has been said ; the condition may readily be
imagined.

American Asylum.—But the glory of Hartford, and
indeed that of the United States, is the American Asylum, for the education of the deaf and dumb. This asylum was incorporated in 1816 ; the first establishment of
the sort, in the United States, and the parent of those
since established, in Philadelphia and New-York. Having mentioned those asylums, now, the third time in these
sketches, a brief historical outline of the art by which
these unfortunate beings are instructed, may not be unwelcome to the reader. "Some years ago, a lady of
Paris had two daughters that were deaf and dumb. Father Farnin, a member of the Society of Christian Doc-
trines, being acquainted with the lady, called at her
house one day when she was out : he found no one in
the house but the two deaf and dumb young ladies, and
addressed several questions to them, not knowing their
misfortune, to all of which they returned no answer, but
studiously pursued their work, without even lifting their
eyes to look at him. He attributed their silence to contempt, and withdrew in a passion, when meeting their
mother at the door, he learned the cause of their silence.
The circumstance filled him with emotions of pity, and
from that moment he resolved to exert himself in teaching them to read and write. Death, however, surprised
him before he had attained any degree of success. The
first conception of a great man is generally a fruitful one.
The attempt was brought to perfection under the amiable Abbe Sicard. Some few years since, the Rev. Mr.
Gallaudet, a citizen of New-England, and a gentleman
of distinguished merit and classical attainments, went
first to England, and then to Scotland, with a view of
acquiring the art of teaching the deaf and dumb. Meeting with no encouragement at either of those places, he
went to France, were he was received with great kindness and respect, by Abbe Sicard. The doors of the

school were thrown open to him, and being familiar with the French language, he soon returned to this country, qualified for the purpose, and bringing with him Laurent Clerc, one perfect in the science, himself being deaf and dumb. They arrived in August, 1816, and the asylum was opened in 1817. The progress of the institution has been beyond conception:—it is patronized by the United States, and many private gentlemen, among which I find the name of the amiable Gen. Van Rensselaer, of Albany. It is under the direction of a president, and twelve vice-presidents, for life, who are gentlemen of the first respectability in the United States. I found about 70 pupils in the asylum, some of whom were engaged in mechanical pursuits. I saw several specimens of their work, which were equal to any performed by other mechanics, such as shoes and cabinet work; but chiefly I was surprised at their literary attainments. Mr. Laurent Clerc, took me into his department, where there were about 30 pupils. He communicated to them my name, place of residence, and my pursuits. While he was doing this, their eyes were fixed on him with deep attention, and the moment he had finished, each turned to his or her slate, and in the twinkling of an eye, I saw my name, the state I was from, &c. written in a fair, legible hand; and out of the thirty there was but one letter wrong. I examined several of them, myself, by means of a slate, upon geography, grammar, history, &c. and found them perfect. The asylum is built of brick, on the finest situation in the city. It stands upon a lofty eminence which commands an extensive view of the surrounding country. The building is amazing large, and handsomly divided into separate apartments. This institution received from congress 23.000 acres of land, lying in Alabama, and many of the states have contributed to its success, besides private donations; yet there are no free pupils taken in here, as at Philadelphia and New-York: this astonished me. Each pupil must pay for tuition and board, $150. A great falling off from the benevolence of New-York and Philadelphia: but they are large cities. Several of the male pupils are learning trades, such as shoe-makers and cabinet-makers.

A number of shops stand round the building, where they attend to their business. This arrangement will be attended with much inconvenience, as some want to learn one trade, and some another; scarcely any two of them wishing to learn the same trade; so that they must have nearly as many instructors as pupils. Several specimens of their composition were shown to me, one of which is the following:—

"*The thanks of the Deaf and Dumb to the Public.*—In the United States there were a great number of schools for children ; but there were none places of instruction for the deaf and dumb. All the parents thought that their deaf and dumb sons and daughters were impossible to learn how to read and write, and were grieved with them. Fortunately the Kind Being brought Mr. Gallaudet to France ; on the purpose for learning how to teach the deaf and dumb. When Mr. Gallaudet applied to Mr. Clerc to come to this country, and incited Mr. Clerc to think those poor deaf and dumb had no idea of God and Christ, and then his consent made Mr. Gallaudet pleasant. They came to the western country by water and arrived in it. They prayed to the citizens and countrymen to give them money for the Asylum and the generous contributed to the helps of the American Asylum. It was worthy that they were benevolent ; so that all the deaf and dumb are thankful to them and think God will prompt the citizens and send the rain to pour out over the farms of the countrymen; to provide them fruits and live in happiness. We are sorry that they visit the Asylum but little ; before they came frequently to attend schools, and if they pass through Hartford and stay at the hotel, they should come to see it ; that they might wonder at seeing the deaf and dumb writing on slates and talking to each other by making signs."

Mr. Gallaudet lives in a handsome house, near the asylum, and has married one of the dumb pupils, (a wise choice ;) she is very handsome, with one of the most expressive faces in creation ! Mr. Laurent Clerc, has married another of the pupils, likewise a very handsome female; she is a sister of Mr. Boardman, of Huntsville, editor of the Alabama Republican. I spent an evening at their house in Hartford, conversing with them by signs and by means of a slate. They are both people of no common information, and possessed of easy and engaging manners. They had a very beautiful child of between two and three years old, who could talk fast enough, but it was amusing to see it hold communication with its parents by signs. They seemed very fond of it though it stood in great awe of its father. Mr. Gallaudet also had one child, though it was not old enough to talk. I would advise all gentlemen who wish to avoid a scolding wife, to go to the American Asylum, where I can assure them they will find a great deal of good sense, as well as beauty. I never did see so great a number of interesting females together.

Manners and Appearance.—From what I had heard of Hartford in the western country, I expected to find a set of sour, contracted, bigoted, Pharisaical, illiberal men; the result proved quite the reverse. In their manners they are affable, open, liberal, and sociable; many of them are people of the first learning and talents. How then could they be bigoted? For politeness and easiness of address, they are inferior to no town I have visited. The ladies in these states are universally handsome as respects shape, countenance, and complexion. The ladies of Hartford, however, have a slight tinge of melancholy in their countenance; it is softened by a shade of placid tranquility. They are very delicate; but the men, particularly the laboring class, are stout and well made. They have not advanced so far yet as to countenance a theatre, though they have a circus, the next step to it. I have no doubt, but in a few years, they will extend their rational amusements as far as the stage, which may perhaps be the means of saving them from the effects of an evil which seems to threaten their morals with a total overthrow; I mean the too free use of spirituous liquors, an evil which is making fearful strides throughout the Atlantic country, and especially in port towns. Many a man, for want of amusement goes to the grog shop. Whiskey in the west, and gin in the eastern states, is to be the Cæsar of America.

Amongst the number of those whose claims to particular attention are indisputable, appears our distinguished country woman Mrs. Sigourney, one of the brightest
ornaments of the present age.   To her we are indebted
for some of the finest specimens of poetry.   She is the
wife of C. Sigourney, of Hartford, a gentleman of reputation, and easy fortune.   This lady is richly endowed
by nature, of rare personal beauty, a vigorous mind and
native talent, improved far beyond her sex.   But these
are trifling qualities compared with her unbounded char-
ities ; diffusing comfort and pleasure to all around her ;
I do not know a more enviable female.   Mrs. S. is a-
bove the common height of females, not too tall, she is
slender with well proportioned limbs ; her complexion
is ruddy, with hair as black as a raven, with the finest
black eye, and teeth as white as ivory.   Her countenance is animated with a pleasant smile, her cheek bedecked with blushes ; she shrinks from the homage paid
to her virtue.   She is the mother of several children, (as
I have been told,) though she does not appear to be
more than twenty-five years old.   I found her engaged
in the domestic concerns of her family ; she received
me with that sort of cordiality which tended no little to
enhance the accounts I had received from others.
I am told she is a writer of the first class in our country,
but extremely averse to being known as such.   Hartford
seems to be a favorite soil of the feminine virtues ; few
cities can boast a greater number of exemplary females,
I shall mention but one other family and conclude.   It
will be recollected that with the clergy of Albany, I mentioned Dr. C. speaking of him to a lady in this city, she
observed that an uncle of the Doctor's lived in Hartford,
and that I must not fail to call on the family, speaking
of them in the highest terms of respect.   Accordingly I
called at Mr. Chesters that evening, and was met at the
door by Mr. C. himself.   He saluted me with all the
ease and warmth of an old acquaintance, and invited me
to walk up stairs, where he introduced me to his family ;
but such a family I never saw before, or ever expect to
see again.

The family consisted principally of females, his wife, several daughters, and a Mrs. E. Philips, who had just arrived from Boston. The reception I met with, the manners and appearance of the ladies, was so different from any thing I had ever seen in this lower world, that I began to think I had fell in with the inhabitants of some other region. It was some time before I could resume my composure sufficiently to reply to the courtesies and caresses with which I was overwhelmed on all sides. The ladies formed a circle around me, the dear old man approached as near as they would let him, while they drew from me my adventures in detail, with which they appeared to be highly gratified. Meantime refreshment was not forgot, the best the house could command was spread before me, they did not forget what was due to a stranger, which too many do. Each face, illuminated with the most suasive sweetness, pressed me to eat and to drink, not in that cold formal manner which we so often meet with from people in their sphere, but with all the familiarity and warmth of old friends. Though willing to bestow some token of respect upon a family who so deeply interested me, and to prefer them as a pattern of imitation, yet the pen of Roscius could not do justice to virtues like theirs.

While I remained in Hartford, which was about a week, I took occasion to attend preaching: being curious to see and hear all that was to be seen, for, as respects my own religion, I do not hold with going to preaching. People (so they say,) go to preaching, or to church, to learn their duty to God and their neighbor; but if they practice their duty, why go to church? What our duty consists in, is plainly enough told to us by our Saviour, viz. "Love the Lord thy God with all thy heart, and thy neighbour as thyself." I do not think it possible for words to be plainer, all that seems to be lacking is the practice. But to use one of Carey's expressions, this is a digression. And so I went to church, and the people came, and the preacher too; he was a Universalist, the first I ever heard. I had consulted my landlady in the morning, on the subject of the different sects, the best orators, and such things, when she replied that " the Uni-

26

versalist was called the greatest orator, but she would'nt
go to hear him if she never heard a sermon;" though
she added, " you may go if *you're a mind to*." Highly
gratified with an opportunity of judging for myself of
this sect, I went to hear the Universalist.   There were
but few people in church when I arrived, but they soon
flocked in till it could hold no more, though it was a
large building.   I looked toward the pulpit, but it was
empty : meantime the organ began to play in the most
melting strains.   I kept my eye upon the aisle up which
the parson must pass to the pulpit, with α view of catch-
ing a full-length sight of his person.   In a few minutes
a spare, thin visaged man, of middling height, with a
majestic air, walked up the aisle and ascended the pulpit.   He was dressed in a neat suit of black broadcloth,
with a fine white cravat tied gracefully around his neck.
His complexion was fair, his features regular, with a retreating forehead, and the keenest blue eye ever formed
by nature.   His countenance shone bright from the beginning, but in the progress of his discourse it burst into
a vivid blaze, difficult to behold.   His text was, " Go
thou and do likewise," in which he painted the priest,
the Levite, and the Samaritan, in their true colours.—
But such a flood of eloquence I never heard from the
pulpit : he began low, rising by a regular climax, now
swelling with celestial pathos, now dropping soft as the
pearly dew; his voice sonorous, his action graceful, his
attitude natural and easy, his style chaste, his reasoning
clear,; in short his whole soul seemed one flame of love.
He drew such a picture of universal charity, as would
have pierced its way through adamant.   The audience
hung upon him with deep attention, maintaining throughout the most deathlike stillness.   This is but a faint outline of the man as a preacher; his character as a christian is unrivalled—of this I had ocular demonstration.
Mr. B. will pardon me for hinting a matter which his
transcendant humility would have forever remain between
him and his God.   Incomparable man! well mayest thou
say, " go and do likewise."   In the afternoon I went to
hear the Rev. Mr. ——.   But here was a great falling
off; I should have supposed he was doing any thing but

preaching. He had his sermon wrote down, as many of
the clergy do in this country, and what between his bob-
bing up and down to look at the words, his ungraceful
person, and his awkward delivery, he made the worst
hand of it I ever heard. The upshot of the business was
that one half of his hearers fell asleep, while he wanted
the courage of the Methodist preacher I heard of once,
to arouse them. A Methodist preacher (I forget his
name) perceiving his audience asleep, cried out with a
loud voice, "fire! fire!" The audience awaking, cried
"where? where?" "In hell," said the preacher, "for
those who sleep under the gospel!" This was different
from the shrewd old parson, on a similar occasion, who
was fond of a nap himself. Discovering his audience
asleep one day, he stopped suddenly, and addressing
some children who were at play in the gallery, in a whis-
pering tone, desired them to be still, or they would wake
the old folks below!

History.—Hartford was settled in 1633. The first
building erected where Hartford now stands, was built by
the Dutch of New-Netherlands, (now New-York.) Previous to this, one of the sachems from Connecticut river,
waited upon the governor of Massachusetts, and invited
him to send some of his people to settle amongst them.
Whilst the governor was thinking upon the matter, and
withal not very anxious to risk the safety of his people
among the savages, the governor of Plymouth, Mr. Winslow, sent some of his people to explore this same country, and discovered Connecticut river to be a fine flowing, capacious stream. Finally, the report of these men
determined him to establish a trading-house, for the present, being afraid to venture farther. In 1638, materials
for a small house were completely prepared, put on board
a vessel, under escort of a company, commanded by Capt.
Holmes, and sailed for Connecticut river. On arriving at
the place, they found they were superseded by the Dutch,
as already stated. They had built a *hortse*, and mounted it with cannon, precisely where Hartford now stands;
they called it the "Hirse of Good-Hope;" it stood on
the bank of the river. On the arrival of Holmes opposite the fort, he was ordered by the Dutch to lower sail

and strike his colours, or the guns would open upon him.
But Holmes, disregarding the threat, passed boldly on,
and landed on the right bank of the river, just below the
mouth of a small stream, now in Windsor, where he set
up his house, and enclosed it with a stockade.   Here he
carried on a lucrative trade with the Indians, who were
highly pleased, and sold them land, and continued peaceably to trade with them.   This gave umbrage to the
Dutch at New-Netherlands, who sent a company to drive
the English from their station ; but they were not to be
drove—and both parties continued to trade with the Indians in peltry, &c.   Thus they went on well, until a
quarrel with those river Indians involved the whites in a
slight war.   Peace, however, was soon restored, and the
whites from Plymouth finally settled Hartford in 1634,
by a company of people from Newtown.   The place
where Hartford now stands, was called by the Indians
"Suckiang."* and the name of the Indians "Pequots."
At this period New-England abounded with moose, deer,
bears, wolves and other animals.   The pigeons were in
such numbers, that they darkened the light of heaven.

Journey to Boston.—After spending a week in Hartford, I set off (in the stage again,) for Boston, intending
to stop a day or two in Worcester.   Upon leaving Hartford, our road still hung upon the river, through a fertile
plain ; for several miles we met with extensive fields,
rich meadows, and droves of the finest cattle to be found
in the United States.   At length we ascend an elevated
country, which commands a prospect of twenty miles in
all directions.   The land, however, is thin but well watered ; the original growth is entirely cut down, and the
country exhibits nothing but farms, villages and churches.
Few sheep, and no hogs, are seen, though I am told
they raise enough for their own use, and some for market.   Although the middle of April, I have seen but one
plough in operation this spring, so backward are the
seasons in this country ; the maples are just beginning
to bud.   The farms and houses look lonesome and gloomy, compared with ours at this season, where all is life

* Hoyt's History of Indian Wars.

and activity. Here you see no one stirring, either in the fields or about the houses. And here I am sorry to remark, for the first time, since I commenced travelling, a bad disposition, and want of principle in the people, dangerous to unprotected travellers ; it is hazardous both in the stage and at the inns. The inn-keeper, where we breakfasted after leaving Hartford, is the greatest ruffian I ever met with in any country, and in every respect unworthy the public patronage. We had ruffians in the stage, and the driver himself was one of the rudest, savage looking men I have seen. There was but one man in the stage who might be said to be a gentleman ; and by our joint threats we made out to arrive safe at Worcester, about three o'clock P. M., having left Hartford at six A. M. For several miles before entering Worcester, the country is nothing but one mass of stones. Nothing but stone fences in this country, from Albany, with slight exceptions, to this town ; and I am told they are universal in the New-England States. They add much to the scenery of the country, by laying it off in squares, by the regularity and symmetry of their appearance.

Worcester.—Worcester is a very handsome town ; very much like Springfield, and about the same size. The streets are wide and straight; the houses (of wood, principally,) are painted white ; and though planted with trees, it has not that rural air which the luxuriant elms give to Springfield. It has a very pompous courthouse, resembling the President's house at Washington city, 4 churches, a prison, an alms-house, 2 banks and 2,962 inhabitants. But it is chiefly remarkable for the residence of one of the most distinguished families in Massachusetts—I mean the Waldo family—judge Lincoln, (same family,) governor elect of Massachusetts, Doctor Bancroft, the celebrated poet, and the American Antiquarian Society. The Hon. judge Lincoln, governor of Massachusetts, (though he does not take his seat till June,) is a man of young appearance, for his age is forty. He might very easily pass for thirty. He is, in his person, tall and finely made ; rather spare, his com-

26*

plexion fair, his features handsome, with a soft blue eye,
his countenance luminous, his carriage light and natural,
his manners that of a perfect gentleman.   He is said to
be a man of the first erudition, and to possess a great fund
of theoretical, as well as practical knowledge.   He ap-
pertains to the same family of the celebrated Gen. Lincoln, of the revolution, who received the submission of
the royal army at Yorktown, under Lord Cornwallis.
Governor L. has a brother, quite a young man, who bids
fair to figure in the politics of his country at no distant
day.
    Doctor Bancroft is celebrated as one of the first writers
in our country.   He is far advanced in life ; I should
think over sixty ; and though he has a slight paralytic,
he walks about and converses with all the facility of
youth.   The Doctor lives in affluence, amidst an amiable family, like himself, possessed of all the affability and
ease common to people of the best society.
    The American Antiquary, I am told, is a rare collec-
tion of the various productions of nature and art, with a
valuable library, consisting of 6,000 volumes.   But from
the absence of Mr. Thomas, the principal proprietor, I
was unable to see it.   Worcester is pronounced Wooster
by the inhabitants ; nor did I dream that Wooster meant
the Worcester in the Geography, until I saw it saw spell-
ed on the signs.
    Having little to detain me at Worcester, I pursued my
journey to Boston, (in the stage,) which is only forty
miles distant.   The land from Worcester to Boston is
diversified with rich and poor, stony, flat, mountainous,
and marshes covered with winter birch, the first I ever
saw.   This birch is of small size, between a shrub and a
tree, and perfectly white ; it is always an evidence of
poor soil.   To this variety of soil we must add numerous
ponds of crystal water, which look extremely beautiful.
When we drew nearer Boston, the face of the country
changed into slight mountains, consisting of pine ridges,
resembling the spurs of the Alleghany, with here and
there an impetuous stream rushing down the declivities.
About eight miles this side of Boston, we passed the beautiful country seat of General Hull, who commanded in

the last war. It was pointed out to me by my fellow passengers. It lies on the right hand side of the road, and for taste and beauty, may, with truth, be styled an earthly paradise. The house peeps above one of the richest shrubberies I have seen, in which art seems to have exhausted her skill. All the country seats, however, from this to Boston, generally, are truly magnificent; but they are completely eclipsed by the far-famed Cambridge, three miles on this side of Boston. Here I must stop! cities, towns, villages, rivers, shrubberies, groves, harbors, edifices, domes, steeples, bridges, and shipping, all bursting upon one at once, the ablest pen would shrink from the task. Cambridge itself unites every thing that can be called great and beautiful, a vast green of some miles in extent, as level as a calm sea, overspread with here and there a cluster of trees, streets and houses. The lofty halls of the University, a master piece of architecture, with the grand squares attached to them, the church, and professor's dwelling houses, may give some idea of Cambridge. But this is only a drop in the ocean; lift your eye from the smooth green lawns of Cambridge, and Boston stands before you, rising up as it were, out of the water; a little to the left is Charlestown, on the right is Roxbury and Watertown. Charles' river is upwards of a mile wide, branching off into different channels; five vast bridges in view; the United States' navy yard at Charlestown, with two ships of the line of an hundred and ten guns each; the shipping of Boston and Cambridge ports, all visible at one view, presents an assemblage of objects beyond the power of any one to describe.

Boston.—Boston rises up gradually from the water's edge on all sides, and terminates upon a lofty eminence in the centre, or nearly so. This gives it a fine display from whatever point it is approached. The state-house, a grand edifice with a lofty dome, stands upon the highest ground in the city, nearly in the centre; this, and the cupolas of Fanueil Hall, the old state-house, and a dozen others, with about 70 white steeples which pierce the clouds in every part of the town, gives Boston a decided advantage over any city, in point of beauty, at this distance.   The bridges mentioned, as my fellow travellers informed me, are called by different names ; one leads from Cambridge to Charlestown, another from Boston to Charlestown, and three from Cambridge to Boston ; one, however, is a causeway, or mill dam, which is crossed as a bridge ; some of them are a mile in lengh. We took the middle bridge, which soon landed us in Boston, where beauty diminished as we drew near ; and still more so when we found ourselves lost in narrow streets, with houses mountain high on each side of us.   I was no little afraid of being dashed to pieces by the stages and carriages which come meeting us, for want of room to pass.

At length I arrived at the exchange coffee-house, (where all the great people put up,) was assisted out of the stage by some of the clerks, and making a sudden stop at the foot of a tremendous staircase, desired the young man " not to put me in one of his little back rooms, where I could see nothing." " O no," he replied, " you shall have room enough," and leading the way up stairs, he left me in a parlour about forty feet square! laughing as he drew the door after him at the idea, no doubt, that he had given me room enough.   It was some time in the afternoon of the following day, before I ventured to walk over the city, which, independent of the scenery that surrounds it, is by no means handsome.   The streets are very short, narrow, and crooked, and the houses are so high, (many of them five stories,) that one seems buried alive.   The side-walks are narrow, and badly paved, and the town is badly lighted ; in this respect, it is greatly behind New-York or Philadelphia.   They have a custom amongst them as old as the city, singular enough ; that is, shutting up their shops at dark, winter and summer, which gives the city a gloomy appearance, and must be doubly so during the long winter nights.   I should be at a loss to conjecture how their clerks and young men dispose of themselves, during their long winters.   New-York and Philadelphia do as much business after dark as they do in the day, and perhaps more ; for the young people then take time to amuse themselves, and the lights which illuminate the shops and stores, give life and activity to the whole city. Broadway, Pearl-street, Chatham, and in fact all that do business, forms one of the most cheering spectacles in the world at night. The site of the city is nearly circular, its greatest width being not more than a mile and a half, or perhaps three quarters; but the houses are closely built, and so high, that they contain a great number of people. There are, however, some handsome streets, such as Washington-street, State-street, Green and Congress-streets : but the glory of streets is the colonnade on the side of the mall. Beacon-street is also, for its length, unrivalled, bordering on the mall likewise, and being on elevated ground, it commands one of the finest views in the city: it runs in front of the state-house. But the scenery of the environs is what distinguishes Boston from any city, perhaps in the world! No one can conceive imagery more rich, or more replete in beauty. From the top of the state-house arises a dome, ornamented with a cupola some hundred feet in height, from which you have one of the finest prospects in the world. Every part of the city, the wide spreading bay, the ocean, Charles' river, the bridges, white sails, Charlestown, Cambridge, South Boston, Roxbury, Dorchester, Quincy, in short, twenty-eight towns and villages may be seen distinctly with the naked eye, with an extensive country, in the highest state of cultivation, splendid mansions, rich shrubberies and gardens, to the distance of twenty miles, with rounding hills of magic beauty, all mingled together ; add to these the numerous islands in the bay, Fort Independence, and Fort Warren, the human mind is incapable of admitting more, the eye is literally surfeited with beauty !—the scenes are lost in rapture ! ! Much as I had travelled, and curious as I had been to regard the scenery of the states through which I passed, never had I seen any thing to compare to this, even my favorite scenery in Washington City, shrinks into nothing beside it. I could extend these remarks to an enormous volume, abounding as it does, with endless materials, but my engagements oblige me to be brief, and I haste to describe the city in a topographical view.

Boston is about four miles in circumference, in shape
an oblong, or nearly circular. It is almost surrounded
by water, being joined to the main land by a narrow
neck, extending in the direction of Roxbury, to which
the buildings join. It is only separated from Cambridge
and Charlestown by Charles' river, and from Dorchester and South-Boston by a part of the bay, over which
there is likewise a bridge. These lie south, Cambridge
lies west, and Charlestown lies north, or nearly so. Boston contains 1 new state-house, 1 old do. a court-house,
a hall for police, Fanueil hall, a prison, an alms-house,
a house of correction, a hospital, a dispensary, a theatre, a circus, a custom-house, a city library, a law library, an athenæum, a museum, 2 market-houses, 6 bridges,
3 wharves and the mall, an observatory, and 7 banks.
It has also 32 houses for public worship, viz. 12 Congregationalists and Unitarians, 4 Episcopalians, 4 Baptists, 4 Universalists, 3 Methodists, 1 Roman Catholic,
1 Friends, 1 New-Jerusalem, 1 Seamen's chapel, and 1
African. The wharves of Boston are among the first
public buildings in the city, and a subject of admiration
to all who visit them : they extend to a great distance in
the water, to wit, central and long wharf, 1,240 feet.
The India wharf is also of considerable length. These
wharves are lofty brick houses, with a street on each
side, for the lading of vessels, the water being too shallow for vessels to come near the shore, as they do at
New-York. The buildings on those wharves surpass
any idea that can be formed of symmetry and proportion :
so uniform in height, that no line can be drawn with
more exactness ; particularly central wharf, the whole
of the buildings being four stories high, built of the best
burnt brick, and occupied for stores. I mean the wharves
are all four stories high, and of brick, but the central
wharf being more recently built, is more showy. Nothing can look more grand than these wharves stretching out into the bay to such an amazing length. The
state-house requires little more to be said. It is called
the *new* state-house, to distinguish it from the old one.
It stands upon a lofty eminence, called Mount Vernon,
at the head of the mall.* It is built of brick, and very

* Pronounced Mal by the citizens.

high in proportion to its relative size. It has a splendid dome and cupola of astonishing height, with stairs
leading many a weary round, out upon the top. It fronts
the mall, with a colonnade of singular beauty. The legislature of the state holds its sessions in the state-house ;
the treasurer of the state, the adjutant general, and secretary of state have their offices there. The governor
and council also sit in the state-house. The interior is
not very splendidly decorated, but quite enough so.
The legislative halls are on the second story, and are
very simple indeed ; the members sitting upon semi-circular seats, without desks ; the speaker's chair is distinguished by no frippery or pomp. From the centre is
suspended a costly brass chandelier, which was presented to them by a relation of mine !—His name, and the
date of the year it was presented, is engraved upon it.
This unexpected memento, which was lowered for my
inspection by my conductor, filled me with emotions
which may easily be imagined. In strolling through the
building, I came across several relics of the continental
war, which deeply interested me.—I remembered that
war !—I remembered the uniform !—A hat worn by the
Light Infantry, another of a non-commissioned officer,
one of the caps worn in the tents, one or two knapsacks,
all of humble materials; the hats were small, coarse,
round crown, bound round with coarse ferret, such as
our dandies would disdain. Besides these, there was a
bayonet, a spur, and the hilt of a sword ; all were rusty,
and showed the marks of time. They were brought to
Boston from West Point, and are carefully preserved in
the office of the adjutant-general. Having mentioned
the mall now the second time, I may as well dispose of
it, while I am in the neighborhood, and have it full in my
eye, nothing but a street between us. Moreover, in disposing of it, I dispose of the most interesting part of the
city. The mall (which is often called the common,) is
an extensive plot of ground, enclosed and designed for
the amusement of the citizens : it is very large, comprising between 11 and 12 acres, nearly square ; it has a
gentle descent from the state-house to the water, which
spreads out into a wide sheet at its lowest extremity. It

is planted with beautiful flourishing trees, and has a large
pond fed by a spring in the centre. Near this pond
stands the celebrated great elm, a drawing of which has
been eagerly sought by the neighboring cities ; this tree
was planted by Mr. Quincy, the father of Mrs. Scott, the
widow of the celebrated Hancock, who signed the declaration of Independence, the same family who gave name to
Quincy, the residence of the venerable John Adams. It
is a tree of great size, but not very high ; the top, however, branches out in great luxuriance. The city of
New-York has offered a premium for the best drawing of
this tree, and several artists are now engaged in the performance : such is the renowned " mall." But the mall
must be seen and enjoyed, to obtain an accurate idea of
it. Here the citizens repair in sultry weather, to breathe
the refreshing breeze from the ocean. Here may be
seen the young and the old of both sexes, particularly of
an evening ; the gay dresses of the ladies are now flutter-
ing in the wind before me. The spruce beau, the pert
apprentice, the statesman, and the beggar, all tread the
mall in the pride of independence ; but I must quit this
pleasing scene for one less pleasant.

Old State House.—The old state-house is a large brick
building, at the head of state-street, which runs east and
west ; it stands about the middle of the city, has a cupola, and looks venerable from age. It is now used as a
masonic hall, and sundry public offices are kept in it.
Formerly the general court, (as the legislature is called
in Massachusetts,) held their sittings in it.

Fanueil Hall.—At the foot of state-street, a little to the
left, stands Fanueil hall, famous in history as the rallying point from whence the adventurous sons of freedom
hurled their thunderbolts upon inordinate ambition.
Fanueil hall is a large building of brick ; the basement
story is now, and always has been, used as a market-
house. It is open on all sides, and filled with butchers
and butcher's meat ; the second story comprises the hall,
with one or two small offices at one end. The upper one,
or third story, contains the city arms. The hall is kept
locked up, except upon particular occasions, such as the
fourth of July, or Washington's birth-day, or some ex-

traordinary meeting of the citizens. The clerk of the
market opened the door, and left me to contemplate, in
silence, this sacred cradle of American liberty—who,
that has read the history of his country, has not
dwelt with interest upon the soul-trying scenes which
passed within these walls! The hall is of considerable
length and looks as fresh as though it were finished yesterday. It is neat, but plain, and without galleries: gentle elevations appear on each side, in different rows, in
the form of steps, reaching from one end to the other,
upon which the listening crowd were wont to stand to
hear the immortal Hancock and Adams. A full length
portrait of Fanueil, who presented the hall to Boston,
in an old fashioned dress, adorns the upper end of the
hall, a little to the right of the humble chair, once filled
by virtue and undaunted courage! The floor on which
I tread was once pressed by the feet of those illustrious
heroes!—yes, from that seat resounded a voice which
shook Great Britain to her centre!—Liberty or death!
Great souls—great in council, great in the field—tran-
scendent men, well do you merit the plaudits of admiring ages! A wreath of flowers and evergreen hangs over
the chair. I left the hall with deep impressions of the
interest I took in its sanctity, and went above to view
the arms. The city of Boston is divided into ten companies; each company is designated by different names,
and different uniforms. The arms, &c. of every company, are deposited in a separate room; these are disposed in the neatest and most complete manner of any companies to be found. Each man has his gun, a cartridge-
box, a knapsack, a tin cup, a hat, (or cap,) and canteen, so
precisely disposed that they may equip themselves at a
moment's warning. Each man has his accoutrements
numbered; this number is legibly marked upon the wall
where he must place his accoutrements, under penalty
of fine. No mistake in these Bostonians. Drums, fifes,
and colors all in complete order. The market is just under them; they have nothing to do, but fill their knapsacks and march.

    Court-House.—The court-house stands between the
old and new state-houses. It is a very handsome build-
27

ing, I should say the handsomest public edifice in the city.
It is built of white free stone, and the work is well executed. It cost $92,000. The courts sit in this build-
ing. The mayor holds his courts in it. It contains several offices, besides a law library, containing about 1,700
volumes entirely devoted to the subject of law!

Massachusetts general Hospital.—The general hospital
is a vast building of stone, at the north west extremity of
the city. It is handsomely ornamented with a glass cupola, and is the most spacious building in the city. It
differs little from the Philadelphia hospital in the neatness and convenience of the apartments. The floors of
the Massachusetts general hospital are painted; those of
Philadelphia, New-York, and Baltimore are not. There
are more patients in the same room in the former, neither are the insane admitted in this as in Philadelphia
and Baltimore, a very judicious improvement. The
asylum for the insane is in Charlestown, and makes a
part of the general hospital, being under the direction of
the same trustees, and subject to the same regulations.
The general hospital was founded in 1811, but did not
go into operation till 1818. Fifty-six gentlemen from
different parts of the state, were incorporated by the
name of the "Massachusetts general hospital," with
power to hold personal and real property to the amount
of $3000 income per annum. The charter constitutes
the governor, lieutenant governor, the president of the
senate, the speaker of the house, and the two chaplains
of the legislature, a board of visitors semi-annually.

The corporation choose a president, a vice president,
twelve trustees, a treasurer, and secretary by ballot, to
serve for one year. The trustees choose (by ballot,)
eight practitioners in physic and surgery, who are called
consulting physicians. They likewise choose an acting
physician, an acting surgeon, a superintendant, and matron, for *each* department, one of each for the hospital,
and the same for the *asylum* for the *insane.*

The corporation meet annually, when all the doings
of the trustees are laid before them. The trustees meet
quarterly, when all reports, books, accounts, and minutes, relating to the general hospital are strictly examin-

ed by them. The trustees are divided into six visiting committees, each to serve one month. Their duty is to visit the hospital and asylum once in every week, examine every patient and every room in the hospital and asylum, to see that it be kept in proper order. The consulting physicians are called on in all difficult cases. The cooking, washing, ironing and bathing departments, are constructed upon a plan superior to any thing of the sort I have seen in the United States.

The institution has not as yet been able to extend relief to paupers ; each boarder pays at least three dollars per week, every thing included.* My limited means of information has not enabled me to say what compensation (or whether any) is bestowed upon the members of the institution, except the superintendents, who receive a yearly salary.

Perhaps there is not an instance upon record, which affords the same evidence of liberality and public spirit, evinced by every class of citizens, in promoting this grand object. One thousand and forty-seven individuals subscribed—of these, three gentlemen in Boston subscribed five thousand dollars each! two hundred and forty-five gentlemen subscribed one hundred dollars each! and above that sum, one hundred dollars, which constitutes them members of the corporation for life. The " Massachusetts humane society" subscribed five thousand dollars. They have received in legacies sixty thousand dollars. The state granted them the " old province house," yielding a yearly income of $2000. These donations may give some idea of the wealth and benevolence of the citizens of Boston. This exceeds New-York. The buildings of the general hospital, and lands attached to it, cost $184,173 45 cts. Annual average expense of the hospital, $1,836 ; do. asylum, $1,-217 36 cts. This extends to the year 1822 : I found no later report on record. Three capital surgical operations have been performed in the hospital, since its commencement ; viz. one of *lithotomy*, one of *popliteal aneurism*, and one case of *phymosis*, all of which succeeded

* The hospital is compelled by law to support 30 state paupers annually.

The institution owns a valuable botanical garden. A-
mong the members of the corporation, I find the honored
names of John Adams, John Q. Adams, Levi Lincoln,
Crowninshield, Strickland, Otis, Philips, Thorndike,
Perkins, and Story. It is made the duty of the visiting
committee to see the wards and rooms in every building, to inquire into the conduct of the officers and attend-
ants towards the boarders, to examine whether the galleries, apartments, beds, linen, &c. are in good order,
whether the provisions are of a good and wholesome quality, and sufficient in quantity, whether the stoves, fires,
&c. are in good order and safe, and whether heat and
ventilation are properly attended to. The attending
physicians and surgeons, with the superintendant, must
reside in the hospital. No operation is performed, but
in the presence of many individuals. Not a medicine is
prepared but by written prescription, which is placed on
record; not a patient remains in the hospital who is not
visited once a week by the visiting committee, and per-
sonally examined by them; no change in food or in disease, and no medical application, but what are noted in
a book, and exhibited to the board of visiters and to the
public. No one can be elected acting physician, surgeon, or superintendent, who is not above twenty-six
years of age, shall have studied physic and surgery sev-
en years or more, and have been recommended by the
consulting physicians as a proper person. A record of
all their doings is carfully kept in a book. There were
but 70 patients in the hospital when I called; I did not
visit the insane.

Alms-House.—Boston has struck out a new path with
respect to the poor. They have attached a large farm
to the establishment, which is worked by the paupers,
and by means of this, and articles furnished for spinning
and making clothes, they are little or no charge to the
city. Many indigent persons who are unable to purchase wood or other necessaries of life, go to the poor-
house, and ultimately prove an advantage to the establishment; these come and go when they choose : the
homeless and all are taken in there. The paupers are
mostly men and women advanced in years, who work a

little every day ; they work at their ease, no one offering
to extort more from them than they are able and willing
to perform. It is surprising to witness how neat their
farm and gardens appear. Massachusetts is famous for
her skill in farming in general, but this farm excels ; it
has the appearance of magic. They plant a great quantity of potatoes, beans and peas, and every species of
vegetables. It is a perfect show to see how accurate the
farm is laid out, and the neat order in which it is kept,
not a weed to be seen. This is the work of the men ; the
women stay within doors, they wash, iron, mend, and
cook. The poor-house is a large stone building in South
Boston, several stories, with a chapel in the upper story,
where divine service is performed every Sunday. From
200 to 300 paupers are supported in this manner, annually, being little expense to the community. I never saw
more happiness, ease and comfort, than exists in the
poor-house of Boston. The amount of expenditures for
objects belonging to this department, from May 1, 1824,
to April 30, 1825, was $25,822 35.

The nett expense of the alms-house, is 1,873 90 ; average number of persons in the alms-house, is 336 ; families relieved in wards, 635 ; pensioners, 158 ; persons
to whom grants are made, 16.

Orphan Asylums.—There are in Boston two permanent orphan asylums, established by the legislature,
though wholly supported by subscription. One of these
is for the support and education of female orphans, supported by the ladies of Boston ; the other is for male orphans, and supported by the gentlemen. Being told
no material difference distinguished these benevolent establishments, I only visited the female asylum. Here
was another evidence of the public spirit and unbounded
charity of the people of Boston, some ladies giving as
high as $400. The ladies of several other towns in the
state are subscribers. But here I must remark, what I
have once before in these sketches, that there are too
many children together. The building is by no means
adequate to the number of children in this asylum. The
slightest observation of the apartments is enough to convince any one of their truth. Besides, there are too ma-

27*

ny in the school-room; it will not, it cannot be healthy where so many living beings are compelled to breathe the effluvia issuing from each other. Neither do I approve of keeping children so very young as those are, (some of them not more than four years of age,) so closely confined: what I mean is, that children of their age are too young to be kept at close study so great a portion of the day, as these children are. Something is wrong in the management of the establishment, I would suppose, from the appearance of the children, they do not look healthy and vigorous. The dear little creatures were all disposed (to the amount of an hundred I should think,) on seats adapted to their size, some knitting, some sewing, some reading and writing; I examined them all, at which they seemed highly delighted. After going through the building and hearing them recite, the lady matron or directress desired them to sing, when the whole troop joined in a hymn, which they sung in strains of the most enchanting sweetness.

State Prison—The state prison of Massachusetts is organized upon the same plan as those of New-York and Philadelphia, with this difference, however, the convicts of the former are more lively and active, perform their work with more cheerfulness, and receive the full amount of their labor. The prison is in Charlestown, and like those mentioned, has a large yard for the prisoners to perform their labor. The out door laborers are chiefly stone-cutters, and never did men exceed them in application to business. The prison-yard is in one continual roar of hammers and chissels. Not a man lifted his head to look at me, as I walked through the sheds, while the dust or sand, raised by the instruments, almost blinded me. The mechanics work in shops, which make a part of the prison wall, some hundred feet in length. In these shops mechanics of every description are at work, even at jewelry, printing, and engraving: many of these convicts clear their expenses, and have money to take with them when they are discharged.

" The state prison, or penitentiary, is built of stone, and stands on the westernmost point of the peninsula of Charlestown, called Lynde's point, a pleasant and

healthful situation, commanding an extensive, rich and
variegated prospect. It consists of a principal building,
66 feet long and 28 wide, containing five stories; and
two wings, each 67 feet long by 44 wide; making the
whole building 200 feet. The centre or principal building, is divided into apartments for the accommodation of
the officers and overseers. The two wings form the
prison, and are four stories high, containing 47 rooms and
cells in each wing. A long entry, 12 feet wide, runs
through each story, the whole length of the wing, and
the cells or rooms are situated on each side of this entry,
and open into it. The rooms of the two upper stories
are 17 feet by 11, and are furnished with square windows, with double grates and a glazed sash. The cells
of the two lower stories are only 11 feet by 8, and have
no windows; receiving air and a small light by means
of crevices or openings through the wall, about 2 feet
long and 4 inches wide. These cells in the ground story, are appropriated for the convicts during their sentence to solitary, and when confined as a punishment for
disorderly behaviour. Half of the upper story of the
east wing is appropriated for a hospital, where the sick
are comfortably situated, tenderly nursed, and skilfully
attended. The other half of this story is the apartments
for the females, who are always locked in, and not suffered to go into the work yard where the male convicts
are.

The foundation of the prison is composed of rocks,
averaging two tons weight, laid in mortar; on this foundation is laid a tier of hewn stone, 9 feet long, and 20
inches thick, forming the first floor. The outside walls
are 4, and the partition walls 2 feet thick; all the joints
in the wall are cramped with iron. The doors of the
cells in the two lower stories are made of wrought iron,
each weighing from 500 to 600 pounds. The entries
have grated windows and sashes, at the outer ends of
each wing, and at the inner ends, grated doors, through
which the prisoners come out and descend to the yard.
On the centre of the building is a cupola, in which the
alarm bell is suspended.

Competent judges pronounce this to be one of the

strongest and best built prisons in the world. It has
these advantages over many other buildings of this kind,
it can neither be set on fire by the prisoner, nor be un-
dermined. The stones of which it is built are of coarse
hard granite, from 6 to 14 feet long.

The work yard is 375 feet by 260, encompassed by a
stone wall, 5 feet thick at the bottom, 3 feet at top, and
15 feet high, on top of which, is a plank walk, or platform, with railings, where the centinels who perform duty by day are stationed. It is guarded at night by 24
men."

The whole of the prison is neatly plastered and white-
washed, even to the floors : from two to four sleep in
one cell, upon straw beds, with pillows and blankets, and
stools to sit on. They eat three times a day, mush with
molasses or milk, for breakfast ; supper the same ; pork
or fish, with beans or peas, and bread, for dinner ; all
who labor hard, drink beer. None are put in for life. It
is under the government of a warden, deputy warden,
commissary, clerk, keeper, three turnkeys, eleven watchmen, and attended by a chaplain and physician. The
number of prisoners in when I called, was about 300—
280 is about the average. They cleared $17,139 46 last
year, (1824,) after paying all expenses. This is the
best prison, and the best kept, of any in the U. States,
at least, that I have seen. The wardens and keepers
are gentlemen of education, and discharge their trust with
great humanity.

Athæneum.—But the pride of Boston is the Athenæum.
Here the citizens " drink deep of the Pierian Spring."
It contains a library of 19,000 volumes, of the best au-
thors, both ancient and modern. Here I saw for the first
time Confucius, Terence, Dante, and Leland's transla-
tion of Demosthenes. Being honored with the privilege
of the Athenæum, I spent some pleasant hours in its a-
partments ; the books are classed in different rooms, and
you have only to name those you wish to read, when you
are shewn into that part of the building which contains
them. No one is permitted, not even the proprietors, to
take a book so much as from one room to another ; those,
and those only, who are proprietors, can go into the A-

thenæum without special leave from one of their number.
The privilege is certainly one of the greatest treats ; the
building being one of the largest in the city, pleasantly
shaded with trees, the rooms spacious, and as silent as
night ; no one is allowed to speak above their breath
lest they might interrupt the readers. Each room is accommodated with chairs, tables, pen and ink, for taking
extracts if you wish so to do. Besides the library, the
Athenæum contains a choice collection of statuary and
painting. For this invaluable treasure, the citizens of
Boston are indebted to the taste, zeal, and indefatigable
research of —— Shaw, Esq. a man of platonic virtue,
and once secretary of the ex-president Adams, to whom
he is related. He was the founder of the Athenæum ;
and to whose politeness I am indebted for my introduction into it ; here the first citizens of Boston repair in
their leisure hours to read. Besides this library, there
are several in the city. The law library has been mentioned ; the city library contains 6060 volumes. The
books in all the libraries are well selected ; want what
author you will, it is to be found in Boston.

Markets.—The market of Boston yields to none, and
in many things it excels, particularly in its fish ; the butter is sweet and abundant, much more so than in New-
York ; but there is no market that I have seen which
equals Boston for its excellence in fish. The meat and
vegetables also are fine and plentiful, with early fruit of
delicious flavor ; but they have no market-house worth
the name. The butchers assemble under Fanueil Hall,
and another place adjoining ; but the venders of vegetables line themselves in rows at random, or sell out of
carts the best way they can ; the fishmongers have a kind
of a shed, with a long bench, near to which they have
large tubs of water with the finest salmon, fresh from the
ocean, and every kind of fish that can be mentioned.
The fish market is exemplary for neatness. But how they
have, with their population, lived so long without a market
house is a mystery. They are now building one, which
is nearly finished ; it would, for length, make about one
square of the Philadelphia market, and wide enough for
two. It is laughable (I mean for those who are not con-

tra disposed,) to see the pains and cost they are at to
construct a building the least calculated for the purpose
intended of any thing else.   It is a massy building of
free-stone, finished in superior style, carried up in a solid
wall, like a house, whereas the beauty is out of the question.   I mean the convenience of a market-house is, to
have it long, narrow, and open on all sides, so that the
articles may be spread abroad, and the people may have
both room and light.   The same money they are spending on this, would have built a complete market-house,
three times as long, and ten fold more to the purpose.
They have the neatest arched windows and doors, all of
the whitest free-stone and first architecture; and instead
of placing this most worthy edifice in the centre of the
city, they have built it nearly at the bay.   I dare say it
will cost some hundred thousand dollars.   Their fire department is also badly organized; this, however, they
are about to remedy.   Boston has only been incorporated a few years; before this, it was governed by select
men, to whose want of foresight on the subject of the
general weal, may be the supposed cause of the city's
being kept rather in the back ground.

Museum.—The museum of Boston is a good collection,
but kept in a slovenly condition, and the subjects badly
preserved.   In this respect it is greatly inferior to that
of Philadelphia or New-York.   It is chiefly valuable for
its specimens in the fine arts, which consist of paintings
and statuary: besides these, an ancient shield, and the
chair used by Gov. Winthrop, when administering justice, were the most interesting objects.   The elephant
that was killed while crossing the bridge, is handsomely
preserved, and standing on its feet, in the museum, though
not enclosed in glass, like the one I saw in New-York;
it is, however, much larger: it also contains a great
Greenland white bear, which, for size, has no equal; also a variety of wax figures, which always disgust me.
Among the paintings is Trumbull's representation of
Gen. Washington crossing the Delaware, after the breaking up of the ice.   He is in the act of giving his horse,
upon which he is mounted, a sudden check by the rein,
whilst with his head turned over one shoulder toward the

river, he is earnestly watching the progress of the army
and artillery over the stream.

The famous treaty of Penn with the Indians is also
represented, though in small design. Penn is standing,
with his head uncovered, under the renowned elm, amidst
an immense crowd of whites and Indians. The whites
are on his left, and the Indians on his right hand, all of
whom have their eyes fixed on him in deep attention;
Penn, with his hands spread in token of sincerity, seems
to have concluded the treaty. A number of trunks are
standing on the ground, and some of the white people
are on their knees unlocking them, taking out the goods
they contain, and distributing them amongst the Indians.
The Gill family (one of the most distinguished in Massachusetts) by Copely, likewise deserves notice. Gill
himself, his first and second wife, his mother-in-law, with
her brother, Nicholas Boylston, are all represented in full
size, in rich attire ; the ladies in full dress of blue satin ;
Boylston has a rich mantle of crimson satin thrown over
him, while he is regarding you with the keenest eye in
nature. This gentleman is celebrated for his wealth, as
also in history for his liberality in bestowing to Cambridge University a library of 28,000 volumes. Here
too, is a full size representation of a French princess, in
the reign of Louis XIV. by Nutter. The left side of her
head is as plain as my hand, the right is curled into ringlets, and twisted high up on the temple, ornamented with
a garland of flowers. Her neck is bare, her bosom full,
and her waist screwed to nothing. Her arms. which are
finely turned, are bare to the elbow, from which drops,
in luxuriant folds, a double tier of the richest lace. Her
eyebrows are arched, her face masculine, but fair, with
much expression and dignity in the countenance. Also
Rittenhouse, with his hair parted in front, from the crown
of his head, and never was any thing more plain and
simple. Likewise a portrait of Chancellor Livingston,
who is looking me in the face with a calm, steady countenance, surpassing the unruffled sea. But the giant Her-
cules frightens the beholder; he is represented dying,
his eyes thrown up to heaven, his masculine limbs. his

grim countenance, his face besmeared with blood; he is terrible even in death!

Manners and Appearance.—Whatever may be the cause, and however strange it may appear, yet it is nevertheless true, that in proportion as one part of society advance in science and civilization, the other part sink into vapid ignorance ; like turbid water, the pure particles rise to the top, while the dregs settle to the bottom. Whether the cause of this difference is to be sought for in the physical or moral structure of the human mind, I leave to those whom it may more deeply concern to investigate. This truth is perhaps in no community more clearly manifested than in Boston. The people differ as widely as tho' they lived on opposite sides of the globe. How happens this ? The means of education are the same to all ; there are not less than an hundred schools in Boston and its vicinity, free to all, many of them without money and without price ; Cambridge is in sight ! Never were the means so ample as in Boston ; the whole state is one seminary of education ; no excuse for ignorance ; the poor are taught gratis.

One part of the community have realized these advantages while the other has not. In no city, perhaps, in America, are to be found a greater body of what may be called gentlemen than in Boston : whatever can be conceived of wealth, whatever can be conceived of talent, or intellect embellished by education or improved by business, is eminently displayed in the gentlemen of Boston. Here the human mind appears to be perfectly unfolded ; most of them, indeed all of them, are men of liberal education, whether professional or not, and by associating constantly together, and reciprocating those delicious waters which flow from the fountain of knowledge, their manners, of course, accords with the excellence of those attainments. They are affable, mild, and liberal, in every sense of the word. They are mostly Unitarians and Universalists in religion, the most humane and benevolent sects I have met with ; the former, however, predominate. The ladies, like the gentlemen, are not exceeded by any on the continent ; in accomplished manners, they possess all the yielding softness of the southern ladies, with warmer hearts, and minds improved by travelling, most of them having made the tour of Europe. Their countenance is diffused with a magic charm of irresistible sweetness, to which they join the utmost grace of gesture and harmony of voice. As to beauty, the ladies of Boston are celebrated throughout the world. But that which deserves our greatest applause, is their unbounded benevolence and charity towards the distressed; " which things the angels desired to look into." All the females, of every class, have a flexible softness in their manners peculiar to them. What may be called the lower class, for their opportunity, are ignorant, proud, and abrupt in their manners, particularly the men; nor do they mix at all with the higher class, or have any intercourse with them, more than with the inhabitants of a distant country. They do not know them in the streets, they are as absolutely separated as though an impassable gulph lay between them. These last, I cannot call them clowns, for a clown though awkward is bashful; but these are presuming, pert, and in some cases rude, nor have they a spark of that yielding charity which distinguishes their more refined neighbors. Their manners and their dialect perfectly correspond, though they can read and write, and many, in fact, all, I am told, go to the grammar schools; a chambermaid will read as correct as the most finished scholar, and yet their dialect is wretchedly defective. Here are a few of their phrases; *had'nt ought*, ought not, *I be*, I am, *do what you'r mine'to*, use your pleasure, *on to it*, on it, with a number of such. But *guess*, and *what'say*, are their favorites, and make a part of every sentencce. It is amusing enough to hear about a dozen of their *what'-says* and *guesses* assembled together. What'say is a substitute for sir or madam, (which amongst them you seldom hear,) and answers to the *how*, of New-York; it is a habit they have contracted from asking a question to be repeated again, although they have heard it distinctly. They have the *hickups* here too. All the learning in the world will never break them of those vulgar habits. Thousands of dollars are expended annually in Boston for no other purpose than to eradicate this igno-

28

rance, and all in vain. But hear what they say of themselves : "The people of Boston be the first people in the world, no city like Boston ; they be all fools in N. Y. they had'nt ought to be compared with the people of Boston." If this be the case in the very emporium of literary taste, all attempts to improve the common people are really disheartening.

History.—Boston was settled by Isaac Johnston, Esq. who married the lady Arabella, sister to the earl of Lincoln, from whom the present governor Lincoln is descended. But we must go back to the history of England, in order to have a satisfactory detail of the history of Boston ; a city which on every account deserves the praise of mankind. When freedom was hunted out of the world it took up its abode in Boston, from which no power has been able to dislodge it. When Queen Elizabeth returned to the government of England, all those who had taken refuge from persecution, returned also. But some of these being more strenuous than others, were, by their brethren, styled puritans ; these last refused to conform to the ceremonies of the church established by Elizabeth, for which, they were rigidly punished. Puritanism, however, spread, and gained ground by persecution. These proceedings called up a question among those learned divines, respecting the established church ; " is she any longer a true church of Christ, and are her ministers true ministers." The result was, that they withdrew themselves, and formed a state church, and elected their own pastors. These are the same with Congregationalists, who have preserved this mode of electing their ministers ever since. In this respect they differed from the Presbyterians of Scotland, whose ministers are appointed by a presbytery. One Robert Brown, of an honorable family, and related to the lord-treasurer, a fiery zealot, travelled through the country, held forth against bishops, ecclesiastics, courts, and ordaining ministers, and gathered a separate congregation. These refused to join in worship either with the regular church or with the puritans, and were called Brownites. Most of the puritans were for keeping within the pale of the regular church, though they disapproved of its ceremonies, and wrote against Brownism. The government, however, imprisoned, fined, and put to death, all non-conformists, without distinction; amongst these the Brownites were the greatest sufferers. About this time they amounted to 20,000. At length a number of religious people, upon the borders of Nottingham, Lincolnshire, and Yorkshire, joined the Brownites. There were now so many of them, and lived at such a distance asunder, that they formed themselves into two distinct societies. The one with which is our concern, had for its pastor the famous John Robinson. The church still being harassed by government, removed to Holland one year after Robinson was elected. After remaining some time in Holland, which did not suit their religious principles, they turned their eyes towards America. With great difficulty they obtained a patent for settling in America, and part of them returning to London, the rest set sail, and entered the harbor of Cape Cod on the 10th of November, 1620: Robinson was not of the party, he returned to England. Before they landed they formed themselves into a civil body politic, under the crown of England, and to the amount of 101 landed at Plymouth, a name which they gave the place in honor of the city of that name in England.* These, however, nearly all died before another ship came over and added to the number. It was years before the plantation amounted to more than 300.

When Mr. Robinson and his church separated from England, they were rigid Brownites. But after removing to Holland, and conversing with men of learning, and being a gentleman of a liberal mind and good disposition, he became more moderate, as did his people; so that the Brownites would not unite with them in worship. Mr. Robinson wrote against Brownism, and was the means of ruining the sect. He is the father of the Congregationalist form of worship, which is at this day used in New-England: Brownism is discarded. Meantime, Mr. John Carver, the first governor of Plymouth, dying,

* They landed the 11th, and the last of the month (November) the wife of Wm. White was delivered of a son, the first child born in New-England. They called it Peregrine.

Mr. Bradford was elected in his stead. In 1621, Governor Bradford sent a shallop, with ten men and three Indians, to make discoveries in the bay afterwards called Massachusetts bay. These men landed under a cliff supposed to be Copp's Hill, in Boston; had an interview with the chief, and formed a friendly intercourse with the natives. In 1629, King Charles incorporated the governor of Massachusetts bay, in New-England, which comprised all the land lying between three miles north of the Merrimack, and three miles south of Charles river. Thus was laid the foundation of Boston. The patent right was purchased by Sir Richard Saltonstall, Thomas Dudley, John Winthrop, and others; Winthrop was made governor, and Dudley deputy-governor. They embarked the following spring, in fourteen vessels, accompanied by several gentlemen of wealth and eminence, to the amount of fifteen hundred; amongst whom was Isaac Johnston, and arrived in Massachusetts bay. Before they landed, they held a court on board the ship Arabella,* (named so in honor of Johnston's wife,) the principal object of which was to provide for the support of their ministers; after which, they landed where Charlestown now stands, and repaired to a large spreading tree, under which Messrs. Phillips and Wilson preached their first sermon; the people sheltering their heads with booths and tents. Shortly after this, they spread themselves over the territory of Johnston, and others settled Boston, (called by the natives Shawmut.) Sir Richard Saltonstall settled Watertown, which is in sight of Boston, between Cambridge and Roxbury; Quincy settled Quincy; Ludlow Dorchester; Pynchon, who has already been mentioned, settled Roxbury. Winthrop, as governor of the colony, settled finally in Boston. I saw his chair, which is still preserved in the museum. I was upon the hill where the tree stood, under which those intrepid people heard their first sermon, though no vestige of the tree remains! I was on the famous Bunker Hill, where they risked their lives in defence of that liberty for which they forsook their native land! I was on the spot where the brave Gen. Warren

* Hence their legislatures still retain the name of courts.

fell!! I saw the remains of the old monument, erected on the spot where he breathed his last. It was a rude structure of brick, which some unknown person has almost demolished, as disgraceful to the country. In a few days hence the corner stone of a monument more worthy the occasion, is to be laid!—I am now standing on the remains of the entrenchment thrown up by the Americans on the evening before the battle; it is scarcely perceivable, being overgrown with grass, and nearly level with the ground. I see the point by which the British approached up the hill, down which they were twice drove by the American fire. The British approached the third time; their ships and field pieces double their fire; the powder of the Americans fail; they receive the British on their bayonets; resistance is made to the last, even with the buts of their guns, which for want of powder they were unable to load—This was "liberty or death," truly! During the dreadful conflict, Charlestown was fired by a bomb from Copp's hill by the British; but the fearless sons of liberty, regardless of the devouring flames, continue the contest to the last. The British carried the redoubt with the loss of one thousand and fifty-four, out of three thousand; amongst whom was Major Pitcairn and Col. Abercrombie: the Americans lost one hundred and thirty-nine. Since I have strolled over the bridge which separates Charlestown from Boston, I will be excused for dropping a remark upon this town. Nothing can be handsomer than Charlestown, on every account: the buildings are splendid, the streets are large and regular, its site elevated and commanding; it rises up from the water's edge to Bunker's hill, part of which is built on, and overlooks Boston, Cambridge, and Massachusetts bay. For health, wealth and beauty, it surpasses any town of its size in the Union. The state prison and lunatic hospital, which I have just visited, are mentioned in their proper place: besides these, Charlestown has 6 churches, an alms-house, 26,598 inhabitants.

Navy-Yard.—The United States navy-yard is likewise located at Charlestown. A few marines are stationed here; the most trifling, abandoned-looking men, from their appearance, to be found. I applied to the

commandant, Major W. for liberty to inspect the interior
of the yard, but this haughty bashaw sent word " *he was
engaged*, and that I must report my business to the lieutenant ;" (rather a reproach to Uncle Sam.) As in duty
bound, I obeyed his highness, and called on the lieutenant, whom I found unqualified to give the information I
wished to obtain, and after undergoing sundry indignities
from those mighty men of war, I had to give up the design.   Through the politeness of Major Binny of Boston, I obtained the following particulars.   The navy-
yard contains 50 42 pound cannon, 170 32 pound do.
100 42 pound carronades, 70 32 pound do., besides a
large number of smaller guns; together with 150.000
round, grape, and shot of various sizes, from 42 to 6
pounds canister.

They are now building two ships of the line, which
are nearly completed, or so far as is suitable to their safe
preservation.   One complete frame for a frigate of the
first class, the keel of which will be laid this autumn, is
now on hand, and will be used in the succeeding spring.
A sloop of war to mount 20 32 pound carronades, will
be launched in the course of the summer ; two other
sloops are to be built next season.   It is contemplated to
build a dry dock at this yard ; the site for which is equal
if not superior to any other.   The navy-yard contains
60 acres of ground.

The line of battle ships are built under ship-houses,
which completely defend them from the weather.   Another is to be erected over the place of the frigate.   This
yard contains ground adapted for the location of a rope-
walk, and every thing necessary to fit out any number
of ships ; and there could be built at one time twenty
ships of war, of various classes.   I walked through one
of the battle ships of 110 guns, and five decks ; one of
the most awful, dread-inspiring machines in the universe!

But to return : Amongst the early settlers of this cradle of American liberty, were the Ludlows, Quincys,
Walcots, Adamses, Lowells, Thatchers, and the great
Otis family ; all of whom were distinguished for talents
and literature : to these qualities, they united courage,
firmness, and a love of liberty that feared no odds.

Amongst those renowned patriots, those defenders of the rights of mankind, shone Samuel Adams and John Hancock, a host in themselves. S. Adams was one of the common people, but having acted as sheriff many years in Boston, and being a man of great natural talents and address, was more popular among the great mass of the people than Hancock. On the other hand, Hancock was wealthy, and liberal as he was rich. He had been educated in ease and affluence, by an uncle who doated on him, and who at his death bequeathed him one million pounds sterling! I had these particulars from Mrs. Scott, his widow, who is now living in Boston. She states that her husband, Hancock, was so generous that he not only gave this great estate away, he threw it away. He came to this fortune at the commencement of the revolution. His high-born soul, fired with the love of liberty, indignant at the attempts of Great Britain to enslave his country, used to hold private consultation with Samuel Adams, whose influence over the people, was greater than Mr. Hancock's; in short, these two used to meet together privately, and lay their plans, which were disclosed to the people by Adams. They found it easy to infuse their spirit into a people naturally brave, generous, and independent. Thus were the citizens of Boston prepared to meet " liberty or death;" nor did they shrink from the high ground they had taken.

Boston was the first to propose a colonial congress to oppose the first tax of Great Britain, on coffee, silks, &c. It was the first to propose the non-importation of British manufactures, addressing circular letters to her sister colonies, to join in the resolution; and it was the first victim of British vengeance. Besides Fanueil Hall, the citizens used to meet in the old south meeting-house, a spacious and splendid building, as best suited to their numbers. When the tea ships arrived in the harbor, the Bostonians in vain endeavored to have them returned, as they were consigned to the governor. Meantime they assembled in the old south, to deliberate what was best to be done, in regard to the tea. They sat from 9 o'clock till 3, when the question was put, " Do you stand to your resolution?" and was answered in the affirmative,

nem. con., and agreed not to suffer it to be landed.
However, they concluded to wait till the owner of one of
the ships (Mr. Roach) should wait on the governor, for
leave to let his ship pass, which being refused, he returned to the meeting. After some disputing, a person in
the front gallery, dressed like an Indian, raised the war-
whoop. Upon this signal, meeting broke up, and seventeen men, in the disguise of Indians, proceeded to Grif-
fin's wharf, and in about ten minutes they hoisted out
and broke open 342 chests of tea, and threw the whole
overboard: they then returned peaceably, not having
spoken a word during the transaction. At this time
there were two British regiments in Boston; and whilst
the tea question was under discussion, an affray took
place between the citizens and the British troops, in
which three of the former were killed, and one mortally
wounded. The fourth man dying of his wounds, all of
them were interred in one vault. The citizens of Roxbury and Charlestown, formed a junction with the corps
in Key-street, and joining the procession, proceeded
through Main-street, followed by an immense crowd of
people ; so numerous that they were compelled to walk
six abreast, and the whole closed by a long train of carriages, belonging to the principal gentry in Boston.
During the procession, all the bells tolled in the most
doleful manner. But this was trifling compared with the
difficulties and mortification they underwent during the
port bill, and the residence of the British in their city.
Beef, mutton, and pork, sold for 1*s.* 1 1-2*d.* sterling, per
lb.—geese half a guinea a piece, and fowls 5*s.* a pair.
But worse than all this, the British turned their beloved
old south meeting-house into a horse-riding school ; converting it into a stable! It was at this time, perhaps,
the most richly furnished meeting-house of any in the
colonies ; the cushions being covered with crimson damask, and other costly meterials, and they stripped it of
every thing, to the walls. The old south, however, is
still standing, and has no appearance of being old. It
is a very large meeting-house, on the corner of Washington and Milk-streets, in the heart of the city, and
strange to tell, scarcely any of the young race know any

thing of its history. It is fitted up in a very superb style, has a large, fine organ, and is still used on public occasions, as well as for divine worship, which is performed in it every Sunday. I had the honor of hearing a sermon delivered in this " TEMPLE OF LIBERTY."

Since my visit to Boston, I have seen many that witnessed those trying scenes of the revolution ; amongst whom is the respected relic of Governor Hancock, (as he is called here.) This lady, after the decease of Mr. Hancock, married a Mr. Scott ; he died also. She is now a widow, a little turned of seventy, though no one would suppose her to be more than sixty ; her fine yellow hair hanging in ringlets over her forehead, with scarcely a gray hair to be seen. She is under the common size, with a light handsome figure ; she has what is called a laughing eye, and is as sprightly as a girl of sixteen. She was married a few days before the battle of Lexington, to Mr. Hancock, and was at Lexington during the battle. She related that " it was with the greatest difficulty she and her aunt kept Mr. Hancock from facing the British on that day, where he must inevitably have been sacrificed to the vengeance of Pitcairn, who had offered a reward for his head ; and such was his ardour to engage Pitcairn, that they (the ladies,) both clung round his neck so tenaciously that he was unable to extricate himself from them." She said he was a hot-headed, rash man, being with great difficulty persuaded by his friends to keep concealed while the British were in search of his person. In order to secure his safety, his friends kept him by force several days and nights, hid in a swamp, without shelter. Mr. H. had no children, and bequeathed his property to the state, (as I have been told.) Let this be as it may, Mrs. Scott is far from being in independent circumstances. She is without a carriage, and had to give up the splendid dwelling of her beloved Hancock, whom she speaks of with the greatest veneration. She keeps his portrait in her parlor, which she showed me with much seeming pleasure. I saw the house she was mistress of ; it is a noble stone building in Beacon street, and overlooks the mall. It is a reproach to Massachusetts, to suffer the widow of a man to whom they owed so much, to remain in her present situation. But she bears her reverse of fortune with the fortitude of a philosopher ; and with two agreeable nieces, who live with her, is as cheerful as though she rolled in splendor. She is the daughter of the celebrated Quincy, whose father settled the village of that name near Boston. Her father's sister was the wife of the ex-president John Adams, and the mother of John Quincy Adams, president of the United States. So little is this respectable female known, that it was a mere accident I heard of her. I likewise called on the Miss Byles's, daughters of the celebrated Mather Byles, a great poet, a great tory, a great clergyman and a great wit. Finding his name in the history of the times, I mentioned the circumstance to a friend, who told me his two daughters lived in Boston. I sought them out, and found them in an old decayed wooden house, at the foot of the mall. The house (which must have seen a century at least,) stood in a luxuriant grass plat, with two beautiful horse-chesnut trees growing near the door ; the whole was enclosed by a decayed wooden paling, which communicated with the street by a small gate with a wooden latch. Upon opening the gate I was within a few steps of the door ; but the looks of the house, the old rotten step at the door, the grass growing through it, not the trace of a human footstep to be seen, the silence that pervaded the mouldering mansion before me, I imagined it could be no other than a deserted house. I knocked at the door, however, and an elderly female opened it immediately ; I inquired for the ladies of the house ; she replied, " she was one of them, and that her sister was sick." Upon my saying something about paying my respects to them, she very coldly invited me to walk in. The house looked something better inside, though poverty and neglect marked it throughout. The parlor was small and ill furnished, having but two old tables, three or four old chairs that looked as though they had served the revolution. Amongst these was one which appeared to be the monarch of the rest ; it was (a handsome chair once, no doubt,) curiously carved, wholly of wood, with a straight high back; upon which was mounted the British crown, supported by two cherubims. This chair of state is carefully placed under the portrait of their father which with another portrait of his nephew, (executed by himself and sent to the ladies from England,) constitutes the remaining furniture of the parlor. The other part of the house I did not see; it had a small back room, and an upper story where I suspect the other sister had retired.

Miss Byles appeared to be about 75 years of age, was thin visaged and wrinkled, very distant in her manners, which were by no means affable or refined. She seemed averse to conversation, and appeared to wish me away. I drew a few sentences from her, the amount of which went to show that she was a warm lover of the British crown and government, and that she despised the country she was in; she said "the Americans had her father, herself, and her sister up, in the time of the revolutionary war, treated them ill, imprisoned her father, and suspended him from preaching, came very near sending the whole of them off to England, just because her father prayed for the king." But she said they were very kind to her and her sister now, that she wanted for nothing, though she complained bitterly against some body, she did not know who it was that had knocked the bark off one of their trees: it was poor spite she said. I saw a few inches of the bark rubbed off, which was doubtless an accident.

Matthew Byles was born in the colony and educated at Cambridge. He was (says the writer of those times,) a scholar, eloquent and accomplished. A gentleman of humor, but sided with the royalists in the time of the war, and had the Americans not placed a guard at his door the populace would have torn him to pieces. The following anecdote was related of him when a young man. "The captain of a vessel, a friend of his, about to set sail, proposed to Byles to go with him as Chaplain; the parson, on some account, was obliged to refuse the office, and told the captain it was out of his power. His friend dropped the subject of chaplain, but insisted upon Byles' spending the evening with him on board the ship; that a number of his friends would be there, and they would

take a parting glass together at least.   Byles accepted
the invitation, and waited on the captain, who, while they
were all making merry, set sail, having given secret instructions to that amount, previous to the arrival of the
parson, and they were a considerable distance from land
before Byles discovered the cheat.   He making a virtue
of necessity passed it off in good humor, and no chaplain
being aboard, he was forced to act.   But when they
came to examine, no psalm book could be found.   The
captain being a man of humor, and withal clothed with
a little power, proposed to Byles, of whose poetic talents
he was apprised, to compose a psalm for the occasion.
Byles submitted with a good grace, and composed a
psalm peculiar to himself and to the occasion.   I have
seen the psalm ; it contains some of the finest strokes of
wit and humour to be found.   But Mr. Green, of Boston,
who possessed more good nature, and an equal share of
wit with Byles, paraphrased the psalm.   This called up
a spirited answer from Byles : which was again replied
to by Green; and thus they continued to write poetry
against each other to the great amusement of the citizens.
Riding in the country one day, he saw a man making a
rail fence some distance from the road, he turned out of
his way to address him with " will you never leave off
railing, can't you live without a fence."
    Whilst speaking of literary characters, I cannot help
adding a brief notice of Miss Hannah Adams, the glory
of New-England females.   She is the authoress of several valuable works, which have long been before the
public, viz. " The History of the Jews," " The History
of New-England," and " Letters on the Gospel."   These
works are said to be ably written, and bespeak her a
woman of piety and learning.   I have seen these works
since my visit to New England, but being unqualified to
judge of their merit, I speak of their general character.
Miss Adams lives in Boston.   She is about seventy years
of age, of low stature, and slightly inclined to corpulency : she is declining in health, though very cheerful,
and walks a good deal in fine weather : her hair is perfectly white, her complexion is fair, her face round, her
features regular and very delicate, her eyes a dark hazel,

(what may be called black,) very small, but soft and intelligent; her teeth are decayed, and disfigure her very much; she lisps in speaking, but has a sweet melodious voice. Her countenance is animated, and the most pleasing I ever witnessed in a person of her age, her face being constantly lighted up with a smile. But the leading trait in her countenance is *innocence ;* the infant at the breast is not more so. Her manners are easy and natural, without one spark of pride or affectation : in short, she possesses a dignified simplicity, with a great share of good nature, which is visible in her whole deportment. I was often in her company, and found her uniformly the same. She informed me that she was upwards of three years in compiling her Jewish History, and that at one time she must have had as many books before her, as would have filled the room we were in. She is a distant relation to the president of the United States. Mrs. Morton, lady of the Lieut. Governor, is also a distinguished writer.

It has already been observed, that the human mind has been thoroughly developed in Boston. This city has made bold advances in the fine arts, in belles-lettres, and in mathematics, philosophy, poetry, theology, and in law, Boston also holds the first rank in our cities. Among the most eminent of her citizens for learning and high literary attainments, may be esteemed the present editor of the North-American Review, the Rev. Jared Sparks, late pastor of the Unitarian congregation in Baltimore. Mr. S. is about 30 years of age,—he may be something over—rather above the common height, neither spare nor robust, and well formed. His complexion is wan, his hair is deep black, his eyes a dark gray, full, calm, and steady. His face is round and features regular. His countenance is contemplative, serene, and as meek as Moses: so gentle, so spotless, he is the admiration of all who know him. As a scholar, and a gentleman, he may possibly have an equal, but in diffidence, charity, and benevolence, he stands alone.

There are many literary men in Boston, of whom I only saw one more, the Rev. Mr. Pierpont: he is said to be a writer of some eminence, both in poetry and

prose. He is an amiable man, of good stature, and elegant manners. The poet Percival lives in the city, but
I had not the good fortune to see him.

The citizens of Boston are at present engaged in making great improvements in the city. They are reclaim-
ing the land from the water, and have succeeded to an
astonishing degree, having realized about 70 acres of
made land where the mill-pond formerly flowed. They
are likewise pulling down houses, widening the streets,
and erecting large and durable buildings. The town is
chiefly built of brick, though there are many elegant
free-stone buildings, which, for beauty and size, excel
any private buildings in the United States. These
stand mostly on Mount Vernon, Beacon-street, and the
Colonade. The buildings in the Colonade are truly
magnificent, having a colonade running in front' of
them, the whole length of the street; these are not only
large, but the workmanship surpasses any thing of the
sort: and here we have not only marble fronts but marble houses. D. Sears, Esq. lives in one of these, which
for beauty and splendor, sets description at defiance, and
is only exceeded by its princely owner. The Appletons
are likewise with Mr. S. in Beacon-street, and like him
live in princely style. But the exterior of the houses is
nothing compared with the costly furniture within them;
plate, China ware, mahogany, the finest cut glass, and
rich carpeting, are paltry things with them; their houses are adorned with nymphs, Naiads, shepherds, cupids
and goddesses, of the finest alabaster; portraits, the finest
paintings, and the choicest books, settees and chairs:
damask curtains, of the richest fashion; every room is
filled with the " softly speaking marble;" these beautiful images meet you wherever you turn: they are standing in niches on the stair-cases and up-stairs, as well as
below. The marble assuming every shape and every
grace: here you see a nymph stretched on a couch,
there a Naiad standing with a gilded cup in her hand,
and a third in the act of dancing. I was particularly
struck with a bowl, upon the edge of which sat two of
the sweetest looking doves; one was in the act of drinking out of the bowl, the other had its head turned, look

ing behind it;—the whole of unequalled polish, and rivalling the snow in whiteness. Another interesting object
was a female figure sleeping upon the skin of a lion. The
skin of the head, with the rough mane, the eyes, and
even the eye-lash, was nature itself. Another object of
interest was a model of the temple of Neptune, which is
in a mouldering state, great part of it having tumbled
down; those parts were substituted with pieces of cork,
and the whole enveloped with moss. The main frame
of the edifice was nothing but a low, square frame,
open at the top, the whole representing every vestige of
a structure in ruins.

In Boston I was also gratified by seeing a portrait of
the renowned Walter Scott, but it was by no means striking; if the likeness was a true one, there is no truth in
countenance, as his was the most vacant imaginable,
without one spark of genius perceptible. It could not
be his, being distinguished by nothing but a simple blue
eye and a most unmeaning smile.

One might spend a year amongst these people, and
still find something new. Many of the ladies have visited France and Italy, from which they have culled the
choicest specimens of the fine arts, particularly from the
latter. Garlands, flowers, fruit, in the finest alabaster,
embodying every grace of form and ingenuity, to a degree beyond the power of the most luxuriant fancy to
conceive. New-York certainly does more business, but
for men of solid wealth, refinement and taste, Boston is
the nonpareil.

Whilst on my visit to Alexandria, I happened in company with a travelling lady, and speaking of the Atlantic
cities, she observed, that " if she was compelled to live in
the United States, (being a foreigner,) she would give
Boston the preference, on account of the taste and refinement, and above all, the hospitality of the citizens."
This shook my prejudice a little, but still I had no intention of visiting Boston, until I went to Albany, where the
account of the lady was confirmed, to my satisfaction; I
therefore resolved to see Boston. On my way thither I
fell in with two of the citizens, whose manners and conversation effectually dislodged the prejudice I had imbib-

ed from infancy, against this city, that it was inhabited
by a sour, bigoted, priest-ridden race—noted for nothing
but psalm-singing, and hanging witches and Quakers.
I was more favorably disposed to New-York, but in
Philadelphia I centred every virtue! See the wretched
effects of prejudice.—In Philadelphia the people scarcely
invited me to sit down; but in Boston, I have been ca-
ressed, and loaded with favors, though a total stranger
to them, without even an introduction. One grain of reflection might have removed this prejudice ; for it is impossible that illiberality and science should exist in the
same place; but so ignorant was I of the resources of
my country, that I was unapprised of the great advantages which its citizens possess, over that of any city in
the Union.

Boston, however, has been losing ground in commerce,
for a few years back; and its merchants are vesting
their capital in manufacturing establishments, upon the
most extensive and comprehensive scale. They have
several grand manufactories of glass, cotton, dying and
calico printing, in which vast sums are vested. The
Chelmsford factory, near Boston, belongs to a number
of wealthy merchants, amounting to a capital of $100,-
000. Only a part of the plan has arrived to effect : it is
confined wholly to the weaving and printing of calico,
which for texture, brilliancy, and durability of tints, are
equal to any imported; in texture it is superior. About
175 pieces are finished per day, but this quantity will
be doubled in the course of another year. The Waltham factory is in complete operation ; it also belongs to
a company of merchants, and is confined to the manufacturing of cotton shirting and sheeting. This factory was
established in 1814 : the capital stock is $600,000. It
employs 400 persons, chiefly females ; has in operation
7800 spindles, 240 looms, and makes about 1,700,000
yards annually. The whole of the machinery is performed by water! The cotton is carded, roped, spun, warp-
ed, sized, beamed, and wove by water power. The
looms are entirely of iron, and make such a noise when
they are in full operation, that it is with great difficulty
you can make yourself heard. This is a most astonish-

ing invention. This factory is on Charles' river, and although not more than nine miles from Boston, it is nothing more than a tolerable creek. I am amazed at the shortness of the streams in this country. Col. Lyman, one of the Waltham proprietors, a gentleman of great wealth and merit, lives on his country seat near Waltham, in summer; and amongst other rare and choice collections of taste and beauty, he has a number of tame swans, the first I ever saw tamed. I could not help stopping the carriage several minutes, to admire those beautiful creatures as they played in a stream near the road side. They moved their snowy necks with such ineffable grace and ease: their bills and feet are perfectly black. Besides the factory just mentioned, there is an extensive bleaching establishment at Waltham, where the cloth is whitened and prepared for market. It also contains a large laboratory, where medicine is prepared. Besides those factories there are the Nashua and Dover establishments, and many others near Boston. Waltham, though a small village, is one of the oldest towns in the vicinity of Boston; the situation is level, handsome, and the country between it and Boston resembles a highly cultivated garden, beyond description beautiful. The famous Lexington is not far from Waltham. There are three extensive glass manufactories in and near Boston. Window-glass is made in the city, and flint glass in South-Boston: but Lechmere-Point, at the end of canal bridge in Cambridge, is the most extensive. Here was made the piece exhibited at Washington, among various others, last spring, which was pronounced to excel any that was presented.

The New-England (Flint) Glass Company, at Lechmere Point, near canal bride, Cambridge, usually employs one hundred and forty men and boys; this embraces the flint glass works, including the blowing and cutting of glass; there is attached an establishment for the manufacture of red lead, a principal ingredient in the composition of flint glass. The amount of glass made annually at this factory, exceeds one hundred thousand dollars. Adjoining the flint glass works, is a crown glass factory, principally owned by the same proprietors.

This factory employs about sixty men, and manufactures at the rate of fifty or sixty thousand dollars per annum.

There is also established at Lechmere Point, Winchester, extensive works, where near ten thousand head of beef cattle are annually slaughtered. Upwards of 20,000 barrels of beef, and 10,000 barrels of pork are annually packed for shipping; and 1,000,000 pounds of bar soap, 500,000 pounds of candles, and many other operations connected with the slaughtering of cattle, are carried on, employing near 60 men a great part of the year. There is also a stone-ware manufactory, an iron foundery, a steam-engine manufactory, and many other kinds of business, employing the whole population, which is now near two thousand, and has increased since 1819, one thousand per cent.

At Brighton, a few miles from Boston, an annual fair is held, where every production of the state is exhibited for sale, but principally cattle. At the same time premiums are awarded to those who bring the best specimens. Also, at the same place a weekly market is held for cattle, whence the butchers supply the citizens of Boston with beef.

The citizens of Boston are remarkably fond of military parade, and have the best band of music in the country. Once in every year the state elect their governor, and his inauguration takes place in Boston, on the first day of June, which is celebrated by every man, woman and child, in the state, who are able to attend. It is then they have their grand military parades, at which time the officers receive their commissions from the governor. The inauguration of His Excellency, Governor Lincoln, took place whilst I was there, and with the citizens I attended the ceremony. The mall, from its size, affords a fine opportunity for the display, and we were favored with one of the brightest suns. The citizens attended, some in carriages, and some on foot, till the mall was covered with such numbers that you might have walked from one end of it to the other on their heads. I did not see the ceremony of the inauguration, which took place in the state-house, lest I might have been crushed to death, so great was the crowd.

Meantime I took my station near the mall, where I could
see the most interesting part of the fete. The guards
with great difficulty preserved a square in the mall
which was accommodated with elegant settees, for the
governor and his suite ; from which seats he was to
present the officers their commissions. The military
were equipped in the most superb style, with the city
band, in readiness to escort the governor from the state-
house to his seat on the mall. The moment he had taken the oath of office, it was announced by the firing of
cannon, and the band began to play ; the escort then
moved to the front of the state-house, where they received the governor, who, with his secretary and the lieutenant governor, all three dressed in the same uniform,
each with a sword by his side, proceeded abreast with a
slow, dignified step, to the seat prepared for them on the
mall. The band was full, and the music exquisitely
fine. They passed so near my carriage that I could
have touched their plumes with my hand. The govern-
or walked between the other two, (you might see that he
" was gentle born,") he wore a plain cocked hat, the
others the same, with lofty black plumes ; fine looking
men, same height and figure. When they gained the
inside of the mall another round was fired ; the govern-
or taking off his hat, passed between the troops to his
seat, and sitting down puts on his hat, his suit uncover-
ing their heads, remained standing; during which the
troops were forming, the band still playing. At length
they all sit, and the troops go through the manual exercise. When this was ended, the governor, with his
suite, walked slowly round the lines, and returning to
his seat ; the officers who have previously been elected
(on the same day) advance to the governor, with their
heads uncovered ; he rises up to receive them, and
hands each man his commission. After this, another
round is fired, and the governor is escorted back to the
state-house, where the troops are disbanded. These
anniversaries are quite a treat to the citizens of Boston,
and religiously observed.

I was likewise present at the celebration of the battle
of Bunker Hill ; the greatest procession probably that

ever took place in the history of America. This procession has been so generally diffused in the newspapers, and if it had not, it so far exceeds not only the limits of this work, but my powers of description, that I
should only sully a subject which I hold too sacred to
profane. I collected the newspapers the following day,
and intended to give the order of procession, but upon
reflection I thought it would be dry, and the greatness
of the throng deterred me from going to Charlestown.
From a window in School-street, I viewed the procession from beginning to end. I should be at a loss to say
with which part I was most pleased ; the whole was
grand beyond conception. The music of all New-England was there, and all the masons, which are numerous
in those states ; the bands were divided, and every
lodge by itself, each leaving a small vacancy, with a
splendid banner, on which was the number and name of
the lodge, and the state to which it belonged. The
Knights all in black, with lofty black plumes waving in
their hats, their black pointed aprons, Gen. Lafayette
in an open carriage, the soldiers of the revolution in
open carriages, (a venerable band,) drove by young gentlemen of the first distinction in the city. It was a moving scene ! But while our extacy was wrought up to the
highest pitch, a dear old man, dressed in an old coat,
and an old hat, passed under us; he was sitting in the
front of the carriage, with his right arm extended, and
in his hand he held an old continental shot bag, with the
same bullets in it which he used at the battle of Bunker
Hill. He gently waved it backwards and forwards from
one side to the other, so that the people on each side
might have a chance to see it ; and continued to do so
throughout the procession. The coat he had on, and the
hat, were likewise those he wore in the battle ; we saw
distinctly several bullet holes in each—the solemn motion of the carriage ! the effect cannot be described !
Gen. Lafayette, and even the Knights, all glorious as
they shone, shrunk into nothing beside this war-worn
soldier ! It transported us fifty years back, and we in
imagination were fighting the battle of Bunker Hill ;
the sacred relic he bore in his hand seemed endued with

speech; its effect, like an electric shock, flew through the lines, and held each heart in fond delusion. Not a word was uttered for several minutes! till, " did you see that?" whispered one to the other, whilst every cheek was wet! The music was ravishing, the masons looked divine, and the Knights Templar like supernatural beings! The whole was not only grand, it was sublime! but our language is too poor for such occasions. The procession was about an hour and a half passing through the street, and supposed to consist of eighty thousand persons, while we were favored throughout with one of the most brilliant suns.

Although Boston is behind New-York in trade and business, it has one advantage, which renders the city much more pleasant in summer than the latter, whatever it may be in the winter, that is its lofty elms, and spreading horse-chesnuts, the streets being mostly shaded with full grown trees, nor do the high houses look so terrifying when one gets used to them, but more especially with those who inhabit them. Nothing hinders Boston from being as large as New-York or Philadelphia, but want of room. The whole of the peninsula is built on to the water's edge, and even into the bay. Were it not that it is hemmed in by the bay and Charles river, Charleston, Cambridge, Watertown, and South-Boston would make a part of the city. Roxbury does join it; the houses extending quite through the neck. It is kept fully as neat as Philadelphia, (though some of the streets and side-walks are badly paved,) and the houses, kitchens, and back yards are exquisitely neat. The city is distinguished by the " north end, south end, West-Boston, and the wharves." Copp's hill, famous in history, is in the north end ; the Mall is in the south end.

I ought to have noticed the churches and fortifications in the topographical description: the churches are remarkable for nothing but their great size and their high steeples. The harbour is defended by nature, the entrance to it being so narrow as not to admit of more than two ships a-breast. Fort Warren stands on one side of it, and Fort Independence on the other. The latter, for

strength, may defy the world, the walls are of such
thickness that no power on earth would be able, from
the water, to penetrate them. It sits on an island, as
does Fort Warren, and makes a fine show from the city.
In fact, the whole bay is diversified with islands of singular beauty. By the way, Uncle Sam is very shabbily
represented in this part of his dominions : the commandant of Fort Independence was not at his post, and his
deputy, a Major something, (I never inquired his name,)
gave me a most ungentlemanly reception, and, had it not
been for the interference of a Dr. M. (the only gentleman on the place,) I believe in my heart, this man of
war would have opened the battery upon me. He
seemed to view my visit with evident signs of mistrust,
and took me, no doubt, for a spy, although I had a letter
stating my business. Seriously, the marines and the
whole pack of them, (except the Dr.) were the most
scurvy set I met with in my travels. It is time those
military despots, those young Cesars, were nipped in the
bud. They are designed to protect, instead of insulting
peaceable citizens. I find that the farther they are from
the government the more assuming they become. The
very females of the place, (they could not be ladies)
stood in the doors and in the yard, gaping at me, as
though I had been an Ourang-outang, without speaking a
word, or shewing the least mark of civility. A great falling off, indeed, after having been honoured, in the most
exemplary manner, by all the officers of the Naval and
War Departments throughout the Union ! Thus these
upstarts bring disgrace upon the government. A gentleman will always treat every one civilly, at least, for his
own sake.

But to return : Boston has improved rapidly since it
became a city. The Mill-dam, mentioned with the
bridges, is a stupendous structure of human industry
and enterprise : it is built across the bay, nearly two
miles in length, at an expense of $500,000 ! The object
was to open an avenue, and create water power, to put
in operation an extensive establishment of tide-mills, and
other waterworks : a great part of the design has been
completed. The Exchange Coffee-house, a recent

building, covers over an acre of ground; and we may reasonably suppose that the land recently recovered from the bay (at an expense incalculable) will soon be crowned with tasteful buildings. Its resources, both in capital and talents, in proportion to its population, are comparatively very great. In short, for refinement, taste, hospitality, and scenery, Boston is the garden spot of the Union.

It will be recollected, that Doctor Franklin was a native of Boston: almost the first object of my curiosity, after my arrival in the city, was to enquire for the spot where his parents resided; but to my great surprise, his family was scarcely recollected! After much enquiry and heart-rending researches, I discovered the place where the house once stood to be opposite the Old South church, in Milk street, though the place was occupied by another building.

The revenue of Boston port custom-house, will be found at the end of the book. It contains about 58,000 inhabitants.

Quincy.—During my visit to Boston, I frequently rode out in the country, if country it may be called, which is covered with towns and villages. In one of these excursions, I paid my respects to the Ex-President Adams, of Quincy. Quincy lies south of Boston about eight miles. Mr. A. does not live exactly in the town, but a little to the right, about two hundred yards from the road, on this side of Quincy. He lives on a farm which is kept in fine order, and fitted out with barns, stables, and carriage houses. My heart beat high as I knocked at his door, which was opened by a servant. I told her I wished to see Mr. Adams, if he was not too much indisposed, (having heard he had been unwell.) "Which Mr. Adams do you wish to see," she replied, "the Judge* or the President." "The President," I answered. She withdrew, and in a few minutes a most enchanting female entered the parlour. I handed her my address, and desired her to present it to the President,

---

* The President's Son

She returned in a moment and asked me to walk up
stairs. I followed her, and took the precedence in entering the chamber of this venerable Patriarch. I found
the dear old man sitting up, before the fire. He would
have arose, but I flew forward to prevent him. He
pressed my hand with ardour and inquired after my
health.

We conversed upon general subjects relating to Alabama, the state I was from, such as its trade, navigation,
and productions of the soil, &c. In answer to several inquiries relative to himself, he replied, " that he was
then, (April, 1825,) eighty-nine years and six months
old; a monstrous time," he added " for one human being
to support." He could walk about the room, he said,
and even down stairs, though he was at that time very
feeble. His teeth were entirely gone, and his eye sight
very much impaired; he could just see the window, he
said, and the weather vane that stood before it, but retained his hearing perfectly. His face did not bear the
marks of age in proportion to his years; nor did he
show the marks of decay in his appearance, with the
exception of his teeth, and his legs, which were evidently much reduced. He had a slight obstruction in his
breathing, from having recently taken cold, and his
tongue seemed to perform its office with abridged vigour. He coughed a little, but said he was free from
pain. He was dressed in a green camblet morning
gown, and his head uncovered, except his venerable
locks, which were perfectly white. He appeared as he
sat in his chair to be about the size of his son, the present president of the United States, and his features bore
a striking resemblance to the portraits and busts I had
often seen of him. The most child-like simplicity and
goodness appeared in the sun-shine of his countenance,
which, while speaking, or listening, became extremely
animated: but when left to itself, subsided into an un-
clouded serenity. When I mentioned his son, (the
president,) and Mrs. A. the tear glittered in his eye; he
attempted to reply, but was overcome with emotion.
Finding the subject too tender, I changed it as quick
as possible. Mr. Adams is represented to have been

a patron of merit and genius, and amongst the most charitable men of the age. His mansion is a large venerable frame building, built as he told me about thirty-six years ago. It is large for a country house, consisting of three apartments, of equal size below stairs, with a gallery leading to the staircase. One of these is a common room, into which strangers are first introduced. In passing to the next room, you turn suddenly to the right, and crossing the gallery enter a parlor, the furniture of which resembled a female Quaker's dress, rich but simple. The chairs were furnished with deep satin, cushions; elegant sofas and carpets completed the furniture. From this in the same direction you enter the third apartment, which contains the family portraits. The portrait of Mr. Adams and his lady when they were young, likewise his daughter and John Quincy. The latter had very little resemblance to the original at this day, but as much like George Washington, his son, as if it had been taken for him. Besides Mrs. Smith, the lady already mentioned, who is a niece of the good ex-president, another niece lives with him; they are both widows! It was truly interesting to see the tender, affectionate attention these ladies paid to the venerable old man; his happiness and comfort engrossed all their care, whilst peace and resignation sat on his brow. Like a calm evening sun, he is imperceptibly gliding to lighten other worlds! His house faces Quincy, looking to the south, and commands a full view of that village. After partaking of a repast, without which no one is permitted to depart from his house, I walked over the village; it is the most delightful spot in Massachusetts. A bold transparent stream runs purling along through the midst of it; it is likewise adorned with lofty elms, grass plats and gardens of inexpressible beauty.

This part of Massachusetts, and the whole way that leads to it from Boston, is one uniform representation of matchless beauty; superb country seats, intermixed with groves and gardens, relieved by luxuriant meadows, with the same stream which waters Quincy, winding its way

30

to the bay. These specimens of art are sometimes heightened by piles of the wildest rocks in nature.

On the road to Quincy, near Boston, stands Dorchester Heights, from which Gen. Washington forced the British to evacuate that city. The old breast-work, or fort, is still to be seen from the road, though partly overgrown with grass. This was the piece of generalship that so much astonished the British—it was erected in one night. Here it was that several thousand barrels of sand were ready to overwhelm the enemy, had they attempted to climb the hill. This must have been, what we, in the southern states, call a yankee trick. The British, however, disappointed their expectations, by evacuating the city, and General Washington, amidst the shouts of the men and the smiles of the ladies, entered Boston in triumph.

It appears that the ladies of these times were truer whigs than the men—they not only threw all the tea they had into the streets, but abjured the name of tea. Gen. Washington, or some of his officers, sending to one of them to borrow a tea-kettle, the lady replied, that "she had no tea-kettle, but she would lend him her coffee-kettle."

Returning from Quincy to Boston, I was agreeably surprised to find in the stage, the brother of Mr. Gales, of Washington city, whose resemblance to him led to the discovery. He was taking an excursion with his beautiful wife, whom he had just married in Greenwich, Mass. and was soon going to North-Carolina, where he resides. See what the fame of our yankee girls effects.

Cambridge.—The site of Cambridge has already been mentioned; it is a perfect level, something lower than the site of Boston, from which it is only divided by Charles river and part of the bay. It is connected with that city by two bridges, and the causeway over the mill-dam, which last is 50 feet wide; its length has been noticed. One bridge is called west Boston bridge, and the other Craney's bridge; the first is 3483 feet long, supported by 180 piers; the other is nearly the same. Cambridge, though very extensive, is very thinly settled; a few houses here and there in clusters, with clumps of trees and shrubberies. It has a port and some stores, and several manufactories on that side next to Boston. The houses are beautifully shaded with the elm and horse-chesnut, the favorite trees of New-England,* which give it a pervading air of rural luxuriance; nor is it cut up into streets, but left to expand in all its native grace. Cambridge is pronounced Camebridge by every body in this country, particularly the learned. It is chiefly remarkable for being the seat of Harvard University, famed for being the first literary institution in the United States. This seminary was founded in 1638, the oldest in America, being not quite twenty years after the first settlement of New-England. It was called Harvard after a gentleman of that name, who was its first benefactor: he beqeathed it 779*l*. It was first called a school, but in 1650 it was incorporated by the name of Harvard college, and finally styled the University. It is the most richly endowed of any literary institution in the Union; and consists of six large edifices, besides buildings for the president, professors, and students. It has a president, twenty professors, six tutors, a proctor, and a regent. It has a library of 28,000 volumes, the largest in America! It has a philosophical and chemical apparatus also, the most complete one in our country; the philosophical apparatus alone cost nearly 1500*l*. It has besides an anatomical museum, an observatory, a cabinet of minerals, and a botanical garden of 8 acres, containing a rich collection of trees, shrubs, and plants, both foreign and domestic. It has usually between three and four hundred students. By a rule of the university, the president is not allowed to exercise clerical functions. The buildings stand three miles west from Boston, though they are very distinctly seen. An exhibition of students took place while I was in Boston, of which I availed myself with no small degree of pleasure. The hall was filled when I arrived, although it wanted several minutes of the time, and it was with difficulty I obtained a seat. But the crowd still continued to squeeze in, both in the galleries and below; the ladies below and the gentlemen

* I have not seen a Lombardy poplar since I left Albany.

above. The musicians also sat in the gallery, music being a part of the exhibition. The president had not made his appearance, and I indulged the interval in viewing the audience, which could not have been short of a thousand; beside a vast number who were unable to get in for want of room. The students, dressed in the richest black silk gowns, sat by themselves under the gallery, except the pierian sodality that were to perform on instruments, who sat above. These were easily distinguished by the uniformity of their dress, and their modest deportment. I never saw such an assembly of fine looking people, not only as respects size and figure, but in mien and countenance : genius and intelligence shone in every face. Meantime my ear was saluted with the most ravishing sounds ; the music in the gallery began to play, and continued till the president of the university entered the hall, and took his seat in the desk. He entered the hall in a flowing robe of shining black silk, like those worn by the students. President Kirtland is of middling age and stature, portly figure, and fair complexion, his face round and comely, with a blue eye, his mouth small, his teeth regular and beautiful, his countenance noble, frank, and intelligent. On his head he wore something which I shall never be able to describe : it was a cap (or something like one) made of black silk or velvet. Supposing this cap to fit the head precisely, upon the top of this, that is, upon the crown of his head, sat something quadrangular in shape, thin as pasteboard, and black as the other. This part of the head dress was about ten inches each way, and adhered horizontally to the sound part. He wore it one corner foremost, from whence dropped one of the richest tassels, which I thought interrupted his Rev. LLDship very much, by getting into his eyes. The whole, however, was very becoming, and gave him quite a dignified appearance. When he had advanced about half way up the hall, he took off the thing, whatever it be, and saluted the audience by a gentle inclination of his head, with great dignity and grace ; he then proceeded up the hall with a slow, majestic step, mounted the rostrum, and stepped from thence into his desk, with the utmost com-

posure and self-possession, while a pleasant smile sat
upon his countenance, and every eye seemed to hail his
arrival. After being seated, he put on his head-piece,
the music stopped, and the students began the exhibition,
the president calling them separately by name in Latin.
The instant they were called, they arose and moved toward the rostrum, with inimitable grace and modesty of
gesture. As they mounted the rostrum, they bowed first
to the president, and then turning round, with a cheerful countenance, bowed respectfully to the audience, and
immediately commenced speaking, perfectly unembarrassed, whilst a thousand eyes were upon them. Sometimes one, but often two, three, or four, would mount the
rostrum together, though but one at a time exhibited.
Some spoke in Greek, some in Latin, and others in English. The subjects were orations upon history, philosophy, and the fine arts ; also dissertations, disquisitions,
and conferences were likewise held by three or four in
debate. Essays, dialogues, astronomical, and mathematical exercises; among others, a dialogue in Greek,
translated from Maliere's Marriage Force, and spoken
by three young gentlemen, one of whom (Mr. Hamilton)
was the son of mine host, " Exchange Coffee-House ;"
and though all Greek to me, it gave universal satisfaction, particularly to the president, who could not forbear
laughing as they seemed to quarrel, and were sometimes
upon the point of fighting. There was no material difference in the performance of the speakers; the whole
was deeply interesting; the easy grace, sometimes the
arm uplifted with the flowing sleeve, sometimes incum-
bent on the breast, whilst the symmetry of their persons
was often visible, under the gently waving robe. An
interval in the exhibition of the speakers, gave place for
the music, performed by the sodality.

I should be at a loss to say which I admired most,
the beauty and modesty of the youths, the richness of
their dress, the display of eloquence, or the sweet rolling
music : from never having witnessed a display of this nature, I was doubtless more affected with the exhibition
than any one present. Amongst the students, I was
particularly struck with Charles F. Adams, son of the

30*

president, George Sheafe, of New-Hampshire, his thin
Cassius face, and eagle eye, betoken something more
than common ; John S. Silbey of Maine, Allen Putnam
of Danvers, Omen S. Keith of Franklin, Jonathan Chapman of Boston, William Morgan of New-Orleans, and
Wm. Dwight of Springfield. But above all, I was cap-
tivated with Benjamin Brigham of Boston ; if I am not
mistaken in him, he is some day to add to the list of native orators. He seemed to have arrived to the age of
manhood ; tall, and finely made, his countenance luminous, his voice melodious, his delivery fluent and suasive,
his action natural and easy. He delivered a disserta-
tion upon the moral effect of the stage, as highly tending
to improve taste, and refine the manners. During the
oration, an irresistible smile played upon his lip ; in
short, his genius, his gestures, and his silver tongue must
succeed !

Before the exhibition commenced, I had an interview
with professor Everett, a well known literary gentleman,
who resides at Cambridge. Mr. E. is quite a young
looking man for his celebrity ; his complexion is fair,
his figure light, and of common stature. His attic countenance abundantly confirms report, indeed his fame is
the only instance that ever reached my knowledge in the
rude west. But I have dealt so much in prodigies
of late, that I confess my very poor stock of language is
exhausted. All I dare venture to say of professor E. is
that he has a more classical look than P. K. and is one
of the most finished gentlemen I have met with.

Journey to Salem.—Having amused myself with every
thing worth seeing in and about Boston, I once more
take the stage for Salem.

Salem is distant from Boston sixteen miles, which we
travel in about three hours, taking a northerly course
over Charlestown bridge. Here we have much the same
scenery, only a little more of the sublime. For the first
time, I saw what could probably be called the Atlantic.*

---

* I had a view of the main ocean at Boston, from the observatory,
through a telescope. It happened to be a boisterous day, and the waves
were running high, the water dashed up to a great height, resembling
smoke issuing from a chimney.

It lay to our right, and was in sight a great part of the way, though we were at no time nearer than two, probably three miles. The day being calm, it was perfectly smooth, and had a blue appearance, resembling the Blue ridge in Virginia. It might not unaptly be compared to a moderate mountain when seen at a distance, the remotest part being (or looked so) elevated. It differed, however, from a mountain in this, that what we may call the summit was unbroken, whereas a mountain is indented. Nothing ever appeared more sublime; but it is impossible to describe my sensation upon beholding this part of the globe for the first time.

Farms and villages, white spires, groves of trees, with rich foliage, extensive meadows, as far as the eye can see, through which the sea flows as clear as crystal, sometimes like a broad river, sometimes in a narrow rivulet, as the ground may happen to lie, form the principal scenery on the road to Salem. These meadows are called salt marshes, and are covered with coarse natural grass, which does not grow very high; it is mowed by the inhabitants and said to be good food for horses. Stakes are drove in the ground throughout these marshes, upon which the hay is placed to cure, as in high tide they are overflowed by the sea. They are not enclosed for the most part, as no cattle or stock of any sort are allowed to run in the streets. The whole state being laid out into towns, the roads are called streets, and people are prohibited by law, from letting their stock run out of their own enclosure. Whether this be the case in the other New-England states, I am not able to say. As we drove on we had a fine view of Nahant. It is about twelve miles from Boston, and much resorted to in summer by parties of pleasure from that city. It is an elevated spot of ground upon the shore of the Atlantic, upon which stands a large house of entertainment, where any one for money may have what he or she wishes to eat or drink; it is seen very distinctly from the road, although it is several miles distant. I had the pleasure of travelling with the sister of Rufus King, Esq. who had been on a visit to Boston, and was then on her return home.

She was a woman of elegant manners, and gave me much satisfactory information on the subjects of my pursuits. Had she not been in the stage, I should have crossed a floating bridge without knowing it to be such. This bridge lies on the bosom of one of those rivers or inlets of the sea, and being fastened at each end, rises and falls with the tide. The weight of our horses and carriages sunk it under water in several places.

Salem.—Salem is the oldest town in New-England except Plymouth, and the second in trade. It is finely situated for commerce, having one of the best harbors on the Atlantic ; it is likewise strongly fortified both by art and nature. It is the wealthiest town, for its population, in the United States, and carries on an extensive trade with Canton and the East Indies. The town lies level and compact, has some splendid houses of brick, though the most of the buildings are of wood ; most of the streets are wide and handsomely paved, and though the site may be called low, it commands an extensive view of the harbor and the adjacent country. Like all the New-England towns, it is planted with shadowy trees : it has a large square of ground in the centre of the town, likewise shaded with trees. This square is ornamented with two massy gates opposite to each other, which are adorned with lofty arches, emblazoned with the emblems of liberty. These sylvan shades give it an appearance of much rural sweetness. It contains a court-house, alms-house, a market-house, 3 banks, the East-India museum, an atheneum of 6,000 volumes, orphan's asylum, and 12 churches, mostly congregationalists, and 12,830 inhabitants. Most of the churches, both here and at Boston, are very erroneously called congregationalists, whereas, one half, at least, of the citizens are Unitarians. Like all the towns in New-England, it is governed by selectmen. All matters relating to the town are regulated by the citizens themselves, at what they call a town meeting. The people of New-England (for what reason I have not understood,) seem to be opposed to corporations , I was surprised to learn that it has been not more than four or five years since Boston was incorporated !

Prison.—The prison is a large handsome brick building, in which the jailor resides ; there were only four felons, and three debtors in the jail. The cells were small, grated windows, which scarcely admit the light, though they were well white-washed, and in good order. These were on the lower story. The debtors apartments were on the second story, large and airy. The debtors were the merriest fellows in the town ; one of them was singing yankee-doodle when I entered, the other two were singing Miss M'Claud, and playing cards. They laughed and sang by turns, and regarding me with some attention, asked me " what news from Alabama." Bidding those cheering fellows adieu, I called a carriage, and set out to the alms-house, which stands about half a mile from the town, from which, however, it is seen very plain. It stands on an elevated situation, and is one of the finest buildings in New-England. This establishment may justly be held a patron of imitation. It has a large farm and gardens like that of Boston, but still better regulated ; instead of being an expence to the citizens, it has the town in debt to it. Salem is the first town in the United States that introduced the laudable plan of furnishing paupers with the comfortable means of maintaining themselves. It is nothing more than an amusement for them to cultivate those fields and gardens. They work at their ease, and just as much as they think proper to perform. Their farms, but especially their gardens present the best specimens of taste and skill to be found any where. Besides the farm a number of mechanics are furnished with tools and work in doors. The cost of the paupers last year was $11,450 25. Balance in favor of the alms-house, $1,886 11.

Museum.—It has already been observed, that Salem carries on an extensive trade with Canton and the East Indies. This trade has been prosecuted with great spirit and enterprize for many years, and has been a source of much wealth to the citizens. Salem owns 34,454 tons of shipping, which is nearly all employed in the India and Canton trade. A society of gentlemen was formed in Salem in 1799, and incorporated in 1801,

by an act of the legislature, with a fund, the chief object of which was, first, to assist the widows and orphans of deceased members ; second, to collect such
facts and observations as may tend to the improvement
and security of navigation. For this purpose, every
member bound to sea must carry with him a blank
Journal, in which he is to insert every thing worthy of
notice during his voyage, and upon his return deposit
the Journal with the society. Third—to form a museum of natural and artificial curiosities, particularly such
as are found beyond the Cape of Good Hope and Cape
Horn. The funds arise from fees of admission, volunta-
ry donations, and annual assessments.

No gentleman can be a member of this society who
has not navigated the seas beyond Cape Horn and the
Cape of Good Hope, either as masters or factors, or su-
percargoes of vessels belonging to Salem. The name
of the society is " *The Salem East India Marine Society.*" The society at this period, (1825) consists of 236
members, under a president, a committee of observation,
a recording secretary, a corresponding secretary, an
inspector, distributor, superintendent, and treasurer, with
a fund of $6,829 49. The officers are elected annually
by ballot. The society meet six times in every year;
one rule is, that " politics, on no account, shall be introduced into the society." Every member is bound,
during his voyage, to notice the variation of the compass, bearings and distances of capes and head lands, the
latitude and longitude of ports, islands, rocks and shoals ;
also, soundings, tides, and currents, enter them on his
journal, and, on his return, deposit the same with the society. It is their duty also, to collect all useful publica-
tions, curiosities, and donations, for the benefit of the society.

The collection is one of the richest in the United
States, and worthy the attention of all lovers and friends
of science. The accumulation since the date of the society has been surprising. They have 67 Journals,
that is, of voyages which embrace the transactions of
one ship : say the ship sails from Salem to Liverpool,
London, Madeira, Columbo, Pondichery, Madras, and

back to Salem, perhaps absent a year, or as it may happen. These long voyages afford opportunities of acquiring a great deal of useful and interesting information. Besides the subjects mentioned, they contain sailing directions, the manner of transacting business at the East-India ports, with the weights, coins, imports, exports. &c. besides a vast fund of observations on the inhabitants of that country and the Islands in the Indian Ocean.

The articles in the museum at this time, amount to 2,269 : consisting of almost every production of the terraqueous globe, both natural and artificial, but principally from the southern part of both hemispheres. The artificial curiosities mostly consist of the implements of war used by the rude Islanders of the Indian Ocean and the southern seas, with their domestic utensils, dresses, and ornaments. Particularly the Island of Japan, the Celebs, the Philippines, Borneo, and the Sundy Isles, the Islands of Africa, with the Polynesia. To which we may add, the different coins, medals, and coats of arms of the known world, both ancient and modern ; cloth wove from the bark of trees ; paper bills of currency ; curious manuscripts ; views, portraits, and alphabets of different languages, and a variety of other interesting objects.

The natural curiosities consist of birds, fish, animals, serpents, shells, insects, coral, gems, ores, and petrifactions. The whole is scientifically arranged, and presents truly an intellectual feast to the naturalist. This museum is worth all the cabinets and museums put together in the United States, at least all that I have seen. Here I saw a candle made of the tallow of the tallow-tree of Japan, (croton subiferum,) it was sticking in a candle-stick made of coloured beads ! Gold and silver ore, with the pure platina of South America ; the camelion, (they, however, are common in Alabama.) An instrument to find the two chief corrections of a lunar observation, a glass brush, magnetic ore, a specimen of oriental writing on palm leaves, branches of cocoa and cinnamon trees, pine of Norfolk Island, busts of Cicero and Shakspeare, sword of the sword-fish, which

was about four (perhaps more) feet long, as hard as iron,
and precisely in the shape of a sword; a saw of the
saw-fish, like the other, except having teeth on both
edges the whole length.   Gold and silver thread, earth-
en pottery, found in Herculaneum, two china tureens in
the form of a swan, four blocks of the giant's causeway
in Ireland; a beautiful shawl, made of red and yellow
feathers from Owyhee, a complete glass ship, gypsum
from Smyrna, &c. carbonate of lime, from Gibraltar, pe-
trified clams from Sicily, found 100 feet deep in a mountain, a humming-bird, with nest and eggs! coffee plants
and fruit, sulphuret of tin, from Madagascar.   The green
viper, from China, the bite of which is mortal, unicorn
fish, (acanthurus unicornis,) horns of an ox from Sicily,
these were amazing both for length and thickness.   Cro-
codile of the Ganges, 136 specimens of Italian marble,
100 different views of Rome, 4to. engraved by Pronti;
lava from Mount Vesuvius and Etna, and gems of all
colours.   A drawing of the *Ado Nulli Cone,* in the British Museum, an extremely rare shell.   But a repetition
of any one specimen in the museum is useless, the whole
is equally interesting, particularly portraits of the principal Chinese merchants, and the most beautiful variety
of coral and pearl.

But the greatest curiosity is an ancient carved box:
this wonderful work of art was presented to the museum
by the Hon. Elias Derby, formerly of Salem.   It was
given to him several years since, by a gentleman of
Westphalia, (Mr. Muller,) who obtained it in Italy.   It
was executed in the 14th century, and supposed to be
the work of a monk.   It is in the form of a globe $2\frac{1}{4}$
inches in diameter.   The upper hemisphere, or celestial
region, contains 58 whole length human figures!   The
other hemisphere is intended to represent the day of
judgment, and hell and purgatory; in which may be
seen various Roman Catholic figures.   In this hemisphere there are 28 whole length figures, and 19 half
length, and 5 heads, making in the whole 110!   A most
extraordinary piece of ingenuity indeed.   The figures
are complete, and so small that you have to look through
a magnifying glass to see them; and there appears, in

every face, a most surprising degree of expression. The globe is made of boxwood. This museum is visited by every one free of expense, though one of the members must accompany those who wish to see it.

Appearance and Manners.—The citizens of Salem are stout, able bodied men, more so than any I have seen this side the Blue ridge, and their ladies excel in beauty and personal charms. This was observed by our friend and national guest, Gen. La Fayette. Both men and women have the true New England round full face, with large black eyes, and a soft bending countenance. Their manners are still more improved than the people of Boston. Besides the affability and ease of the Bostonians, they have a dignity and stateliness peculiar to them. In short, the gentlemen of Salem may be said to have arrived to maturity in all those perfections, which are derived from education and a knowledge of the world. Most of them are largely engaged in commerce, and from their great wealth, have it in their power to gratify an inclination to improve by travelling. You find few gentlemen in Salem, who have not visited almost every part of the world, and who do not possess more general knowledge than those of any other town in the Union. It is, moreover, the seat of some of our first men : the Crowninshields, Putnams, Storys, Endicotts, Peabodies, Flints, Pickerings, and Judge White, uncle to the amiable Mrs. Peabody, of Springfield ; among which I must not forget the celebrated Doctor Prince, one of the brightest ornaments of the present age. He is a nephew to the celebrated writer of that name, and is himself an author of distinction. It is surprising how virtue and knowledge comes to have so little influence upon the world. From the early accounts of Salem, I never thought of that town without horror. These accounts had never been softened, and when I heard of the reception given Gen. Lafayette, I was astonished that any thing good could come out of Salem. It is needless to repeat what no American ought ever to forget, the superior address of Judge Story on that occasion, and the memorable words, " we could not forget them if we would, we would not forget them if we could ;" to which the people replied, " no, never." This was worthy of Greece and Rome in their greatest splendour.   Amongst many other instances, this is sufficient to show that education alone is not able to remove prejudice.   That to cure the errors imbibed in our youth, travelling is indispensable. In short, to judge accurately of men and things, they must be seen.   I had heard one part of the history of Salem, that is, all the evil that ever it had done, without any of the good : the same of Boston and Hartford. This had created a prejudice, which vanished the moment I came to see and judge for myself.   The opinion I had formed of Salem in particular, was as diametrically opposite to the truth, as the darkness of midnight is to the meridian sun.   Neither ought it to be decried for a delusion, which at one time pervaded and still pervades many parts of the world.   I mean the delusion of witchcraft ; it was the delusion, more properly speaking, of the age.   How many of those supposed witches were burnt about the same time in England, a country famed at this time for refinement and liberality ! with as much reason we might abjure Paris for the massacre of St. Bartholomew ; and where is a place of more refinement ?   But whatever Salem has been heretofore, I was sensibly struck with admiration at their Virgilian eloquence, (if I may so express it,) and the well bred ease of their manners.

History.—Salem was settled in 1626, by John Endicott. He came from England, and was accompanied by three hundred people, including servants. I had the pleasure (and it was one I never shall forget,) of seeing a descendant of Mr. Endicott.   Gen. Putnam of the revolution, of whom it was said " that he dared to lead where any dare to follow," was of this town.   I never left a city or town with more regret.

Journey to Providence.—After spending about a week with those truly interesting people, with whom I had formed an universal acquaintance, notwithstanding the shortness of my visit, and resting a few days in Boston, I took my final leave of that city, and set out for Providence, Rhode-Island.   Providence lies westwardly from

Boston, between forty and fifty miles, which is travelled in about nine hours. This road being the common route from Boston to New-York, it requires several stages daily to convey the travellers from Boston to Providence; where they take passage in the steam-boats, proceeding down Providence river into the sound, thence into East river, which brings them to New-York. The distance from Providence, is upwards of two hundred miles, for which you pay fourteen dollars, including board. We met with nothing worthy of remark on the road to Providence, with the exception of the Pawtucket falls, and some straggling human beings, of whom my fellow travellers gave me a singular account; whether true or false I know not. It has so much of the marvellous in it, that I gave it no credit. The circumstance is as follows : as we were driving on pretty brisk, one of the passengers cried out, " yonder, look at the pilgrims," pointing towards the left. I turned my eyes that way, and saw a number (perhaps about twelve in all,) of ragged people, great and small, walking up a steep hill, about three hundred yards from the road. They were dirty, and all bareheaded. To the inquiries respecting them, two of the gentlemen in the stage stated that " there were some hundreds of them in the woods; that they subsisted by rapine, and whatever they could kill or procure in the woods ; that they lived in caves and amongst the rocks promiscuously; that they were regularly descended from the first settlers in New-England. Their predecessors were part of those who settled Plymouth, and not approving of the form of government drawn up for the church, separated from it, and betook themselves to the woods, to avoid the penalty of the laws imposed on them ; and that, becoming enamoured of a vagrant life, they found means to subsist ever since." Such is the story of those persons we saw. My informants added that several attempts were made within their knowledge, to catch and tame them, but all attempts were vain; they ran with such swiftness that neither man nor horse could overtake them. Upon expressing my doubts upon a subject so strange, the passengers said it was noticed by Morse, in his History of the United States.

Upon reflection, I recollect a circumstance which goes
to confirm this story, however fabulous it may appear.
The circumstance is this : travelling once in Ohio, I put
up at a small town, where, upon my arrival at an inn, I
was shewn into a room where I found other travellers.
After some introductory conversation, the travellers asked me if I had heard the news? I replied that I had not.
Upon which they gave me an astonishing account of a
new sect that had just arrived in the neighbourhood of
the town, where they were that evening encamped.
The report was, that between thirty and forty men, women, and children, wretchedly dressed, all on foot, were
travelling, it would seem, towards the lakes ; that they
called themselves pilgrims, were destitute of the means
of travelling, and almost naked, being covered with old
rags, skins, and pieces of old blankets, great part of
which had been given to them out of charity, by the
people of the country, as they travelled. That they all,
men and women, slept promiscuously, and the filthiest
looking human beings imaginable. The beards of the
men were unshaven, and the whole of them crawling with
vermin. That the people of the country gave them
provisions, and before they were apprised of their situation, used to admit them into their houses and suffer
them to sleep on their floors ; but their fame preceding
them, the people were compelled, in their own defence,
to refuse them the rites of hospitality. Such were the
people who were said to have arrived in the suburbs
of the town. A number of the citizens filling their pockets and pocket-handkerchiefs with biscuit, cheese, and
bread, were then actually going to see them, upon
which, one of the travellers joining the party, all set out
to see the strange people. When they returned, they
gave nearly the same account, making it rather worse.
They stated " that the children were so wild, that no entreaty could prevail with them to approach near enough
to receive the provision; and finally, they were obliged
to throw it at them, upon which, they snatched it up and
swallowed it, with the eagerness of ravenous dogs."
Some attempts were made to take those people up under
the vagrant law, but the lawyers, when consulted, repli-

ed that they were effectually protected by the Constitution of the United States, which guarantees free toleration to all sects of religion, and this being their tenets, they were free to enjoy it.   These were said to be either from the state of Maine or New-Hampshire, (I do not recollect which.)   They called themselves the *pilgrims.* Their tenets were continual travelling and trusting to the Lord, or to chance, for subsistence. I have not heard of them since : they were said to be grossly ignorant and immoral.

We passed the celebrated falls of Pawtucket, about 12 o'clock, at a small village of the same name.   Pawtucket river forms the line between Massachusetts and Rhode Island.   Pawtucket village is on Rhode Island shore: opposite to which are the falls.   The river is quite an ordinary stream, not larger than Elk River, in Virginia, or Little Sandy, in Kentucky.   The water falls over a rock, which constitutes a natural dam, running quite across the bed of the river, in a semi-circular form. The fall is said to be about fifty feet, nearly perpendicular.   Of this, however, I was unable to judge, as the bridge, upon which we cross the river, is built partly over the falls, and by this means, the nature and beauty of the falls are almost wholly concealed.   They are seen to most advantage below the bridge.   Though the falls were to me a matter of little curiosity, they seem to variegate the scenery of the place, which is highly romantic.   These falls are the means of much wealth to the citizens of Rhode-Island, by enabling them to establish sundry manufactories of cotton, iron, flour, &c.   I rode over to see these factories during my stay at Providence.   They are somewhat like the Waltham factory, but greatly inferior in the machinery.   At Pawtucket the spinning part is performed by the movement of a machine, which requires the aid of two persons.   They weave ticking, shirting, and sheeting.   They also print calico, but it is miserable stuff.   I found no person in the shops, or out of them, that was either able or willing to give any satisfactory information as to the capital stock, or quantity of cloth manufactured.   One of those

31*

who attended the looms, said they wove (that is, each
loom) twenty yards per day.

Providence.—Providence is a very romantic town, lying partly on two hills and partly on a narrow plain,
about wide enough for two streets. It is divided by
Providence River, (over which there is a bridge,) on
both sides of which, on the margin, are the principal
houses of business. On one side of the river the ascent
is sudden, on the other, it is gradual. It contains 14
houses for public worship, a college, a jail, a theatre, a
market-house, 8 banks, an alms-house, part of which is
an hospital, and 12,800 inhabitants. The churches are
very splendid, and the jail is tolerable ; but the poor-
house does not deserve the name, and the hospital is a
wretched abode, disgraceful to the town. I found about
half a dozen prisoners in the jail, in all, some of whom
were confined for debt. These, however, bore the
marks of humane treatment. The poor-house is an old
building, in the most unwholesome part of the town.
There were about twenty paupers in it, the dirtiest set
of beings I ever saw. I found five maniacs in the hospital, lying on straw upon the floor, which looked as
though it had not been swept or washed for years. The
citizens, however, are engaged in measures to render
those establishments more comfortable. Providence is
mostly built of wood, though there are many fine brick
edifices in it. The Presbyterian church is ornamented
with a handsome dome and collonade, and is one of the
finest buildings in the United States. The streets are
wide and regular, and most of them paved, with handsome side-walks, planted with trees. It is a very flourishing beautiful town, and carries on an extensive trade
with the East Indies. They have, besides this, a number of coasting vessels employed in the cotton business.
The town of Providence alone owns 6 cotton factories,
2 woollen factories, 12 jeweller's shops, where jewelry
is manufactured for exportation. It has also, many iron
founderies, where those iron looms for the cotton factories are made ; likewise a bleaching establishment,
where 12,000 yards are finished per day. It employs 60

hands and has a capital of $40,000. Rhode-Island is
the greatest manufacturing state in the Union, having, at
least, 150 cotton factories, and the whole business of
these is done by Providence. Besides those articles,
Providence manufactures various others. The citizens
are mostly men of extensive capital. The firm of
Brown & Ives is among the greatest in New-England.
I made several attempts to visit Brown University, but
was finally disappointed. I called several times at the
house of the President, but never found him in. The
buildings stand on the highest part of the town, in a
beautiful situation, but they are not extraordinary, either
for size or architecture. I saw but two old brick buildings, with much of the glass broken out of the windows,
and every appearance of neglect and decay ; and, worse
than all that, I saw a specimen of the politeness of the
students, which reflects no great honour upon the Institution. I am told it is well endowed, has a president
and 10 professors, and averages 150 students. By a
rule, the president and majority of the trustees must be of
the Baptist religion. This sect is the prevailing religion of Providence.

Manners and Appearance.—The citizens of Providence are mild, unassuming, artless, and the very milk of
human kindness. They are genteel, but not so refined
as the people of Boston. Most of them are deeply and
closely engaged in business, and they have not that leisure to improve by reading, which the Bostonians have;
nor do they travel so much as the citizens of Salem.
They are an industrious, enterprising people, and have
all the hospitality and frankness of the New-Englanders.
They are stout, fine looking men ; the ladies, particularly, are handsome, and many of them highly accomplished. Both sexes are remarkable for plainness, and have
a very independent carriage.

History.—Every one knows the story of Roger Williams : he was not only the founder of Providence, but
of Rhode-Island. Roger Williams was a clergyman,
who came from England to Massachusetts in 1631 ; and
being charged with holding a variety of errors, was forced to fly from the state suddenly, leaving his house,

wife and children, in Salem, and in the midst of winter
took up his abode at Seekhonk, without the limits of
Massachusetts. But Seekhonk being in the bounds of
Plymouth colony, Governor Winslow advised him, in a
friendly manner, to go on the other side of the river,
which was uncovered by any patent. Accordingly, he
and four others crossed Seekhonk river, in 1636, and
was hospitably received by the Indians ;* and laid the
foundation of the town, which, in gratitude to his Maker,
he called Providence, after purchasing the soil from the
natives. Here he was soon joined by others, who, like
himself, fled from persecution. Among these gentlemen
were Messrs. Coddingham and Fenner. From the mildness of their government and the free toleration in respect to religious opinions, Providence soon became the
asylum for persecuted sects of every description ; and is,
at this day, the most mild and tolerant republic in New
England. It is the only state in New England whose
citizens are not compelled by law to support religion.
All the other states oblige every citizen to pay so much
annually, to support some clergyman, leaving the choice
of the sect to the citizen ; but at all events, he must support some minister, (as they call him.) To return :
Williams and his friends suffered greatly from cold, fatigue, and want ; having no friends among the human
species but the Indians, who were ill supplied themselves. They, however, enjoyed liberty of conscience
which has, from that day to this, been inviolably maintained thoughout the state. So little has the civil authe-
rity to do with religion, in Rhode-Island, that no con-
tract is binding between a clergyman and any society,
Neither are the people compelled by law to support
schools, and yet the dialect is less corrupt than in any
part of New England, which I have seen : I mean that
of the common people ; all people of education speak
alike, in every state. Rhode-Island leaves the human
mind perfectly unshackled, the effect of which is visible
in the independent deportment of the citizens. It has

* After such a lesson as this, it becomes us truly to send missionari,
among the Indians.

also been noted for its patriotism and courage, since it has been a state, and has the honour of being the birth place of the celebrated General Green.

The Hon. Judge Martin, of Providence, has been at much pains to rescue from oblivion much of the biography of Mr. Williams and his adventurous companions, which he has committed to paper, and read a great part of it to me. I saw the place where this sage built his first rude cabin. I saw the hill upon which his remains are interred; being pointed out to me by the Judge, who is an enthusiastic admirer of the singular fortitude, talents, piety, and philanthropy of the founder of Providence. He walked with me to the spring from which he used to quench his thirst; where, weary, and forlorn, an outcast from a society calling themselves christian, he could, at least, drink the waters of peace. It is the choicest spring I have seen east of the Alleghany. I spent much of the short time I stopt at Providence in the company of J. M. whose pleasant and winning manners, but particularly those of his lady, almost persuaded me to prolong my visit. All our talk was of Roger Williams. I saw an original letter, written by R. Williams to "Neighbour Whipple," dated the 8th of July, 1669. It was written in the old English style, and evinced great boldness of genius and energy of intellect, and disclosed the sentiments upon which he and his more rigid brethren differed.

Providence is also the residence of his Excellency Governor Fenner, a descendant of the faithful Fenner, who, with his life in his hand, accompanied his friend R. Williams, and with him took refuge among savages, from the cruelty of pretended christians. G. F. lives in the edge of the town, upon the same lofty eminence with the University, commanding an extensive prospect of the town, the surrounding country, and Providence river, which spreads out to a great width before his door, its glassy bosom elevated, as it were, above the horizon, which, with the shrubbery, lawns, and flower gardens of the Governor, almost rivals the scenery of Boston. He has the handsomest flower garden I have seen in my travels. G. F. is a middle aged man, of good size, and great

benignity of countenance. His manners are distinguished by the same simplicity and native independence as
his fellow citizens. He lives in ease and affluence, and
appears, in every respect, worthy the place he holds.

The place where Providence stands was called by the
natives Mooshausic. The state takes its name from an
Island within it, which at first was called the Island of
Rhodes, from its resemblance to the Island of that name;
but in process of time, it became reversed to that of
Rhode-Island. Providence River is navigable to Providence for ships of 900 tons. The revenue of the custom house, and amount of shipping, will be found in the
table at the end of the book.* It is the smallest state in
the Union, except Delaware.

Return to New-York.—Anxious to return to New-
York, from which I had been absent nearly five months,
I hastened the time of my departure from Providence,
and taking leave of my friends, took a passage in the
steamboat accordingly. Stepping down into the cabin,
I found but one passenger aboard, a lady whom I had
often seen and conversed with, in Boston, but to this
moment I never knew her name. To pass off the time,
I took a book from the library, (usually kept on board
those boats) and turning over the leaves, I found the following remark of Lord Byron on criticism : " Every
thing now must pass the fiery ordeal of criticism, compared with which, walking on red-hot plow-shares would
be recreation. A critic, like the tiger, attacks all
whom he can master, and kills for the dear delight of
butchering." This made me quake for my sketches:
if that be the case, there will scarcely be a mouthful for
one of them. Whilst I was pondering upon their probable fate, my attention was attracted by the arrival of the
passengers, who came down the steps of the cabin to
the number of twenty or thirty, but this was a small part

---

* I was highly gratified in Providence by meeting with a Mr. Southwick, brother to a friend of mine in Alabama, and nephew to Mr. S. of
Albany. Nor must I overlook the singular marks of respect paid to me
by the citizens, particularly upon my arrival, which was honoured by a
turn out of the band. ,

of the sum total : the greater part of whom remained on deck. I also returned upon deck, the better to breathe the fresh air, (the day being exceedingly warm) as well as to enjoy the prospect, the boat being now under way. I happened to take a seat by a charming young lady, a Miss C. of Boston : she had a book open in her hand, which appeared to be nothing more than a brief description of the Western part of the state of New-York, to which she was bound on a party of pleasure, together with her father, mother, a female cousin, and a large party of gentlemen and ladies. They were upon an excursion to the Falls of Niagara, the springs, and wherever choice or fancy might lead them. The whole party were from Boston, and proved to be people of the first respectability. This, she told me, was her inducement to purchase the book, which I found her reading. Reading, however, amidst such a crowd, was out of the question, and we turned our attention to the surrounding objects.

This was an interesting voyage to me : the more so, as it was the first time I ever was at sea ; being told we were to pass through the sound, and that we were to be completely out of sight of land. In the mean time, the river began to widen rapidly, till at length we could scarcely see the shore, while, in the course of the evening, we had a fine view of Newport, the Forts, and Newport harbour, which is said to be the best in the United States. Newport is a post-town of some magnitude : it is situated on our left while passing down the river. It is the capital of Rhode-Island. It stands 30 miles from Providence, on Providence river. The harbour is strongly defended, which answers likewise for the defence of Providence. Newport makes a fine show when seen from the water, and is said to be a place of much fashion and style, though not equal to Providence in population and commerce.

Whilst I was wholly engrossed in viewing the great expanse of water, which now surrounded us, the fast receding shore, and the numerous vessels, by which we seemed to fly, sitting at the stern, with my back towards the company, which had insensibly withdrawn from around

me, a gentleman, neatly dressed in black, of an interesting mien, came and seated himself upon the edge of the
boat, immediately in front of me, and appeared to regard
me with more than common attention. Thinking he was
a citizen of the country, I addressed a few general remarks to him, adding, that being from the Western
states, every thing in this part of the country was to me
an object of curiosity, particularly the ocean, which was
now in sight. He replied, that he also was from the
west,* that he lived on Red River, in Louisiana, though
he had formerly lived in Salem. Say what you will
about philanthropy, a citizen of the world, and all that,
every heart of any warmth will expand towards those of
their own country : the moment I heard he belonged to
the states I was from, I felt a paramount partiality for
this interesting stranger. His pleasing manners and enlightened conversation soon discovered him to be a gentleman of no ordinary pretensions, and from mutual
feeling, we became attached to each other during the
voyage.

We had conversed but a short time, before another
gentleman stepped forward from the crowd and saluted
me by name ! Surprised to find myself known where I
thought I was a total stranger, I returned the salute, and
apologized for my want of recollection : " My name is
Flint," he replied ; " I had the pleasure of seeing you at
Salem." It was the Rev. —— Flint, of Salem, to whom,
I am proud to acknowledge the deepest obligation ! It
gave me unspeakable pleasure once more to meet a man
of his worth, with whom I had thought I was parted forever ! But this was not all, my friend of Louisiana was
a cousin of his, also a clergyman, and of the same name !
These gentlemen are both men of high classical attainments, and rank equally high, as writers and divines. The Louisianan, in delicate health, was on
his way to the Saratoga Springs, accompanied by his
friend and mine. Night coming on, deprived me of seeing much of the ocean, though we felt its effect, the most

* We of the western country universally call all that part of the Union west of the Alleghany, west ; and those states on the east, Atlantic,
or eastern states, without farther distinction.

of us, being very sick; and after laughing at my companions, I slunk into my birth, sick enough, but kept it to myself, lest they might return the first. Next morning we were close under Long Island on our left, having the state of Connecticut on our right. We kept nearly a west course, having Long Island in view the distance of an hundred miles. This Island belongs to New-York; is 140 miles long, and only 10 wide. We landed about sun-down at the foot of Fulton-street, in New-York; and agreeably to the custom of steam-boat passengers, separated without ceremony, and (though not on my part,) without regret.

West Point.—Not having it in my power to take West Point in my regular tour, and being told that it was the most interesting spot of all the places I had visited, I took a trip there after my return to N. York. West Point is celebrated as the seat of the United States Military Academy, situated on Hudson river, 60 miles above New-York; it is also celebrated in history for the treachery of Arnold. General Putnam, mentioned in these sketches, may be called the father of West Point.— When Fort Montgomery was captured by the enemy, in 1777, it was resolved to erect another fortification on Hudson river. Gen. Washington left it wholly to the judgment of Gen. P. to fix on the spot, who decided on West Point, and (as his biographer remarks) " it is no vulgar praise to say, that to him belongs the glory of this rock of our salvation," termed (by the British) the Gibraltar of America. West Point was stampt by nature as a rallying point for American liberty! It is a question whether that place on earth exists, where sublimity, beauty and utility, are so happily blended, as at West Point. An extensive green, of several acres, level to a nicety, washed in front by one of the noblest rivers in the world; behind it rises suddenly up one of the wildest craggy mountains, crowned with a huge castle, commanding a view of thirty miles in extent! This formidable fortification is called Fort Putnam; it stands upon a plane of rocks, out of which it is built, and, for size, might itself be taken for a mountain. The foot of the

mountain is skirted with flower gardens of unutterable
beauty, in front of which, in a single row, stand the
houses of the academic staff, with a wide street running
in front, between them and the public green.   Not a
house stands on the green, but those appropriated to the
cadets, where they diet, lodge and parade, beyond the
limits of which they are not allowed to pass without special leave.   The barracks of the military post stand on
the margin of the green, at the bank of the Hudson.   No
one has liberty to settle at the point, but those gentlemen who compose the staff, so that no grog-shops are
kept there.   It is the only place, I venture to say, in the
Union, where there are half a dozen houses, that one of
them is not a grog-shop.   The mountain is called the
highlands, and is the commencement of the Blue Ridge.
The whole place has a martial air.

The military academy at this place, is under the direction and instruction of a superintendant, a professor
of natural philosophy, and two assistants—a professor of
engineering, and an assistant—a professor of mathematics, and four assistants—a professor of ethics and belles-
lettres, who is also chaplain to the academy—a professor of chemistry and mineralogy, and one assistant—an
instructor of tactics, who is also commandant of cadets,
and has two assistants; a teacher of the French language, with one assistant; a professor of drawing, an instructor of artillery, a quartermaster, a paymaster, an
adjutant, a physician and surgeon, a store-keeper, and a
sword-master.   These are wholly under the control of
the secretary of war, whose duty it is to visit the academy once a year,, and to him all returns and estimates ap-
pertaining to the institution are to be made, through the
superintendant.   Under him, the commandant of the U.
S. corps of engineers is inspector of the academy.   It
is also subject to a Board of Visitors, consisting of not
less than five gentlemen, of distinguished military science, in common with science in general.   These constitute a board of annual visitors, whose duty it is to examine the progress of the cadets, the state of police and
discipline, inspect the whole establishment, and report
the same to the secretary of war.

The number of cadets now at West Point (Oct. 1825) is 221. These are divided into four classes, annually, agreeably to their merit, corresponding with their course of study, which comprises four years. That is to say, all cadets employed in the first year's course, constitute the 4th, or lowest class; those of the second year, the 3d class; those of the third year, the 2d class; and those of the fourth and last year, constitute the 1st class.—They are examined every 4th of July.

The course of literature is as follows :—*First year,* French language, and mathematics begun. *Second year,* French language continued, mathematics completed, and drawing begun. *Third year,* drawing completed, mechanicks, experimental philosophy, astronomy, and the first course of chemistry and mineralogy. *Fourth year,* geography, history, moral science, engineering, and the science of war, chemistry and mineralogy, completed.

The practice of military instruction is collateral with the literary course, as follows :—*First year,* school of the soldier, guard, and police duties of privates. *Second year,* school of the company, and the duties of corporals. *Third year,* school of the battalion and the duties of sergeants; also the exercise and manœuvres of artillery pieces. *Fourth year,* evolutions of the line, duties of orderly sergeants and commissioned officers, including those of the battalion staff, and of officers of the day; also the remainder of the instruction in artillery, and the sword exercise. The cadets have an encampment annually, from the 1st of July till the 21st of August; this is called field exercise, and the instruction is exclusively military.

The literary course of instruction extends to the pronouncing and translating the French language, and translating English into French. Drawing embraces the human figure—landscape with the pencil, shading, and finishing in India ink—topography, &c. Geography is extended to the knowledge of the grand divisions of the earth, with the boundaries, productions, commerce, manufactures, naval and military strength, &c. &c. of the different countries on the globe. History comprises universal history, and the political history of the United

States. Moral science includes moral philosophy, and
the elements of national and political law. Chemistry
and mineralogy extends, 1st, to chemical philosophy, including the theory and practice of analysis, &c.—2d,
application of chemistry to arts, &c. Mineralogy and
geology includes the classification and description of
minerals, rocks, general structure, analysis and uses of
minerals, &c. &c. The course of mathematics is complete, embracing every branch of that science. The
course of mechanics embraces statics, viz.—the equilib-
rium of force and rest, centre of gravity, stress of materials, and theory of arches, dynamicks, hydrostaticks, hy-
drodynamics, pneumatics, &c. Experimental philosophy is extended to the illustrations of the physical prop-
erties of heat, principles of light and colours, refraction
and reflection of light, theory and use of the senses, &c.
&c.; also magnetism, common and galvanic electricity.
The course of astronomy is complete.

The military course embraces the whole science of
war. Engineering comprises field fortifications, such as
fortifying lines, erecting batteries and redoubts, calculating labour, time and materials for construction, different
field works, military bridges, field defilements and practical operations on the ground. Also permanent fortifications, viz.—attack and defence of fortified places;
analysis of the system of Vauban, Cohorn, Cormon-
taigne, and later improvements; constructing mines,
fougasses, &c., construction of works, art of defilement,
and armament of forces.

The science of artillery comprises the knowledge and
use of ordinance, military projectiles, gunnery, &c. &c.;
also grand tactics, viz.—organization of armies, marches,
order of battles, battles, &c. Also civil and military
architecture, viz.—elementary parts of buildings and
their combinations, orders of architecture, construction
of buildings, arches, canals, bridges, and other public
works, machines for construction, the execution of a se-
ries of drawings, consisting of plans, elevations, and sections, to illustrate the principal parts of the course.

Practical Military Instruction.—This course embraces
the system of infantry tactics, established for the army

of the United States, commencing with the elementary drill of the soldier; including the school of the company, school of the battalion, evolutions of the line, exercise and manœuvres of light infantry and riflemen, duties in camp and garrison of privates, non-commissioned officers, commissioned officers, &c. This course likewise includes artillery instructions, sword exercise, the cut and thrust, or small sword, and many things beside.

No cadet is received at the military academy, who is deformed, or under four feet and nine inches in height. They must also know how to read well, and write a fair hand, and likewise be perfect in figures. When they are perfected and fit for the army, they receive a diploma, and are promoted by lineal rank. The establishment is under very strict rules, consisting of two hundred, in all, exclusive of the following, viz. revellie at dawn of day, next the roll is called; police of the rooms, cleaning of arms and accoutrements. and rooms inspected: all this must be done in thirty minutes after the roll is called. From sun-rise till 7 o'clock they study; breakfast at 7, parade at 8, from 8 to 11 recite, from 11 to 12 attend military lectures, from 12 to 1 literary lectures, dine at 1, recreate till 2; from 2 till 4 study, from 4 to sun-set, military exercises; dress, parade, and roll-call, at sun-set; from sun-set to half an hour past, supper; signal (a gun fired) to retire to quarters immediately after supper: from half past sun-set till half past 9, study; half past 9, tattoo; inspection of rooms, and signal to extinguish lights at 10 o'clock.

During all this time, they are under the eye of the most able masters. So minute is the discipline, that it extends to a tooth-brush, and their rooms, even to a towel, are inspected twice a day. Any disobedience of orders, or disrespect, is subject to the rules of war; the offender being tried by a court-martial. The sentence extends to dismission and confinement; no corporeal punishment being allowed.

The uniform is a coatee of gray cloth, single breasted, with three rows of eight gilt bullet buttons in front; button holes of black silk cord, herring-bone form, with a festoon at the back end; a standing collar; cuffs four

32*

inches wide; the bottom of the breast and hip buttons
range; the collar is ornamented with cord and buttons;
cord-holes proceed from three buttons placed lengthwise
on the skirts, with three buttons down the plaits; the
cuffs are likewise ornamented with black cord and buttons.   The vest is of gray cloth, single breasted, having
yellow gilt buttons, and trimmed with black silk lace.
The pantaloons are also gray, trimmed down the sides
with black silk lace, and an Austrian knot in front.   The
cap is of black leather, with a bell-crown seven inches
high, and a semicircular visor, highly polished; gilt plate,
of a diamond shape; black plume, eight inches long;
leather cockade, two inches in diameter, with a small
gilt eagle; in front are gilt scales to fasten under the
chin.   The whole expense is discharged by the government, and the number of cadets (if I am not mistaken,) is
limited.

This is certainly the greatest establishment for young
gentlemen in the Union; it is impossible for them to be
vicious.   If I had twenty sons, I would send nineteen of
them to West Point academy; under the eye of the first
gentlemen, whose example alone would fix their manners and form their taste.   But the greatest care is taken
by the provisions of the institution not only to inculcate
every virtue, but even the shadow of vice is interdicted.
They are not allowed to play at any game whatever, read
novels, take newspapers, play on any instrument, throw
stones, throw water, snow ball, bathe, or swim in the
river; but this is out of the question, for they are not
permitted to go off of the public ground, not even to visit any family at the port, unless it be on Saturday evening.   They are not allowed to receive money, even
from their parents, without leave from the secretary of
war!   In this respect it has a decided advantage over
most seminaries.   But to see them on parade, is a most
imposing sight; all arranged agreeably to height, their
nodding plumes, uniform dress, while the best band in
the United States fairly cheats one out of his senses,
sometimes rolling towards you on the green, sometimes
echoed from Fort Putnam, it would almost stir the dead.
Meantime their glittering arms, the magic movement of

their limbs, such touching grace in their evolutions, whilst not the least noise interrupts either the eye or the ear. It is surprising to see how the human form can be moulded to such perfection. They have an inspector at their meals, to which they march in sections : not a word is spoken, and every arm moves at the same instant at the table. They have carvers during meals—no unnecessary talking is allowed.

I would advise all parents to send their sons to West Point. If they would have them acquire just ideas of the Deity, if they would have their passions brought under a proper subjection to reason, and the nicest sense of honor, if they would have them free from frivolous affectation, if they would have them perfect in every social, moral, and political duty, in short, if they would have them free from every vice, and accomplished in every virtue, send them to West Point. They need be under no apprehension whatever ; the guardian angel of America stands sentry there. If such be the cadets, what must be their instructors ! where our government found such men is really wonderful. Col. Thayer, the present superintendant, I am told, studied at the military academy in Paris. Let him be educated where he may, he is doubtless one of the most fascinating men in the world. But in saying this, perhaps I am doing injustice to the others, for I never saw a set of men resemble as they do. Col. Thayer, Maj. W. the Rev. chaplain, Capt. Douglas, Maj. A. and the Dr. are all that I became acquainted with : indeed my time there was limited to two days only. If I admired the generosity of New-York, if I was charmed with that of Boston and Salem, I was transported with the manners of the people of West Point. Such equiformity of demeanour, such minute attention to every point of politeness, such effulgence of countenance, no parade of authority, nothing volatile, but the most pleasing mildness ; they have a winning sweetness peculiar to them, for which that line of Pope must have been made. "Like the sun, they shine on all alike, in graceful ease and sweetness void of pride."

Rape of the Lock.

One of the days I spent at West Point, happened to be
Sunday; of course I went to church, and the moment I
made my appearance, the officers of the staff rose from
their seats, and remained standing until I was seated.
Different from the reception I met with at Charleston
navy-yard, and Fort Independence, but nothing more
than was to be expected from men of their accomplished
manners; in doing this they honoured me greatly, but
they honoured themselves much more. I had not sat
long when the cadets entered the chapel, with all the dignity of sages. It was truly an interesting sight, to see
such a number of the finest young men, such vestal
sweetness displayed in every countenance, their glossy
locks and military dress, each armed with a short sword,
while modesty sat " foremost on each brow."

Some have gone so far as to say that we are doing
wrong to encourage this institution, inferring that these
cadets may in time turn their arms against their country.
But I am far from entertaining this opinion. No, if ever the liberties of our country are endangered, it will be
done by the ignorant. We find that when the liberty o
Rome was overturned it was done by the ignorant and
vulgar, while all the men of polite literature rallied on
the side of liberty.

New-Haven, Conn.—Paying an occasional visit to
New-Haven before this work went to press, I was led to
expunge other matter in order to make room for a few
remarks on that beautiful city. It stands at the head of
a fine bay which sets up from Long-Island Sound; distant from New-York city 76 miles, from Boston 134,
from Hartford 36, and is the semi-capital of the state of
Connecticut. Its relative situation from New-York is
north-east. In whatever point of view New-Haven is
considered, whether for topographical beauty, the utility of its institutions, or the scenery of its environs, as a
town, it is decidedly the Eden of the Union ! It sits on
an even plain of about three miles in circumference,
which is surrounded by mountains, hills, and rugged
rocks, excepting only where it faces the bay. These
eminences assume an endless variety of whimsical fig-

ures, where nature seems to revel in sportive wantonness. In some places a solitary rock of stupendous dimensions presents a bold perpendicular front ; others present naked bluffs of amazing height, while others meet at right angles, and run off in a thousand arbitrary directions. Some are covered with cedar and pine, others are perfectly bare ; some are round craggy points. They all, however, unite in the form of an amphitheatre, by which nature evidently intended to guard her favorite spot.

These bold features of nature, contrasted with the smooth plain, covered with delicate white houses, solemn churches, lofty steeples, extensive greens, wide streets, of undeviating straitness, lined with spreading elms, and the stately buildings of Yale College, gives New-Haven an over-powering charm ! Its public buildings are the Colleges, and 7 churches, viz :—2 Congregationalists, 1 Episcopalian, 1 Baptist, 1 Methodist, 2 African, 2 Banks, a court-house, (in which the Legislature sits,) a jail, an alms-house, 3 academies, 2 insurance offices, a custom-house, and 9000 inhabitants. The citizens are building a great public hotel, which is nearly completed, that for size equals, if it does not surpass, the Exchange Coffee-House in Boston. The public burying ground also deserves particular notice. The houses are mostly built of wood and painted white, with a few handsome brick buildings ; the churches are also with one or two exceptions handsomely built of brick, ornamented with steeples and bells. The streets are wide, straight, and cross at right angles, each adorned with two rows of lofty elms of uncommon beauty, whose exuberant branches form a most delightful shade ; almost all the houses have gardens attached to them, which are laid off in a style of inimitable taste and beauty, adorned with trees, flowers and summer houses ; but its chief ornament is a great square called the green, in the centre of the city, occupying the front of the colleges. New-Haven is an incorporated town, and governed by a mayor, aldermen, and common council.

Yale College.—But New-Haven is principally distinguished for being the seat of Yale College, one of the oldest and most respectable literary institutions in the United

States, and has produced some of our first men. The College edifices consist of 11 buildings, viz :—North College 108 feet by 40, Middle College 100 by 40, South College 104 by 40, Lyceum 56 by 46, Chapel 50 by 40, and a Laboratory ; the commons, which contain two large dining rooms for the students, with a kitchen in the basement, a Medical College, and 3 dwelling houses. It has a president and 10 professors, viz :—Rev. Jeremiah Day, S. T. D. LL. D. President, and professor of mathematics and natural philosophy ; Æneas Monson, M. D. professor of the institutes of medicine ; Nathan Smith, M. D. C. S. M. S. Lond., professor of the theory and practice of physic, surgery and obstetricks ; Benjamin Silliman, professor of chemistry, pharmacy, mineralogy, and geology ; James Kingsley, A. M. professor of the Hebrew, Greek, and Latin languages ; Eli Ives, M. D. professor of materia medica and botany ; Jonathan Knight, M. D. professor of anatomy and physiology ; Rev. Nathaniel W. Taylor, Dwight professor of didactic Theology ; Rev. Eleazer T. Fitch, A. M. professor of divinity ; Rev. Chauncey Goodrich, A. M. professor of rhetoric and oratory ; Denison Olmsted, A. M. professor of mathematics and natural philosophy ; Josiah W. Gibbs, A. M. librarian, and lecturer on sacred literature. Besides these, it has 8 tutors, and 21 resident graduates, and averages about 360 academical students, besides medical and theological. These are divided into 4 classes, viz :—Senior, Junior, Sophomore, and Freshmen. At this time there are students from every part of the United States, and many from the West-Indies ; most of them are sons of our most distinguished citizens ; amongst whom I find two sons of General Van Rensselaer, of very promising appearance. The College has a cabinet, a philosophical and chemical apparatus, which are said to be complete, particularly the chemical laboratory, supposed to be the best in the Union. The mineralogical cabinet, I am told, consists of 2,500 specimens ; independent of this, a cabinet has recently been purchased of G. Gibbs, Esq. of Boston, consisting of 24,000 specimens,* said to be the best collection in the

* The original cost of this cabinet is said to have been £4000 sterling

country. Not having had the pleasure of seeing either the cabinet, or the apparatus, I speak of them from report. It also has a library, consisting of 10,000 volumes, and the students have two libraries amounting to 3,500 more, making 13,500 in the whole.

The Medical College is connected with Yale College, though the building stands in a different part of the town. This institution has three professors, viz :—one of materia medica, one of anatomy and surgery, and one of the theory and practice of physic. The medical students attend chemical lectures in the laboratory of Yale College, but neither diet nor lodge in the college. At the head of the Medical College, stands the celebrated Dr. N. Smith, already mentioned. The average number of medical students is about 70 ; they usually attend in winter. The Theological School has but recently commenced, and the number of students is inconsiderable. The local advantages peculiar to this institution, and the ability with which it is conducted, will render it one of the most desirable places for the education of youth in our country.

Yale College was founded in 1700, by a number of clergymen, and was incorporated in 1701, under ten trustees. It was first located at Saybrook in 1702 ; five young men received the degree of master of arts. From this period till 1718, the prosperity of the institution was greatly hindered by disputes between the trustees and the community, respecting the final establishment of the seminary. Both parties were equally disunited ; but a majority of the trustees finally removed it to New-Haven in 1718. It was called Yale College out of gratitude to Elihu Yale, Esq., one of its principal benefactors. E. Yale was born in New-Haven, but left it very young for England ; he afterwards went to Hindostan, where he acquired great wealth, part of which he sent to this infant college. From this period Yale College began to flourish, and in 1745 the trustees were, by a new charter, erected into a faculty of " the president and fellows of Yale College." In the mean time they received numerous donations from the colony, and private individuals also, both of this country and Europe ; amongst whom I find the respectable name of Dr. Berkley, Dean of Derry, in Ireland, and afterwards bishop of Cloyne. Likewise Sir Isaac Newton, Sir Richard Steel, Doctors Barnet, Woodward, Halley, Bentley, Kennet, Calamy, Edwards; the Rev. Mr. Henry and Mr. Whiston, presented their own works to the library : many other respectable gentlemen made similar presents. But to come nearer our own time : His Excellency, the present governor of Connecticut, and formerly secretary of the treasury of the U. S., presented the college $2000 for the purpose of increasing the library ! In 1792 the Legislature of the state, appointed the governour, lieut. governor, and six senior counsellors, additional members of the board of trustees, which has been attended with the happiest consequences. But such is the reputation of the college, and the number of students is such, that the funds are still insufficient for an adequate number of professors; consequently some of them have fallen a sacrifice to their arduous duties; others have resorted to travelling to recruit their broken constitutions. Thus, while thousands of dollars are daily devoted to other puoposes, this nursery of science, which has contributed so largely to the benefit of mankind, is wholly unnoticed, and left to struggle between nature and duty. Out of the many hundreds who have been benefitted at this celebrated place, no friendly hand is stretched out to lighten the burden of the faculty. Connecticut has acted a generous part towards it, so far as she was able, but this state is too small, singly, to support an institution of such magnitude.

No situation could be more happily chosen for an institution of this nature, than the one occupied by Yale College. The five first named buildings stand upon a gentle elevation, and range at the head of a beautiful green. The three colleges are four stories high, handsomely built of brick, and ornamented with venetian blinds, which give them a very pleasing appearance; while the morality of the place, its classic green and sacred shades, fanned by the zephyrs from the bay, and its romantic scenery, all tend to elevate the mind and chasten the taste.

Grave-Yard.—The grave-yard is called the new cemetery: this is a large field, smoothed, enclosed, and divided into parallelograms, neatly shaded, and separated by alleys of sufficient breadth for carriages to pass between. Each parallelogram is 64 feet in breadth, and from 100 to 180 feet in length. These are laid out into family burying grounds, each with an opening left to admit a funeral procession. The lines of division are planted with trees, and the name of each proprietor is marked on the railing. This field is covered with tombs, tables, slabs, monuments, and obelisks, mostly of marble, and in several instances from Italy. The obelisks are ranged universally on the middle line of the lots, successively, throughout each parallelogram. Thus this cemetery presents a novelty of taste and design, unequalled in either hemisphere. The names, dates, &c. of the deceased are engraven on the monuments, in most instances in large gilt letters: the whole is one representation of unequalled magnificence, and excites the wonder and admiration of all who visit the place. I am told that New-Haven is indebted for this, as well as the various ornaments of taste and skill, with which it is adorned throughout, to that Hon. sage, Hillhouse.

Literary Men.—New-Haven is a very hot-bed of literary men. Besides several of the faculty, who have long been distinguished in the literary world. Here I met with Jedediah Morse, D. D. A. A. S. the father of American geography; also the famous Noah Webster, L. L. D. author of Webster's spelling-book, &c. &c. &c. Nothing could equal the pleasure I felt at the prospect of seeing 2 men with whose names and celebrity I had long been acquainted. Of all the Atlantic writers, these have rendered the most essential benefit to the western country: and the first person I called on in New-Haven, was the Rev. J. Morse, whom I had long since thought was numbered with the dead. I found him, however, alive and well; quite a lively and genteel man, not only polite, but friendly, sociable, and condescending; nor does he look so old as one would expect. Mr. M. in his person is rather over than under six feet in height, remarkably slender and straight; he appears a little turned of seventy; his visage is thin, long, and features rather delicate, with a fine, full dark eye; his hair is plentiful, parted from the crown to the forehead, and drops off on each side; it is gray but not perfectly white; his head is remarkably small, rather more oval than common.   He is quite an active man for his years, and still pursues writing geographies; but our country increases so fast, that the old gentleman hardly gets one geography out before it is out of date, and he has to commence a new.   He speaks very slow and soft, without the least ostentation of learning.   I called upon him often in his study, and found him always pleasant and communicative; he lives in plain style; his first wife is living, and quite as agreeable in her manners as her husband.   He told me he had three sons living in New-York, and one on his travels in Europe. He dresses in a plain gown, and looks very venerable. After Mr. M., the next man I called on was the celebrated Mr. W.   I knocked at the door with more than common enthusiasm; for though we back-woods folks are not learned ourselves, we have a warm liking for learned people.   In a few minutes, a low chubby man, with a haughty air, stepped into the room; his face was round and red, and by no means literary looking.   He was dressed in black broadcloth, in dandy style; in short, he comes nearer the description of a London cockney, than any character I can think of; he eyed me with ineffable scorn, and scarcely deigned to speak at all.   I am sorry for his sake I ever saw the man, as it gave me infinite pain to rescind an opinion I had long entertained of him.   He appears to be about sixty years of age.

The next person I waited upon was President Day, who gave me a reception worthy the principal of Yale College.   This celebrated man is of middle age, tall, and well made; his complexion inclining to dark, his face is oval, with a keen hazel eye, his countenance grave and dignified, and plainly marked with the lines of deep thinking; his features are regularly proportioned, manly and striking, with a high smooth forehead; his manners are those of a perfect gentleman.   With respect to President Day's natural and acquired abilities, it is superfluous to say any thing, as he is universally known to be a man of general science, and one of the first mathematicians of the present age. Professor Silliman is in appearance very like President Day, about the same age and size ; his complexion fairer, with the same hazel eye, but a shade darker, sparkling with genius; his countenance more luminous and striking, and his manners more captivating. As a writer, chemist, and mineralogist, Professor Silliman ranks among the first men of this or of any other country. He visited Europe when a young man, with a view of prosecuting his studies, particularly of chemistry, where he travelled three years; during which he wrote a journal of his travels, a rare and invaluable work, which does honor to the American character. His remarks in this work are concise, but pointed, and display the most striking evidence of talent, industry, and research, to be found; nothing dry nor volatile, not a line in the whole work, which is considerable, but conveys both pleasure and instruction. He delivers lectures on chemistry in Yale College, during the winter months, which, for elocution, science and sentiment, are said to afford a perfect intellectual feast. I was honored with a ticket of invitation to attend the lectures whilst I remained in New-Haven, but was prevented by indisposition, a circumstance I deplore, the more so, as the opportunity is lost for ever, it being the last lecture for the season. These gentlemen, with Professors Smith, Taylor, Kingsley, and Knight, are all of the faculty I had the pleasure to see. Doctor Smith is one of the finest men in the world. I do not speak of his abilities, as the whole faculty is one constellation of learned men. But Dr. S. is so singularly good, so easy and simple in his manners and conversation, as much like Dr. M. of New-York, as one man can be like another; about the same age, though Dr. Smith is tall and thin visaged, but fair, with a soft blue eye. Professors Knight and Taylor were also men of very engaging genteel manners. Professor K. did not strike me particularly : I thought him rather stiff and formal, though he is remarkable for his personal endowments, and he is said to be equal, if he does not surpass any of the faculty, for talen and profound learning.

There are several more literary men in New-Haven, but my limits compel me to conclude.

Beside these, New-Haven is the seat of several distinguished families, viz. the Ingersolls, Edwardses, Kimberlys, Whitneys, Hillhouses, and Bristols, have their residence in this town. The celebrated Whitney, who invented the cotton gin, now deceased, was of New-Haven.

Besides the college, New-Haven has three academies, and several grammar schools, which are well conducted, and yet the dialect is subject to the like exceptions with other places. I think it rather an improvement, upon that of New-York and Boston, for they have a great many *on'um* here, with *alhwhile* and *alltime*, besides swarms of *bes;* and *guess* has taken such deep root, that one might as well attempt to overturn the Andes as to eradicate this word from the dialect of New England, and yet I should think a few well directed lectures in the common schools might be attended with happy consequences, for although the yankees cannot be drove, no people are more easily led. But one fact is settled, that, excepting these vulgarisms, they pronounce the English language with great distinctness, clearness, and uncommon melody. The citizens of New-Haven, in manners and appearance, differ little from the neighboring towns; same hospitality peculiar to New-England. A town, however, is no correct specimen of national appearance. Great disparity as to size, is visible between those who are brought up in towns, and those who are reared in the country, the latter being much the stoutest men. The Legislature of the state is now in session in New-Haven, and amongst the members, are many from the country, who are elegant looking men, of good stature.

The Inauguration of the governor took place on the day previous to the meeting of the Legislature, which was celebrated with great military eclat. His excellency Gov. Wolcott, former secretary of the United States treasury, is descended from the distinguished family of Wolcotts, mentioned in these sketches, who settled Massachusetts; a man of unblemished reputation, and unequalled generosity, the worthiest of the worthy, and the best amongst the good. I was much gratified to witness the honors showered upon his gray hairs, by an enlightened, brave, and generous people. Gov. Wolcott is far advanced in life, the whole of which has been devoted to his country.

New-Haven was settled by a company of gentlemen, the principal of whom were the Rev. John Davenport, and Theophilus Eaton, Esq. in 1639; the natives were called Quinnipicks. This town is famous for giving refuge to the regicides Goff and Whalley, who were concealed many years in a cave, under one of those large rocks already mentioned, called the west rock; also famous for the residence of a hermit, who lived on it many years, and at length was found dead in his hut : it is said he was partially deranged. I was on the east rock, which is 370 feet in height; it stands nearly two miles from N. H. and commands a prospect of thirty miles, not so richly diversified as the prospect from the statehouse of Boston, but much more romantic and picturesque.

The following is a statement of the duties and tonnage of the towns and cities visited by the author, for the year 1824.

Baltimore	$1,183,294 60
Philadelphia	4,325,427 16
Wilmington, (Del.)	1,098 20
New-York	11,227,794 94
Boston	4,216,325 45
Salem	436,966 08
Providence*	250,474 19
Newport	54,063 10
Richmond	75,612 38
New-Haven	94,334 60
Alexandria	97,383 01
Georgetown	12,743 97

* Providence lost over a million of dollars worth of shipping by a rise of the river, a few years back, of which it will not recover for many years to come.

Statement of the tonnage of the shipping belonging to the following districts on the 31st December, 1824.

	tons.	95ths
Baltimore - - - - -	84,905	53
Philadelphia - - - - -	90,168	35
Wilmington, (Del.) - - - -	10,977	65
New-York - - - - -	281,148	08
Boston - - - - -	148,672	58
Salem - - - - - -	38,881	52
Providence - - - - -	20,538	57
Newport - - - - - -	10,419	73
Richmond - - - - -	7,224	55
Alexandria - - - - -	14,156	70
Georgetown - - - - -	4,853	70

THE END.

CPSIA information can be obtained
at www.ICGtesting.com
Printed in the USA
BVHW041921030321
601628BV00014B/280